FROM WELFARE STATE
TO REAL ESTATE

Also by Kim Moody

An Injury to All: The Decline of American Unionism

Workers in a Lean World:
Unions in the International Economy

FROM WELFARE STATE TO REAL ESTATE

REGIME CHANGE

IN NEW YORK CITY,

1974 TO THE PRESENT

Kim Moody

THE NEW PRESS

NEW YORK
LONDON

Requests for permission to reproduce selections
from this book should be mailed to:
Permissions Department, The New Press, 38 Greene Street, New York, NY 10013.

Published in the United States by The New Press, New York, 2007
Distributed by W. W. Norton & Company, Inc., New York

LIBRARY OF CONGRESS CATALOGING-IN-PUBLICATION DATA

Moody, Kim.
From welfare state to real estate : regime change in New York City, 1974 to the present /
Kim Moody.
p.   cm.
Includes bibliographical references and index.
ISBN 978-1-59558-088-7 (hc.)
1. New York (N.Y.)—Politics and government—1951–   2. New York (N.Y.)—Economic
conditions.   3. New York (N.Y.)—Social conditions.   I. Title.
F128.52.M58 2007
974.7'1043—dc22   2006028786

The New Press was established in 1990 as a not-for-profit alternative to the large, commercial publishing houses currently dominating the book publishing industry. The New Press
operates in the public interest rather than for private gain, and is committed to publishing,
in innovative ways, works of educational, cultural, and community value that are often
deemed insufficiently profitable.

www.thenewpress.com

Composition by dix!
This book was set in Walbaum MT

Printed in the United States of America

1   3   5   7   9   10   8   6   4   2

To Sheila . . . for our time in New York

Here I was in New York, city of rose and fantasy, of capitalist automatism, its streets a triumph of cubism, its moral philosophy that of the dollar. New York impressed me tremendously because, more than any other city in the world, it is the fullest expression of our modern age.

—Leon Trotsky, *My Life*

CONTENTS

Acknowledgments   xi

Introduction: The Neoliberal Transformation
of New York City   1

1. The Crisis in Context   9

2. From Crisis Regime to Mayoral-Business
    Coalition: The Rise of Koch   62

3. Globalization and the Underdevelopment of
    New York: The 1990s   93

4. Politics in the 1990s: Soft Cop, Hard Cop   114

5. The Bloomberg Phenomenon   155

6. Behind the Skyline:
    New York's Elite Remakes the City and Itself   196

7. Beneath the Skyline   243

Conclusion: Neoliberal Triumph   284

Notes   293
Index   325

ACKNOWLEDGMENTS

This is a book with many contributors. Most of them are not aware of their contribution. They include friends, colleagues, students, and people I met in New York. So many are they that I won't attempt to name names. Rather I will acknowledge groups, places, and institutions and hope that they recognize themselves among these. The order of acknowledgement is not necessarily by the size or importance of the contribution; they all helped.

I probably wouldn't have written this particular book if I hadn't been one of two winners in a competition for original research papers on the New York City fiscal crisis of 1975 sponsored by the School of Public Affairs of Baruch College in 2003–4. I certainly wouldn't have even entered such a contest if I hadn't been teaching New York City politics in various forms first at the City College Center for Worker Education and then in the political science department of Brooklyn College. I owe much to the faculty, staff, and students of those institutions. While I taught labor studies and history at Cornell University's labor studies program in the city, I nevertheless learned much about the working-class city from students, faculty, and staff there as well.

On the ground and over the years, many activists taught me about life in the city. Among the groups they belonged to are: *Labor Notes*, the Association for Union Democracy, the Teamsters for a Democratic Union, District Council 37 and several of its local unions, Transport Workers Union Local 100, the Progressive Staff Congress/AFT, the United Federation of Teachers, Communications Workers of America Local 1180, Make the Road By Walking, New York Taxi Workers Alliance, Chinese Staff and Workers' Association, the Latino Workers Center, the Northwest Bronx Community and Clergy Coalition, the Brooklyn Greens, and New York Solidarity, whose members overlap with many of these organizations.

Research requires accessible institutions and helpful staff. Those that made institutional research on this book a pleasure include: the marvelous state-of-the-art open-stack library at Brooklyn College; the Internet archives at Baruch College, which gave me access to the MAC papers and the video interviews with major fiscal crisis players made in 1995; and my two favorite low-tech and thoroughly accessible libraries, the City Hall Library on Chambers Street and the Cadman Plaza branch of the Brooklyn Public Library, which still has the microfilm files of the *New York Times* and the same microfilm machines I used over thirty years earlier. Finally, there are the neighborhood newspapers, which tell the tales that don't fit in the *Times.*

There would not be this book if it weren't for the folks at The New Press, past and present, including my editor, who had many positive suggestions. Naturally, any mistakes are my own.

Introduction:
The Neoliberal Transformation
of New York City

Cities change. For its first two hundred years New York was a merchant city, a key port in the Atlantic economy, where goods were bought and sold domestically and internationally, but only occasionally made and those mostly for local consumption. In the nineteenth century New York saw work and residence separated and neighborhoods sorted out by class. As the century progressed, Manhattan rapidly filled in the grid plan drafted in 1811. Beginning in the 1840s or 1850s, New York, along with other cities in the Northeast, began the process of becoming a center of industry. It was not a city of big industry, but of many smaller, often specialized firms.

By the time of the Civil War, the city's commercial and financial faces turned west as well as seaward. As industry spread westward across the Great Lakes and down the Ohio Valley, meeting the Mississippi at St. Louis, and as western agriculture became mechanized, New York financed and shipped much of the swelling output of the new industrial power that was the United States. Reaching from the Great Plains to Europe, the city's role at the center of the Atlantic economy grew and its population exploded. From 1870 to 1910 the population of Manhattan alone grew by one and a half times to reach 2.3 million.[1]

In the 1880s, immigrants began to arrive in waves and from farther away in eastern and southern Europe than the earlier migrant groups. In 1898, the city's geography changed dramatically as

Brooklyn, Queens, and Staten Island united with Manhattan and the Bronx (which had been annexed piecemeal in 1873 and 1895), expanding its industry as well as its size and population, which reached almost 5 million by 1910 for the combined city. By the 1940s, it was the biggest manufacturing center in America. It was still, of course, a commercial city and already a financial center. Each phase of its development was a response to larger national and international economic change and each incorporated much of the last, but the central economic dynamic changed. In this way, it remained a diversified economy.[2] While each of these changes was in line with general developments in the country and broader world, human agency was at play with each transition. All of these transformations were battlegrounds socially, economically, and politically.

Martin Shefter described the rhythm of these later battles as the "machine/reform dialectic." In the face of fiscal crises, usually the result of a combination of economic "panic" and the excesses of Democratic machine rule, the city's respectable elite would forge a fusion ticket to oust the crooks and re-establish fiscal responsibility. This scenario would be repeated in 1894, 1913, and 1933, each reform movement, whatever its unique features, under control of the city's business elite. After 1937, Shefter argues, the city's political regime became "pluralist," mainly because labor unions and sometime independent parties they organized (American Labor and Liberal) became important.[3] The regime that would begin to emerge following the fiscal crisis of 1975 we will call neoliberal.

Beneath and behind these political changes, however, were class forces, new and old, engaging in a tug of war over the city's space, resources, and wealth. The city's clubhouse system of machine politics that formed the core of Shefter's "machine/reform dialectic," as he shows, was largely a response by Tammany Hall to the emergence of an independent labor movement that made its mark on the 1886 mayoral election. He writes, "The defections Tammany had suffered to the United Labor Party in 1886 encouraged its leaders to strengthen their district organizations by establishing a network of clubs that involved the machine in the social lives of

Democratic voters."[4] Both 1913 and 1933 were years of working-class upsurge in the city as in the nation. The last of these produced the administrations of Fiorello La Guardia, who implemented the New Deal in New York and also unleashed Robert Moses to reshape the city with public money. La Guardia and his successors presided over the acceleration of New York's unique "social democratic polity," or welfare state. This was economically supported by federal money and the city's industrial base, and politically pushed for by its industrial working class with its broad variety of organizations, as described in Joshua Freeman's *Working-Class New York.*[5]

The city, however, began to change once again after World War II. African Americans from the South and Puerto Ricans from the island arrived in growing numbers. At the same time the manufacturing and transportation jobs they hoped for began leaving. Before there was white flight, there was industrial exodus. These goods-making and -moving industries were reduced by competition from more efficient facilities inland; driven or zoned out by bankers and developers who saw more valuable uses for the land they occupied; rendered obsolete by new technology; plowed under by Robert Moses's bulldozers; or swallowed up by what we call globalization. The city lost population, particularly white population, as more and more whites left for the suburbs and beyond. If Robert Moses drastically altered the built environment, migration, in and out, transformed who did the city's work and who filled its neighborhoods. With these changes and the rise of the United States as a world economic, political, and military superpower came new political currents: the civil rights struggles of the 1950s and 1960s; Black and Puerto Rican nationalism; the women's movement; the antiwar movement of the Vietnam era; and the upsurge and organization of the city's huge public-sector workforce, its hospital workers, and others. All of these forces expanded and deepened the city's public provision, adding to the "social democratic polity" shaped by earlier generations of working-class people. The city became the site of a complex web of class, race, gender, and anti-imperialist conflict, replicating in new form the old fight over space, resources, and wealth. This story has been told often in many different ways, sometimes as an explanation for the city's social problems, sometimes as a prelude to the fiscal crisis of 1975, frequently in an effort to blame the victims.[6] We will refer to it often, but not attempt to retell it in detail. The focus of this book is on what happened during and after 1975.

Class and Race

A few years ago, a colleague of mine at Brooklyn College asked me if I thought class was still a meaningful framework in which to look at politics. It was an obvious question given that most attempts to analyze or untangle New York City politics do so in terms of race and ethnicity. New York was classically the American city of ethnic politics. After the demographic transformation mentioned above, it certainly could lay claim to be a prime example of the centrality of race in urban politics in the United States. Class seemed to have faded or been pushed into the background as the social struggles that began in the 1950s in the United States focused on racial and gender oppression. One need not make the whole leap to postmodernism to accept the reality of racial politics in urban America. Nor can one deny that even class oppression or exploitation is often experienced as racial oppression by working-class people of color. In New York City, as elsewhere, housing, education, employment, even entertainment, are allocated as much or more by race as by class. The interaction of the two in these fields of life is so intimate as to defy any strict delineation or separation. Race is central to American life—period. Why, then, insist on using class as an analytical framework as well as race?

My answer is: because class won't go away. It is imposed on politics and life by the actions, behavior, investment, and political priorities of capital and the incredibly powerful social class it reproduces globally, nationally, and in our cities. If the working class in the United States is fragmented, disorganized, in retreat, and bamboozled by business gurus, politicians of all stripes, religious demagogues, and often its own leaders, the ruling capitalist class has been on the organized offensive worldwide for three decades or more. Despite its own internal contradictions, capital has shaped and imposed the neoliberal agenda for the world. However complex the process by which capital gets its political act together, it seems rather obvious that nationally, and even globally, it has done so, and it has succeeded in imposing much of its agenda on the United States and a good deal of the rest of the world. The resistance to it takes many different forms, but it is usually the working and/or other subordinate classes that form the bulk of that resistance whether in their own name or not. So it is in New York City, the metropolis at the center of much of this global neoliberalism.

To impose its agenda in New York, the city's business elite had to reassert its influence over city affairs in the era of social movements. Exasperated by the cost of this "welfare state" in one city, by the apparent capitulation of the politicians to the new unions and social movements in the 1960s, and by the seemingly unquenchable demands of these new forces, the city's ruling class, its business elite, its "permanent government," reacted in a highly unified and organized way to establish more direct control of "their" city in the mid-1970s. So, although race remains central and ethnicity important, and though immigrant status adds another dimension to race and ethnicity, class won't go away. The bulk of this book looks at how the business elite of that portion of the global capitalist class that lives in and around New York organized, maneuvered, and manipulated the city's politics, budgets, resources, and ultimately the living and working possibilities of the other classes. And it looks at the conditions and resistance of New York's diverse working class.

The Uniqueness of New York City

It can be argued that all that has changed in New York City since 1975 simply reflects what has happened in the country as a whole. Isn't the city's experience just part of the bigger picture? It is, of course, part of the bigger process both nationally and globally. But it is precisely its character as a "global city" that has made the implementation and results of the neoliberal regime that was launched in 1975 distinct, and even different, from most other cities. Although we will return to these facts again, it is worth bearing in mind that New York's poverty *rate* is today almost twice that of the nation at about 22 percent: in Manhattan the income of the top 20 percent of earners is fifty-two times that of the bottom 20 percent as opposed to about ten times for the country, while the Bronx was named the poorest urban county in America.[7] So, something about New York is unique.

Of course, New York is unique in many other ways. By most accounts it is America's most exciting city. The very outlandish wealth of its business elite has made it a cultural, entertainment, and lifestyle mecca. If you have just enough money to buy access to some of this, it is a great place to live. Yet, the writers, social critics, historians, and social scientists who live there and wouldn't live any where else almost always write from a critical standpoint. One thinks of the late Jack Newfield, an investigative journalist whose love for the city he grew up in was always manifest, but whose criticism of its social conditions and politics was ruthless. So, as they might have written in the clichés of a travel book in the age before the Rough Guide, it is a city of contrasts—wealth and poverty being one of the most salient, and love of the city and anger at the conditions it produces and tolerates for so many being another.

There is also the matter of just what we mean by New York City. Today it is fashionable, and certainly legitimate, to speak of metropolitan economic and social ecosystems. I have not taken this ap proach, however, because what seems most important about New York's economy are its global connections far more than its relationship to the surrounding region. Politically, the city is more affected by state politics as a whole than by those of the scores of nearby cities and towns. So, the focus will be on New York City itself. Many books about New York, on the other hand, focus almost entirely on Manhattan, home and workplace to much of the city's global business and cultural elites. Most images of it, as well as the covers of books about it, display the Manhattan skyline of one or another era. It is said to be an island city. In fact, it is a city of islands, many of them, and even of wetlands and wildlife not in its zoos. It has miles of sandy ocean-front beaches like L.A.—some created by Robert Moses. Most importantly, however, it has four additional boroughs in which the vast majority of New Yorkers live. These are where the majority of the city's working-class population lives—largely segregated by race and ethnicity, always fighting over the spatial edges of their neighborhoods with gentrifiers and developers and with each other. This is where the mass base of the city's unions live and where most of its community-based working-class organizations are found.

As we shall see, growing parts of these outer boroughs, as they were named by some Manhattan-centric person years ago, are the battlegrounds of the latest stage in "development"; that is, the highly profitable building and owning of expensive high-rise residential and office space. Development of this sort was, until not too long ago, primarily a Manhattan venture. Now it is crossing bridges and borders to seek profit on a very large scale in the low-rise communities of Brooklyn, Queens, the Bronx, and, to a lesser extent, Staten Island. There is no public figure like Robert Moses behind this and no public agency planning it—only enabling it. It is the "market," meaning the profit-driven, mega-developers, bankers, lawyers, and countless other interests who stand to make a buck over the "Manhattanization" of large parts of the outer boroughs, which is behind this change in the city's skyline and built environment.

It is here that global capital meets local capital. For the city economy rests very heavily on international financial speculation and the services it requires, and that activity has brought in vast amounts of money that are headed for more speculation. Real estate in New York is a major form of such speculation. Its upscale development also satisfies the demands of the city's growing cadre of well-to-do professionals, traders, hangers-on, etc., who seek the upscale lifestyle New York offers, but who are being priced out of Manhattan by the even wealthier layer above them. Left in the wake of this development is a vast working class almost half foreign-born, some of it well paid, but much poorly paid, poorly housed, and poorly educated. The workforce shaped by the demand for services holds down income, while the pressure of development has pushed up the cost of housing for everyone. There is another side to this, however. While union membership and density has been declining in the United States for decades, in New York City both measures have held steady. And, while some of the old working-class institutions that helped make New York unique are long gone, new types of community-based working-class organizations have arisen. The potential for resistance to the neoliberal agenda exists even though it has not yet been exercised on a mass scale.

How did this neoliberal ascendancy come to be? How did the extremes of New York's economy evolve? How did both its capitalist class and the professionals who serve it change? How did the city's vast working class change? That is the economic, social, and political story told in this book.

1

The Crisis in Context

In 1974–75 the world plunged into the deepest economic downturn since the Great Depression. Production, profit rates, and trade contracted and the international financial system came under stress. The consequence of an endemic fall in the rate of profit, economic growth among the Organization for Economic Cooperation and Development (OECD) countries (the world's twenty-four richest nations) ground to a halt—falling from just over 5 percent growth in 1973 to 1 percent in 1974 and zero in 1975. In the same period the European OECD member nations dropped from 6 percent growth to 2.5 percent to −1 percent. The slump of industrial production in the OECD countries was even greater, going from a growth rate of 9 percent from 1973 to 1974 to −9 percent by 1975.[1] From 1973 through 1975 the U.S. real gross domestic product fell by about 1 percent, the industrial production index fell from 70.6 to 63.4, or by 10 percent, and the rate at which industrial capacity was used fell from 88.4 percent to 74.6 percent. From 1973 to 1974 domestic corporate profits fell by 8.6 percent.[2]

At the center of the slumping world economy was New York City. First dubbed a "World City" by Le Corbusier in the 1930s, it was reanointed by the Twentieth Century Fund as one of a handful of cities at the center of international financial activity.[3] As a world financial center, New York would be affected by more than the temporary impact of recession, as important as that was. For the recession would reveal deep changes and weaknesses in that very global financial system. The world banking system, for example, was going through what Martin Mayer termed a "revolution." This revolution was one in which the new electronic technology that was enabling a globally integrated financial system was running well ahead of U.S. banking practices, increasing the velocity and forms of money, and creating a dangerously unstable situation.[4] The whole underlying financial system was shaky. As Mayer had warned in his 1974 book, *The Bankers*:

> There are billions of dollars in potentially lost loans in the system, and the clock ticks toward the moment of their detonation. The present banking structure *can* collapse; the larger the regulatory apparatus permits it to grow, the more catastrophic the collapse will be.[5]

An example of this was the relatively new Real Estate Investment Trust that borrowed from the banks. By 1974 the value of REIT assets had grown to $20 billion, with several banks holding their own REITs, including Chase, which held $1 billion. In 1973 a Florida REIT filed for bankruptcy, which set off a recession in the real estate and construction markets. By 1975, the REITs lost 80 percent of their value and, from 1974 to 1978, plunged from $420 billion to $13 billion. The banks were hit with defaults, Chase lost $169 million and First National City Bank had to write off 10 percent of its REIT loans.[6]

Beginning in 1973, as a result of U.S. pressure on Saudi Arabia during the oil crisis, petrodollars flowed into the New York banks, providing vast new sums for investment in a world that was heading into recession. The funds would not go to U.S. industry, where profitability was already in a slump, but to the governments of developing nations hungry for capital. These nations would, in turn, open their markets to U.S. investment, accelerating the process of globalization. With inflation still high and monetary policy pushing interest rates up, this new explosion of petrodollars would eventually produce the Third World debt crisis of the early 1980s.[7]

In the mid-1970s the developing nations would be one of a number of alternative paths of investment.

In the context of the world economic downturn and a shaky banking system, the financial markets went from jittery to semi-panicked. Even before the recession in the early 1970s, 130 brokerages "merged, folded, or moved out of state," pointing to the instability in the securities industry.[8] When the recession hit, the stock market slumped; the Dow Jones dropped 18 percent from 1973 to 1974, while the broader New York Stock Exchange index fell by a quarter.[9] The New York bankers had recently seen and participated in the failed attempt to save the sinking Franklin National Bank and had watched Germany's Herstatt Bank go under, while a Congressional Budget Office report warned of more financial instability. Then, in the fall of 1974, Chase revealed that the value of its investment portfolio had been overstated by $40 million or more.[10] Falling securities prices in the midst of the world recession had devalued Chase's portfolio and underlined the vulnerability of the banks and the city that housed them. New York's banks seemed headed for trouble.

In the early 1990s, Saskia Sassen would name New York, along with London and Tokyo, as one of the three global cities at the center not only of world finance, but of the important and high-priced producer services that increasingly fed the expanding corporate world. For Sassen, a global city was one of a number of nodes in the world economy that provided these key services.[11] More recently, Taylor, Catalano, and Walker defined world cities as part of a network of some 316 cities, 10 of which stood out in terms of their provision of such services and their "connectivity" to the other world cities. In this network, New York stood second only to London and well ahead of the other top ten.[12] By the mid-1970s New York City was exporting 68 percent of the value it produced to the rest of the country and the world.[13] While it is well to remember that New York is also rooted in the U.S. economy and political system, it is clear that a city so tightly integrated into a wounded world economy could not help but being hurt and having its own financing rendered more difficult.

New York's centrality in the global economy, however, was also a source of long-term decline in other areas. If globalization secured the city's place in finance, producer services, and communications, it also contributed to the decline of its once vibrant industrial base. Historian François Weil summarized this well when he wrote:

> Paradoxically, New York actually profited little from the international economic order established after World War II. Worse, industrial activity in the metropolis experienced a worrisome decline. Henceforth, the advantages New York offered, in terms of quick access to information especially, were not always enough to compensate for the costs of production, so much higher than elsewhere. In addition, direct and indirect imports grew enormously in the 1960s to the detriment of New York–based firms. In a few years, numerous Manhattan clothing workshops closed their doors. Brooklyn's factories and breweries followed, and even, in 1966, the Navy Yard, pride of the entire borough. Between 1968 and 1977, 600,000 industrial jobs disappeared.[14]

New York would remain an export city, as we have seen, but what it exported changed dramatically in a short period of time. As Eric Darton writes, "During the time span of the planning and building of the World Trade Center, New York lost much of its port and manufacturing capacity, crippling the city's ability to simultaneously finance, manufacture, and distribute goods and products."[15] Instead of goods, it became by the 1970s an exporter of producer services. These no longer required ships, tugboats, or docks, all of which virtually disappeared from the city's shoreline. The Port Authority would remain an importer and exporter of goods, but the docks would be in New Jersey.[16] Along with the disappearing industries went thousands of decent-paying jobs on the docks and in the streets of Manhattan and Brooklyn—and with them the tax revenues of a once stable working class and the businesses that employed it. Air transport jobs made up for only about half the loss of other transportation jobs from 1965 through 1973.

Other gain were in telecommunications and broadcasting, but the big gains for that whole period were in lower-paying service jobs.[17] New York's exports now left the city by wire, airwaves, or, when they had to be performed in person, by plane. They were largely intangible and dependent on the demand of other businesses the world around. There was here a chain of dependency and vulnerability. Finance at the center, vulnerable to the changing world system, and business services largely dependent on finance, on the one hand, and its own exports on the other. These, in turn, affected the city's important real estate market.

Central to the development of the financial center and the services it spawned was the tidal wave of new office construction in downtown Manhattan built to house these expanding businesses. Between 1967 and 1973, 66.7 million square feet of office space was built in Manhattan, two-thirds of it from 1970 through 1972.[18] This symbolized the rapid shift from industry to finance and producer services and composed the fixed capital of these industries— arguably the most profitable investment in town. But it was also subject to rapid rises in vacancies when recessions hit the tenants and, hence, a source of vulnerability. This profitable, highly vertical sunk capital was also at the heart of the city's financial and fiscal problems. Much of this real estate was tax-exempt, notably the World Trade Center due to its ownership by the Port Authority. The office boom of the early 1970s pushed up the price of land and rents without increasing city revenues proportionately. When the building boom collapsed in 1974, it contributed to a fall in city revenues. The Temporary Commission on City Finances, set up to locate the causes of New York's fiscal problems, noted that "the city's corporate office complex historically has been immune to recessionary forces."[19] But by the 1970s, the process we now call globalization had advanced to the point where New York's financial sector was vulnerable to a worldwide downturn such as that of 1974–75. Not only did jobs in securities get hit hard, but the office space, much of it new, that housed these jobs slumped. Office vacancies soared and midtown Manhattan rents dropped by a third from 1970 to 1976 in real terms. New office space construction dropped from 17.4 million square feet in 1972, to 4.9 million in 1974, down to 1.6 million in 1976. Measured in real value added, the city's economy declined by 2.7 percent from 1970 to 1975, more than twice the drop of the national economy.[20] All of this necessarily impacted the city's tax revenues. Although real property tax income rose to pay off debt, other tax levy revenues (commercial rent tax, sales tax, etc.) fell by 15 percent from 1974 through 1976, or by 28 percent when adjusted for inflation.[21] What was supposed to be the global city's economic salvation had contributed to its financial woes.

Turning Points

In little more than a decade and a half the economy of New York was transformed from a diverse production site in which 45 percent of its workers made or moved tangible goods and structures to one in which only half that proportion did so. The city's economy had become more and more dependent on the export of financial and other producer services, which accounted for almost half the value produced in the city in the mid-1970s.[22] The shift was even clearer in New York's globally connected export sector. According to the Temporary Commission on City Finances, manufacturing lost 12,159 export-based jobs in 1965–69 and 41,987 in 1969–73—just before the big recession of 1974–75. Transportation saw slight gains in 1965–69 due to air transport, but a net loss in all transport of 10,226 in 1969–73. The financial sector gained 59,242 jobs in 1965–69, but 18,657 were lost in 1969–73. Over the whole period in the export sector, manufacturing had lost 54,146 jobs net, while finance picked up 40,585 and other services remained flat, losing only a few jobs.[23] In terms of the city's crucial export sector, New York became less economically diverse and more vulnerable to fluctuations in the world economy. The 1960s were a turning point in the New York economy against which the financial and fiscal problems and crisis of the 1970s must be understood.[24]

The early and mid-1970s were also a turning point in the world economy and international and domestic politics. In 1971 the Bretton Woods system of currency exchange was dismantled. By this time Germany and Japan were becoming serious competitors against U.S. industry. And the 1974–75 world recession set off a decade or more of economic stagnation among the major industrial nations.[25] The recession and the prolonged stagnation that followed discredited the Keynesian foundations of American liberalism and European social democracy in the eyes of many, leading to two important political shifts. The first was a general move to more centrist, even austere economic policies by the Democrats in the United States, and eventually by the European left. In the United States, at least, supply-side economics became a catch-phrase even before Ronald Reagan took office. Next was the rise of a new, harsh conservatism and its election to government in the United States, Britain, and much of continental Europe by the early 1980s.[26] This trend was prefigured in the United States by Nixon's New Federalism, which was continued by Ford and his treasury secretary, William Simon, although the thrust of this early policy direction was blunted by an uncooperative Democratic Congress and partly derailed by Watergate and its aftermath.[27] Nevertheless, neoliberal economic policy was taking shape.

In the United States in the early 1970s big business organized itself around a common political agenda. Thomas Byrne Edsall described this effort in his 1984 study of the forces underlying the Reagan revolution when he wrote:

> During the 1970s, business refined its ability to act as a class, submerging competitive instincts in favor of joint, cooperative action in the legislative arena . . . the dominant theme in the political strategy of business became a shared interest in the defeat of bills such as consumer protection and labor law reform, and the enactment of favorable tax, regulatory, and antitrust legislation.[28]

At the center of this development was the Business Roundtable, pushing what would become the Reagan economic policy agenda. The Roundtable, founded in 1972 by 125 of the nation's largest industrial, commercial, and financial corporations, aggressively lobbied the federal government for tax reductions on business, deregulation in transportation and finances, labor law "reform" designed to weaken unions, and austere fiscal policies. The neoliberal agenda was given further definition and an organized social base. The Roundtable was supported by conservative think tanks such as the Heritage Foundation, founded in 1973, and by a variety of ad hoc business-based coalitions such as the Consumer Issues Working Group, which helped defeat the Consumer Protection Agency, and the National Action Committee on Labor Law Reform, which aided in the defeat of labor's attempt to improve labor law.[29] Many of the top corporate executives who founded the Roundtable and some of the other organizations lived or worked in the New York area. Directly or indirectly, their ideas provided a backdrop to the city's policy options just as they did in Washington, D.C.

These same global trends affected America's other ailing cities as well, causing widespread fiscal distress, but given New York's central place in the world economy, they hit New York harder and at a sharper angle. Furthermore, the forces of global recession hit a city already vulnerable to financial and fiscal crisis. By May 1975, New York edged up to default on its bloated short-term debt.

For New York's powerful business elite, this crisis offered an opportunity to roll back a decades-old tradition of social spending and provision far in advance of other American cities. In the 1930s, the city's welfare provision and public sector grew enormously under the fusion-reform regime of Fiorello La Guardia as a result of New Deal money that flowed into the city, first to pay for "home relief" the city could no longer afford. The federal Civil Works Administration, Public Works Administration, and later the Works Progress Administration provided millions to rehabilitate the city's parks and build bridges under the guidance of Robert Moses, as well as to build its first public housing project.[30] As Joshua Freeman has shown in his *Working-Class New York*, by the 1940s the city provided a unique cluster of urban social institutions that he characterizes as a "social democratic polity." This included a public hospital system that had twenty-two hospitals at its height, an expanding City University system, extensive public housing, significant union-provided cooperative housing, rent control long after it was eliminated in other cities, and civil rights legislation before most other cities. All of these were fought for and defended by the city's vibrant labor movement and left-wing parties.[31] To this was added the new or expanded social programs of the 1960s: Medicaid, Medicare, the War on Poverty with its community participation setup, and growing welfare rolls. Promising still more strains on the city's budgets were the social movements of that era and the new, initially militant municipal unions.

For New York's business elite the growing costs of the city's "social democratic polity" and Great Society programs had, with the changes in the city's economy and its place in the new global marketplace, come to clash with long-held priorities for city expenditures. Although some of New York's business elite had backed many of these more recent reforms and their major political champion, John Lindsay, their costs now seemed exorbitant and the corporate price tag too high. The whole experience of the late 1960s and early 1970s seemed to many in the business elite to be a threat to the city's position in the global economy as well as to their own economic priorities. In a 1971 report from Chase Manhattan Bank, David Rockefeller, a central actor in New York's and the nation's elite, wrote, "It is clear to me that the entire structure of our society is being challenged." In a closed-door meeting of top business executives in 1973, one concluded, "If we don't take action now, we will see our own demise. We will evolve into another social democracy."[32]

Business's "developmentalist" view of city finances had called for fiscal restraint on social programs and largesse on infrastructure projects and spending that underwrote the upward and outward expansion of the city's central business district. The social movements and the new programs that came in their wake had shifted the city's financial priorities even further from its own. The fiscal and financial troubles of the mid-1970s were the call to action and the opportunity to act. The city's fragmented politics, along with the decline of the social movements and the relative "maturity" of the municipal unions, cleared the way for a reversal of priorities via the establishment of a "crisis regime," a series of state-sponsored organizations and offices imposed on the financial governance of New York City.

As David Harvey has pointed out, New York City in the mid-1970s was a sort of rehearsal for the larger neoliberal reorganization of national priorities that would take place in the United States under Ronald Reagan and in the United Kingdom under Margaret Thatcher. Restraint on social spending, privatization, deregulation, and, most importantly, the reassertion of class power by the nation's capitalist class are at the center of the neoliberal project. The word was not yet in wide use in the mid-1970s, but the sense that the city's business elite, themselves at the center of the national and global capitalist class, had lost power and with it control of the city government's priorities was strong. The crisis regime shaped in 1975 would in many ways be an example of how government could be used to reassert class power and shift priorities toward both the traditional goals of business and the newer ideas that would be known as neoliberalism.[33]

Political Fragmentation, Interest Groups, Coalitions, and Elites

New York's style of "interest group governance" described long ago by Sayre and Kaufman was unique in several ways.[34] First, the political structure of the city undermined the "strong mayor model" many thought embodied in the city charter. The borough presidents, seated on the Board of Estimates, brought the demands of not one political machine but five, plus the minimachines of the Republican, Liberal, and Conservative parties. They competed for city jobs, judgeships, capital projects, vending and supplier contracts, zoning variances, etc., all of which bid up the budgets, while they simultaneously sought to keep taxes on their constituencies low. Unlike Chicago, with its unitary Daley machine, New York City had no central disciplining force other than the mayor and the two other citywide members of the Board of Estimate who still relied on the cooperation of the county organizations to get elected.[35] While Tammany was alive and well, candidates for citywide office could be negotiated by county leaders. The fragility of this setup had already been demonstrated when the Brooklyn machine challenged Tammany candidate James Walker in the 1925 Democratic primary. Although the challenge failed, it was a warning shot. But after the defeat of Tammany's candidate in the 1961 Democratic primary, its position as first among equals declined terminally. Indeed, the county machines had lost power over the years. La Guardia's 1938 charter revision had strengthened the mayor by extending his appointment and dismassal authority over most department heads, and limited the patronage powers of the county organizations by centralizing much of the contract award system. Further charter revisions limited the role of the borough presidents, and first New Deal and then Great Society programs replaced some of the old functions of the machine with bureaucratically managed redistributive programs. Additionally, as Mollenkopf points out, the county organizations came to rest on taxpayer-supported legislators and their staffers more than the clubhouse. By the 1970s, the centrality of the media further weakened the role of the county organizations in mayoral elections.[36] Still, the regulars controlled most county organizations, which in turn controlled access to the ballot for locally elected city and state offices and could create a margin of victory in citywide elections as well as in each borough.[37] Even reformer Lindsay, with no real machine, was forced to distribute patronage largely on the recommendation of the county Democratic organizations.[38] As always, the county organizations expected something in return for their efforts beyond the depleted supply of patronage jobs, and that something had to do with suppliers, contractors, vendors, and consultants. Some of those were "earned" through the small banks, insurance companies, and law firms controlled by "regular" Democratic district and county leaders who fed off the capital and expense budgets.[39] Part of it came through the city agencies the county organizations still influenced and through which some of the supplies, equipment, fees, and contracts were purchased. With such a competitive dynamic, reining in spending in large parts of both the capital and expense budget seemed a task for Caesar, not clubhouse denizens or well-intentioned reformers. A city situated so deeply in the global economy—like a nation—is less able to shape its future the more decentered its government.

Then there were the interest groups. Sayre and Kaufman envisioned a city with countless interest groups competing with one another for resources and preventing the rule of an elite. A sort of ultrapluralism was said to contribute to the weakness of government, something analogous to neoclassical economists' view of the market as an infinite number of more or less equal players. As Fuchs, Bellush, and others have pointed out, however, all interest groups are not equal nor is the system of political and social conflict as unstructured and fluid as Sayre and Wallace argued.[40]

As Fuchs put it: "Power is not evenly distributed in the fiscal policy arena, and even when a city has a high degree of interest group activity, like New York, groups do not have equal access to the process."[41]

Furthermore, most interest groups are embedded in deeper social class and race formations that determine the level and type of access, available resources, and the ability to build effective coalitions. The contention here is that at that time, particularly given the financial nature of the crisis, access to the policy process and the resources to impact it were highly uneven, the overwhelming advantage lying with New York's business elite. I say business rather than banker or financial because, as I will argue, the intervention that created the crisis regime involved major players from much of corporate New York. I say elite because the vast majority of the city's small businesses had no real access and because even big business tends to be represented by those activist leaders whose access to policy making is regular and influential.

The other potential actors, mainly the black and Latino communities and organized labor, failed to have decisive influence over the outcome because they failed even to contemplate, let alone undertake, the construction of a broad coalition based on some alternative resolution of the crisis more favorable to working-class New York. Because both the unions and New York's black and Latino community activists had some influence on the city's social and political priorities in the 1960s, there has been a tendency to exaggerate their actual political power in the 1970s.

The period of the mid- to late 1960s certainly produced some high-profile activities and movements, as they did throughout much of the country. Actual political representation of African Americans in city politics proportionate to their share of the population, however, would come later. As Charles V. Hamilton argued, institutional gains from the period of the social movements in New York came largely through community corporations and the various agencies associated with the War on Poverty, rather than through gains in the electoral process or in representation in city and state government.[42] As late as 1989, when whites composed only 48 percent of the city's voting age population, they held three-quarters of the seats on the city council and 82 percent of the votes on the Board of Estimate. Such black and Latino representation as existed was mostly encased in the county organizations, which ultimately played little role in the formation of the crisis regime.[43] It was also a time in which community action and other antipoverty programs, where blacks and Latinos had made gains, were being cut back. The power of the black community had been in the streets and there the demands were more representational than redistributive: school integration, community control, construction jobs in Brooklyn and Harlem were among the major goals of the 1960s.[44] The notable exception was the welfare rights movement. In New York, however, this movement, which gained steam and organizational presence in 1966, peaked in 1968 and was all but dead by 1970.[45] In fact most of the radical organizations of the late 1960s, such as the Black Panther Party and the Young Lords, had declined or disappeared by the early 1970s. The most obvious institutional legacy of the more radical movements was open admissions and the expansion of the City University of New York (CUNY) and the system of community boards, which became law in its contemporary form in 1969.[46] The potential power of the black and Latino communities lay in coalition among themselves and with the municipal unions, many of which already contained significant numbers of African Americans, including officials at the local level and, in some cases, higher. While there was resistance from the black and Latino communities, particularly against cuts in the city's public hospital system, the black and Latino communities did not have the access to shape the crisis regime. Other than some black politicians and union leaders, there was not the institutional power to have a decisive impact without a broader coalition.[47] This did not happen.

The New York labor movement was deeply divided over such questions as urban development, civil rights, the Vietnam war, and even, frequently, which candidates to support. Like the public-sector workers, those in the private sector followed the national pattern of militancy, the 117-day strike of New York Telephone workers in 1971–72 being a prime example.[48] Neither private- nor public-sector union leaders, however, were able to consolidate effective coalitions prior to the crisis. The role of labor in city politics was fragmented, contradictory, and largely reactive.

The municipal unions that arose in the 1960s, of course, played a large role in the resolution of the financial crisis, but not one that shaped the crisis regime. The explosion of public-sector unionism across the country in the 1960s had its epicenter in New York. The two powerhouses of municipal labor were District Council 37 of the American Federation of State, County, and Municipal Employees (DC 37) and the United Federation of Teachers (UFT). Also important, though it did not negotiate directly with the city, was the Transport Workers Union (TWU) Local 100. Important in bargaining directly with the city were the uniformed service unions, the Uniformed Sanitationmen's Association, the Police Benevolent Association, and the Uniformed Firemen's Association. For most of the period examined here, TWU Local 100, with almost 40,000 members, led the system of pattern bargaining established in the 1960s. DC 37 had grown from about 20,000 dues paying members in the 1950s to 79,000 in 1970 and 106,783 in 1974–75. The UFT went from 5,000 (out of 40,000 teachers) in 1961, when it called its first strike, to nearly 71,000 in mid-1974. By the eve of the crisis each of these two unions spent over $12.5 million a year.[49] District Council 37 and the UFT, in particular, were not only large but well organized with significant professional staff and a clear-cut hierarchy. In addition, in the 1960s DC 37 had developed an effective political operation headed by Norman Adler. It was certainly an exaggeration to say, as the Bellushes did, that DC 37's electoral machine was a replacement for the clubhouse, but it was a sign of the role unions played in bypassing and to some extent diminishing the centrality of the county organizations to electoral politics. Adler, his staff, and local union volunteers also lobbied both city hall and Albany.[50]

Although prior to the crisis the unions sat together in the Municipal Labor Committee, they did not bargain together or cooperate directly in Democratic primaries to push labor candidates. Victor Gotbaum, executive director of DC 37, and UFT president Albert Shanker were cool, sometimes hostile, toward one another. Shanker had from time to time raided some DC 37 jurisdictions. Gotbaum had disagreed with Shanker when the UFT struck the Ocean Hill–Brownsville experimental school district three times in the fall of 1968 in opposition to community control. Gotbaum had joined with a group of black and liberal union leaders to pressure Central Labor Council president Harry Van Arsdale to get Shanker to call off the strike, a strike which rendered any alliance between the city unions and the black community problematic, to say the least.[51] Thus, for all the power and organization of the municipal unions, they did not present a united front until the crisis was upon them. Then, as we will see, Gotbaum became the recognized leader who most others followed willingly, Shanker and the police and fire unions hesitantly. It was only after the crisis was well under way that the municipal unions engaged in coalition bargaining with the city, and in 1977 the established a statewide political coalition of public-sector unions, the Public Employees Conference.[52]

The municipal unions, like much of the black and Latino communities, were embedded in the city's huge working class and to a lesser extent among those middle-class professionals in the public sector. In this sense they shared certain common interests in the way the city spent money. Their priorities (schools, housing, health care, parks, sanitation, etc.) were different from and frequently in conflict with those generally ascribed to New York's business elite, who saw capital infrastructure improvements that improved land values, restricted spending on social programs, restrained city worker wages and benefits, low property and business taxes, and tax breaks on office and luxury apartment construction in the central business district as priorities.

New York's working class, however, like that of the nation, was badly divided along racial lines and frequently competed along those lines for housing, jobs, and city resources. Potentially breaching that division was a rising cadre of black union leaders in both the private and public sectors. This was particularly true of DC 37, where ascendant leaders like Lillian Roberts, Charles Hughes, Charles Ensley, Stanley Hill, and others had already made their mark.[53] Despite this, no broader coalition was ever sought for working-class New York.

A Special New York Interest:
Its Business Elite

The most powerful interest groups were those based in New York City's unique business elite, itself the social and economic center of America's corporate capitalist class. While the members of this elite may have lived in the suburbs as much as in the city, they made their business homes within the confines of Manhattan from Sixtieth Street to the southern tip of the island, the core of the city's central business district (CBD). At the heart of this community in the mid-1970s were the corporate headquarters of 84 Fortune 500 firms (down from 140 at its height, to be sure), and the headquarters of over 450 national companies altogether, including the nation's largest financial institutions and other giant producer and business service firms that earned New York the title of global city.[54] According to Matthew Drennan's calculations, in 1976 New

York was home to firms that accounted for 24 percent of the sales of the Fortune 500, 41 percent of the assets of the nations largest commercial banks, 34 percent of those of the largest insurance companies, and 29 percent of the biggest diversified financial outfits.[55] The number, size, and concentration of these firms gave them and those who ran them an influence even when they did not appear to intervene. Through both their market leverage and permanent and occasional organizations, these large business interests and their representatives affected city fiscal and financial affairs day in and day out.[56]

Furthermore, this business elite possessed a number of resource-rich institutions that had permanent access to city fiscal, financial, and political power centers. Among these were the City Club; the Citizens Union; the Real Estate Board of New York; the Commerce and Industry Association; the Rockefeller-led Downtown–Lower Manhattan Association; the Regional Plan Association; and the Citizens Budget Commission (CBC). Most of these organizations had sizable professional staffs and the full backing of the business elite. When Sayre and Kaufman wrote about the CBC it had six hundred affiliated business corporations and cooperated with most of the above organizations.[57] Shefter outlined the policy agenda of these groups and its relationship to past crises:

> Generally, when New York has been faced with a fiscal crisis or demands for the construction of new transportation facilities, a substantial part of the downtown business community has united behind a program calling upon the municipal government to: (1) stop financing current expenditures with borrowed funds; (2) balance its budget by slashing current expenditures rather than by raising taxes; (3) use its borrowing power capacity to improve the city's transportation infrastructure rather than for other purposes (such as building new schools); and (4) cover, to the greatest extent possible, the debt service with user-charges (fares on subways, tolls on bridges) rather than with local tax revenues.[58]

Alongside this, of course, is the role of big money in city elections. Money became central in the 1960s. In 1969 John Lindsay and his two opponents spent $3 million. By 1977 the cost for both the primary and general election was $6.5 million, with Koch alone spending $2.1 million. In his race for a third term in 1985, Koch spent a whopping $7.2 million, most of it from real estate and financial interests.[59] In New York City, just about every major business is involved in real estate development and politics in one way or another.

Matthew Drennan, in the *Setting Municipal Priorities* series, has called the dense network of large businesses on which the city's business elite is based the corporate headquarters complex. This complex included "headquarters offices, firms servicing headquarters offices, and ancillary services provided to the individuals who perform the headquarters and corporate service activities."[60] According to his econometric model, this complex accounted for 46 percent of the city's private economy in 1975, measured in terms of value added. The biggest slice of the corporate headquarters complex in 1975 was in producer services, which accounted for 83 percent of the complex. The value added produced by the firms in this complex came above all from what the city exported to the rest of the country and the world, composing 68 percent of the value added produced in the city. Drennan's complex accounts for two-thirds of this exported value added.[61] Manuel Castells describes the economic dynamic this way:

> It is because Manhattan is the CBD of New York, and New York is the corporate center of the largest economy in the world, holding what is still the most important international currency, that capital flows tend to converge on the location of the leading financial institutions.[62]

In other words, the city rests not primarily on its local or regional economy, but on the world economy in which New York's business elite is a major player. Thus, the dependency of city officials on its business leaders goes far beyond campaign contributions. There is the power to take its export-created income, capital, and jobs elsewhere either in whole through relocation or in part through outsourcing—the twin Damoclean swords always hanging over the city's tax policies and practices. There is also, as we shall see, the power to simply withhold capital or services even while staying in the global city.

The Highly Integrated Corporate Complex

Complex is a good word for what underlies New York's business elite, for this corporate community is highly integrated as a business network and as a group intensely interested in the city's land use and value, taxing and spending priorities, and general business climate. Global city theorists, like Saskia Sassan and Manuel Castells, in particular, point to the integration of the financial sector and producer services, including telecommunications. New York is the center of both in the United State. It is precisely as industrial production decentralized and internationalized that "agglomorations" of producer service firms arose in the world's three global cities.[63] In particular, Sassen points to New York's centrality in telecommunications, a fact more likely to be overlooked than the role of finances in the international economy. And, as she wrote, "New York has at this point the largest concentration of telecommunications facilities in the United States."[64]

Then there is real estate. Nowhere in the country is land so valuable as in New York City. And virtually all the components of the corporate headquarters complex have a deep interest in these values. Urban land values are not so much set by supply and demand, since the supply of land is fixed in most cities, expanded only occasionally and marginally by landfills in the case of New York. Rather they are, as one urban economics text puts it, "determined by productivity (or profitability), which is highest at the place of maximum accessibility, that is, the central business district."[65] This conforms to the Regional Plan Association's "law of urban rent," laid out in its 1927–31 *Regional Survey of New York and Its Environs*, which argued that valuable land in lower Manhattan ought

to be used for the most valuable pursuits.[66] Under a growing economy, building more and more office space in Manhattan is extremely profitable because you can build so high and charge high
rents. Unlike land, office space is affected by supply and demand,
but also by locational considerations—Sassen's "agglomeration"
located in the central business district. Here is how Drennan rhap-
sodically describes what this means for his corporate headquarters
complex:

> For the most dynamic and most internationally oriented part
> of New York's export base, the corporate headquarters com-
> plex, the most important parts of the capital stock are the
> office buildings clustered in Manhattan south of 60th Street.
> That 14-square-mile area, the central business district
> (CBD), contains 286 million square feet of office space. No
> city in the world has a CBD with such extraordinary density
> of office space—20.4 million square feet per square mile.[67]

The CBD is so dense because it is so vertical and so high, which
means as long as occupation holds up it is highly profitable to the
owners of the land and or buildings. But there is more to it than
that. Every addition to this office space draws in a legion of interests: banks to finance it; developers to assemble it; engineers and architects to design it; contractors to build it; lawyers to protect it;
insurance companies for titles, construction operations, and the
structures themselves; and so on. Once built, there are the firms
that service the office space, above all the utilities, themselves big
business and a central part of the corporate headquarters complex.
When in the early 1970s a firm like Con Edison saw new office skyscrapers going up, they saw millions in new business. A dramatic
example of this was the rise of the World Trade Center, which
"consumed wattage for a city of a hundred thousand."[68] This was
even truer for New York Telephone/AT&T (now Verizon). With
the residential telecommunications market long saturated, it was
not simply a matter of more phones in the WTC, but of "a multi-
million-line Nynex (New York Telephone) switching station" and

the new digitally based data-transmitting services that were becoming the heart of their profit vistas. This new technology was also key to the rapid internationalization of banking and the accelerating growth of multinational corporations.[69] For all the distinct and sometimes conflicting interests of the firms that make up the complex and inhabit the CBD, they have longstanding common interests in the growth of the CBD, on the one hand, and in the city's property tax and capital budget, on the other.

The property tax is important to all because it affects the rent the corporations and financial institutions must pay. It is in a very real sense a cost of production to the producer service firms, even though much of the cost of these taxes is exported along with the services these firms provide.[70] For capital-intensive outfits like New York Telephone (now Verizon) and Con Edison, who have sunk capital all over the city and cannot export much of these costs or leave the city, the real property tax is very important. During the first half of the 1970s, the property tax level rose significantly despite shrinking assessments and an increasingly poor collection rate, which fell from 95 percent in 1970 to 90 percent in 1975.[71] From FY1969 to FY1975 total revenue from the property tax rose by 86 percent to $3.3 billion. The effective tax rate, that is the rate on assessed value, rose from 5.5 percent to 8.2 percent during that period. So, although the rate on full value remained relatively flat in those years, companies with large property holdings would have experienced a sizable tax increase.[72] This, of course, would have strengthened their resolve to hold to their traditional advocacy of tax and spending reductions. The irony here is that the cause of the rate increase was the rising interest on the short-term debt that was funding the city since property taxes could only be raised above 2.5 percent to pay off debt. The other side of this irony, of course, was that it was precisely the relentless pressure from business that kept property assessments low and exemptions and abatements high, that created the revenue side of the city's long-standing fiscal problem. Looked at from a business perspective, the priority of the corporate headquarters complex was bound to be immediate budget cuts, layoffs, "decapitalization" of the expense budget, and tax reductions, not tax increases on itself. Looked at from the ordinary citizen's point of view, some changes in the property tax might have seemed reasonable, but this idea was literally drowned out by the blare pointing to the expense side of the budget.

Since 1932, the CBC has been an aggressive and highly professional organization representing, as Sayre and Kauman put it, "the large revenue-providing groups in the city," i.e., the corporate headquarters complex that had been advocating budget restraint and tax reductions.[73] Other business-backed or socially elite groups like the City Club, the Real Estate Board of New York, and the Economic Development Council, as well as the CBC, were vocal in calling for mass layoffs and the renegotiation of union contracts in early 1975. In February, the Real Estate Board attacked Mayor Beame's suggestion of an increase in the real estate tax and called for pay cuts. In May, City Club chair Joel Harnett demanded a 5 percent pay cut and the CBC called for a "total wage and jobs freeze."[74] Also important because of their advocacy of aggressive CBD development were the Downtown–Lower Manhattan Association and Regional Plan Association. The *New York Times* and the *Daily News* joined the chorus, demanding labor sacrifices and focusing on city spending.[75]

Prelude to the Crisis Regime

Charles Brecher and Raymond Horton, both associated with the Citizens Budget Commission and both involved in the crisis policy debate, described what happened in the spring and summer of 1975 as they saw it:

The year 1975 was a turning point for the City of New York. In that year the city's economic leaders forced its elected leaders to change longstanding municipal priorities. Henceforth, the municipal labor force would shrink; its real wages would fall; less income would be redistributed to the poor; taxes would be cut; borrowing to pay for expenses would be eliminated. The overall objective was to balance the City's budget and restore its access to the public credit markets.[76]

Of course, balancing the budget in the way described above would do more than restore access to the market. It would "change long-standing municipal priorities," as the "economic leaders" had long advocated.

The question arises: was the formation of the crisis regime a bankers' or a businessmen's coup? Jack Newfield and Paul Du Brul called it a "revolution in the governance of New York City." Robert Bailey referred it as a "regime change," a term less loaded then than now, and characterized it as "the politics of creditor intervention."[77] It lacked the one-act immediacy of a true coup, but interestingly enough, when the state legislature enacted the Financial Emergency Act in September 1975, it used the language of martial law. The act read in part:

> [The] situation is a disaster and creates a state of emergency. . . . The state must undertake an extraordinary exercise of its police and emergency powers under the state constitution, and exercise controls and supervision over the financial affairs of the city of New York.[78]

Although the state legislature acted at the behest of the business elite on a program demanded by it, the regime change was also supported by the mayor and, most significantly, New York City's municipal unions. This coup, it would seem, was supported not only by those who might benefit, but by some of its victims as well.

There is a difference between this "creditors intervention" and previous ones that gives it the character of a genuine regime change. As Shefter has argued, in what he calls the "machine/reform dialectic," there was a long history of fiscal crises or scandals presided over by Tammany followed by the city's banking community, or its good-government representatives, forming fusion campaigns, taking over the city, straightening out its finances, and then being voted out of office after a single term, with the exception of Fiorello La Guardia. In 1894, 1913, and 1933, the bankers put up fusion candidates, won in the conventional manner of city politics, and then enacted their priorities.[79] In 1975 things were different and not at all conventional. There was no mayoral election in 1975 and the city lost much of its home rule capacity, something that hadn't happened before. When the next election came, the new administration was not a reform one and did not disappear after one term, nor was it anything like La Guardia's reign. After the crisis was resolved on terms favorable to the corporate headquarters complex, the new institutions of the crisis regime remained but relinquished control in a manner not usually associated with coups d'état. If New York in 1975 was not Chile in 1973, it was not business as usual either.

According to Dale Horowitz, senior managing director at Salomon Brothers and a municipal bond specialist at the time, the first warning shot for the investment bankers came in July 1974 when they floated an offering of city notes that no one bought and on which the underwriters lost money. Bailey says that at a meeting of the Comptroller's Technical Debt Management Committee on October 7, 1974, "the potential for severe financing problems to the city was first seriously discussed." In fact, warnings had been sounded well before this. In the early 1970s Karen Gerard, an analyst for Chase, presented a paper full of warnings to a meeting of Clearing House bank leaders. In 1973, the Rockefeller-appointed Scott Commission said the city was overspending but was ignored. At an April 1973 meeting of the Regional Plan Association, Walter Wriston of First National City Bank (FNCB) said much the same thing and helped set the tone of the near future by blaming the city workforce and its "financially ruinous" pension plans.[80] Horowitz observed on CUNY-TV in 1996, "A lot of people should have known and should have done something about it."

In October 1974, the city reported a huge deficit and Mayor Beame briefed DC 37 chief Victor Gotbaum about the city's financial problems. In that same month he ordered a hiring freeze, and in December layoffs, but they didn't stick. At the end of 1974, the banks further reduced the share of city paper in their portfolios, indicating they knew there was a problem. In December, Horowitz met with Governor Hugh Carey to discuss New York's "financial problems." This is when, he said, the bankers and investors started to worry about the city's ability to pay. Internal memos at Morgan and Bankers Trust warned that the market for city paper was flooded.[81]

The next step was the formation of the Financial Community Liaison Group (FCLG). After an informal meeting with Mayor Beame on January 9, 1975, leaders of the major banks formed the FCLG, headed by Ellmore Patterson of Morgan. It pushed for four things: (1) to protect the banks interests and investments; (2) to avoid open conflict or controversy, that is, to do things behind the scenes as much as possible; (3) to demand a wage freeze, major spending reductions, and less reliance on money markets; and (4) to get control over the debt of the special districts and authorities. These authorities, like the Triborough Bridge and Tunnel Authority, City University Corporation, Housing Authority, and Battery Park City Authority, were important because their paper competed with city, and soon Municipal Assistance Corporation (MAC), paper. It was hoped these four demands would, in Bailey's words, "force a new way of making political choices on the city's government."[82] The FCLG itself did not succeed in this hope. This was the creditors' intervention and it didn't do the trick. As a private group it lacked the authority to force the city's hand.

In March and April, the city couldn't get anyone to buy its bonds or notes and in May the market closed to the city and the bankers publicly announced they would not underwrite any more city paper. Whether acting simply as prudent bankers or to push their agenda, this was a demonstration of the power to withhold capital and was the first moment of actual crisis. As Fuchs argues:

> While chronically unbalanced budgets and extensive borrowing through the municipal bond market are signposts of a city heading toward insolvency, these conditions themselves do not necessarily precipitate a fiscal crisis. A full-

fledged fiscal crisis requires that the city be locked out of the bond market.[83]

This is, of course, just what happened and the city was in crisis.

Was this a political move by the bankers or just the market speaking? It may well have been both, but it certainly was what bankers do when they are faced with potentially huge losses. Their previous behavior indicates they were already responding to market problems. They, along with banks all over the country, had been selling off New York paper since the summer of 1974, $2.3 billion of it by March 1975. There were a number of reasons for this behavior. For one thing the New York banks now faced competition from brokerage houses with their newly developed money market funds. More important, however, was the transformation of the municipal bond market. Once the domain of the big New York banks, it had exploded in the previous fifteen years, growing from $7 billion in 1959 to $22 billion by 1974, with some nine hundred firms trading in these unregulated securities and providing still more competition for New York paper and New York banks. Another force intensifying competition in the markets for government bonds was none other than former New York State governor Nelson Rockefeller, who had created forty-one bond-issuing (tax-exempt) authorities during his reign, driving their debt to $12 billion by 1974. The temporary default of one of these, the state's Urban Development Corporation, in February, provided more jitters among public securities underwriters.[84] The federal government had not seen fit to regulate this market. Given the antiregulatory drive of the Business Roundtable, the deregulatory recommendations of the 1971 Hunt Commission, and the 1973 legislative proposals they inspired from Treasury Secretary Simon, regulatory tightening was the last thing likely to happen. In 1975, the SEC faulted the city as well as the "practices of the bonds counsels, underwriters and counsels," but did nothing.[85]

It is worth remembering, as well, that the leaders of New York's business elite were international businessmen, not simply operators in the city, and their world was in trouble, reminding us that the acceleration of financial globalization mentioned earlier provided an alternative investment target in Third World debt. One writer said of Citibank (then First National City Bank) chief Walter Wriston, "Walter's heart really belongs to the world."[86] The same could be said for David Rockefeller, founder of the Trilateral Commission and member of the Council on Foreign Relations; Pat Paterson; Felix Rohatyn; and most of the leading characters in the crisis regime. As Mayer observed in the early 1970s, "New York's First National City already finds more of its profits overseas, and with the growth of multinational enterprise more and more banks feel a need to be in place to service their customers worldwide."[87] They saw municipal bonds and notes in the context of a global investment market in which they had more and more of a stake. When they began dumping New York paper in mid-1974, they were simply behaving like bankers in a troubled world market and protecting their assets. But the spring of 1975 offered an opportunity as well as the threat of default. It may have been simple self-interest to push the state toward taking charge of the city's finances, but it was a political agenda coupled with the desire to reassert their class power over city affairs that informed the programmatic content and goals of the crisis regime demanded by New York's business elite. The opportunity to do what they had long wished done was too much to resist.

Crisis Regime Change

The FCLG having failed to produce anything, the financiers took the next step on May 26, 1975, Memorial Day, at the home of Richard Shinn, president of Met Life, not only a big financial firm, but a major landlord in the city. Felix Rohatyn of Lazard Frères and Frank Smeal of Morgan were also there. According to Newfield and Du Brul, here is where the "concept, structure, and powers of the Municipal Assistance Corporation was worked out."[88] Of course, the proposal needed an official panel to legitimize it, so Governor Carey appointed a three-person panel—Richard Shinn, Donald Smiley of Macy's, and Rohatyn. The legislation was drafted by Simon Rifkind, a retired federal judge with deep Democratic Party connections and a partner in the law firm Paul, Weiss, Rifkind, Wharton, and Garrison. He would become a member of the MAC board, and his law firm its legal counsel. Governor Carey called the legislature to order on June 5, and five days later the Municipal Assistance Corporation (MAC) Act passed into law.[89]

The central mission of the MAC was to sell its own bonds as a state agency. These would be backed by the city's retail sales and stock transfer taxes, collected and held by the state. It would retire the city's short-term debt by exchanging it for its own long-term bonds. As described in its first annual report, "the Act requires the City to adopt the State Comptroller's uniform system of accounts for municipalities, to phase out its practice of including certain operating expenses in the capital budget, and to reach a balanced budget by fiscal year 1978."[90] The city did change its accounting system, it reduced but did not eliminate the capitalization of the expense budget, and it failed to balance its budget by 1978.

Governor Carey appointed to the board Rohatyn; Rifkin; Thomas Flynn of Arthur Young; Robert Weaver, former HUD secretary and one of the very few African Americans to play a role in the crisis regime; and Donna Shalala, a political science professor from Columbia. Mayor Beame added another dimension by appointing not only financiers John Coleman and George Gould, but Francis Barry, president of the Circle Line and a fund-raiser for the Bronx Democratic Party, and William Ellinghaus, president of New York Telephone and soon to be vice chair of AT&T. Ellinghaus not only represented "industry," but was chair of the Regional Plan Association as well as a director of Bankers Trust, J.C. Penney, and International Paper. In addition, at various times he was vice chair of the New York Chamber of Commerce and Industry and a member of the Economic Development Council of New York City.[91] Truly a man of his class, Ellinghaus brought something to the crisis regime the bankers and brokers couldn't: experience in dealing with unions. In 1971–72 Ellinghaus had faced the 117-day strike by New York Telephone technicians mentioned earlier. MAC represented not only finance, but major business services (legal, accounting, and telecommunications), tourism, and retail.

MAC ran into trouble right away. Authorized to sell $3 billion in bonds from June through August, its first $1 billion offering sold only $550 million. MAC could not sell enough bonds to cover city expenses or interest payments. On August 25, MAC informed Carey it could not raise "the cash necessary to meet the maturing obligations of the City and the operating expense requirements for September and beyond cannot be raised through the sale of MAC bonds."[92] The city was headed for default.

MAC had other problems as well. Its board was not of one mind. By July 18, MAC's staff, headed by Herb Ellish, had come up with a program to make the city attractive to the market. It was a classic restatement of what the city's business elite had always wanted, with a few new demands thrown in. Its eleven points included: a wage freeze; layoffs of ten thousand employees; a 10 percent across-the-board salary cut; a four-week furlough for all city workers, meaning they would work fifty-two weeks, but be paid for forty-eight; 10 percent cuts in all supplies and purchases; a transit fare hike; tuition at CUNY; a 10 percent reduction in pension benefits; cancellation of new and existing capital projects; cuts in welfare and Medicaid (difficult because of state and federal mandates); and finally, management reforms.[93] This last item became the Mayor's Management Advisory Committee (MMAC), chaired by the omnipresent Richard Shinn. How hard and how much to push for MAC's new austerity package were, apparently, controversial. The hawks included Ellinghaus, whom, at Rohatyn's suggestion, Carey appointed chair at the July 21 board meeting, demoting the more indecisive Flynn.[94] But as the city careened toward default in September with no hope of MAC raising sufficient funds to head it off, something with more power than MAC was needed to enforce MAC's and Carey's agenda.

That something was given shape at a meeting in the offices of William Ellinghaus on August 20. In attendance were representatives of Chase and Morgan, Rohatyn, Governor Carey, and, of course Ellinghaus, the hawk. Ellinghaus's immediate targets were CUNY tuition, a transit fare increase, and a reduction in welfare payments.[95] MAC, now chaired by Ellinghaus, also contributed a 111-page financial plan written by Rohatyn and released in early September. As Rohatyn tells it in the MAC 1976 *Annual Report*:

> On the basis of the Corporation's [MAC's] recommendations, Governor Carey called the State Legislature into Extraordinary Session on September 25, 1975. The Legislature enacted the Financial Emergency Act for the City of New York, which was signed into law by the Governor on September 10, 1975.[96]

The Emergency Act brought the "police and emergency powers" of the state to the side of the business elite's agenda, about as close to a coup as events ever got. It had several key elements. First, a complex financial bailout that would carry the city through November and which officially brought the state and city pension funds into the bailout. In fact, DC 37 trustees had already authorized the use of pension fund money on September 4, indicating that the unions were on board with this new development in the crisis regime. The act made Beame's wage freeze state law. It provided a court-monitored debt restructuring. It protected anyone involved in the financial plan from court suits. It imposed a special deputy comptroller for the city responsible to the state comptroller, in effect, a watchdog over the city comptroller. Finally, it created the Emergency Financial Control Board (EFCB). What all of this meant was that repayment to investors was the bottom line to which all other questions deferred. The only opposition to the act came from upstate Republicans who didn't like using state funds to bail the city out. They lost.[97]

The EFCB was to be composed of the governor and state comptroller, the mayor and city comptroller, and three private members appointed to serve at the pleasure of the governor. The first three private members were Ellinghaus; David Margolis of Colt Industries, whose headquarters was still in the city then (but would move within a few years); and Albert Casey of American Airlines, representing another of the city's major industries. No bankers! Casey, however, was replaced early on by Rohatyn, who was simply too central to the process to not be at the new seat of power. The powers of the EFCB extended not only to the city's budget, but to those of the "covered agencies," that is CUNY, the Health and Hospital Corporation, the Housing Authority, etc. Its major power was to limit the size of the total budget of the city and the autonomous agencies. It also required approval for any borrowing the city or the agencies might wish to do. It seems likely this was meant to reduce or limit competition with MAC bonds. The board was not empowered to dictate any single budget item, only to reject budget or plan totals or contracts that would exceed the limits. After some disagreement over the EFCB's relationship to the city Board of Estimate, state attorney general Louis Lefkowitz ruled in December that the EFCB had "final review" on the matter of city contracts as well as the overall budget. The act also included a continuation of collective bargaining, though this was severely crimped by the limits imposed on the budgets and would, in fact, be transformed. In addition, the city was required to draw up a three-year plan for city finances and spending.[98] This setup led to a lot of complex bargaining between city and state, city and agencies, city and unions, etc.

A good example of this process was the way in which tuition was imposed on CUNY. It was not done by simple fiat from EFCB. As the city had its "austerity," and then its smaller "crisis," budgets rejected by the EFCB, it turned to reducing funds for CUNY by $32 million. Since state funds for the university were matching funds based on the city's contribution, this would mean a total loss of $64 million at a time when CUNY was expanding. EFCB also stopped CUNY's capital spending. The Board of Higher Education was in a tight spot. It proposed a four-week furlough to make up the lost money, but EFCB rejected it on the grounds that it was a one-shot deal and not a permanent saving. In May 1976, CUNY closed down for lack of funds. It was finally the New York State Legislature that forced the hand of the Board of Higher Education by making it clear that any state aid was contingent on CUNY charging a tuition, preferably at par with the state university system. Higher Education Board chair Alfred Giardino and four other board members resigned rather than implement the tuition. The state simply appointed a new chair and replaced the resigned members with those who dutifully did what the EFCB could not: impose tuition. The legislature quickly approved funds for CUNY. The fight over cutbacks in the city's hospitals was even more bitter and racially charged.[99]

Though the process was never one of simple dictate, the EFCB would eventually shift the city's spending priorities in a direction business had sought for decades but had found so hard to achieve. As an institution, it represented not only the city and state political leadership, but a broad section of New York City's business elite. In addition to the four members first appointed, it would include: Kenneth Axelson of J.C. Penney; Francis Barry of the Circle Line and MAC; Gilroye Griffen of Bristol-Meyers; Stanley Shuman of Allen & Co.; and John Sawhill of New York University, not only a school but one of the city's biggest landlords.[100] Manufacturing, retail, tourism, real estate, and private higher education were all represented along with finance. The major missing business group was the media. But, at least in print form, the media played an active role in defining and shaping the debate for the public. In fact, DC 37 complained over and again that the *New York Times* and the *Daily News* had picked up big business's demands for cutbacks.[101]

The other important actor in the crisis regime was, of course, the federal government. Everyone involved understood that ultimately the situation required federal assistance on a scale grander than the state could provide or anyone could squeeze out of the city's budget, no matter how austere. A parade of petitioners from the city, business, and labor had traveled hat in hand to Washington, only to be turned back empty-handed again and again. The greater powers given to the EFCB were, in part, meant to convince Washington that the once profligate city was going to mend its fiscal ways, like it or not. The man to convince was Treasury Secretary

William Simon. According to Walter Wriston, when he tried to by-pass Simon in order to speak to then–vice president Nelson Rocke-feller, Simon called him and said:

> "Do you know the way to the Oval Office?"
>
> "Yeah," replied Wriston, "it runs through your front door."
>
> "That's right," said Simon, "Always remember that. I'm in charge of this thing."[102]

And why not? Simon was the quintessential Wall Street insider. Simon was, until he went to Washington, a senior partner in Salomon Brothers in charge of municipal and government bond sales. He had been a member of the New York City Comptroller's Technical Debt Advisory Committee, where he advised the city on bond sales in 1970–71. Now, like his fellow New York bankers and businessmen, he wanted the city to straighten out its fiscal priorities and he had the leverage to do it. So he withheld any loans or credits.[103] Simon must have known that a default on New York City paper would have had disastrous ripple effects across the nation and possibly the world. A November Federal Reserve report showed that 546 banks in twenty-six states held $4.2 billion in New York city and state paper. Another 179 banks in twenty-four states had half their assets in New York bonds. A later report revealed that, in fact, 954 banks in thirty-three states held $6.5 billion in New York paper.[104] A New York default would indeed have had serious national and international implications.

On November 26, Ford and Simon agreed to seasonal loans, loans that had to be paid back within the same fiscal year, of $2.3 billion, and by December 9, Ford had signed it into law. Disaster was averted for the moment. In fact, near crises would continue, and the city's three-year plan to balance the budget would fail. In 1978, both MAC and the EFCB were renewed until 2008. More federal and state aid was needed and was forthcoming, but the budget was not balanced until 1981, and even this was more a technicality than a reality. The sale of MAC bonds didn't end until 1985.[105] Before examining who got what out of the crisis regime, I turn to the complex role of the municipal unions.

The Municipal Unions

The course of events described above could not have happened without the cooperation of the municipal unions. While the unions lacked the power to direct matters, they had the power to disrupt and, thereby, influence them. At times they used that power, but for the most part they, or at least their leaders, accepted the policy and institutional framework proposed by business and implemented by the state as the crisis regime. The leading force in this direction was DC 37's Victor Gotbaum. Gotbaum had been convinced early on that the city's financial problem was real. He agreed to concessions on pension fund contributions, summer hours, and interdepartmental transfers as early as January 1975. In February, he told his union's newspaper, "The crisis we just went through was real, is real, and will continue to be real."[106] Acceptance of the framework and the degree of concessions, however, did not come at once.

Into June, Gotbaum and others still talked tough and resisted proposals for layoffs of civil service workers. From January through April, DC 37 pushed for a march on Washington, which was eventually scheduled for April 26. DC 37's call for such a march was picked up by the Industrial Union Department of the AFL-CIO. As the crisis became more evident the demand for $5 billion in aid to U.S. cities was added to demands for full employment, lower interest rates, and other national demands. Of the sixty thousand union members who marched in Washington, DC 37 claimed it had brought twenty-five thousand. City union leaders followed this up with a meeting with New York State's congressional delegation.[107] On June 4 Gotbaum led a march of ten thousand union members to Wall Street to protest calls for wage cuts from FNCB's Walter Wriston and demanding that the city not pay the banks interest. In May, Gotbaum had dubbed FNCB the "No. 1 enemy" of the city and called for a boycott. Sanitation workers struck when the layoffs of three thousand were announced. City hall was besieged with union demonstrations against layoffs. The Brooklyn Bridge was blocked by laid-off police. An alliance of two DC 37 locals, Local 1930 in the New York Public Library and Local 371 in the Department of Social Services, held an unauthorized demonstration of about three hundred after Gotbaum refused to back a second demonstration.[108]

But as the possibility of default became clear, Gotbaum became convinced that the crisis was real and that the municipal workers would have to make some sacrifices. By late July, the *New York Times* could report a split among the municipal unions, with Gotbaum and DC 37 at the head of the moderates.[109] He also became convinced that city worker pension funds could and should play a role in preventing default.

The person who convinced him was Jack Bigel. Bigel had been an activist in the left-led United Public Workers and, after that union was destroyed by red-baiting and loyalty oaths, had become a financial consultant to the Uniformed Sanitationmen and DC 37 on pension and welfare fund matters. Bigel saw that the possibility of default was real and feared this would lead to federal bankruptcy, which would threaten collective bargaining. Convinced of this possibility, Gotbaum formulated a bottom-line program: whatever happened had to be negotiated; collective bargaining had to be preserved; and job reductions had to be achieved by attrition, not layoffs. Soon the Municipal Labor Committee, which Gotbaum chaired, put forth a positive alternative to the mayor's plan for a wage freeze and mass layoffs: cut remaining "provisional" (non–civil service) employees; cut contracting out by 20 percent, promote early retirement; agree to productivity increases; press for more state and federal aid; and allow the municipal pension funds to purchase up to $400 million in city bonds.[110] This last amount would turn out to be laughably inadequate.

The fear that moved the labor leaders to suggest using pension funds to buy city paper and to eventually make greater concessions was the unknown waters of federal bankruptcy. Barry Feinstein said, "We were just scared to death of all the questions default and bankruptcy evoked."[111] Many years later, Gotbaum and Bigel both said on CUNY-TV that they felt they had to do almost anything to avoid bankruptcy.[112] The question is, why did they think bankruptcy was so likely? Default and bankruptcy are not the same thing, although the words were often used interchangeably. Default on one or more series of city notes might have had serious implications but would not necessarily have signaled any institutional change other than what happened; i.e., state control over city finances in order to restore investor confidence. It was highly unlikely the city would enter Chapter 9 of the federal bankruptcy code. For one thing, as Bigel himself later pointed out, you would need permission of a majority of creditors, which would be almost impossible, given how widespread city paper was. For another, a city cannot simply sell off assets like a private business. In any event, true municipal bankruptcies under Chapter 9 were rare. From 1940 through 1983, there were some 330 municipal bond defaults, but only 9 bankruptcies.[113] Another reason to doubt that bankruptcy was a likely course for the city or state was that the bankers opposed it. Rohatyn went so far as to write a opinion piece for the DC 37 newspaper opposing bankruptcy.[114] What they wanted was a MAC with teeth, but Beame had blocked that. When even the more muscular EFCB couldn't head off default in November, the bankers supported, reluctantly to be sure, the interest moratorium Rohatyn and Rifkin dreamed up as a stalling tactic that would delay default until federal aid could be squeezed out of Simon and Ford. As Wriston said years later, they opposed bankruptcy and "felt very strongly this city should not be run by a federal judge." While he put this in terms of democracy, it is obvious that the bankers stood to lose significantly under bankruptcy. In fact, the only people who seemed to really want bankruptcy, according to Bigel, were the *Wall Street Journal*, the *Village Voice*, and Herman Badillo. Nevertheless, Gotbaum and others took the threat of bankruptcy seriously.[115]

Seldom mentioned in most accounts of the crisis is the behind-the-scenes role of Central Labor Council president Harry Van Arsdale in convincing Gotbaum, Shanker, Feinstein, and others to "tone down the rhetoric that was going on in the early days," as David Rockefeller put it, and to commit pension fund money to head off default. He was particularly important in convincing the reluctant Al Shanker to commit the teachers' pension fund, which he finally did in late October. Van Arsdale was on the Mayor's Management Advisory Board, set up in September 1975 as part of the crisis regime, and would later participate on the Temporary Commission on City Finances, which recommended much of the austerity and development program the city would adopt. Van Arsdale also played a key role in forming the Business/Labor Working Group in early 1976, a labor-business coalition he co-chaired with David Rockefeller. Van Arsdale took a cooperative rather than adversarial line throughout the crisis and helped persuade the public-sector union leaders to do the same.[116]

Having convinced themselves of the danger of bankruptcy, and been convinced by others to follow a cooperative course, the majority of union leaders severely limited their actions and possibilities. Lacking an alternative plan, they accepted both MAC and, later, the EFCB once they were granted guarantees of formal collective bargaining. DC 37 and most municipal unions had negotiated a new contract that called for a 6 percent increase in FY1976, which began in July 1975. At first they resisted Mayor Beame's suggestion that they defer the 6 percent increase due on July 1. But from late July through September 15, the unions negotiated the extent of the first round of concessions at the Americana Hotel, with Ellinghaus and Rohatyn participating. In September they agreed to a wage freeze and to defer the 6 percent increase to 1978, *if there was money available at that time.* The deferral was graduated by employee income; i.e., only the highest-paid lost the whole increase. The union leaders also agreed to let the city reduce payments to the welfare fund by $8 million. The city agreed to reduce its workforce by attrition but later turned to layoffs anyway. Gotbaum and the other leaders felt they had little choice by this time. But, although the total package was said to equal $1 billion, it seems clear that the concessions were meant to encourage investors to buy MAC bonds in the belief the city was finally doing something.[117] In any case, the Americana agreement was a turning point for the unions—away from potential opposition to one of cooperation, a stance that would affect collective bargaining for years.

This is not to say that bargaining went smoothly in 1975. The United Federation of Teachers struck for four days in September 1975 and won some gains. As soon as it was created, the EFCB revoked the teachers' new contract, demanding further concessions. Then, the crisis regime revealed one of its fissures when the mayor; the new deputy mayor appointed as part of the crisis regime, John Zucotti; and the Board of Education sided with the UFT in an assertion of city power, while Governor Carey sided with the EFCB. The tug-of-war went on until February 7, 1977, when the EFCB gave in and approved the UFT contract.[118]

In the fall of 1975, the city had faced another shortfall. The unions this time played a more substantial role as savior by putting up their pension funds to buy MAC bonds. It's not clear who first proposed this. City Comptroller Harrison Goldin discussed the idea with a pension fund trustee in late July. Van Arsdale had also proposed this. In any case, it was Jack Bigel who came up with the plan to use the $8.5 billion in city pension money to borrow $4 billion from the banks in order to buy MAC bonds over the remainder of the three-year city financial plan. The banks charged 8 percent and the bonds paid 11 percent. Although the pension funds eventually made money off the deal, it was very risky at the time. As Bigel put it in one of the CUNY-TV *Oral History* series, "City paper had no market, hence it was worthless. We were its only market." Again the motivation was fear of bankruptcy. "We moved heaven and hell to avoid bankruptcy." In the initial deal the unions put up $2.5 billion. In the end, the pension funds bought $3.8 billion worth of MAC bonds.[119] The ostensible purpose of the union concessions, EFCB, the new city financial plan, and the pension fund and state borrowing was to convince Washington that the city was mending its ways. It worked, along with ongoing pressure from the banks, and Simon and Ford agreed to the $2.3 billion seasonal loans through 1978 that ended the near-term threat of default, if not the city's financial problems.[120]

The agreement to use employee pension funds as a banker for the city had far-reaching implications. The banks and the unions changed roles, as the banks' share of city paper dropped to 1 per-

to continue aid. As Martin Shefter put it, "the chief significance of MUFL lies in what it has *prevented* its members from doing—namely advancing or defending their interests in ways that the city's other creditors would not tolerate" (emphasis in original).[127] Although the union leaders and bankers didn't agree on everything, for example, the extension of an EFCB on steroids, MUFL did encourage cooperation. Its output, however, was not evenhanded. Like the private sector Business/Labor Working Group, it advocated the business elite's program of tax reductions and capital construction, in particular the convention center and Westway.[128]

Thus, by mid-1977, the crisis regime had essentially put the business elite's agenda in place. In addition, they had convinced much of the public as well as the municipal unions that their view of the crisis was correct and their solutions virtually inevitable. But was this vision of a city spending uncontrolled fortunes on municipal workers, poor people, and luxuries unknown in other cities what had really happened? Was there another way to view New York's financial and fiscal troubles? A more detailed look at the city's finances tells a different, more subtle and complex story.

The Blame Game: The Causes of Insolvency

The fiscal crisis was accompanied and followed by a blame game that attempted to pin the fault for insolvency on everyone but the business elite. The poor in general, and the blacks and Puerto Ricans who had migrated to the city in the 1950s and 1960s in particular, were blamed for bloated welfare rolls. City workers and their unions were said to be the cause of soaring city costs. The unique institutions that made New York different, like its public hospitals and housing as well as the City University, were added to the list of fiscal offenders. But were these really the causes of insolvency? Was the rate at which New York's budgets grew really faster? Was its "social democratic polity" the cause of the crisis? What were the factors behind the city's growing deficits?

New York's position as a world financial and producer service center, and its consequent lack of economic diversity, on the one hand, and its age, on the other, made it unique among U.S. cities. At the time, David Gordon noted that "old cities," defined as those that reached economic/industrial maturity before World War I, spent 42 percent more on average per capita than "new cities." Ten of the eleven cities with the highest spending were old cities. Fourteen of the sixteen most indebted cities, including New York, were "old."[129] New York, as the quintessentially "old" American city, followed the pattern of higher expenses than new cities. (But the growth of its budgets in the years leading up to the fiscal crisis did not outpace those of the nation's cities as a whole.)

New York's expenditures rose by 392 percent from 1961 to 1975, according to the Temporary Commission on City Finances (TCCF). But expenditures by all state and city governments in the United States rose by 374 percent in the same period. So New York was only slightly ahead of the national average. In addition, the city budget's rate of growth actually slowed down from 15.9 percent a year in 1966–71 to an average of 10.2 percent a year in the first half of the 1970s. In real terms the drop was even sharper: from 10.8 percent to 3.2 percent.[130] New York's underlying problem lay in the structure of its spending more than in its acceleration. New York City spent more per capita than any other city but Washington, D.C. In functions performed by most cities New York ran ahead of Chicago and Los Angeles by 50 percent. This was largely explained by its status as an "old" city, on the one hand, and by the fact that some costs borne by New York, such as public hospitals, schools, and community colleges, are carried by counties or special districts in other cities.[131]

One frequent explanation of New York's higher spending at the time was the growth and cost of the municipal workforce, which occurred largely as a result of the Great Society expansion of redistributive programs. Although labor costs are the largest part of the city's budget, as they are for any city, this explanation is not convincing. From 1961 to 1975 the municipal workforce grew by 46.7 percent. But state and local employment across the country grew by 89 percent, almost twice the rate of New York City. In this same period the city's total costs of wages, benefits, and pensions rose by

313.6 percent. Since this was significantly slower than the 392.7 percent growth of all city operating costs, it couldn't be the driving force behind budget imbalances. Furthermore, the rate at which the city workforce grew slowed down from 23 percent from 1961 to 1966 to 14.7 percent from 1966 to 1971 and 4 percent from 1971 to 1975, less than 1 percent a year. Similarly, the average annual rate of growth in labor costs slowed from 18 percent from FY1966 to FY1970 to 7.8 percent from FY1971 to FY1975. In real terms labor costs fell from 9.7 percent a year in FY1966–70 to just over 1.2 percent a year FY1971–75. As a proportion of the operating budget, labor costs, including the pension and welfare funds, fell from 56.4 percent to 47.4 percent in those years.[132] Although a series of high-profile strikes (SSEU, TWU, UFT, USA) from 1965 through 1968 gave the municipal unions a reputation for militancy, the formalization of collective bargaining with the city's 1967 Office of Collective Bargaining and the state's 1968 Taylor Law in fact narrowed the scope of bargaining, reduced strikes, increased orderly contract administration, and generally moderated the outcomes of bargaining.[133]

Another frequently mentioned suspect was the city's AFDC roll. From 1961 through 1975 the city's welfare rolls multiplied by four times, just as they did nationally. Furthermore, New York City welfare rolls had risen rapidly during the 1960s, 32 percent a year from FY1966 to FY1970, but from FY1971 to FY1975 they grew modestly by 6.9 percent. In 1974, the proportion of people on AFDC in New York (12 percent) was not significantly higher than in other major cities. In fact, Boston, Philadelphia, Newark, and St. Louis, also older cities, all had a higher proportion of their residents on welfare. As former Lindsay administration official Charles Morris showed, the city's caseload growth rate was less than the national average after 1970. Payments mandated by the state, however, were higher in New York, as were city welfare worker wages due to a higher cost of living.[134] Nevertheless, according to Brecher and Horton's calculations, welfare declined as a proportion of the expense budget by 6.2 percent from 1969 to 1975. Indeed, redistributive spending, which had accounted for 48.7 percent of budget growth in 1961–69, composed only 9.7 percent of the total increase in 1969–75.[135] Thus, it is difficult to place primary responsibility for the actual crisis either on programs for the poor or on the city workforce. These were large pieces of the budget, to be sure, but their costs were being brought under control and their growth rates were not sufficient to explain what pushed the city over the brink in 1975.

Two institutions that stood out as unique to New York and central to its remaining "social democratic polity" were its public hospitals and university system. The hospitals, however, were heavily financed by Medicaid and Medicare. As a tax-levy expense they grew by less than half the rate for the whole expense budget.[136] Employment at CUNY grew by 300 percent from 1961 through 1975, while employee salaries also tripled because so many CUNY employees were necessarily fairly well paid professionals. Only half the cost of CUNY was met by federal and state aid. In spite of open admissions after 1970, the growth of enrollment in CUNY had actually been faster in the 1960s, at 10 percent a year, than in the first half of the 1970s, at 7.6 percent. The staff, which had grown three and a half times from 1960 to 1970, grew by a third from 1970 to 1974. The cost of expanding facilities did not come from the expense budget, but from bonds issued by the CUNY Construction Corporation. The total cost of CUNY had grown at over twice the rate of the city budget, but, at $537.3 million by 1975, it still only accounted for 4.6 percent of the total expense budget. As a local tax-levy expense in 1975 it was $192.2 million, or 2.7 percent.[137] As city officials and others argued at the time, CUNY was part of the long-term solution, a road to better employment for thousands of low-income New Yorkers. To see CUNY, as many did, as simply another form of welfare was certainly shortsighted. The cost was undeniable, but scarcely enough of the budget to be the cause of the crisis.

Another aspect seldom examined in relation to the crisis is the contract, supplies, and equipment line of the expense budget—the focus of pork barrel politics as practiced in New York and most large U.S. cities. From FY1961 to FY1975, the contract, supplies, and equipment budget grew by 620 percent, almost twice the rate of the expense budget and significantly faster than the workforce that would have used the supplies and equipment. By FY1975 this portion of the expense budget amounted to $1.3 billion, two and a half times the expense of CUNY, and accounted for 11 percent of the total. In 1961 it had been 7.6 percent of the expense budget, and in FY1971 7.5 percent. The rise in the Consumer Price Index in those years was 80 percent; it cannot explain this phenomenal growth. Looking in more detail, the contractual services item of the expense budget alone almost tripled from FY1965 to FY1974, growing by 285 percent compared to 218 percent for the city expense budget, partly a function of Lindsay's practice of substituting outside consultants for city employees.[138] But from FY1971 through FY1975 it had slowed down to 7.6 percent growth a year from 35 percent during the previous five years. What had accelerated were the supplies, materials, and equipment lines, which had actually declined slightly from FY1961 to FY1971, but grew by over 18 percent a year from FY1971 to FY1975, nearly twice the rate of the total budget. Despite the slowdown in contracting, the combined contracting, supplies, materials, and equipment lines represented more of a push on expenses than CUNY. It seems most likely that it was the city's decentered and politically accessible contracting and purchasing systems that allowed these items to rise so fast and to push up city costs.

Finances

There were other city spending practices, including financial and budgeting tricks (rollbacks, the magic window, shifting from capital to operating budgets), and heavy reliance on short-term debt, that need to be considered in finding the causes of the crisis. The city's annual debt service, which accrues off the capital budget but is paid from the expense budget, grew by 350 percent from FY1965 to FY1975, not quite as fast as the total budget.[139] Yet, most of this growth occurred after 1970, so from FY1971 to FY1975 it rose from 10 to 15 percent of the expense budget and amounted to $1.8 billion. Combined, debt service and the contract, supplies, materials, and equipment lines almost equal welfare spending and are larger than the education, higher education, and libraries items combined.[140] None of these two items went to the city's employees or welfare recipients and very little to the black and Latino communities. The debt service went to the banks and other major investors, and the other items to the city's contractors, suppliers, and consultants—some of it via the mayor and Board of Estimate, remnants of the county organizations, borough presidents, and other politicians. Since debt service is the child of the capital budget, we must look more closely into that. According to Morris's figures, from FY1965 to FY1970 the capital budget rose by 137.7 percent compared to 117 percent for the expense budget.[141] From FY1971 through FY1975, however, capital expenditures rose by an incredible 341 percent compared to a 49 percent increase in the expense budget.[142] Much of this, of course, is the result of shifting expense items into the capital budget. If we remove the "capitalized" expenses ($26 million in FY1965 and $722 million in FY1975) and compare the adjusted capital budgets for FY1965 to FY1975 the increase is a little over 100 percent.[143] But the long-term debt that paid for capital projects was being pushed upward at an accelerating rate.

Responsible for at least part of this was an innovation of the 1960s used across the country: this was the use of bond-raised city money for private projects with a "public" dimension. In other words, the practice of subsidizing CBD development was increasing and putting more pressure on long-term debt, magnifying the effects of increased short-term debt. This practice had pushed up the ratio of new long-term debt to capital spending nationally above its traditional rate of 50 percent a year to 67.5 percent in 1973 and 118.7 percent in 1977.[144] Something similar occurred in New York in the same period, where this was carried out mainly through the Public Development Corporation, founded in 1966, and the Industrial Development Agency, set up in 1974 to provide low-interest loans to private developers. The city's long-term debt rose by a mere 4.3 percent from 1966 through 1970. But from 1970 through 1975, it rose by 48 percent, more than ten times as fast, coinciding with the office tower boom. This meant that the debt floor under the short-term debt that was the major immediate cause of the crisis had risen dramatically in the years leading up to it. Had the practice of shifting expenses to the capital budget and of increasing long-term debt to subsidize CBD construction been avoided or discontinued early enough by increasing property tax assessments on commercial and industrial property even fairly modestly, the reliance on short-term, high-interest debt would have been much less, the debt service burden been significantly lightened, and the fiscal crisis quite likely avoided. But this was not to be.

From the last term of Robert Wagner Jr. through Abe Beame's midterm, when the problem became a crisis, both comptrollers and mayors accelerated the practice, allowed by state law, of funding operating expenses from money borrowed to fund the capital budget, while issuing more and more short-term notes: revenue anticipation notes, tax anticipation notes, bond anticipation notes, and urban renewal notes, all based on dubious estimates of future revenues. The amount of short-term debt issued each year grew from $4.4 billion in 1970 to $8.4 billion in 1975. Short-term debt went from a negligible 2.3 percent of total debt in 1961 to 10 percent in 1965, 20 percent in 1970, and 36 percent in 1975.[145] As a result, as we have seen, debt service rose from 10 percent of the expense budget in FY1971 to 15 percent in FY1975 on the eve of the crisis.[146] The rise of short-term debt was the financial cul-de-sac in which the city put itself and the main financial reason why the banks eventually refused to underwrite any more city paper. The debt route to covering deficits was bound to fail in a national market awash in high-interest government paper from all levels.

One of the problems with a number of past studies of the fiscal crisis is the failure to break down the periods of the 1960s and first half of the 1970s. As Table 1-1 shows, when these are broken down it is clear that beginning in the 1970s the city was reducing the rate at which spending grew. When inflation is factored in the reduction in growth is substantial. Furthermore, some of the usual suspects in the fiscal crisis blame game do not really fit the profile, most of them growing at the rates below that of the total expense budget. In addition, many of the big items were at least partially funded by the state and federal governments. Federal and state aid became a source of deficits when the rate at which they grew slowed down in the 1970s, largely a consequence of Nixon's and Simon's attempts to cut back on social spending. Reducing the largely mandated programs was all but impossible, and the use of short-term debt to plug the holes accelerated rapidly. The use of short-term debt instead of increased revenues was bound to produce a financial problem and, if unattended, a crisis.

TABLE 1-1
City budget by periods, 1966–71
and 1971–75

	FY1966–71	FY1971–75
Total expense budget	17.9%	10.7%
Social services	37.6%	6.9%
Labor costs	15.0%	9.7%
Health services	14.4%	10.5%
CUNY	10.0%	7.6%
Debt service	6.8%	24.7%
Contractual services	29.4%	7.8%
Supplies & materials	2.6%	18.4%
Equipment	–0.4%	18.7%

Real annual average growth rate of selected items
(1982–84=100)

Total expense budget	11.0%	3.1%
Social services	26.8%	1.5%
Labor costs	8.1%	1.2%
Health services	8.2%	3.0%

Sources: *Report of the Comptroller of the City of New York, 1974–75*, 155; *TCCF Final Report*, June 1977, 124; *Economic Report of the President 2002*, 92. Table mixes items by function and cost for illustrative purposes. For example, labor costs cut across CUNY and social services.

The other side of the problem was tax revenue. Interest and principal on the debt had to be paid out of the expense budget, and the debt service had risen from $402 million in 1961 to $676 million in 1970, an increase of 68 percent, and then to $1.9 billion in 1975, a jump of 188 percent.[147] Tax revenues had not kept pace, even though Lindsay had instituted a few new taxes, including personal, commuter, and business income taxes—over strenuous opposition from business.[148]

One cause of inadequate revenues was the loss of industrial jobs, discussed earlier. Another was the acceleration of white flight and suburbanization in the first half of the 1970s. The recessionary period that began in 1969 and lasted almost unabated in New York City through 1975 halted the in-migration of African Americans and Puerto Ricans, but drove the flight of many presumably middle- and higher-income whites to the suburbs and beyond. Fully half a million left the city between 1970 and 1975.[149] Although many still worked in the city, they no longer lived there, paying no income taxes and less sales tax than before. While Lindsay had asked Albany for a commuter tax equal to the income tax paid by city residents, the state had limited it to one-fifth of the resident rate, causing a significant loss of revenue.[150]

Another problem was the political change that caused the flow of intergovernmental revenue to slow down significantly. Federal and state aid had risen from 25 percent of total expenses in 1962 to 48 percent in 1974, allowing the city to pay for programs it could not have funded on its own.[151] Most of this increase was a consequence of the expanded national social programs of the mid-1960s. But the rate of growth of these intergovernmental revenues slowed dramatically after 1970. During Lindsay's first term, 1966–69, intergovernmental funds, particularly federal money, grew at an annual average of 35 percent. During his second term they grew by only 12.4 percent a year on average, and during Beame's first two years by 16.7 percent.[152] The new fiscally conservative winds blowing through Washington had stranded the city.

Yet another problem, as well as a potential solution, was the real property tax. As in most cities, this had long been New York's core source of revenue. This tax would fall less on the poor and more on big real estate owners and developers, and the Manhattan-based corporations, all politically important groups. While the amount brought in by the real estate tax levy rose by 181 percent from 1961 to 1975, its rate of increase remained flat, slowing down slightly from about 7.9 percent a year between 1966 and 1971 to 7.8 percent from 1971 through 1975. This led to its decline as a percentage of local tax levy revenue from 59 percent in 1966 to 55 percent in 1971 and 50 percent in 1975. The real estate tax dropped from 42 percent of total revenues in 1961 to 24 percent in 1975.[153] This, despite the building boom of the early 1970s!

The problem was that the one local tax that was least affected by the business cycle and by the relatively low incomes of many New Yorkers was growing more slowly than expenses and shrinking as a proportion of revenue. It shrank not due to any slump in real estate values, which doubled from 1960–61 to 1970–71 and grew by another third by 1974–75, but from a drop in the assessment of that value from 82.2 percent of market value in 1960–61 to 57.6 percent in 1970–71 and 48 percent in 1975.[154] Since it had long been city policy to assess outer-borough home owners at a much lower rate than commercial or industrial property, and since reassessments on homes were infrequent, the declining assessment rate of the 1960s and early 1970s had to reflect an easing of assessment on much of the new central business district office space in Manhattan. In addition, businesses like Citibank, Morgan, Met Life, the New York Stock Exchange, and Con Edison routinely applied for reductions in their assessments. District Council 37 bitterly pointed to the big business "line up each spring at the Tax Commission to get lowered assessments."[155] A 1980 New York University study concluded that raising assessments to full value, as state law required, would have increased revenue on the property tax by 50 percent.[156] Even a more modest increase, if implemented early enough, could have averted the fiscal crisis.

To underassessment must be added the extensive tax abatements and partial exemptions that subsidized the office tower boom of the Lindsay years. As the New York University study said, "Most nonresidential exemptions for purposes of economic development go to commercial structures in Manhattan."[157] The theory of urban development by tax incentive has been challenged from many corners. As Brecher and Horton put it:

> The housing and development [tax relief] programs have been criticized for subsidizing projects that would have been built without exemptions. In such cases the tax subsidy only enriches the developers without yielding broader social benefits.[158]

In addition, the proportion of real estate that was totally tax exempt rose from 28 percent in the mid-1950s to 40 percent by 1976. This was due in large measure to the growing practice of putting large private development projects like the World Trade Center (completed), Battery Park City, and Times Square (both on paper at that time) under state-created authorities (Port Authority for World Trade Center, a subsidiary of the Urban Development Corporation for Times Square renewal, and for Battery Park City, its own authority) that were tax-exempt, even though the city paid for much of the underlying infrastructure. In addition, when the World Trade Center failed to fill up, occupants were lured in with more tax incentives. The lost taxes from the World Trade Center alone were estimated at $700 million by 1979.[159] Overall, New York's reliance on the real property tax was way below that of most other large cities. In 1972, property taxes accounted for a little over 50 percent of New York's total local revenue compared to almost 80 percent for the nation's twenty largest cities.[160] We can see, also, in Table 1-2, that real estate revenues grew more slowly than either local levy revenues or total revenues. The sales tax, lifted somewhat by the effects of inflation, grew more rapidly but composed less than 7 percent of total revenues. A more realistic assessment and taxation policy for commercial and industrial projects and property

TABLE 1-2
Average annual growth rates of major revenue sources

	FY1966–71	% of Total '66	FY1971–75	% of Total '75
Total revenue	16.8%	100.0%	12.3%	100.0%
Total local levy	9.8%	53.1%	10.6%	48.3%
Real estate tax	7.9%	38.1%	7.8%	24.1%
Sales tax	4.8%	10.3%	12.0%	6.6%
Business taxes	1.8%	8.6%	12.8%	6.0%
Federal aid	53.0%	8.3%	18.4%	20.6%
State aid	22.3%	27.3%	11.6%	31.1%

Average annual real growth rate selected revenues
(1982–84=100)

Total revenue	10.1%	4.3%
Total local levy	4.5%	3.0%
Real estate tax	3.0%	1.0%
Sales tax	0.5%	4.1%

Source: TCCF, *Final Report*, June 1977, 97. *Economic Report of the President 2002*, 392. Does not include all revenue sources.

would have made the scramble for short term loans far less necessary. This didn't happen because of the intense ongoing pressure from the city's uniquely powerful business elite.

The argument against increasing property or any other taxes on business is that firms would leave the city or move much of the work elsewhere. As we shall see later, however, most of the large financial and producer service firms that had become the core of New York's big business community by the mid-1970s exported not only their services, but their high rents and much of their tax burden as well. Landowners, developers, construction firms, and utilities, all of whom also compose a large section of the business community, simply could not move. The most likely candidates for relocation, for whatever reasons, were the multinational industrial corporations whose actual production was elsewhere in any case.

And, of course, many had left for one or another suburban area. But it was not necessarily taxes that sent them packing. For example, when GTE left in 1970 for Stamford, Connecticut, its stated reasons were not taxes, but "availability of housing, and construction and land costs."[161] Also, in some measure, as Matthew Drennan argues, the flight of industrial headquarters also reflects the decline of that sector and, I would add, numerous mergers and acquisitions in the industrial sector. Looked at in terms of the rising service sector there was and has been growth in its office functions in the city, reflected in the office tower booms of the 1960s and 1980s. This includes the trend of foreign firms to open offices in New York. Indeed, in the aftermath of the 1975 fiscal crisis, what Drennan calls the city's corporate headquarters complex grew 124 percent by 1982, measured in value added. All despite New York's high, though temporarily frozen, tax rates and a half decade of economic recession, indicating that locational decisions are made on many bases.[162]

In 1975, however, power trumped fact or analysis. The crisis regime succeeded in shifting the city's financial priorities and halting and even reversing New York's "social democratic polity" and its Great Society offspring. But the emergency crisis regime, with its denial of home rule and its transparently business-dominated agencies, could not be justified forever. It had to leave a legacy that would institutionalize the agenda of the corporate headquarters complex and the business elite more generally.

2

From Crisis Regime to Mayoral-Business Coalition: The Rise of Koch

While the various organizations that composed the crisis regime were central to the eventual resolution of the crisis, the EFCB, MAC, and even the MMAC did not run the city day-by-day. The mayor still mattered, and few wanted a second term for Abe Beame. Just what electoral coalition, however, was to bring a credible administration to office remained to be seen. The old Democratic coalition of clubhouse, working-class ethnics, and minority communities had shattered during the Lindsay years. The clubhouse coalition that took back city hall under Beame was inadequate to govern or, in all likelihood, even to elect again at the citywide level. The city unions were a somewhat new factor in electoral coalition building. The African American and Latino communities were alienated by their exclusion and by the rapid decline of services in their neighborhoods.

The disarray of the Democratic Party became apparent as seven candidates lined up for the 1977 primary. The candidates reflected many of the disaffected constituencies of the city. Facing Beame were: Ed Koch, erstwhile liberal reformer appealing to the increasingly conservative white ethnic vote; Mario Cuomo, liberal Queens Democrat backed by Governor Carey and endorsed by the Liberal Party; Percy Sutton, Manhattan borough president and a mainstream spokesman for the black community; Congressman Herman Badillo, representing the city's Puerto Rican population; Bella

Abzug, outspoken feminist; and Joel Harnett, wealthy publisher and president of the City Club. Beame, Koch, and Cuomo all spent over $1 million in the primary and runoff. In the primary, the turnout was high and the vote split more or less evenly among the five leading candidates, with Koch first at 20 percent, Cuomo just behind with 19 percent, and Beame trailing third with 17 percent. The runoff was between Koch and Cuomo. Koch got most of the county organizations, except Queens, which backed Cuomo. He also got Badillo's backing and that of most of the city's black politicians. Cuomo got most of the union endorsements. Koch won the primary but again faced Cuomo, running on the Liberal line in the general election. Koch won, with 50 percent of the vote to Cuomo's 41 percent. The ethnic vote split, with a majority of the Jewish vote going to Cuomo and the two splitting the Italian vote—in other words, voters did not follow ethnic lines to the degree they once had. The unions also split in the general elections, with the public-sector unions backing Koch and the Central Labor Council and building trades backing Cuomo. The county organizations, however, all backed Koch, including those that had supported Cuomo in the primary.[1]

The fragmentation of the Democratic constituencies, the split among the unions, and the long-term decline of the county organizations all meant a city government even more splintered and permeable than its already decentered structure provided. But this occurred in the context of a centralized setup imposed by the crisis regime. The MAC, EFCB, the Office of the Special Comptroller, the MMAC, etc. all brought the central authority of the state into city affairs. At the same time, as Bailey points out, they all focused on the mayor. Thus, ironically, the mayor's importance was magnified at the expense of the Board of Estimate (and hence the county organizations) and city council. In particular, the major financial functions of the comptroller and the Board of Estimate were, in effect, limited by the EFCB, which dealt directly with the mayor.[2] On the one hand, the mayor was in alliance with the crisis regime. But the regime, though the creature of the state, was also in large measure the possession of the city's business elite and its priorities were theirs. The mayor also became more accessible to those whose power had grown as a result of the crisis regime—namely, the city's already disproportionately powerful business elite. This accessibility was not only that which had long been a factor via the City Club, CBC, Downtown–Lower Manhattan Association, Real Estate Board of New York, etc., nor even the enhanced power via MAC and the EFCB, but by personal ties to the new mayor, which it turns out were many and growing. Given the centrality of the mayor in the crisis and post-crisis regimes, it was virtually inevitable that the business elite or various sections of it would focus more on him.

Until his downfall during his third term, Koch would be funded by the business elite as no mayoral candidate before him. By 1985, when he ran for his third term, Koch would raise $11.9 million, of which over $7 million was spent on the Democratic primary. Altogether, from 1981 through 1986, the Democratic candidates for citywide office, along with the county organizations, raised $30 million. Most of this came from the usual coalition of real estate, finance, and large corporate donors. The top fifty contributors accounted for a quarter of the total, and 70 percent of them had business before the Board of Estimate, which had a say in construction and infrastructure projects, albeit within EFCB limits. The top 435 contributors to Koch's 1985 campaign provided almost half the $7 million he spent on the primary.[3]

Perhaps the symbol of Koch's unity with CBD New York was the fact that the private swearing-in ceremony for his third term was held at the home of Colt Industries chief and EFCB veteran David Margolis. What kept Koch in office, besides pandering to racial prejudice, was, according to Newfield and Barrett, "a governing coalition of real estate, finance, the Democratic Party machine, the media, and the recipients of city contracts."[4] Mollenkopf correctly adds middle-class white ethnics in the outer boroughs, not all of whom were regular Democrats.[5] Koch's coalition was, for a while, even broader than that. In his run for second term in 1981, Koch had won the nomination of both the Democratic and Republican parties, the latter without a primary. To attract middle-class and working-class ethnic votes, "Ethnic Ed" used the standard "white backlash" codes of the day. To diminish any opposition from the black and Latino communities he abolished the anti-poverty organizations that had been strongholds of black and Latino political activists, notably the Council Against Poverty and the community corporations in early 1978.[6]

In 1985, perhaps sensing the loss of support among his big business donors, Koch proposed a campaign finance reform law that imposed limits of $3.6 million each for the primary and general elections. Individual contributors were limited to $3,000. The law was passed by referendum in November 1988 and was in effect for the 1989 election. Although the new law undoubtedly stopped the escalation of election costs, spending would remain high. Koch spent $4 million in the primary, while victor David Dinkins spent $7.2 for the entire campaign. Limits had been imposed and much public money substituted for private funds, but even with the city's four-to-one public financing formula, the bar for private money had been raised far beyond the meager $2.6 million spent by all candidates in the 1969 election.[7]

While clearly dominated by the business elite, Koch's governing coalition included the county organizations, which gave him influence over the borough presidents and hence "developmental" projects requiring Board of Estimate approval. In addition, Koch neutralized one potential source of grassroots opposition by pouring city money into the many nonprofit organizations that provided some of the city's social services. Thus, while cutting back on city services to the poor, he increased money to the professionals who ran these private agencies, making their officials think twice about advocacy actions that might annoy the mayor. The patronage character of this funding was revealed in the fact that 40 percent of these contracts were issued on a no-bid basis. Between 1980 and 1989, service contracts rose in value by more than a quarter in real terms, reaching $2.6 billion by the time he left office.[8]

Koch and the Shift in City Priorities

As Bailey argues, "Businessmen became directly involved in the oversight of New York's management through the MAC, EFCB, Mayor's Management Advisory Committee, and the new deputy mayors."[9] Here Bailey is referring to their role in bringing greater efficiency to city operations, which, given the later revelations of widespread corruption, could not have reached too deeply. These business activists also promoted their agenda for a shift in city priorities. That agenda came in many forms, some old, some new, but an important version was that of the Temporary Commission on City Finances' final report, *The City in Transition: Prospects and Policies for New York*, published in June 1977. The TCCF included among its members participants in the crisis regime such as academic and MAC member Donna Shalala, investment banker and MAC member John Coleman, construction and real estate magnate Robert Tishman, labor leader Harry Van Arsdale, and, of course, the ubiquitous Richard Shinn. While the report was published under Beame, many of its recommendations would be followed by Mayor Koch over his three terms.

The TCCF's major policy recommendations were listed under Part III of the report, "Developmental Policies for the Future." The thrust was the familiar one that the city must promote income-producing businesses by lowering taxes and providing various incentives. It stated, "In the future, the City's tax policy must be reoriented so that it promotes rather than retards the local private economy, even if this means further contraction of the local public economy." In addition to a staggering list of taxes to be abolished or reduced, the report called for the end to rent control, which, it argued, would increase real property tax collections. It also called for cutting those pension benefits not mandated by state law and cutting city hospital beds by five thousand. Not all of its recommenda tions were favorites of the business elite and not all their favorites were included, but the thrust of "developmentalism" was clear.[10]

Another indicator of the new direction for city policy can be found in the MAC *Annual Reports*. In his opening letter to the governor in the 1978 report, Rohatyn makes the following statement concerning the capital budget:

> The near bankruptcy of New York City was as much due to improvident capital spending as it was to budget gimmickry. The enormous sums lost on its Mitchell-Lama middle-income housing had to be made up by reduced services and higher taxes; the municipal hospital system could still bring the City down.

In the next paragraph he writes that over half the $4.5 billion to be raised by MAC during the city's four-year plan would be spent on capital projects. "This money," he writes, "together with State agency funds for such projects as a new convention center and Westway, is the key to the city's economic future."[11] Housing and health care were seen as a drag on the city, while tax-abated construction projects were its future. Yet, both Mitchell-Lama housing and the city hospitals were income-producing services. The hospitals, as we saw, were mostly subsidized by Medicaid and Medicare and their burden on local revenues grew at only half the rate of the expense budget. Nevertheless, the budget priorities of the Koch administration would follow the lines of TCCF and MAC recommendations, with some exceptions.

As if to make sure this would be the case, New York's business elite regrouped in the late 1970s. In 1977, the year the TCCF published its report, the Chamber of Commerce and the Chamber of Industry Association merged to create the powerful Chamber of Commerce and Industry, with David Rockefeller as chair. The merged chamber recruited business leaders to serve as advisers to city government in hopes of making it more businesslike. Rockefeller also chaired the Economic Development Council, an older elite business governmental pressure group. In addition, he founded the New York City Partnership in 1979, an organization of executives from the city's top 150 corporations united to push development as they understood it.[12]

To measure the policy shift, it is important to look at the allocation of spending during the first crisis period and the subsequent years. As Table 2-1 shows, the first crisis period, June 1975 to June 1978, saw a rise in welfare and other redistributive budget items due to the lingering impact of the recession and the effects of city worker layoffs. Total spending, including both expense and capital budget, rose by a very modest 6.1 percent, or 1.5 percent a year. Welfare rose by 13.8 percent, while developmental functions dropped a sizable 37.1 percent, due to a freeze on capital projects. Clearly, this first period, mostly under Beame, did not reflect the goals of the business elite, MAC, EFCB, etc., but a necessary, though unsuccessful, transition toward a balanced budget. During the period of 1978 through 1982, with Koch as mayor, the shift in priorities became apparent. Total expenditures rose by 25 percent, or 4 percent annually; welfare was cut by 0.9 percent, or just under 0.2 percent annually. Although overall redistributive functions increased by 20.8 percent, or 4.2 percent a year, this still ran behind total expenditures, though slightly ahead of the expense budget's growth. Developmental functions, however, grew by 72.1 percent, or 14.4 percent a year, almost twice the rate of total spending. This latter is due entirely to capital spending. This was the $2.5 billion Rohatyn promised to devote to the convention center and Westway (the latter was eventually defeated) and similar business-backed CBD projects.[13] Measured in real terms from 1978 through 1982, the expense budget declined by almost 16 percent, while the capital budget rose by 85 percent. The portion of the capital budget spent on infrastructure, the preferred expenditure of the corporate headquarters complex, rose from a mere 10.8 percent in 1976, reflecting the freeze on new capital projects, to 60 percent by 1981.[14]

The Koch administration would continue to reflect the priorities of the crisis regime throughout its second and third terms. From 1983 through Koch's last year, capital spending rose 121 percent, or 17.3 percent a year. Total spending in that period rose 62.4 percent, or 8.9 percent a year, less than half the rate of the capital budget. In terms of the proportion of total spending in the period 1983–89, redistributive functions dropped from 33.2 percent of the total to

TABLE 2-1
Average annual growth of NYC budgets, 1975–82

	1975–78 %	1978–82 %
Capital budget	–8.1	5.1
Expense	4.5	4.0
Total expenditures	1.5	5.0
Redistribution	3.4	4.2
Welfare	3.5	–0.2
Allocative	1.9	7.1
Developmental	–9.3	14.4

Source: Brecher & Horton, *Setting Municipal Priorities*, 1984, 243, 246.

30.8 percent, while developmental items rose from 8.4 percent to 9.5 percent. Most allocative functions declined slightly, except criminal justice.[15]

The developmentalism of the Koch era was different from the mega-projects of the age of Robert Moses. For one thing, the private sector not only benefited, as always, but also directed things. For another, federal money dried up as the Reagan administration cut all urban programs. Federal regional and urban development funds fell from a 1980 peak of $19.8 billion to $8.7 billion in 1990.[16] In 1980, one out of every five dollars the city spent came from the federal government. By 1990, it was one out of ten.[17] Central business district development would have to be funded by a combination of public and private money directed at projects initiated by private developers, banks, and big business generally. To clear the way for private developer/banker leadership, the City Planning Commission and the Department of City Planning, which had already lost their power over the capital budget during the crisis regime, became rubber stamps for the mayor, only approving or disapproving projects assembled by private operators.[18] The public contribution came in the form of huge tax breaks and generous subsidies from the city treasury and capital budget.

Koch's tax policies closely followed crisis regime/corporate headquarters complex lines. During his reign business taxes were lowered, as was the property tax rate and the commercial rent tax. The stock transfer tax was neutralized through rebates to those who paid it, bringing an annual loss of $480 million. Although the tax levy on commercial and industrial property grew, market value continued to far outstrip assessments. From 1983 to 1989 total property market value increased by 174 percent, and taxable assessments by 45.5 percent. As a percentage of all local tax revenue, real property taxes dropped from 53.6 percent in 1975 to 34 percent in 1983. Exemptions through 421a's for new residential building and J-51 exemptions, extended to co-ops and condos in 1975, were costing the city a total of $250 million a year by 1983. These programs of exemptions and abatements, known as tax expenditures, amounted to hundreds of millions a year and would rise to $655 million in 1991. The Citizens Budget Commission reported that from 1976 to 1981 total property tax expenditures had grown by 28 percent to reach $2.5 billion in FY1981. Perhaps most remarkable was the fact that during the Koch years the city did not use the total limit the state imposed on the real property tax. The value of the unused margin of the property tax was about $144.5 million in 1975. With the need to pay off huge amounts to short-term debt, this margin fell between 1975 and 1978, then rose again and fell in 1982 to $3.4 million. After that, however, this gift to the corporate headquarters complex and real estate interests rose to $1.8 billion in 1989, Koch's last year. It would go up even more later.[19]

The impact of this on the effective tax rate of the different tax classes is indicative of how Koch benefited big business develop-

TABLE 2-2
Property tax 1983–89 ($billions)

	1983	1989	% Change
Taxable assessed value	43.8	63.7	45.4
Taxable market value	129.9	355.4	174.0
Tax levy	3.99	6.2	55.7

Source: *Comptroller's Report, FY1992*, 245.

ment. But it also reveals how he gave a break to outer-borough home owners and renters in small buildings with one hand, while taking away in a less visible form with the other. In 1981, the state legislature amended the code to make tax assessments below market value legal. At the same time, it created four classes of property: (I) one- to three-family houses; (II) all other residential real estate, including apartment buildings, condos, and co-ops; (III) utilities; and (IV) office buildings, and industrial and commercial buildings. From 1983 to 1989, the effective tax rate for Class I fell by over 50 percent, clearly a benefit that many outer-borough residents, particularly outer-borough home-owning ethnics and gentrifiers, would feel in their pocketbooks. The effective rate also fell by 22 percent for luxury apartment buildings, condos, and co-ops, a boon to well-paid professionals working in the CBD. But the effective rate for Class III, utilities, actually rose. This increase, however, was easily passed along to homeowners and renters in monthly bills, not from the city, but from the companies, a more invisible tax on owners and renters alike. Finally, the effective tax rate on Class IV businesses fell by 23 percent over the same period.[20]

To these gains were added new tax breaks through the Industrial and Commercial Incentive Board, (ICIB), created in 1977. By 1982 the ICIB was handing out $47 million a year to CBD office construction. Another giveaway program was the Industrial Development Agency (IDA), created in 1974, just before the crisis. It issued tax-free bonds and used these revenues to make low-interest loans to firms, ostensibly to create jobs. By 1983, however, 38 percent of companies receiving IDA loans had produced no jobs, and 45 percent, fewer than promised. To top all this off, another boom in CBD office space was bypassed as a source of revenue as real property tax assessments dropped from 34 percent of total market value in 1983 to 18 percent in 1989. This meant that while the tax rate on assessed property values remained just above 9 percent for this period, the rate on full value fell from just over 3 percent in 1983 to 1.7 percent in 1989.[21]

Newfield and Barrett described some of the results of this largesse:

Koch presided over a building boom in white Manhattan. Between 1982 and 1985, sixty new office towers went up south of 96th Street. Real estate values in gentrifying neighborhoods in Manhattan and Brooklyn went soaring, and the exodus of major corporations from New York was stopped. A new convention center was built, a half-dozen luxury-class hotels were financed with tax abatements, and tourism increased, injecting revenue into the Manhattan economy of theaters, hotels, and restaurants.[22]

To this list must be added Battery Park City and the beginnings of the Times Square renovation, conducted under the protection of tax-exempt state authorities. The cost in lost taxes and subsidies of the Times Square Development Project alone rose to $400 million by 1985, well before it actually took off.[23] The new office towers, luxury apartments, midtown cleanup, and gentrified neighborhoods reflected another lurch in the city's economy toward business services and away from manufacturing and transport.

The impact of the crisis regime and post-crisis Koch era on working-class New York was severe. The increase of the transit fare from 35 cents to 50 cents was accompanied by a tripling of subway breakdowns and a 25 percent rate for out-of-service buses. CUNY tuition brought a 30 percent reduction in enrollments, while the layoff of fifteen thousand public school teachers increased class size by 25 percent. Five city hospitals and twenty-eight drug rehab centers were closed. Overall, the city workforce was reduced by 20 percent, with parks workers cut by 25 percent in 1975 and 29 percent more in 1984. Sanitation was down a whopping 48 percent, the police by 14 percent.[24] Income inequality grew: the share of the lowest 20 percent of households dropped from 15.4 percent in 1975 to 11.6 percent in 1987, while that of the top 10 percent grew from 43.8 percent to 49.2 percent in those years.[25] Middle- and working-class neighborhoods were poorer, dirtier, less safe, less healthy, and harder to get to.

Writing in 1980, fairly early in the process, Brecher and Horton described the outcome of the crisis regime priorities as follows:

These policies yielded a balanced budget, but at what cost? The greatest burden was born by the city's poor, whose standard of living was reduced. Federal food stamp benefits, which are linked to price changes, helped the poor maintain their nutritional standards, but the basic welfare grant of $258 a month for a family of four, available in 1975, now is worth $129 due to inflation. The shelter allowance of the poor was also frozen at its 1975 level.

The consequence of these reductions in living standards was that by 1980 there was a $1 billion gap between housing costs and the income of the city's poorest residents. The result was further abandonment and deterioration of the city's housing stock, with negative consequences for property tax collections.[26] In the 1980s this produced a homeless population of sixty thousand, and from 1977 through 1985 the poverty rate rose from 17 percent to 25 percent, despite the economic upturn. Nevertheless, from 1983 to 1989 public assistance transfer payments as a percentage of the budget dropped by 2.9 percent, while from 1986 through 1990 annual public assistance payments per person fell from $2,900 to $2,600 in real terms. From 1977 to 1986, the real incomes of New Yorkers fell 10.9 percent for the bottom tenth and 6.6 percent for the next decile. The city's top tenth saw a 22 percent increase in real income.[27]

The city's employees also suffered. Layoffs of 20 percent, which hit the lowest-paid hardest, sent some sixty thousand to the unemployment and welfare lines. All city workers lost real income well into the 1980s. From 1978 through 1980 city clerical workers, custodians, and motor vehicle operators lost 15 percent. Between 1975 and 1982, police and firefighters lost 20 percent. By 1985, city workers were winning contracts that would exceed inflation. DC 37 won a three-year contract with gains of 5 percent and 6 percent, while the uniformed services got thee 6 percent increases. In real terms, however, most city workers did not make up what they had lost. From 1976 through 1982 civilian employees, excluding teachers, lost 17.7 percent in buying power, but from 1982 through 1991 they gained only 7.7 percent. Teachers and police came out slightly ahead in real terms, with a gain by 1991 of 4.1 percent and 1.7 percent, respectively. But the institution of collective bargaining remained a shambles. It had become common practice by then for city employees to be without contracts for a year or more as negotiations dragged out. The 1985 DC 37 contract negotiators, for example, took from January 1984 to April 1985 to reach agreement.[28]

Development for Some, Underdevelopment for Others

Urban development necessarily involves the clash of classes and various economic and social interests over space. For the speculators, financiers, developers, and builders, the stakes are high. From at least the mid-eighteenth century large landowners began dividing their estates into plots for sale. A young John Jacob Astor arrived in New York in 1784, already rich from his fur trading, and began speculating in Manhattan land, thus becoming the richest man in America. By that time, the city was already sorting itself out by social class. The old eighteenth-century city, "one oriented to the waterfront, one in which work and home, employer and employee (apprentice and journeyman) were all in a single building" and where "the upper and lower classes had jostled together on the street, in the market place" changed shape. As Weil describes it, "Beginning in 1780, lower Manhattan began to be divided into commercial streets—where stores and offices were concentrated— and residential streets."[29]

This sorting out into the shape of a commercial capitalist city also involved the separation of classes. The upper class moved away from the port and the cluttered city center, first to Bowling Green, then beyond Canal Street and later beyond Houston. As the modes of transportation allowed, the middle class followed suit. Washington Square became home to the rising capitalist class in the 1840s, and, shortly after, the truly rich built the first mansions on Fifth Avenue above Fourteenth Street. The working class lived in converted buildings left by the middle and upper classes and in boardinghouses. The city also sorted out by race, as free black communities took root in Manhattan and Brooklyn with their own churches and institutions. As Lewis Mumford described the process, in reference to London, "the dissociation of the upper and lower classes achieves form in the city itself. The rich drive, the poor walk. The rich roll down the grand avenues; the poor are off-center, in the gutter; and eventually a special strip is provided for the ordinary pedestrian, the sidewalk."[30]

All along the way money is made and people are displaced. At first it is Native Americans and farmers, then the African American community that occupied part of what became Central Park; eventually it would be the working class, poor and not so poor, in the path of Robert Moses's bulldozer. The matter of land speculation was made easier by the Commissioners' Plan of 1811, which laid out Manhattan as a grid of 2,028 rectangular blocks from Houston Street to 155th Street (excepting Greenwich Village). While it would be decades before that space was filled by urban development, its merit, according to surveyor John Randel, was the "ease it allows in buying, selling, and making a profit" on Manhattan land.[31] New York became not only the nation's premier port and commercial center, but also the administrative center of the country's new corporate capitalism. Thomas Bender wrote that "the skyline marked not only growing Manhattan dominance but corporate ascendance too. Gradually corporate values and Wall Street financial power reshaped the metropolitan economy and with it the conditions of innovation."[32] The development of the skyscraper would once again transform the fight over space as the profits to be made from central business district development soared like the buildings themselves.

By the Koch era, of course, most of the land, not only in Manhattan but in the outer boroughs as well, was occupied. Hence, the struggle over space had a zero-sum character. In this struggle, New York's lower-income working-class families were caught in a three-way vise of housing abandonment, CBD and luxury housing development, and gentrification. The first reduced available low-cost housing, while the latter two pushed prices up on existing and future housing. Massive abandonment, torching, and tax evasion in the 1970s led to the loss of tens of thousands of housing units, mostly in low-income neighborhoods. By 1980, 3.5 percent of the city's residential properties, including 26 percent of its rental apartment units, were in arrears, while countless others had been abandoned or burned down. Most of these were in tenements or multiple-unit buildings in low-income neighborhoods: Harlem, the South Bronx, Bedford-Stuyvesant, Brownsville, and the Lower East Side. The net loss of housing units from 1970 through 1984 was 360,000. Although the number of units grew in the second half of the 1980s, it only reached its 1975 level in 1987, while the population had grown by about a quarter of a million.[33]

Roger Starr, housing commissioner under Lindsay and Beame, thought this fine and called for "planned shrinkage": the withdrawal of capital and services from such neighborhoods in hopes the devastation would drive the poor from the city. He could hardly have been more blunt about what he meant. He wrote:

> Stop Puerto Ricans and the rural blacks from living in the city. . . . Our urban system is based on the theory of taking the peasant and turning him into an industrial worker. Now there are no industrial jobs. Why not keep him a peasant. Better a thriving city of five million than a Calcutta of seven million.

Starr needn't have worried because redlining and a change in New York State banking law that allowed savings and loan banks to invest outside the state had done the job and would continue to make low-cost housing scarce.[34]

Gentrification joined office tower and luxury apartment development to push up the value of real estate to new highs, further squeezing the working class and devastating the poor, more of whom became homeless. For example, prices in Elmhurst-Corona, Queens, rose from $43,000 for a single family home and $56,000 for a two-family dwelling in 1977 to a starting price of $180,000 in Elmhurst in 1985 and $190,000 in Corona in 1987. By 1989, prices reached from $240,000 in Corona to $265,000 in Elmhurst.[35] For renters matters were even worse. The income required to rent a median-priced apartment now surpassed the actual median income of renters by $2,000 by 1987. The median monthly rent of vacant units had grown from $240 in 1981 to $450 in 1987. The percent of renters living below the poverty line hovered just below a quarter of all renters in 1987, down only one percentage point since 1981.[36]

The impact of gentrification can be seen in the residential countertrend of the 1980s. As population grew as a result of Latino and Asian immigration, the natural tendency was for more areas in the city to increase their nonwhite population. Indeed, the city's housing and vacancy survey, taken every three years, showed that forty-three out of fifty-four "subboroughs" increased their nonwhite population. Gentrification, of course, would reveal the opposite trend, an increase in white residents. DeGiovanni and Minnite concluded:

> The nonwhite to white racial transition appears to be linked to gentrification in at least 7 subboroughs: Brooklyn Heights/ Fort Greene, Park Slope/Carroll Gardens, Sunset Park, [North] Crown Heights/Prospect Heights, South Crown Heights, and Williamsburg/Greenpoint in Brooklyn, and East Harlem in Manhattan.[37]

Although they inhabit too small an area to show up on the housing and vacancy survey, the plight of low-income renters was well illustrated by the impact of gentrification on the Puerto Rican population of the Lower East Side east of Avenue A, also called Alphabet City. This old immigrant area became a destination for Puerto Ricans moving from the island in the 1950s, as the older European immigrant groups moved out. By the 1970s, however, young whites, often professionals, began moving into Alphabet City and transformed the neighborhood. From 1980 to 1990, the number of blocks in which 50 percent or more of the residents were classified as Hispanic had dropped from twenty-two to thirteen. In addition, this area faced serious disinvestment as residents lost factory jobs in the declining garment industry. As property values dropped, developers bought up lots and buildings to sell for a neat profit.[38]

Gentrification was not simply a natural process of artists, hippies, and "pioneers" seeking affordable housing to populate and/or renovate in the 1960s and 1970s. It was the safety valve for the vast army of well-paid professionals who populate the city's central business districts and attendant cultural organizations. It was aggressively encouraged by changes in the city's tax-incentive programs discussed earlier, namely the creation of 421a's for new residential construction and the extension of J-51s to condos and co-ops. As William Sites explains:

> It was the economic and political reinvestment in New York's core business district during the second half of the 1970s that put real muscle behind renewal in the East Village. Spatial analysis of the city's new tax-incentive programs, such as the 421a and J-51 initiatives, shows that their use was first concentrated near the Midtown area, then spread outward to nearby neighborhoods. By 1980 developers were converting or upgrading more than 3,700 East Village housing units to higher-income use with the help of J-51 subsidies.[39]

On an anecdotal note, I recall returning in 2001 to a tenement on Fourteenth Street between Avenues B and C where I had lived during the early 1970s, when it was still a slum with the bathtub in the kitchen and the toilet in the hall. It was cheap and we exposed the bricks and built an elaborate loft bed. By 2001, the building had been completely refurbished, shower and toilet inside, and the tiny apartments were renting for $1,500.

In his last term, Koch did launch a major push for new housing and the renovation of the vast numbers of in rem buildings seized by the city for nonpayment of taxes or abandonment. The ambitious $4.2 billion ten-year program was supposed to create 252,000 units, of which 24 percent were for homeless and low-income families. In the end, it produced 43,000 new units and several thousand more renovations, only about 5,000 of which went to the homeless by 1989. These latter units were clustered in buildings solely for the homeless and located in low-income communities, further contributing to slum intensification.[40]

Given the sizable tax breaks, the huge unused margins of the property tax, most of which were benefiting the corporate headquarters complex, on the one hand, and the sacrifices made by city employees and low-income New Yorkers, on the other, it is hard not to conclude that the crisis regime had, indeed, turned the city's priorities around and that its employees and working-class residents had financed both the return to fiscal health and the CBD building boom of the 1980s.

The crisis regime formally ended on June 30, 1986, when the Financial Control Board relinquished direct control over city finances, though it would remain as a "watchdog" until 2008 and briefly bark when Mayor Dinkins had budget problems. The city had adopted the generally accepted accounting principles and made other reforms in the budgeting process. Its budget showed surpluses and city paper was selling on the market. By the time the FCB went dormant, however, the coalition that had been held together by Mayor Koch and the institutions of the crisis regime crumbled in favor of a "greed is good" free-for-all by some members of the city's financial and real estate interests. Koch had invited such favored personalities as Ivan Boesky, Carl Icahn, and Donald Trump to his final inauguration in January 1986, as if to symbolize this new mood that swept the country, but had its roots in the global city. A series of scandals involving various raids on the city treasury and job pool would hurt not only Koch, but also the county Democratic organizations largely responsible for them.[41] The unions would continue to split their political endorsements and support. The city's governmental structure came under judicial attack and a charter commission was set up that would, after the Supreme Court struck down the Board of Estimate, give the city a new, more centralized structure in which the mayor, not the council, would gain "residual power"—and most of the power over the budget. As one study noted, New York was the only city in the United States in which residual power went to the mayor, not the city council.[42] In that sense, it was the child and heir of the crisis regime. Charter Commission chair Frederick A.O. Schwarz, scion of the toy retailing family, pushed to give the mayor final say on land use and total control of the $5 billion contract budget, as well as the abolition, rather than reform, of the Board of Estimate. Not surprisingly, the Real Estate Board of New York praised the scheme. The City Planning Commission was to be appointed, not elected, and its eleven members would serve five years. Later it was revised to have a chair and twelve members: the chair and six members were appointed by the mayor, giving him a majority; five were appointed by the borough presidents, and one by the public advocate. In the end, Schwarz didn't get all he wanted and the city council was given final vote on land use, but the concentration of power in the mayor's office, now freed of the Board of Estimate, had been substantially increased.[43] Regime change had become permanent.

The Unions Under Koch

New York City's huge labor movement might have resisted much of the damage done to the city's working class and its neighborhoods by acting together and/or in coalition with the city's African American and Latino communties. On the face of it, organized labor appeared as large as ever, and even reviving from the shock of the fiscal crisis. On Labor Day, September 7, 1981, for the first time in over a decade, two hundred thousand union members marched up Fifth Avenue. Spirits were high. While unions across the country were losing members, those in New York could claim the same numbers, roughly a million, as a quarter-century earlier. It had maintained twice the union density of the country, constituting a potentially awesome political force.

The numbers and spirit of the day, however, hid a different reality. For one thing, former giants like the ILGWU and the ILA had shrunk dramatically as manufacturing and dock jobs disappeared or moved elsewhere. Replacing them in the figures were the public-sector unions, still on the defensive and penned in by the crisis regime, and the growing hospital workers union, District 1199. For another, the city's unions were politically divided. Many of the private-sector unions and the Central Labor Council backed an electoral challenge to Koch in the campaign of Frank Barbero, a left-leaning state assemblyman and former longshoreman. Barbero got 36 percent of the vote in the Democratic primary. In an unusual move, Barbero ran in the general election as an independent with labor backing. He got only 13 percent of the vote in the general election, however. The public-sector unions remained neutral in the primary or backed Koch. Most jumped on the well-funded Koch bandwagon in the general election.[44]

For the public-sector unions, the Koch era brought continued problems, a broken system of collective bargaining and settlements that didn't surpass inflation for anyone until the mid-1980s, and then only for some. In 1977, just before Koch was elected, the Mayor's Management Advisory Board, or Shinn Commission as it was called (yes, after the omnipresent Richard Shinn), proposed that the Office of Collective Bargaining (OCB) be replaced with a setup that would give the mayor the power to set the rules for and determine the outcomes of bargaining. This was stopped by OCB chair Arvid Anderson, who nevertheless let it be known that "the principle issue at the bargaining table today is what is to be given up or taken back."[45] Indeed, in his first round of bargaining with the city unions in 1978, Koch played the tough guy, proposing some sixty concessions. For the first time, however, the unions stuck together and bargained as a coalition. They were able to beat back most of the concessions and establish through arbitration that the 6 percent pay increase postponed in 1976 should be paid back someday, but the wage increases of 4 percent per year for two years did not beat inflation.[46]

Another sign of difficulties in the public sector emerged in the 1980 negotiations between the thirty thousand–strong Transport Workers Union Local 100 and the Metropolitan Transit Authority. The key negotiators here were Richard Ravitch, former Bowery Savings Bank chair and CBD developer, who was then head of the MTA, and John Lawe, president of TWU Local 100. In the style of

Mike Quill, Lawe began negotiations with a demand for a 30 percent wage increase to make up for wages lost to inflation and the fiscal crisis regime. But Lawe barely commanded his executive board. His attempt to work out a Quill-style cliffhanger, in which the MTA produced a prearranged last-minute "breakthrough" of 7.5 percent, failed when his executive board rejected this second and final offer. A twelve-day strike followed in which, as Lawe put it, the members got "the restlessness out of their systems." With nearly two dozen days of pay lost by the workers under the no-strike terms of the Taylor Law, the MTA bought peace with a 20 percent increase over two years. Although half his executive board voted against it, Lawe declared it passed on April 11, and the exhausted and heavily fined members voted to ratify.[47]

Koch had urged Ravitch to resist a costly contract lest it set a pattern for city employees. Adept at political circus, he made the strike an opportunity to show he was in charge by encouraging businesses to stay open and greeting workers who walked across the Brooklyn Bridge to go to work. He made it clear he would once again play hardball in the city-worker negotiations that came up later in 1980. And, indeed, DC 37 and others received much less than the transit workers. Koch's tough stance took its toll on an already dysfunctional bargaining system. By 1988, coalition bargaining had collapsed and the surviving system of uneven pattern bargaining, usually stretched out way past contract expirations, took hold. By the end of the Koch era most city employees saw their annual income at or below where it had been in 1975. In constant 1982 dollars, the lowest-paid city worker saw a 2.4 percent increase from 1975 to 1991, while middle- and higher-paid workers saw decreases of 9.5 percent and 11.4 percent, respectively, despite slightly better contracts in the mid-1980s. Teachers made a 1 percent gain over that decade and a half.[48] Clearly, Koch's mayoral version of the crisis regime had done its job for New York's demanding business elite.

During the 1980s, many of the municipal unions saw a transition in leadership. Prior to this time, powerful leaders like Gotbaum of DC 37, Shanker of the UFT, Guinan of the TWU, Feinstein of Teamsters Local 237, and DeLury of the Sanitationmen's Association had held on through the fiscal crisis into the era of recovery without much in the way of internal opposition. The transitions of that decade were mostly smooth and well-orchestrated, a symbol of how institutionalized and bureaucratic most of these unions had become. In some cases, they brought the gender or race composition more in line with that of an increasingly black, Latino, or female membership. In 1986, Albert Shanker handed the reigns of the UFT to Sandra Feldman, and Victor Gotbaum turned DC 37 over to Stanley Hill, an African American who had been president of the Social Service Employees Union in its calmer years after the merger with AFSCME Local 371. Despite the gender and racial changes, the pragmatic leadership styles of the new chiefs reflected more the compromises of the crisis era than the militancy of the founding period.[49]

One transition that was not so smooth was that of the president of the Central Labor Council. In 1986 long-time CLC leader Harry Van Arsdale died. His heir apparent was his son, Thomas, like his father an official of International Brotherhood of Electrical Workers (IBEW) Local 3. DC 37's Victor Gotbaum decided to contest the election, assuming the backing of the public-sector unions. The contest was, in some respects, a reflection of the political differences within organized labor in that era. Gotbaum represented the liberal wing of labor, while Thomas Van Arsdale stood for the more conservative unions. The election itself, however, did not shape up along those lines. Key liberal and public-sector unions, including 1199, UFT, Communication Workers of America (CWA) public sector locals, and the postal workers backed Van Arsdale. Gotbaum had miscalculated.[50]

Other unions faced the problem of leadership transition as well. Leadership change and competition is generally a good thing, a sign of health. The newer public- and service-sector unions, furthermore, had majority black and Latino memberships, while the old leadership remained white. Some unions, notably the ILGWU, resisted the transition to minority leadership. Others, like DC 37 and 1199, embraced it. But the problems of such a transition could be painful when the old leader, long in office and reluctant to share power, tried to hand the reins to those with much less experience and little opportunity to gain it. This was the case with 1199 during the Koch years.

The hospital workers union had grown to one hundred thousand members by the early 1980s. It was still led by Leon Davis, a Communist until the 1970s, who had been present at the birth of the union in the 1930s and had launched the organizing of the private "voluntary" hospitals in the 1950s. Like many union leaders of his generation, he had grown up in the sophisticated radical working-class culture of the 1930s and 1940s. He had led the union from its origins as an organization of pharmacists to a giant industrial union of hospital workers. He held on to the presidency until he retired in 1982, providing a highly centralized and personalized leadership over a union that had become majority black. Davis knew the union needed minority leadership, and he handpicked two black leaders, Henry Nicholas, who was proposed by a black caucus, for the national union in 1981, and Doris Turner for District 1199 the following year. Conflict between Davis and Turner over contract demands emerged even before she assumed the presidency of District 1199. Distrust grew and the local fell into a period of internal factionalism that lasted until 1989, when Dennis Rivera was elected president at the head of the Save Our Union slate. As a union of some of New York's lowest-paid workers, 1199 might have played a decisive role in opposing many of Koch's priorities, but the rough-and-tumble leadership transition precluded this. It would, however, play a role in Koch's electoral decline.[51]

In the older private-sector unions another sort of trouble emerged: corruption. While corruption was not new to New York labor, it showed up in some unusual places. One was Painters District 9, a union that had been led at various times by communists and socialists. In the 1970s, District 9 fell into mob hands via the leadership of Jimmy Bishop. Backed by the Painters International, crooked local leaders, and the Luchese crime family, Bishop had defeated a rank-and-file reform movement led by socialist Frank Shonfeld. In 1990, Bishop was murdered by a rival faction of the Luchese family.[52] Also among the once more respectable unions were ILGWU Local 10 and Hotel Employees and Restaurant Employees Local 100, whose leaders were caught taking bribes and kickbacks from employers. Less surprising was corruption in the building trades. Freeman summarized the breadth of corruption there: "The Mason Tenders, Cement and Concrete Workers, Carpenters, Laborers, and the Teamster local which had jurisdiction over construction supply deliveries also had serious problems with corruption and mob control."[53]

In 1989, New York was the site of a number of mass and active strikes that seemed to indicate a revival in the private sector. In March, 8,500 mechanics at Eastern Airlines walked out after months of mediation and little progress. Their picket lines were honored by pilots and flight attendants in what looked like a promising start in a bitter fight with EAL boss Frank Lorenzo that ended in the bankruptcy and collapse of Eastern.[54] On August 6, 60,000 telephone workers at NYNEX (Verizon today) struck across New York State and New England. About 12,000 were in the city where the strike was highly active and militant. On August 14, Dennis Rivera, newly elected president of 1199, led the first in a series of successful brief strikes by 47,000 hospital and nursing home workers. Rivera got the backing of the otherwise conservative Cardinal John O'Connor and the Catholic Church. The summer and fall would find the three groups gathered in mass rallies, joined by striking coal miners from Pittston facilities in western Virginia. A huge rally was addressed by Jesse Jackson. As one telephone worker put it, "It almost feels like a real labor movement." The strikes at the New York hospitals and NYNEX were victorious and highly visible in the streets of the city.[55]

The NYNEX strike particularly innovative and hard-fought. The issue was cost shifting of health care benefits, a matter that had come up in 1986 but remained unresolved. This time CWA District 1, representing the NYNEX workers, began preparations a year before the contract expiration, mobilizing members and training as many as three thousand strike coordinators. During the strike some 400 workers were arrested, 250 were fired or suspended, and two were killed. The union launched mobile pickets to reinforce weak picket lines, while members took it upon themselves to organize "stranger" pickets to minimize firings by dispatching strikers to work sites other than their own. District 1 took the fight to the state's Public Service Commission (PSC), where the union opposed a company request for a $360 million rate increase. The longtime involvement of District 1 director Jan Pierce in city and state politics paid off when 130 members of the state legislature signed an ad in the *New York Times* opposing any rate increase during the strike. After the strike, a PSC administrative law judge actually turned down the rate increase and called for a full investigation of NYNEX. Most importantly, the strike beat back the company's cost-shifting demand.[56]

The victories at NYNEX and the city's private hospitals, however, did not overcome the deep problems of so many unions. New York City labor was in deep disarray. The fiscal crisis and the mayoral regime that followed weakened and divided the public-sector unions, while key private-sector unions representing New York's newer workforce, above all 1199, were facing bitter internal conflict. Much of the city's older workforce and unions were paralyzed by corruption. While labor would turn against Koch in his third term and play a role in his downfall, it would not be the leading role. That job fell to his own cronies in the county "machines," on the one hand, and to a mobilizing black community, on the other.

The Downfall of "Ethnic Ed"

Koch began his third term in high spirits at a private celebration at Colt Industries CEO David Margolis's East Side apartment. On the stage at his official inauguration were Democratic county leaders Stanley Friedman of the Bronx and Donald Manes of Queens, along with one hundred or so other business and political figures. By the end of the year, Manes would be dead by his own hand and Friedman would be on trial in Connecticut. Manes had been caught taking kickbacks from contractors of the Parking Violations Bureau (PVB), while Friedman passed out bribes to get PVB and other agency contracts for Citisource, a company he claimed made handheld computers. Friedman got twelve years in federal prison. Brooklyn party boss Meade Esposito was convicted of links to organized crime, but his two-year sentence was suspended due to his advanced age. Koch's consumer affairs czar and campaign sidekick, Bess Meyerson, was convicted in 1988 of trying to influence a judge in her daughter's divorce trial. And the scandals just kept coming. Victor Botnik, Koch's chief of the Health and Hospitals Corporation was forced to resign when it was revealed he did not possess the college degree he had claimed. In 1989, the city hall "talent bank," set up as an affirmative action program of sorts, was discovered to be a patronage machine run by Friedman associate Joe De-Vincezzo.[57] Claiming ignorance and innocence, Koch the erstwhile reformer had appointed a legion of hacks, given the county bosses a free hand so long as their minions on the Board of Estimate backed his development program, and generally presided over the political equivalent of the "greed is good," insider-trading, junk-bond ethics of his business friends.

Then there was Koch the erstwhile racial liberal. The one-time freedom rider had climbed to office by race baiting and hadn't let up. His regime was characterized by a series of police shootings of innocent African Americans. He had closed Harlem's Sydenham Hospital after promising not to. Members of a white mob that killed a black transit worker in 1982 were not convicted of murder. By the end of 1986, one of those high-visibility instances of unprovoked, extreme racial violence exploded in Howard Beach when a dozen white youths chased one black man onto the highway, where he was killed, and severely beat two others. Koch denounced the attack, but made no special deal of it. More and more of the city's blacks began to see Koch not just as a lapsed liberal and a racial loudmouth, but as an aggressive enemy.[58]

In October 1987, the stock market slumped and many a developmental dream went up in smoke. Although the fall of the dollar and the subsequent withdrawal of Japanese and German capital, not the antics of Ed Koch, set off the crash; its impact on New York was devastating as it helped cause, and flowed into, the recession of

1990. The financial sector itself lost jobs by the end of 1989. By 1996, it was still nine thousand jobs below its 1987 level. Altogether, between mid-1989 and the end of 1991, the city lost 190,000 jobs. From the vantage point of Koch's financial and developer supporters, perhaps the most alarming figure was the 53 million square feet of vacant CBD office space, with more to come during the recession.[59]

If Koch could not be held personally responsible for the stock market crash and its aftermath, the scandals and the string of violent racial attacks came closer to his doorstep. So did the declining state of so many neighborhoods, including those where many of his white supporters lived. Ethnic Ed's popularity began to fall among all groups. A *Daily News* poll in early 1989 showed that 63 percent of New York voters said they would definitely not or probably not vote for Koch later that year. His approval ratings among whites fell from 73 percent in 1985 to 43 percent in 1988. His disapproval ratings jumped from 20 percent to 30 percent as the 1986 scandals became public knowledge. After he told Jewish voters they would have to be crazy to vote for Jesse Jackson in the 1988 Democratic primary, it rose to 40 percent. By mid-1989 it hit 50 percent[60] Koch's electoral coalition was collapsing and he was becoming a political liability, not only to what was left of the Democratic county organizations but to the business elite as well. The symbol of desertion by the bankers and developers was the Democratic primary run of Richard Ravitch, himself a banker and developer.

Black Underrepresentation and Mobilization in Liberal New York

New York's reputation as a racially liberal city was largely a myth. This was not simply because of police brutality or the mobilization of working-class whites against black hopes and gains. It was the Democratic Party in particular that had thwarted the advancement of African Americans, Latinos, and Asians in electoral politics and the city's political institutions. This will sound counterintuitive to anyone who looks at the city council in 2007. In the realm of electoral politics prior to 1989, however, New York's African Americans achieved greater representation in the state assembly and U.S. Congress than in the city council or Board of Estimate. By the early 1980s there were only six black council members and three Latinos out of thirty-five members. Although whites dropped from 58 percent of the voting age population in 1980 to 48 percent in 1990, in 1989 whites still held 82 percent of the votes on the Board of Estimate and 74 percent of city council seats, reflecting no change for the entire decade.[61] The reason for this was that both regular and reform club and county organization leaders held on to their power and positions well past the demographic changes that should have shifted representation toward blacks and Latinos. Donald Manes, Stanley Friedman, and Meade Esposito were leading party organizations in boroughs with large minority populations by the time the scandals took them down. New York's myth of racial liberalism rested mainly on Manhattan, where, as Table 2-3 shows, blacks composed only 16.8 percent of the population by 1988 (actually down from 20 percent in 1980), but held the borough presidency for much of the time from Hulan Jack's election in 1953 to David Dinkins's election in 1985. In Brooklyn, where the black population was almost a third of the total, or the Bronx, where it was 28.5 percent, no such breakthrough in city office holding occurred, although, of course, Herman Badillo did become Bronx borough president.[62]

TABLE 2-3
Population of the boroughs by race, 1988
(population in millions, race in %)

	City	Bronx	Brooklyn	Manhattan	Queens	Staten Island
Pop.	7.3	1.2	2.3	1.5	1.9	0.3
White	45.4	25.3	42.5	47.7	51.3	83.4
Black	24.0	28.5	32.8	16.8	19.3	7.5
Latino	23.7	41.5	19.5	28.5	18.8	4.9
Other	6.9	4.8	5.2	7.0	10.7	4.1

Source: Department of City Planning, *Analysis of Demographic Changes Since 1980*, May 15, 1990.

Part of the problem was the number and size of council districts prior to the 1989 charter revision. There were thirty-five council seats as opposed to sixty-five state assembly seats from the city. Prior to the "reform" charter of 1937, when the black population was smaller and limited mainly to Harlem, there had been sixty-five seats on the old Board of Aldermen. In 1937, it was cut down to twenty-five and proportional representation was instituted in order to weaken the Democratic majority. Ironically, the proportional representation scheme allowed the Communist Ben Davis to be elected as the city's second African American council member, taking Adam Clayton Powell's place. Proportional representation was abolished by 1949 and the council eventually increased to thirty-five, but it was still easier for a black politician to get elected in the smaller assembly districts. David Dinkins, for example, was elected to the state assembly in 1965. Until 1989, council districting was done by the politicians, who had no desire to let the new black and Latino migrants who poured into the city in the 1950s and 1960s take over.[65]

What they did do, however, was incorporate some blacks into the machines, particularly in Manhattan, and then Brooklyn. For example, Hulan Jack became the first African American Manhattan borough president in 1953, to be followed by Percy Sutton in the 1960s and David Dinkins in the 1980s. They were mentored by Harlem machine boss J. Raymond Jones, the leader of the Carver Club. Known as "the Fox," Jones negotiated his way within Tammany, eventually to lead it in 1964. As Martin Shefter has argued, however, incorporation of new groups into mainstream politics inevitably involves the weeding out of the radicals and rebels. The process of inclusion is also one of exclusion and domestication. Thus, black leaders such as Sutton and Dinkins tended to be more cautious in their rhetoric and practice than Powell or Shirley Chisholm, who were based more in Congress than in city politics per se. The process was further facilitated by the demise of the three powerful county leaders after the 1986–88 scandals. This made it easier for blacks and Latinos to challenge for state assembly seats at a time when the offices of assembly members with their staffs and budgets had already replaced some of the functions of the clubhouse as a seat of influence in borough politics.[64]

Much has been written about the constant feuding of the city's black political leaders, notably between those in Manhattan and Brooklyn. But the 1980s were also a period of mobilization of the black electorate. The Jackson campaigns of 1984 and 1988 set off efforts to register blacks and turn out the vote. In Brooklyn, in 1984, state assemblyman Al Vann had worked with other black leaders to form the Coalition for a Just New York, which registered thousands of African Americans to bolster Jackson's primary run for the presidency in 1984 and to play a role in the 1985 mayoral election. In fact, by September 1985, the black voter registration rate, when adjusted for age and eligibility (citizenship), at 66.3 percent surpassed both white Catholics and outer-borough Jews, at 57.7 percent and 64 percent, respectively. Only liberal whites, meaning white assembly districts in Manhattan below 110th Street and the gentrified western side of Brooklyn, had a higher rate, at 69.9 percent. Between 1982 and 1985, black voter registration had increased by over 150,000, numerically more than any other group.

While the 1985 mayoral contest saw a low, if standard, turnout of 32 percent, the 1989 race saw more than half the city's registered voters cast a ballot in the primary, and slightly more in the general election. This was an election in which turnout, not money, was the determining factor. Not only were there spending limits for those who accepted public financing, which all the Democrats did, but Koch actually spent twice as much on television ads in the primary as Dinkins, $2.4 million to $1.2 million.[65] African American turnout was the highest of all groups, at 56.7 percent in the primary. In the general election it was 65.9 percent, with only outer-borough Jews voting at a slightly higher rate of 67.5 percent. There is no doubt that the two Jackson campaigns had spurred such a large turnout. Jackson had carried New York City by a plurality in 1988, and a large turnout in the black neighborhoods had made the difference. Inspired by Jackson's success, and offered a black candidate against Koch in the primary and Rudolph Giuliani in the general election, New York's black communities put David Dinkins in office and Ethnic Ed out to pasture. The unions, too, helped defeat Koch. As John Mollenkopf described it, "Particularly Local 1199 of the hospital workers, the United Federation of Teachers, Teamsters Local 237 of housing authority workers, and District Council 37 of city workers, emerged as an effective substitute for the Democratic party."[66] But it was the black community that rallied in numbers great enough to elect David Dinkins.

In the general election, however, Dinkins won just 48 percent of the vote, defeating Giuliani by only a little over 47,000 votes out of 1.9 million cast. Dinkins carried predominantly black assembly districts by 89 percent, but white liberal assembly districts saw only half their votes go to him. Outer-borough Jewish assembly districts, heavily Democratic in registrations, cast 29 percent of their votes for Dinkins, and white Catholic assembly districts, 26 percent. The racial divide that Koch had inflamed, though hardly created, had further undone the Democratic coalition. Republican mayors, in this most Democratic of cities, would now be a fixture for the foreseeable future as many white Democrats voted their race over their class and party registration.[67]

3

Globalization and the Underdevelopment of New York: The 1990s

The 1990s would see far-reaching changes in New York City. The global city would become even more drawn into the world economy. Its industrial makeup would shift even more toward financial and business services and the diversity of its economy would narrow further. At the same time, it would experience growing competition in these services from other cities at home and abroad. The explosion of the stock market, as well as the export of financial and business services, would hollow out the economic middle and create an extreme inequality of incomes well beyond that experienced in the rest of the United States. The demographics of the city would change significantly as the flow of immigrants from many parts of the world increased, while many whites left. The newcomers filled the growing low-wage labor market and beneath it fell into an expanding informal sector inextricably linked to the regulated economy. By the end of the 1990s, the whole edifice of the city's economy rested on the underdevelopment of its workforce and the neighborhoods it inhabited. Politically, New York's economic and political elites would accelerate their developmentalism as a means to beat the competition of other cities and find some type of diversification. Much of this would rest on the continued growth of an impoverished population and on the increased social control of its most dispossessed.

Globalization Accelerates

The 1980s through the early 2000s saw the escalation and deepening of global economic integration. As Table 3-1 shows, the major economic measures of globalization, world GDP, trade, foreign direct investment, and transnational corporations and their overseas affiliates, all grew dramatically. World GDP doubled from 1982 through 2003 despite recessions in the early 1990s and 2000s. Exports of goods and services grew at twice that rate, by more than four times, while the accumulated stock of foreign direct investment (FDI) multiplied by almost fourteen times and its annual outflow by over twenty times. The number of transnational corporations (TNCs) grew by two-thirds, while the number of their affiliates expanded by more than four times. The sales of foreign affiliates grew by over four times, while cross-border mergers and acquisitions (M&As), not even recorded before 1987, almost doubled from 1990 to 2003.[1]

TABLE 3-1
Indicators of global economic integration ($billions)

	1982	1990	2003	% Growth '82–'03
World GDP	11,737	22,588	36,163	208
Export goods & services	2,246	4,260	9,228	311
FDI outflows	28	242	612	2,086
FDI outward stock	590	1,758	8,197	1,289
Number of TNCs	37,000	60,000	61,000	65
TNC foreign affiliates	170,000	500,000	900,000	429
Sales of foreign affiliates	2,717	5,660	17,580	547
Cross-border M&As	N/A	151	297	97 ('90–03)

Source: UNCTAD, *World Investment Report*, United Nations, 1993, 1995, 2004.

The near halt in the number of TNCs from 1990 to 2003, when coupled with the dramatic rise in foreign affiliates and the appearance of cross-border M&As, indicates not a slowing of globalization but a growing consolidation of TNCs on a world scale. The concentration of global capital is further indicated by the jump in the value of the assets of the foreign affiliates of nearly fourteen times, from $2.1 trillion in 1982 to $30.4 trillion in 2003, compared to a four-and-a-half-fold increase in their number. All of these cross-border mergers and proliferation of affiliates, as well as the growth in assets, had to be financed. Indeed, world financial FDI outflows grew from $48.5 billion in 1989–91 to $157.3 billion in 2001–2, a threefold increase, about 90 percent from the developed nations and a good deal of that from New York.[2]

The acceleration of trade and global investment was enabled by the multilateral organizations at the core of the Washington Consensus, the set of ideas that requires of all nations not only openness to trade and investment, but privatization of public services or production, deregulation of finance and other economic activity, and increased protection of property, including intellectual property. These organizations include the International Monetary Fund and World Bank, which impose structural adjustment programs on developing nations, often with disastrous results, and the World Trade Organization, which enforces market openness and the main goals of the Washington Consensus.[3] Altogether, these goals reinforced the dominant position of the richest countries and of the global cities within them, including, of course, New York.

The content of foreign direct investment shifted heavily toward services in the 1990s, a trend that helped the United States somewhat and was of great significance for New York City. Services as a proportion of FDI stock had risen from about a quarter in the 1970s, to just under half in the 1990s, to 60 percent of the total by 2002. Inflows of service investment accounted for two-thirds of total FDI by 2002. Business services FDI, even more a part of New York City's growth in the 1990s, grew by five and a half times in that period, to $137 billion, with hotels and restaurants growing almost twenty times worldwide, to just under $8 billion. The outward-bound side of this growth in overall services FDI had once been an almost total monopoly of the United States, but by 2002 the European Union nations and Japan had become significant players, and even a small number of developing nations garnered 10 percent of FDI outflows in services. The bulk of the inflow of FDI still went to the developed nations, although less than in the past. The share of FDI going into developed nations was 52 percent in manufacturing in 2001–2, down from 75 percent in 1989–91, reflecting the growing tendency to send such work offshore. In the growing service sector, the developed nations' share of outward FDI went from 88 percent in 1989–91 to 76 percent in 2001–2, down but still the lion's share. It should be remembered, however, that much of this shift simply represents the shifting of facilities by TNCs based in the developed nations. Another potential problem for New York lay in the shift of services from finance and trade, from 59 percent of worldwide FDI service outflows in 1990 to 35 percent in 2002. The 2002 percentage, however, may reflect the stock market slump that hit the United States in 2000 and/or simply the fact that other services grew faster. Other New York–based services, such as telecommunications and business services, were becoming more prominent in the global process of capital accumulation.[4]

The United States deepened its position in the international economy in a number of ways. From 1992 to 2000 U.S. exports grew from $617 billion to just over $1 trillion. The share of services remained flat, however, at 28 percent of the total, but still showed a positive balance compared to goods, where the big deficits came. Imports outran exports, rising from $657 billion in 1992 to $1.5 trillion in 2000, leaving a trade deficit of nearly a half-trillion dollars. U.S.-owned assets abroad grew from $2.2 trillion in 1990 to $7.2 trillion in 2000. Foreign-owned assets in the United States increased from $2.4 trillion to $9.3 trillion in those years. The U.S. economy had become more dependent on the export of services, on the one hand, and foreign purchases of U.S. Treasury bills, corporate stocks and bonds, and currency, on the other.[5] Investment trends in the United States followed suit with private investment in plant and equipment, doubling from about 12 percent of total U.S. investment to 25 percent between 1975 and 1990. It would slump with the stock market crash of 1987, but recover in the late 1990s.[6] All of these developments tended to bolster New York City's financial and business service sectors.

Services had already dominated the U.S. economy, and in the 1990s its proportion of GDP rose from 53.7 percent to 55.3 percent by 2000. The fire, insurance, and real estate (FIRE) sector alone rose from 18 percent to 20 percent during the 1990s. As a source of employment, manufacturing declined from 17.5 percent of the employed workforce in 1990 to 13.9 percent in 2000, while services rose from 33.1 percent to 38.8 percent in those years. FIRE declined as a proportion of those employed, from 6.6 percent to 6.1 percent, reflecting both the technological advances in much of those industries and the growing international competition for that work.[7] Employment in the country's big cities followed the same trend. In seven large northeastern and midwestern metropolitan areas manufacturing fell from 14 percent to 12 percent from 1990 to 2000—and from 26 percent in 1970. FIRE, which had risen as a percentage of the workforce in these cities from 7 percent in 1970 to 9 percent in 1990, fell to 8 percent by 2000. Services grew from 24 percent in 1980 to 31 percent in 1990 and 36 percent in 2000.[8]

Measured against the national economy and the seven metro areas above, New York City followed a similar pattern, but with very different proportions. Manufacturing had fallen to just below 5 percent of the workforce—less than half the 12 percent of the seven cities. Services jumped from 37 percent in 1989 to 44 percent in 2000, well above the seven cities' average. FIRE fell slightly, as it did for both the national economy and seven metro areas, but at 13.4 percent it was well ahead of the 8 percent for the seven metro areas. As we will see below, however, the securities sector of FIRE grew faster than that total sector or than the city's economy, accounting for 87.7 percent of the growth in real earnings from 1992 to 1998. From 1995 to 1997 alone, the securities industry added 10,000 jobs to itself and another 7,800 indirectly to businesses that serviced it. Another way to measure the growing centrality of the securities sector was the fact that New York's metropolitan area had over nine times the proportion of people working in securities than in the nation as a whole. Clearly, the stock market boom of the 1990s was pushing the city's economy toward more dependence on Wall Street. Another growth area in those years was in entertainment, culture, and tourism, which rose from 6.8 percent of the workforce in 1989 to 8 percent in 2000, gaining nearly fifty thousand jobs.[9]

New York's longstanding position as a world financial center led it to emphasize those activities in which it already had a competitive advantage, namely, financial speculation and the financing of world trade and investment. This in turn led to the growth of those business services that supply Wall Street and corporate command and control centers, along with the real estate on which they locate in the central business district. The city's attachment to the world economy in this manner, and the increasing proportion of the city's income that depended on it, meant, as Savitch and Kantor put it, "the economy's role in the international marketplace causes it to lurch between boom and bust cycles."[10] It also meant that New York was in a competition with other cities for the location of many of these financial and business services that would become more intense as the global economy grew, experienced booms and busts, and technology enabled the geographic decentralization of much of this activity.

Trouble in the Midst of Growth

New York City is both a shaper and receiver of these global trends. Capital flows into and out of its banks, exchanges, and brokerages to finance trade flows and worldwide investment. Robert Brenner argues that the stock market bubble of the late 1990s, egged on by Federal Reserve chairman Alan Greenspan, in fact, held up both the United States and the world economies for a time. He wrote:

> In order to keep the U.S., and the world, economy from serious disruption, the Fed thus had little choice but to depend

upon the continued ascent of the stock market to maintain the accelerated growth of domestic U.S. consumption and investment. In effect, the Fed was sustaining a new form of artificial demand stimulus by means of increased *private* debt, both corporate and consumer, made possible by the rise of equity prices and the resulting wealth effect, rather than relying on the traditional old Keynesian formula based on public debt.[11]

Indeed, the world economy had slowed to an annual growth rate of only 1.3 percent from 1996 to 2000, while the U.S. economy grew by about 4 percent, held up after 1998 in part by stock prices and capital gains. A good deal of the wealth effect that Brenner argues was behind continued growth was concentrated in New York State, rising from just over 3 percent of the state's adjusted gross income in 1991 to almost 12 percent in 2000. In those years, capital gains income in the state, most of it originating in the city, grew from $8.7 billion to $53.5 billion.[12]

The boom was, indeed, huge. From 1990 to 2000, the number of shares traded each day rose from 170 million to 1.2 billion, for a total capitalization of $7.2 trillion, almost the equivalent of the 1995 U.S. gross domestic product. If looked at from the vantage point of the *increase* in real earnings (inflation-adjusted wages, salaries, and proprietors' income), the city's overall export sector rose from 57 percent of total earnings gains in the years 1983 through 1989 to almost 90 percent in the years 1992 through 2000. Securities and commodity brokers alone accounted for 48.4 percent of the total increase in city real income, up from only 15.6 percent in the 1980s. Business services rose from 6 percent of the total increase to 14 percent by the 1990s.[13] According to one study using input-output data, the rise in stock prices added 118,000 jobs, $13.6 billion in personal income, and $21 billion in business profits. The biggest winner in this growth was, of course, the FIRE sectors, which garnered $4.4 billion in personal income, and $16.9 billion in business profits, or 80 percent of the total of the stock market effect.[14]

Part of this boom, in turn, was due to the dot-com explosion of the 1990s and the rise of Silicon Alley. Ironically, the Alley, which ran up Broadway from downtown to midtown, filled up the relatively cheap office space in the 1990s due to the sharp fall of office space rents resulting from the collapse of the real estate market during the 1989–91 recession. The number of these new media firms doubled from 1997 to 1999 and their trade organization, the New York New Media Association, grew from eight members in 1994 to seven thousand in 2000. By the late 1990s the new media were creating 870,000 jobs a year nationally, with venture capital investment growing from $49.5 million in 1995 to $536 million in 1999.[15]

The stock market boom and the dot-com bubble burst in March 2000, revealing just how dependent the city had become on its financial sector. Economists James Parrot and Oliver Cooke calculated that during the recession of 1989–90 the city had eight industries that accounted for more than 5 percent each of the growth prior to the recession, while Wall Street had been responsible for only 16 percent of that growth. In the 2000–2001 recession, however, Wall Street accounted for 48 percent and there were only three industries that amounted to more than 5 percent of growth.[16] The city was becoming more and more a one-horse town.

The Competition of Cities

Beginning in the 1970s competition accelerated among cities for new work as old industries died or moved on to cheaper sites. Furthermore, the nature of the competition changed from one for federal funding, as in the urban renewal era of the 1950s and early 1960s, to one for private investment in which business interests played a leading role.[17] In the United States, this competition intensified as the traditional midcentury division of labor between cities (Pittsburgh steel, Detroit cars, Chicago meatpacking, L.A. movies and defense production, etc.) broke down and all these cities sought new sources of employment. One study by Savitch and Kantor rated New York "high" in all areas of market competitiveness it studied. This included the forces of agglomeration as well as a high proportion of services. The advantage of agglomeration and face-to-face collaboration argued by Sassen in *The Global City* as well as by Savitch and Kantor and so important to New York's business services producers diminished to some degree in the 1990s as other global cities and even other secondary cities competed for these businesses. Their competition was facilitated by advances in information technology that made location, and hence agglomeration, less important for a number of key business services.

This was not a competition that Adam Smith would recognize. The tools in this competition were wielded by governments in response to business demands, above all an acceleration of tax incentives and subsidies to businesses, and cheap labor, both of which would become New York specialties during the 1990s. In a recent study, Greg LeRoy estimates that American cities and states gave corporations some $50 billion a year by the early 2000s to attract or retain their business, with little to show for it in terms of jobs. New York alone contributed $3 billion a year by 2003. As we have seen, Koch was not hesitant to employ this approach in the cause of real estate development. If the cities and state used tax "expenditures" to lure business, the corporations employed an army of location and "business climate" experts to extort these subsidies and incentives.[18]

Despite giant tax giveaways and the growth of the low-wage labor force in the 1990s, New York did lose ground in some of what should have been its growth industries other than finances and business services. For example, while from 1991 to 2000 airline passengers increased an average of 51 percent in fifteen of the worlds biggest air traffic markets, New York registered a mere 1.6 percent gain. The big international winners were Paris, Amsterdam, and Seoul, while in the United States, Los Angeles, Houston, Miami, and Detroit all surpassed New York in both growth rate and the number of passengers. In air cargo the story was the same: the average growth from 1991 to 2000 was 130 percent but for New York it was only 26 percent, the lowest recorded gain. As historian Mike Wallace pointed out, JFK's cargo facilities were allowed to become outmoded and its leading position lost by the 1990s. Major express firms like FedEx and UPS moved to Newark.[19]

Communications and media are also industries in which New York held a dominant position. In 1997, these industries employed 233,444 people, with a total payroll of $15.5 billion, according to a 1998 Citizens Budget Commission report. Measured by employment, New York was still well ahead of the second U.S. cities, invariably Los Angeles or Chicago, in advertising, publishing, network television, recording, news syndicates, public relations, and commercial art and design. But, despite the rapid growth of Silicon Alley, as of 1996 the city was still well behind San Francisco, Boston, Seattle, and Los Angeles in computer programming, systems design, retrieval services, and prepackaged software.[20] Some of this gap would be closed by the dot-coms toward the end of the 1990s, but it would not last.

The rise of new services and technology in telecommunications also created problems for the city even where it held on to its lead in infrastructure. According to a Council on Foreign Relations study, New York was losing ground as the leading cybernetic node in world business. The study sounded a note of alarm in 1997, "Once the data processing capital of the world, New York has experienced a serious erosion of its position." The study cites the loss of online banking, back-office work, claims processing, data entry, and similar work as major New York–based companies moved this type of operation elsewhere, anywhere from New Jersey to North Dakota, and later to India.[21] Another Citizens Budget Commission report noted that both Hong Kong and Singapore had developed superior telecommunications infrastructures and provided lower-cost service. Domestically, New York was ahead in fiber optics and digital switching, one of the key aspects of holding onto its financial and business services. It also noted that while the United States led the world in Internet infrastructure, New York was not the primary center of this.[22] Even within the precincts of its growing FIRE sector, trouble appeared. Whereas in the 1960s New York had 12 percent of the nation's insurance workers, by the mid-1990s it could claim only 2.3 percent.[23] The city also saw declines in its share of employment in business services. From 1978 through 1993, its share in legal services dropped from 9.5 percent of the country's total to 7.6 percent, while its share of accounting jobs fell from 8.5 percent to 5 percent in the same period.[24] Clearly, the pressure on New York to find ways to compete in all these areas was strong.

In terms of employment, the New York metropolitan region lost ground within the U.S. economy in many of these crucial services. In finance, for example, the city's share of jobs in the United States fell from 10 percent in 1975 to 6.8 percent in 1996. This, however, represented more the proliferation of ATMs and the movement of back-office jobs to other regions than a loss of business or market share for the city's business elite. Financial earnings for the metro area, which had slumped from 16.2 percent on the U.S. market in 1969 to 13.6 percent in 1975, when the recession hit the city harder than the nation, recovered to about 16 percent in the 1980s and 1990s.[25] Again, however, it was the explosion of equities in the second half of the 1990s that held this proportion up.

Looked at within the New York metropolitan area, however, New York's central business district in Manhattan did not lose much ground to the surrounding suburban region. Since one of the central arguments for the growing quantity and value of tax and other subsidies was that businesses would relocate some backroom functions, or their entire operation, to the nearby suburbs, this is an important fact. Looked at over the long run, Manhattan had 26.9 percent of the jobs in the Consolidated Metropolitan Statistical Area (CMSA) in 1983. This percentage fell slightly for most of the 1980s and 1990s, began to rise in 1998, reached a high point of 24.5 in 2001, then fell to 23.9 percent in 2002 as a result of the recession and 9/11. So, there was a loss of 3 percent to the suburbs or outer boroughs. This is significant, but not a sea change. In terms of output, measured as gross product, Manhattan's position within the CMSA actually improved. During the 1980s and early 1990s Manhattan's gross product fell as a proportion of the CMSA from 38 percent in 1983 to a low of 33.7 percent in 1991, but then rose, reaching a new high of 39.4 percent in 2001 and 38.5 percent in 2002. Obviously, there was a shift in employment and output from some of the declining industries mentioned above, but overall the output per job in Manhattan rose much faster than that of the outer boroughs, the CSMA minus New York City, and the United States as a whole. Table 3-2 summarizes the trend. In terms of gross product output per job, a measure of productivity, Manhattan far outstrips the outer boroughs, the suburbs, and the nation as a whole.[26] Nevertheless, the relative loss of some industries to other cities or nations drove the "permanent government" to push their development agenda in hopes of regaining lost global ground.

Like many other cities in the United States in the 1980s and 1990s, New York entered the competition for new areas of income and work. The 1980s and 1990s were the decades of "downtown" revival based on convention crowds, sports fans, and tourists. In those years U.S. cities raced to build convention centers, sports arenas and stadiums, and festival malls. By the late 1990s, the nation's cities boasted 409 convention centers, almost half built during the 1980s and 1990s, all competing for the hordes of conventioneers that would, the theory said, revitalize the city. During those years cities fought for and traded sports franchises and built arenas and stadiums to hold them and to attract suburbanites back into the city, at least occasionally. From 1990 to 2002, thirty North American cities built some seventy-two new sports stadiums or arenas. Other cities turned waterfronts or old districts into malls full of shops and restaurants, many designed by James Rouse, like Baltimore's Harborplace, and Boston's Quincy Market. New York fol-

TABLE 3-2
Gross product per job: Manhattan, outer boroughs, CMSA and the United States, 1983–2004 ($1996)

	1983	2004	% Change
Manhattan	$92,900	$178,500	93
Outer boroughs	53,000	67,000	26
CMSA	56,300	91,500	63
United States	57,600	81,700	42

Source: Hill and Lendel in Howard Chernick, ed., *The Resilient City: The Economic Impact of 9/11*, 2005.

lowed suit in some respects with the Javits Convention Center and its own Rouse project, the South Street Seaport, under Koch. The grand tourist project of the 1990s would be the Times Square renewal, that of the 2000s the failed West Side and later Queens stadium and the likely successful Brooklyn Nets arena. While New York's efforts in attracting tourists were largely successful, the city remained eighth in the percentage of conventioneers it attracted.[27] The shift to tourism was one factor, along with the explosion of the stock market in the second half of the 1990s, that contributed to the growing inequality of income in the city.

Growing Inequality: Shaping a Low-Wage Workforce I

From 1991 through 2000 the city's economy grew at a real rate of 4.2 percent a year, a respectable rate, but one based heavily on the stock market boom. Employment, however, grew by only 1.6 percent a year. As the financial and business services sector grew, older industries declined even further. Table 3-3 shows the shift in em-

TABLE 3-3
Employment by industry, NYC, 1989 and 2000

	1989	2000	% Change
Goods, transport & wholesale	783,266	618,325	−21.1
FIRE	520,439	484,767	−6.9
Business services	230,120	281,667	22.4
Communications, media, information	135,002	178,409	32.2
Entertainment, tourism, culture	238,846	288,450	20.8
Health & social services	365,549	494,406	35.3
Other services	339,059	350,885	3.5
Retail, except eat & drink	264,445	273,146	3.3
Government	582,643	545,762	−6.3
Total	3,532,892	3,607,665	2.1

Source: James Parrot in Mollenkopf et al., *Rethinking the Urban Agenda*, New York, 2000.

ployment by industry from 1989 through 2000. Many of the losses were in middle-income industries, notably the production and moving of goods, while many of the gains were in industries with large proportions of low-paying jobs, such as entertainment, tourism, and health services. Taken together, the figures on job loss, steady market share, and rapidly rising real earnings in finance and business services indicated a growing income gap between those high in much of the city's business world of Manhattan and the white-, blue-, and no-collar working class mostly in the outer boroughs. As gentrification in areas like Harlem, the Lower East Side, and parts of Brooklyn joined job loss and lower wages, this inequality would take on an increasing geographic form, with 80 percent of Manhattan employment in professional and managerial jobs, compared to 36 percent for the city as a whole.[28] These factors go part of the way to explaining why incomes in all the outer boroughs fell from 1990 to 2000, but rose in Manhattan. As Table 3-4 shows, only Manhattan and Staten Island exceeded the national median family income by 2000.[29]

One result was a rise in the inequality of incomes. In real terms from the late 1980s to the late 1990s, four-fifths of the city's families saw their incomes drop despite substantial growth in the city economy during the 1990s. The poorest fifth of New York families saw their income drop by $1,164, or 13 percent, the next poorest fifth lost $3,901, or 16 percent, while the middle fifth lost $5,083, or 12 percent of their income; even the fourth fifth lost $3,020, or 5 percent. By contrast, the wealthiest fifth gained $23,373, or 18 percent. According to another study, the top 5 percent gained $63,580, or 31 percent. As the *New York Times* put it, "the rich are getting richer and the poor are growing in number."[30] Clearly, the fairly high growth of the 1990s had accrued to the city's business elite, above all to Wall Street.

At the same time, from 1989 through 1999, middle-income jobs, defined as those paying $30,000–60,000, declined by over 68,000, shrinking from 35.2 percent of total employment to 29.6 percent by 1997. The proportion of blacks in the middle- or upper-income groups fell from 37 percent in 1989 to 31.8 percent in 1997, while

TABLE 3-4
Median family income, 1990–2000 ($2002)

	2000	% Change 1990–2000
USA	$54,011	9.5
Manhattan	54,202	5.1
Bronx	33,113	−7.2
Brooklyn	39,055	−7.1
Queens	52,459	−7.3
Staten Island	69,429	−2.1

Source: Fiscal Policy Institute, *State of Working New York 2003*, 2004.

Latinos dropped from 32 percent to 25 percent. Lower-income employment, defined as jobs paying less than $30,000 a year, grew by 52,434 jobs from 1989 to 1999 to become a quarter of the workforce. Ever since the 1970s, the city's poverty rate had risen above the national rate, with the gap widening for most of the 1990s. By 1999, it was 21.8 percent compared to 11.8 percent for the country. The poverty rate for New York children hit 32.9 percent in 1999.[31] Clearly, the city was gaining a good deal of whatever competitive advantage it sought through the formation of a growing low-wage workforce.

Demographic Transformation:
Shaping a Low-Wage Workforce II

Globalization is much more than the economic indicators listed at the beginning of this chapter. It includes the disruption of domestic economies and destruction of previous forms of production, whether by market forces or structural adjustment programs; civil wars frequently fought to claim resources that sell well on the world market; wars of intervention by developed nations to resolve civil wars and protect investments; wars of aggression to capture resources, such as the U.S. invasion of Iraq; famines; the unnatural consequences of the forces of nature when resources are scarce or withheld; etc. By the 1990s, according to the United Nations, 130 to

145 million people were legally registered as living outside their own country—the real number was certainly much higher. By another estimate, 120 million people moved from one country to another in one year alone, 1994.[32] The World Bank estimates that the net migration from low-and middle-income nations to high-income nations, from south to north, was about 14 million people from 1995 to 2000.[33] Far from the many predictions that globalization would lead to a "global village," it had led to increased chaos, poverty, and flight. The world had become an extremely unsettled place.

The United States has long been a prime target for immigration as whole populations were uprooted by conflict and social change. As Oscar Handlin put it long ago, "In the century after 1820 some 35 million people were displaced by the collapse of an age-old social order in Europe and were transported to the new world."[34] The ethnic content of that epoch of migration changed from primarily Western European and, to a lesser extent, Asian prior to 1880 to predominantly Southern and Eastern European after that until the 1920s, when it was largely cut off. This last wave of immigration reached its height between 1901 and 1910, when 8.8 million people entered the United States.[35]

The United States has also been a nation characterized by huge internal migrations. The internal migrations of the 1940s, 1950s, and 1960s were the result of dislocation due to economic changes in the South and on the island of Puerto Rico. From the 1940s through the 1960s, 4 to 5 million African Americans moved from the rural South to the industrial North, while more than 2 million Puerto Ricans left the island for the mainland. By 1970, New York's African American population reached 920,000, while Puerto Ricans numbered 847,000. By 1970, this migration came to a virtual halt.[36]

With the passage of the Hart-Cellar Act in 1965, the door opened to increased migration from outside the United States. The subsequent series of immigration acts meant to control the flow failed to stop or slow down the enormous movement of desperate humanity. By official count, about 9 million immigrants entered the United States legally from 1991 to 2000, and another 7 million came without documents in those years. From 1992 to 2002, 931,972 entered New York City legally. Others entered without documents or let their visas lapse but stayed on. By 2000, 35.9 percent of New York City's population, or 2.9 million residents, were foreign-born.[37] This immigrant population was highly diverse. From 1992 to 2002, for example, 179,596 Dominicans entered New York legally. The second largest group, those from the former Soviet Union, numbered 140,016 in those years. Third were the Chinese, at 102,304. Taken together, English-speaking West Indians accounted for over 100,000, while Guyana provided 54,488, and Haiti 38,885. Immigrants from the Indian subcontinent numbered another 100,000 in those years, while the Philippines sent 29,047, and Korea 16,606. Also represented in significant numbers were Mexicans, South Americans, and Africans.[38] In this same period about 1 million people left the city, mostly whites in what some called the "new white flight." By 2000, non-Hispanic whites composed only 35 percent of the city's population. Their places were taken by the new immigrants, and the population grew in the 1990s by 9.2 percent to reach just over 8 million.

The distribution of these new immigrants was not even across the city's five boroughs. By the late 1990s, over two-thirds lived in Queens (37 percent) or Brooklyn (31 percent). These huge flows disrupted old ethnic clusters. For example, Dominicans replaced Puerto Ricans as the main Latino group in Washington Heights, Manhattan, while Chinatown spread into Little Italy and then out to Sunset Park in Brooklyn and Elmhurst in Queens. Indeed, the ethnically Chinese population of New York grew by 50 percent between 1990 and 2000, to 372,000. Central Brooklyn became Caribbean rather than just African American.[39] In this period, immigrants also spilled out into the suburbs of New York as housing in the city became difficult to find and/or too expensive. By 2000, about 1 million immigrants lived in the nearby suburbs, composing 21.8 percent of their population, and another 995,000 lived in the

peripheral suburbs, where they were 12.6 percent of the population.[40] Largely because of immigration the city escaped one of the
country's more pronounced trends—the population shift from city
to suburb. By 1980, 45 percent of the U.S. population lived in suburbs and only 30 percent in actual cities. While the city population
rose by 12.5 percent from 1980 to 2000, its metropolitan area
(CSMA) shrank between 1980 and 1990, from 18.6 million to 16.9
million. From 1990 to 2000 the metro area rose to 18.6 million,
with over half of that gain in the city, due mostly to immigration.

As in the past, the new wave of immigrants to New York would
work. Whereas they were 35.9 percent of the city's population in
2000, they represented 47 percent of the workforce. As workers
they could be found in large numbers in eating and drinking estab-
lishments, construction, hospitals and health care, grocery stores,
garment manufacturing, transit, and domestic work. Most of these
were low-wage sectors of the economy, and immigrants could be
found in the lowest-paying parts of those sectors. They composed
62 percent of those who earned from $5.15, the minimum wage, to
$7.10 an hour.[41] Like earlier immigrant groups, African Americans,
and Puerto Ricans before them, the new immigrants tend to work
in ethic enclaves. Sometimes they come to replace other groups
that have moved on to other occupations. So, for example, Latino
immigrants tended to replace African Americans, who moved into
the public sector, in hotel work. By 1990, 60 percent of the hotel
workforce was foreign-born.[42] Wherever the majority of new immigrants ended up, it was likely to be a low-paying job with few if
any benefits.

Richard Wright and Mark Ellis identify professional and business service jobs as the "main engine of growth" in the labor market, having grown 77 percent from 1970 to 1997. This is consistent
with the growth in finances and business services discussed above.
It is obvious, however, that with notable exceptions most immigrants have not made it into those occupations. Rather, they have
replaced African Americans and Puerto Ricans in remaining manufacturing jobs, rehab and repair construction, retail, and other services that fall in the city's low-wage workforce. For example, the

share of native Latinos in the declining manufacturing sector dropped from 25 percent in 1980 to just 9 percent in 1997, while the share of foreign-born Latinos rose from 14 percent to 18.6 percent in the 1980s. This "share-shift" is one reason immigrants can still find work in declining sectors.[43] But overall, job growth from the late 1980s through the 1990s was slim. From 1989 to 2000, as Table 3-3 shows, the city gained only 74,773 jobs. But the population had grown by 685,714, with almost two-thirds of that in Queens and Brooklyn, the most immigrant-dense boroughs.[44] As we have seen above, job growth was in either high-paying jobs, mostly professional or managerial, or in low-paying jobs, the ones most open to immigrants.

With job opportunities limited, the city's informal or underground economy grew. While the informal economy is something we often associate with Third World countries, it is alive and well in the United States, and nowhere more than in immigrant cities like Los Angeles and New York. Leaving aside drugs, theft, and violent crime, here were the unlicensed repair workers, street vendors, the countless off-the-books food service workers, nannies, cleaners, dog walkers, floor finishers, painters, and more. Immanuel Ness defines the informalization of economic activity as the moving of work from the regulated economy to the unregulated netherworld of off-the-books work and subcontracting to the point of official disappearance. But the work itself does not disappear. The informal economy is, as Ness argues, connected to the formal economy. He writes:

> Finance, insurance, real estate, media, retail, and even technology have had long histories in the city. But these industries did not just get larger. They altered the way they did business. Most importantly, through subcontracting and outsourcing they have stimulated the development of highly competitive markets for various business and consumer services. Firms have broken down their work into smaller parts and farmed them out to weaker, marginal firms who compete on the basis of cheap labor.[45]

At the end of this chain are off-the-books entrepreneurs and workers: garment sweatshops, grocery delivery contractors, "independent contractors," etc. They populate the kitchens and back rooms of the trendy restaurants, clubs, bars, and theaters frequented by the city's far better paid professionals and managers. They fill domestic worker agencies and sometimes stand on street corners in the unregulated day labor market. While measuring the informal economy is difficult, if not impossible, Ness cites a Los Angeles study that found 42.8 percent of domestic workers, 30 percent of construction laborers, 28 percent of cleaning and building maintenance workers, and 25 percent of food workers to be informally employed. Gus Tyler of the ILGWU once estimated the informal sector of the entire U.S. economy in the mid-1980s equaled about one-third of the U.S. GDP.[46] A more detailed investigation of informal work covering the 1980s was carried out by Saskia Sassen. She found extensive informal labor in the alterations and renovations end of the construction industry in New York. She cites a four-block survey in Manhattan by the Department of Buildings that found 90 percent of interiors had been rehabbed without a permit. She cites an ILGWU study that found three thousand garment sweatshops employing fifty thousand workers and another ten thousand home workers. Another estimate found that 10 percent of footwear production was informal. Virtually all of these types of informal work were performed by immigrants.[47]

Not only had the city been transformed racially and ethnically, but the growth of the financial and business service core of its corporate headquarters complex had been made competitive and its well-paid professional and managerial workforce served and entertained by a huge pyramid of low-wage labor that ran down through legitimate service suppliers to shadow contractors in the depth of the underground economy. In short, to a larger extent than most imagine, the commanding heights of the global city's economy rests on this vast, low-paid, largely immigrant workforce.

While we have no real figures on the informal workforce, even those in the formal low-wage workforce tell us a lot about who the working poor are. While the number of poor working families in the United States grew by almost a quarter from 1986–89 to 1995–97, in New York City their number increased by over 80 percent. By 2001 about 20 percent of the city's workforce earned $8.10 an hour or less. Some 40 percent work in services, 21 percent in manufacturing or transportation, and others in retail or clerical jobs. Just over half of these workers were women and eight in ten were black or Latino. Nine out of ten were adults, while three-quarters worked full-time. Two-thirds were foreign-born, almost half of whom had entered the United States since 1989.[48]

These, along with their statistically invisible counterparts in the informal economy, formed the backbone of the economy that took shape in the 1990s and continues to this day. It is a workforce that competes with itself and others for these low-wage jobs, as well as for housing, social space, education, and government services and benefits. Like the crowded working or unemployed anywhere, it is a potentially explosive mix of humanity. Most of the explosions are small in scale and short in time: street fights, petty crime, strikes that don't make the papers, and occasionally a riot that does. As we shall see, the working poor are not always passive. While much of this workforce is outside mainstream politics, now and then it appears to make a difference. Politics in the 1990s focused heavily on development with a new twist, on the one hand, and how to control the city's workforce, above all the working poor, on the other.

4

Politics in the 1990s:
Soft Cop, Hard Cop

In the midst of the wreckage left by Ed Koch and the social turmoil wrought by globalization and the further shifts in employment, many in the city looked for someone and something new at city hall. In that context, David Dinkins became the hope of many: the hope that racial tensions and conflict could be diminished, the hope that resources would flow more in the direction of black, Latino, and working-class neighborhoods in general. Dinkins himself had called the city a "gorgeous mosaic" and promised a regime of racial healing. He had promised to stop the massive tax breaks to developers and corporations, and to do something about housing for low- and moderate-income families. Almost none of these promises would be kept. *Daily News* columnist Juan Gonzalez famously remarked, "My sense is that you get a people's movement that develops, it elects a people's candidate, and then you get a coup, right?"[1] But was it a people's movement and a people's candidate?

As already noted, it was a black electorate mobilized in large part by the excitement of the 1984 and 1988 Jackson campaigns along with the work of voter registration activists that put Dinkins over the top. The momentum held up long enough for blacks to have a very high level of registration. The voter mobilization counted because the demographics of the city had changed. As Table 4-1 shows, whites had declined in both absolute numbers

TABLE 4-1
Changing demographics of New York City

	1970	%	1990	%
Total population	7,894,862	100.0	7,322,564	100.0
Non-Latino white	4,972,509	63.0	3,163,125	43.2
Non-Latino black	1,525,745	19.0	1,847,049	25.2
Latino	1,278,630	16.0	1,783,511	24.4
Asian and other	115,830	1.5	489,851	6.7
Foreign-born	1,437,058	18.0	2,270,000	31.0

Source: Asher Arian et al., *Changing New York Politics*, Routledge, 1991.

and as a proportion of the population, while blacks and Latinos had grown, together outnumbering whites. Whites were still the largest group, but among white Democrats the vote for Dinkins was low: 12 percent of white Catholics, 25 percent of white Jews. The turnout in predominantly black assembly districts in both the primary and the general election, however, was high at 56.7 percent and 65.9 percent, respectively. In the general election, black assembly districts voted 89 percent for Dinkins. Another key factor in the defeat of Giuliani in the general election was that the vote in Latino assembly districts shifted significantly to Dinkins in the general election. Whereas Latino assembly districts had voted 60 percent for Dinkins in the primary, they went to him by 76.7 percent in the general election.[2]

While the Jackson factor remained dominant, at least in the black communities, several unions played a big role in mobilizing blacks, Latinos, and such working-class whites as did vote for Dinkins. The unions that backed Dinkins reflected the change in the demographics of these unions and their leaders from white males to black, Latino, and women leaders. Stanley Hill of DC 37, Dennis Rivera of 1199, and Sandra Feldman of the UFT all actively supported Dinkins in 1989. Barry Feinstein of Teamsters Local 237 also backed Dinkins. *Times* writer Frank Lynn wrote, "Labor is a major part of the Dinkins financial and political base—more so than any political campaign in memory."[3] Early in his administration Dinkins seemed to reciprocate the support labor had given him. When the workers at the *Daily News* went on strike in October 1990, it soon became a cause celebre across the city. *News* columnist Juan Gonzalez emerged as a leader and brought in Dennis Rivera. Rivera, in turn, brought hundreds of 1199 members to picket lines and demonstrations and solicited the support of Cardinal O'Connor. Jesse Jackson came to town to support the strikers. For weeks the streets of New York were filled with picketers closing down news kiosks that sold the *News* or stopping delivery trucks. For a while it looked like some of the core elements of the Dinkins electoral coalition had taken to the streets in a fight many saw as crucial to the future of organized labor. To his credit, Dinkins openly supported the strikers, even though the strike at times became violent.[4]

In 1991, in what appeared to be a continuation of both the electoral coalition and the alliance in the streets, Rivera and Deputy Mayor Bill Lynch formed the Majority Coalition, which included many of the groups that supported Dinkins and the *News* strike. Its main immediate purpose was to intervene in the newly redistricted city council elections in hopes of a further shift in city politics, in particular reducing the influence of City Council Speaker Peter Vallone. Vallone was an anti-tax, pro-police, anti–social spending Democrat who claimed to speak for the "middle class," meaning outer-borough whites. He was, of course, an irritant to the Dinkins administration. With fifty-one council districts, rather than thirty-five, nineteen of which had no incumbent, it was hoped they could elect more insurgent minority and union candidates. The Majority Coalition endorsed twenty-three candidates, but the effort largely failed and the Majority Coalition faded away until the next mayoral election. According to Mollenkopf, one reason for the failure was the unwillingness of both the politicians and the union leaders to involve community organizations in actual decision making.[5] The *Times*, in addition, noted that huge amounts of money were being raised as 250 candidates battled for a place in the general election. Vallone's Council Political Action Committee had raised $192,000 well before the primary. Even before the council elections, a disillusioned Rivera said that Dinkins, by his surrender to the business agenda, "has demobilized the coalition that elected him."[6]

The first problem was that insofar as there was a movement, it was limited to an electoral mobilization. Even Rivera's Majority Coalition had that limitation. This was not the kind of movement in the streets that had shifted the political agenda in the city as in the nation, in the 1960s and early 1970s. Furthermore, it was safely within the limits of the Democratic Party. With the partial exception of Manhattan, the party had never been a hotbed of progressive social and political ideas. Radical and progressive ideas and movements in the outer boroughs in earlier times—the Socialist Party, the Communist Party, the American Labor Party, and various black and Latino civil rights and nationalist groups—came from outside the Democratic Party. The outer-borough county organizations had resisted black or Latino leadership or even the sharing of leadership as long as possible. Their basic focus was winning office by distributing such patronage and pork as they still had. They were not centers of electoral mobilization. On the contrary, they aimed to turn out only loyalists. Until the 1980s, they were exclusionary ethnic enclaves in which successive ethnic groups fought one another for leadership and loot. Only in the 1980s, and especially after the scandals gutted their leadership, did the outer-borough county organizations open up to blacks in a significant way. In any event, these machines were now badly wounded, and with the reformers tamed there was no organized citywide alternative. Citywide offices were now sought by individuals with political support from temporary electoral coalitions with financial backing from one or more groups within the city's business elite.

Soft Cop, Hard Developer

David Dinkins had won, but who was he, what was his political pedigree, and just what hope did he offer? Dinkins, who was borough president of Manhattan at the time, was recruited to run against Koch in the Democratic primary by black and Latino leaders, including union leaders Dennis Rivera, who had just become president of 1199, and Stanley Hill.[7] While they had sought a black candidate, they also wanted to avoid the mistake that Al Vann and the Coalition for a Just New York had made in 1984–85 when they picked Assemblyman Herman "Denny" Farrell, who ran an ineffective primary campaign against Koch.[8] Dinkins was seen as more mainstream and personally dignified, but he was hardly a "people's candidate." Dinkins had come up through the ranks of the Manhattan Democratic organization. Unlike Adam Clayton Powell, Ben Davis, Al Vann, or Major Owens, Dinkins did not make his political career as an insurgent. He made his way into city politics via J. Raymond Jones's 70th Assembly District Carver Democratic Club, the influential Harlem Tammany clubhouse. J. Raymond Jones, commenting from retirement just before the 1989 general election, noted, "Dinkins understood the rules and played according to the rules. It's no surprise, is it, that the Harlem man—not one of those Brooklyn militants—is the one to do the job." As one study described his early career:

> The Carver Club's connection to the Manhattan county organization, together with the growing importance of black votes, enabled many of Harlem's regular black politicians to achieve upward mobility. Dinkins became an assemblyman, board of elections member, and county clerk through Jones's auspices.[9]

In 1985, following in the path of Hulan Jack and Percy Sutton, he would be elected Manhattan borough president and be the lone African American on the Board of Estimate during Koch's last term. In all of these capacities, Dinkins would necessarily rub shoulders with the city's political and business elites. In 1984, Governor Hugh Carey appointed him to the Urban Development Corporation (now known as the Empire State Development Corporation). This was one of many state "public benefit corporations" created by Governor Nelson Rockefeller in the 1960s to push development and, when necessary, overrule local opposition. On the

UDC board, Dinkins, wrote journalist Jim Sleeper, "disappointed reformers by voting in favor of the power brokers' massive Times Square renewal program." During his tenure as borough president, as Sleeper put it, "Dinkins had also proven himself to the more conservative 'permanent government' of realtors, developers, and contractors who'd always been close to his mentors in Harlem. His vote for the Times Square plan marked but one of many occasions over the next few years when housing advocates felt Dinkins had gone over to the developers."[10]

To be sure, he had also consorted with reformers and even supported insurgent black candidate Major Owens in his Brooklyn race for Congress against black regular Vander Beatty in 1982.[11] But by that time the distinction between reformers and regulars had lost much of its edge. Anyway, it was just sensible party politics. He had supported Jackson in both 1984 and 1988 and, no doubt, benefited from the Rainbow mobilization in his 1985 race. But unlike Jesse Jackson, Dinkins was a politician and not a leader with a movement background.

For the city's financial and real estate elite Dinkins was a known quantity. Sam Roberts wrote in the *Times* shortly before the 1989 election, "New York City's business community, without an incumbent for the first time in sixteen years, is largely following the public opinion polls and finding a familiar face in David Dinkins, the Democratic candidate." Roberts quoted one former Koch backer and real estate developer saying of his support for Dinkins, "Better take the guy we know than the guy we don't know," who was Rudolph Giuliani. Another former Koch fund-raiser, Joseph Flom, was by then raising money for Dinkins. Jack Rudin, a major real estate developer and landlord, said, "He's a very responsible guy. David is up to calling it as he sees it for the good of the city as a whole."[12] In the coded language of the day, this meant not putting the interests of the black community first and going with the development agenda. To be sure, Giuliani also got a good deal of business support, and at least one big player, Donald Trump, decided to hedge his bets and contribute to both. A long-term permanent government associate of Dinkins was Sid Davidoff, a former Lindsay official but now a big-time lobbyist whose firm would make $8.8 million in 1991 lobbying the city.[13] His previous record and the rush of business money to the Dinkins campaign should have raised questions about just how much of a "people's candidate" David Dinkins really was. When he was inaugurated on January 1, 1990, he held a big reception for his financial backers in the World Financial Center. On January 2, the only appointment on his public schedule was with Felix Rohatyn and some of his Wall Street friends. It was as the rest of Juan Gonzalez's famous quote said of the "city's establishment": "they grabbed Dinkins so fast that he still hasn't stopped turning around."[14]

In fact, Dinkins also grabbed for them. Dinkins appointed former Koch deputy mayor and president of Lincoln Center Nathan Leventhal as head of his transition team. This move was characterized by a *Times* reporter as a "public relations effort to signal that the Dinkins Administration would be mainstream and establishment."[15] Moving beyond public relations, his first deputy mayor would be former Koch sanitation commissioner Norman Steisal, then working at Lazard Frères, Rohatyn's investment firm. Sally Hernandez-Piñero, Koch's former financial services director, also became a deputy mayor. Of course, Dinkins had some of his own loyalists as well, such as Bill Lynch and Barbara Fife, two African Americans with a history with him.[16] What seemed clear, however, was that while David Dinkins was not Ed Koch, his administration would not be a radical departure in its attitude toward development and the business elite. Indeed, in December 1989 before he took office, the *Times* reported that his appointments had "less to do with change and more to do with continuity." At the same time, *Times* columnist Sam Roberts wrote that a speech Dinkins gave to a business group could have been given by Koch.[17] The problem was you could not both address the problems of New York's various working-class communities and follow the business elites' development agenda at the same time.

At first Dinkins did try to deliver on some of his promises. Notably, he expanded Koch's ten-year housing program during his first year, reinstituted affirmative action in city contracts, and revitalized committees representing various racial groups. He established a civilian review board over the police and expanded community policing. But as one scholar put it, "By the end of its first 18 months in office, the Dinkins administration was pursuing a fiscal approach indistinguishable from that of the Koch years—except by the strange coupling of harsher austerity with expressions of sympathy for his victims."[18] Aside from the internal pressures in such a direction, two things intervened to turn him toward austerity. The first was recession.

Dinkins had the bad luck to take office as a national recession unfolded. For New York, the recession of 1990–91 began with the stock market crash of October 1987. Dinkins inherited an economy already in trouble. Growth in real gross city product had slowed to 0.5 in 1989 and 0.4 percent in 1990. Then the national recession hit in June 1990 and things got worse. In 1991 real city gross product fell by 4.4 percent from $315 billion to $301 billion. The city's unemployment rate grew from 4.5 percent in 1988 to 11.6 percent in 1992. In New York the recession would last forty-five months and destroy 361,200 jobs, as corporate downsizing followed Wall Street downsizing. Employment losses, at 6 percent of the workforce, were over three times that of the nation, once again reflecting the dependence of the city on Wall Street and real estate.[19] By mid-1991, 49 million square feet of office space lay vacant, virtually canceling out the 43 million built during the Koch years. By 1993 it was 65 million. Vacancy rates in Manhattan were between 16 and 20 percent during Dinkins's term. In that same period, the price of Class A office space in Manhattan slumped from $52 a square foot to $32 in midtown and $30 downtown by 1993.[20]

Dinkins put considerable energy into trying to get money out of Washington in the last years of the Bush administration and the first year of the Clinton administration. In 1990, he promoted the National Urban Summit, which pulled together an impressive list of mayors in November 1990. In line with the general contradiction in mayoral policy across the country, the summit was sponsored by outfits like Merrill Lynch, American Express, Paine Webber, Time Warner, and First Boston. In 1992, as the presidential election approached, he participated in a May 2 March on Washington to demand federal aid for the cities. The event drew only about thirty thousand people. In any case, it was overshadowed by the upsurge in L.A.'s South Central in the wake of the acquittals of the officers who had beaten Rodney King.[21] But Dinkins and the other mayors were bucking a trend already a decade old as federal urban aid dried up. Regional and community development money would drop steadily from its 1980 high of $19.8 billion to $8.7 billion in 1995 and continue to drop slightly thereafter. Urban development action grants dropped from their high in the mid-1980s of around $400–500 million a year to a nominal flow of $3 million in 1994.[22] There would be no salvation from outside.

That was the second problem. Dinkins soon faced the active intervention of the real estate and financial interests. As the recession rapidly created a fiscal crisis and the mayor's Executive Budget proposal for fiscal year 1991 (which began on July 1, 1991) showed a $1.8 billion shortfall, Felix Rohatyn, still head of MAC, pressured the new mayor to cut his housing program along with the usual list of social cuts. The state's Financial Control Board threatened to take over if deep across-the-board cuts were not instituted. Dinkins submitted without a fight.[23] The sanitation department went from 26,000 to 18,000 under Dinkins, while parks and recreation saw a 28 percent workforce reduction.[24] In 1990, David Rockefeller's New York City Partnership issued a policy proposal calling for the abolition of the city's land use procedure, which gave local community boards, borough presidents, and the city council a say in development projects. In 1993, the partnership issued a joint statement with the Chamber of Commerce and Industry suggesting that the city's fiscal difficulties "may be creating a more receptive climate for privatization." The Real Estate Board of New York also made its demands known by warning that the mayor's early position against the use of ICIP incentives would threaten his relationship with the business community.[25]

The interventions worked. By early 1992, Dinkins was reported to have renewed the ICIP, though in reality it never seemed to have stopped at all. In 1990, at least partially under his watch, developer

William Zeckendorf got a $100 million break for his Worldwide Plaza, while Solomon Equities got $70 million for its building at Forty-seventh Street and Broadway and Bruce Eichner got $63 million for his building a block south.[26] From 1990 through 1993, ICIP would grant an average of $144 million in tax reductions per year, twice the level granted under Koch and much of it for the Koch-era Times Square renewal project. In 1992, Dinkins extended ICIP largesse to the previously excluded downtown and East Side areas. When former Koch aid Sally Hernandez-Piñero suggested that such incentives were not the best way to seek economic development, Ronald Shelp, head of the New York City Partnership, wrote a *Times* op-ed piece suggesting that she be replaced as deputy mayor by "an experienced and distinguished business executive." And so she was in 1992, by long-time Chase, i.e., Rockefeller, veteran Barry Sullivan, who was at that time head of First Chicago Corporation.[27] The Chamber of Commerce's wish for privatization was realized when the city handed forty-three acres of Flushing Meadows in Queens to the United States Tennis Association for ninety-nine years. This was negotiated for Dinkins by Sid Davidof, a tennis partner of the mayor's and an active lobbyist, and Norman Steisal, the first deputy mayor from Lazard Frères.[28]

The tax expenditures did not stop or slow down—they grew. In his last two fiscal years Koch had handed out $1.1 billion and $1.3 billion in exemptions or abatements on the real property tax. In Dinkins's first full fiscal year he gave away $1.5.[29] During Dinkins term of office J-51s for rehab amounted to $842 million and were extended to include upscale co-ops and condos. The 421a exemption for new housing construction amounted to $718 million over his four years and it, too, was extended to new areas of downtown and midtown. This housing would not be for the humble. To lessen the tax on buildings with no plan for rehab or extension, assessments were lowered on Manhattan office space. Industrial Development Agency and Public Development Corporation subsidies were also increased, amounting to $123 million and $36 million, respectively, over his term. The Dinkins administration even came up with something new, the "designer package" of tax incentives, subsidies, and energy credits meant to retain business and jobs. These were designed by Barry Sullivan, who crafted twelve of them at a cost of $471 million in 1992–93. Eight went to FIRE firms and four to media outfits. Chase, for example, got $234 million to move 4,600 backroom employees to Brooklyn's MetroTech center, presumably instead of to New Jersey. Prudential got $106 million to fill the empty space at the old Chase building in Manhattan. NBC got $50 million for doing nothing.[30] And so it went.

Rudy Giuliani would later take credit for the "renewal" of Times Square, but it was the Rockefeller Brothers Fund and Koch that had set the plan in motion and Dinkins who closed the deal that accelerated construction and land values at the "crossroads of the world." It was Barry Sullivan who actually negotiated the memorandum of agreement between the city and Michael Eisner of Disney. This was signed on the very last day of Dinkins's term, December 31, 1993. Eisner, however, preferred to make the announcement at Giuliani's side on February 4, 1994. The abatements for Prudential mentioned above brought them into the Times Square plan and they were followed by Bertelsmann, Viacom, and Morgan Stanley, all during the Dinkins administration.[31] The state's Urban Development Corporation, through its subsidiary, the 42nd Street Development Corporation, plowed under 240 businesses to clear the way, all before Giuliani took office. And, as a sort of prelude to the Giuliani era, Dinkins's police commissioner Ray Kelly swept the streets of the city's seventy-five (by police count) squeegeemen by the end of 1993.[32]

The question arises, why, with the new ultra-strong mayor model embodied in the 1989 Charter in place, did Dinkins seem unable to push an agenda that many of his initial supporters believed or hoped he would carry out? The economic context and the rapidly arriving budget crisis certainly provide some of the answer. For one thing, it was not truly a social movement that put Dinkins in office, but rather a loose and temporary electoral coalition, which was by this time typical of New York City's mayoral elections. To put it another way, Dinkins did not have a governing coalition sufficiently strong, well organized, and determined to counter the enormous pressure from the usual suspects in the business elite. Indeed, one of the challenges of electoral movements for social change is that almost inevitably they put their faith in the candidate rather than in the independent actions of the coalition. A bigger problem in this case was that the coalition did not remain organized beyond the election and did not have any idea of the strength and power that globalization had bestowed on the city's unique business elite. As one writer put it, "The Dinkins campaign had not combined its message of 'racial healing' with a critique of the special powers and priorities of banks and bond-rating agencies nor with an alternative set of development and planning initiatives."[33] While this growing dependence on Wall Street and real estate weakened the city's economy by creating a sort of monoculture, it greatly strengthened the hand of capital and its various organizations to a degree that few understood.

Most of Dinkins's implementation of the business elite's development agenda went unnoticed by the average New Yorker, who was more worried about jobs, neighborhood decay, and crime. What the average New Yorker did notice was that the "gorgeous mosaic" remained the site of racial strife. Dinkins did make an effort to improve things. He set up Offices of African American/Caribbean, Asian American, European American, and Hispanic Affairs and instituted affirmative action and contract set-aside programs for minorities and women. His deputy mayors included two Jews, an Irish American, two blacks, two Puerto Ricans, and, for the first time, an Asian, an administration meant to "look like New York."[34] But this kind of diversity effort did nothing to address the roots of competition for jobs, housing, and space between all these groups across the city. Dinkins would fail as the healer, not just because he was indecisive, but because he was unable to address the deeper issue that underlay racial tension and conflict.

Racism, of course, was the problem. This was not simply a matter of attitudes on the part of whites, as problematic as that was. It was the legacy of decades of institutional racism composed of redlining, housing discrimination, and the intensified ghettoization imposed by urban renewal and bad public housing locations. It was also the daily humiliations in the stores and streets of the city, the police brutality, the blatant inequality between school districts, and the complex web of job discrimination and niche employment. The term "white flight" is often pictured to mean the simultaneous departure of a white ethnic group and the seamless entrance of new groups of migrants or immigrants of color into that neighborhood. But the departure of the whites was not all at once, nor was their replacement without friction. In his book, *How East New York Became a Ghetto*, Walter Thabit describes how between 1960 to 1966 "200 real estate firms worked overtime to turn East New York from white to black." In just six years, the community went from 85 percent white to 80 percent black and Puerto Rican by an active process of blockbusting, redlining, and city neglect.[35] The chronic housing shortage remained unresolved for low-income working families and was made worse when Dinkins abandoned his initially ambitious plan. The new immigrants had arrived at the worst of times. The remaining white ethnics held onto communities on the periphery of the city in areas like Howard Beach and Bensonhurst, which they defended as racial fortresses. In Harlem, the Lower East Side, and northern Brooklyn, well-heeled whites gentrified old working-class neighborhoods. In Brooklyn, Queens, and the Bronx, new and old groups of whites, blacks, Latinos, and Asians fought for economic, social, or cultural space. The clash of black customers and Korean greengrocers in Flatbush in 1990 was sparked when a grocer beat a Haitian woman but soon focused on the fact that the grocers weren't hiring blacks. In Park Slope, where white professionals were pushing the remaining working-class Puerto Ricans down past Fifth Avenue, the murder rate went up, tripling in Dinkins's first two years. The clash of Hasidic Jews and blacks in Crown Heights, Brooklyn, in 1991 with the deaths of two young men also challenged the "gorgeous mosaic" metaphor, as two sides, sharing the same neighborhood, wanted to know why the mayor didn't recognize their side of the story. This was followed by a 1992 police shooting of a Dominican in Washington Heights and subsequent clashes between Dominicans and the police. Later that year, ten thousand off-duty police rallied and then rioted at city hall, hurling racial epithets and carrying racist signs. They were protesting a proposal for a civilian review board, an event that Rudy Giuliani attempted to use for political gain. Dinkins, the healer, appeared unable to satisfy anyone, much less stop the racial clashes and killings.[36] With the failure of the "soft cop" the door was opened to the "hard cop."

Racial Politics in the Race to City Hall

Like Koch, Giuliani began his adult life as a liberal. His transition was slow and incremental. As a prosecutor he had gone after big business types like Boesky and Milken. Whatever personal forces moved him toward conservatism and the Republican Party, it was the rise of a New York–based neoconservatism that took shape in the wake of the fiscal crisis of the 1970s that would shape the central idea of his administration. Like the national trend, this New York trend was different from traditional Republican conservatism in that it had a certain populist style and was directed to middle-class and even working-class whites, rather than Upper East Side patricians. The institution that gave it shape and energy was the Manhattan Institute, founded in the late 1970s. Its founding director was Bill Hammett, a former Wall Street analyst. His idea was to bring around a new generation of right-wing intellectuals and to provide alternative analyses and policies to what he, more or less correctly, saw as a moribund liberalism. He had little use for the old-line Republicans of the city, who he said were "just a bunch of rich brain-dead assholes who liked to complain about things." The Manhattan Institute would publish neoliberal economic studies. It even attracted disillusioned liberal Democrats. In the early 1990s Hammett founded *City Journal*. It was through both the institute and *City Journal* that these populist neocons introduced the "broken windows" theory that influenced Giuliani and led him toward a focus on what were called quality-of-life issues.[37]

In the mayoral race of 1993, Giuliani ran a campaign full of racial code words, harping on "competence" despite the fact that he had no experience as an elected official. His "One City/One

Standard" slogan said to whites that blacks and Latinos would no longer get the special treatment that most whites imagined they got. He made a point of appearing at the anti–civilian review board police rally at city hall and saying, after they rioted, that it was more important to support the police too much than not at all. But he also tried to appeal to Latinos and Jews by running on a slate with Herman Badillo, former Bronx borough president and erstwhile Democrat, for comptroller, and Susan Alter, an Orthodox Jewish pro-choice Democrat from Brooklyn, for public advocate. He also sought and finally received the endorsements of Ed Koch and Robert Wagner Jr. In addition, he was endorsed by the Liberal Party, which by now was little more than a personal patronage machine for party boss Ray Harding, who was an enthusiastic Giuliani supporter.[38] Badillo and Harding were partners in an outfit that lobbied the city. With Giuliani in office the number of clients for whom they lobbied the city rose from three to sixty-eight.[39]

In the racially polarized general election Giuliani won by 53,581 votes out of the 1.82 million cast, a margin of 2.9 percent. His victory came as a result of a shift of just over 97,000 votes compared to 1989. The turnout was only slightly lower than in 1989, but all of that small decrease occurred among Dinkins supporters. Turnout in black assembly districts dipped by 2.4 percent, mixed minority assembly districts by 2 percent, Latinos by 5.6 percent, and white liberals (Manhattan and brownstone Brooklyn) by .01 percent. At the same time, the percentage of those groups that voted for Dinkins, rather than Giuliani, also fell slightly in comparison to 1989, so that the total fewer votes from these groups amounted to a shift of 41,116 away from Dinkins. Conversely, both turnout and percentage among the main supporters of Giuliani in both elections, white Catholics and outer-borough Jews, increased their vote by a total of 56,040. About 20,000 of those votes were attributed to an unusually high turnout in Staten Island due to the referendum on that borough's proposed secession from the city, for which Giuliani had expressed sympathy. This was responsible for a rise in the percentage of white Catholics in the electorate from 24 percent in 1989 to

30 percent in 1993.[40] By itself, however, this Staten Island vote could not have changed the outcome without the decrease in support from the core groups in the Dinkins electoral coalition. The Liberal Party, with a traditionally Jewish base, gave Giuliani 62,351 votes and may have made a difference.[41]

Giuliani's electoral strategy for 1993 was consciously predicated on the racism of outer-borough whites. As investigative writer Wayne Barrett put it in his biography of Giulani, "Rudy would not have run in 1993 if David Dinkins were white." That is, he thought he could beat Dinkins because he was black. In a memo to staff in November 1992 giving the results of a survey he commissioned, Giuliani wrote, "It was observed that between 1989 and 1992, registration held up in African American and Latino assembly districts, but had fallen in all white ADs." But, as one of his surveys showed, whites were still a majority of registered voters. He reasoned that all he needed to win was a bigger turnout among whites or perhaps a shift of Latino voters. In fact, the actual turnout in 1993 was 60 percent white. He managed to make Dinkins's expected 95 percent black vote into an issue, while playing down his efforts to get as big a white vote as possible.[42]

TABLE 4-2
Percent of votes by race and party identification, 1989 and 1993

	1989		1993	
	Giuliani	Dinkins	Giuliani	Dinkins
Total	48	50	51	49
Non-Latino white	71	26	77	21
Black	7	91	5	95
Latino	35	64	37	60
Democrat	30	70	33	67
Independent	62	38	69	31
Republican	81	17	93	7

Source: CBS/*NYT* 1991; Voter Research Exit Poll 1993 in Halle, ed., *New York and Los Angeles*, 2003.

Using the survey data in Table 4-2, where the percentages will be somewhat different than the assembly district figures above, there is a significant shift of whites to Giuliani, from 71 percent in 1989 to 77 percent in 1993. Blacks, of course, shifted the other way, from 91 to 95 percent for Dinkins. The Latino vote for Dinkins, however, fell from 64 percent in 1989 to 60 percent in 1993, with the accompanying rise for Giuliani from 35 to 37 percent. Dinkins's Democratic vote also slipped from 70 to 67 percent. The Independent vote shifted even more so, while the Republican vote shifted in a major way for Giuliani.[43] Again, the conclusion to be drawn is that the 1993 election was even more racially polarized than 1989, and that simply based on the proportion of registered voters this worked against Dinkins and for Giuliani.

Disappointment in Dinkins was, no doubt, part of the explanation. In 1993, the city was still hurting economically. But polls showed that much of the electorate was not happy with either candidate. Overall, 43 percent said they were not happy with the choices they faced. A surprising 41 percent of white Catholics expressed dissatisfaction and another 8 percent said they were unsure. Among blacks, 32 percent were unhappy about the choice and 13 percent unsure. It was also the case that old party loyalties and identities had collapsed among white working- and middle-class voters. In an exit poll, fully 69.8 percent of white Catholic voters and 45.5 percent of "nonliberal" Jews answered that they regarded themselves as "Loyal Republican/Conservatives." Among white Catholics, 17.9 percent said they were "Democrat Defectors," as did 40.8 percent of nonliberal Jews.[44] In addition, there were no big policy issues and, as in 1989, the campaign was largely one of personalities and racial code words. Giuliani ran a hard law-and-order campaign on quality-of-life issues, meaning not the lost jobs, the housing shortage, or declining incomes, but problems of petty crime, "aggressive" panhandlers, graffiti, and the like. Lacking either party organization or an articulated programmatic choice, most people, with the partial exception of white liberals, voted their racial preferences, prejudices, and/or fears.

The voter coalition that put Giuliani in office looked a lot like the former Koch coalition, but there were differences. Koch had the backing of the Democratic county organizations, at least until 1989. Giuliani owed nothing to them. For his first two terms Koch had the backing of the public-sector unions; Giuliani didn't in 1993. As a Republican, he owed little to any part of the old Democratic coalition, even those that supported him, like the white Catholics and Jewish Democratic defectors. With race the central focus of city elections, he had no reason to deliver to any working-class constituency. What seemed to be at the center of his electoral strategy was the recognition that there were no permanent coalitions, that class could not, in this racially polarized city, provide an alternative as it once did to some degree. The city was overwhelmingly working-class, but it did not see itself that way. The divisions were too many, some too new as with immigrant groups, and in the case of race, too deep to be patched over by electioneering. Efforts like the Majority Coalition did not provide a permanent grassroots alternative. Thus race was the key to Giuliani's success even more than it had been for Koch. Furthermore, the majority of registered voters were still white and would remain so throughout his two terms, despite the enormous demographic changes.

The election also demonstrated, once again, that by this time, electoral coalitions in New York had little permanence or organizational and programmatic glue. Enthusiasm for Dinkins among the unionists had faded. Sandra Feldman, whose UFT endorsement had helped Dinkins eat into the Jewish vote in 1989, made no endorsement in 1993. Rivera's Majority Coalition was revived but could not deliver enough for a margin of victory.[45] This demonstrated that creating coalitions with no real life outside of election time or outside the Democratic Party, such as the Rainbow Coalition at the national level and the Majority Coalition locally, is not enough. Compare these efforts to the way in which the New York capitalist class organized itself. Not only did it possess the constellation of pressure groups described earlier, but it created, as needed, permanent coalitions of the commanding heights of the city's social and economic structures with highly programmatic agendas. These were not and did not need to be electoral vehicles since the social power of these groups could be expressed in various ways, from campaign contributions to threats to leave the city.

If the Downtown–Lower Manhattan Association had been such a coalition for an earlier age, the New York City Partnership (later renamed the Partnership for New York City) would be the business elite's major developmentalist pressure vehicle for the 1990s. Run during this period by Ronald Shelp, who we met earlier and who succeeded founder David Rockefeller as its head, the partnership included not only all the big financial, real estate, and business service firms, but the Real Estate Board of New York, itself a nine-hundred-pound gorilla. Shelp, who was an expert in business services and saw them as the global city's "engine of growth," also believed that the city's biggest problem was "high labor costs." The partnership not only pushed for more and more development via tax breaks, but even raised its own $100 million investment fund to seed development projects it favored. The major goal of the partnership was to place control of development firmly in private hands.[46] In this, they would succeed.

The Bulldozer and the Billy Club

Mayor Giuliani's priorities became clear from the start. He had inherited a $2.3 billion budget deficit and rather than raise taxes he would cut them and slash spending and jobs. In February, he announced an immediate tax cut of $55 million, including the hotel tax, and promised another $750 million within four years. The New York City Partnership had asked that fifty thousand city jobs be eliminated. Giuliani set about the task. The $350 million city subsidy of the Health and Hospitals Corporation was cut and a plan to cut 2,200 jobs was announced. Schools chancellor Ramon Cortines reluctantly announced a reduction of 2,000 jobs. His budget was cut by $1.3 billion. Cortines would be driven from office in 1995 for dragging his feet on job elimination. By 1997, the mayor would cut the city workforce by 21,000 jobs—in the midst of an economic boom. Subway cleaning jobs were reduced, and the parks department slashed. Some of these jobs would be taken by subminimum "home relief" and "workfare" workers paid their welfare checks. CUNY tuition was raised by a third. The police and fire departments were exempted from cuts.[47] While slashing budgets, the new mayor would accelerate the tax expenditures the city's financial, corporate, and real estate interests had come to expect.

Under Giuliani's watch, development continued its turn toward tourism, with Times Square renewal as its centerpiece. As mayor, he contributed two things to this development. The first, of course, was ever more in tax breaks and incentives. In his first year in office the whole alphabet soup of abatements and incentives (J-51, 421a, IDA, PDC, and ICIP) came to $600 million, up slightly from $594 million in Dinkins's last year. Giuliani continued the "designer packages," dispensing $650 million in twenty-two deals. These were negotiated with a variety of Wall Street and media firms by Clay Lifflander of Smith Barney, who confessed that about 40 percent of the jobs "created" went to commuters. In any case, much of the effect of the first wave of incentives went to downtown firms for job retention, which simply shifted midtown jobs to the cheaper office space in lower Manhattan.[48]

Giuliani's own personal gift to development, however, was the tying together of competition for tourism, increased tax giveaways, and a massive police crackdown on quality-of-life crimes and on the homeless in Manhattan. It was an effort to combine development and social control. Times Square renewal was the geographic center of this fusion of tourist development and law enforcement, although the latter would have its major impact in communities of color throughout the city. As we saw, Times Square development began under Koch, the first Rockefeller Brothers Fund plan being approved by the Board of Estimate in 1984. It then accelerated under Dinkins, whose administration closed some of the first deals and, with the help of the state, demolished scores of buildings. The *New York Times*, through its publisher Arthur Sulzberger Jr., got into the act in 1992 by founding the Times Square Business Improvement District (BID), one of many privately run, city-chartered business organizations that maintain private cleaning and security forces. In 1993, this BID, with an annual budget of $7 million, opened a visitors center and launched a $1.4 million sidewalk lighting project. By the late 1990s, the Times Square BID would employ forty-seven private security guards and fifty street cleaners.

In 1993 the Times Square plan was redesigned by Robert Stern of Yale to give it the "honky-tonk diversity" and "jumbled, kinetic, dazzling and loud" ambiance that it has today. Then in 1994 followed the train of big-time developers, all receiving sizable incentives. Bruce Ratner, Giulani's biggest campaign fund-raiser, convinced the mayor to let him go ahead with a 335,000-square-foot complex that would house, among other things, Madame Tussaud's. Next came Douglas Durst, another mega-developer, who would build a $1.5 billion tower in which Condé Nast would be the first signed tenant. The Rudins followed, as did Morton Zuckerman and the Tishmans. It was a virtual who's who of New York developers and real estate magnates. By 1996 there was a "bidding frenzy" by commercial users and by 1997 20 million people visited the Forty-second Street area.[49]

Despite the generous incentives, it was not Giuliani who was the main political force behind the project. This role fell to Republican governor George Pataki. The state's Urban Development Corporation, to be renamed the Empire State Development Corporation, set up the 42nd Street Redevelopment Corporation as a bond-issuing subsidiary. The 42nd Street Development Corporation had the power of eminent domain, which it used to demolish some 240 buildings, and spent $241 million on buying up properties during the Dinkins years. The state's development corporation also provided tax subsidies. The developers followed in short order.[50]

Giuliani's major contribution to Times Square renewal was his theory and practice of law enforcement. The theory was the broken-windows thesis of George Kelling and James Q. Wilson that came to Giuliani largely through the Manhattan Institute. The theory said that small crimes or signs of disorder, like broken windows, lead to greater crimes, creating an atmosphere in which crime is sanctioned. William Bratton had worked with Kelling from 1990 to

1992 and subscribed to the theory. As Dinkins's head of transit police, he carried out the theory by a practice of busting turnstile jumpers, panhandlers, and graffiti artists. Bratton was hired by Giuliani in 1994 as commissioner of police specifically to do the same for the city as a whole. He gave the practice a name: zero tolerance.[51] The initial targets included beggars, unlicensed street vendors, prostitutes, public urinators, small-time drug sellers, and others who fit the broken-windows mold. (The squeegees, you will remember, were already gone.) But zero tolerance and petty crime in Times Square were only a small part of the change in law enforcement that Giuliani demanded.

The first sign of the problem occurred even before Bratton had time to settle into his new job. On January 9, eight days into his mayoralty, Giuliani ordered the police to storm Muhammad Mosque No. 7, Louis Farrakhan's New York mosque. Responding to a 911 call that the mosque was being robbed, police had rushed up to the third floor only to be repelled by the Nation of Islam's defense corps, the Fruit of Islam, who threw them down the stairs and took one cop's gun and radio. Giuliani reportedly demanded the cops go back in and make arrests. Apparently, even tough-guy Bratton was astonished. Fortunately for them and everyone else involved, a truce was negotiated by the police on the scene, the gun and radio returned, and almost certain bloodshed averted.[52] But race relations, already polarized by the election, worsened. Zero tolerance and the bigger law enforcement offensive would make matters worse.

Once on the job, Bratton initiated the computerized COMPSTAT program. COMPSTAT identified high-crime areas and held local precinct commanders responsible for lowering that crime rate. This implied targeted aggressive tactics that replaced the preventative community policing strategy of the Dinkins years. The target was not, as one might have thought, serious felony crime, but in line with the broken-windows theory, petty crime. Under zero tolerance and COMPSTAT, the pattern of law enforcement changed dramatically. Misdemeanor arrests would rise rapidly, while felony arrests remained flat and even declined between

1993 and 1999. From 1993 to 1999, misdemeanor arrests rose from 129,404 a year to 197,320, most of these for petty drug offenses. More important, perhaps, was a basic change in how misdemeanor arrests were handled. Prior to 1996, those arrested for misdemeanors were issued a summons, known as a desk appearance ticket (DAT), to appear in court. They were not detained unless they possessed something illegal or had a prior record. Now, under Bratton, a growing proportion of people arrested for misdemeanors were detained in precinct jail cells and sent to holding pens at court. The percentage of those arrested who did not receive DATs rose from 48 percent in 1995 to 85 percent in 1998. In other words thousands of people were being held in jail prior to trial for petty crimes. Furthermore, the number of people spending time in jail after arraignment also rose from 28,175 in 1993 to 47,223 in 1999. As one study put it, "The surge in arrests and detentions of an overwhelmingly minority population helps explain the antipathy toward and fear of the police that many members of the city's minority communities feel."[53]

During the 1990s the city's crime rate, like that of the nation, did fall. This decline began during Dinkins's term of office. From 1990 to 1993, murders dropped by 13.7 percent, robbery by 14.6 percent, burglary by 17.6 percent, and auto theft by 23.8 percent. This is generally credited to the hiring of additional police and to the community policing program.[54] During that time, felony arrests had risen by about 10 percent. After that, from 1994 to 1999 the number of felony arrests actually fell by 15 percent. Felony indictments fell by almost 30 percent in those years. Furthermore, the number of inmates in the New York State prison system, which is where those convicted of serious crimes would go, fell by 33.8 percent between 1993 and 1999. This is the opposite of the national trend in which incarceration went up by 41 percent in those years. The city's crime rate also dropped in those years. From 1993 to 1999 the rate of reported felonies dropped by 50 percent, the rate of violent crimes by 51 percent, and the rate of murders by 66 percent. This compared to a drop in violent crimes of 26 percent nationally.[55] Naturally this would boost Giulani's political chances for reelection in 1997. And he never failed to take credit for the decline. In fact, when Bratton also took credit and was praised by the *Times* in January 1996, Giulani dumped him for Horward Safir, the fire commissioner and on old friend of the mayor's from his Justice Department days.[56]

The combination of the bigger police presence and the more aggressive practice of zero tolerance increased a sense of siege and rage in the black community. A closer look at zero tolerance reveals why. It wasn't just—or even mainly—about getting the panhandlers and prostitutes away from Times Square. It wasn't even the outrageous high-profile police shootings of Amadou Diallo and Patrick Dorismond or the sodomizing of Abner Louima. Police shootings, which had dropped 44 percent in Dinkins's last three years, rose by 36 percent during Giuliani's first three years. They would drop after that but not cease. Then there was the stop-and-frisk or "Terry frisk" for guns. A report by state attorney general Eliot Spitzer analyzing 175,000 stop-and-frisk cases found Latinos frisked 39 percent more often than whites, and blacks 26 percent more often. In 1997–98 there were 45,000 Terry frisks. In 35,000, nothing was found. There were 9,500 arrests, half of which were dismissed for lack of evidence. Two-thirds of those frisked were black or Latino. Some fifty thousand people were illegally strip searched when arrested for minor crimes. Civilian complaints about police behavior rose by 75 percent between 1994 and 1998. Giulani's second police commissioner, Howard Safir, nullified two-thirds of the civilian review board cases. Giuliani attacked a federal investigation into police abuse as political because it came from the Clinton administration.[57] In other words, zero tolerance amounted to an attack on minority communities in hopes of producing social control over those communities.

But was this aggressive policing actually the cause of falling crime rates? It is impossible not to note an anomaly in the figures above. Felony crimes dropped, but so did arrests, convictions, and incarceration. Clearly law enforcement over serious crimes was not driving the reductions. There was also the fact, pointed out by *Village Voice* journalist Wayne Barrett, that some of this improvement in crime rates involved reclassifying crimes to less serious categories.[58] The figures, dressed up or not, reinforce the idea that the real goal of Giuliani's zero tolerance approach was social control over the city's most oppressed and poorest residents. Their low pay and ability to survive made them invaluable to sustaining the lifestyle and the chain of firms and contractors that reached from the offices of Wall Street and midtown down to the restaurants, bars, clubs, sweatshops, labor pools, and informal economy on which the global city ultimately rested. These figures also beg for an alternative explanation of the drop in crime besides Giuliani's aggressive law enforcement philosophy and practice. Advocates of the broken-windows theory might take credit. Misdemeanor arrests were up, as was time in jail for petty crimes. Perhaps all this emphasis on petty crime did head off bigger ones. There are, however, more convincing explanations. The larger size of the police force, rather than its aggressive tactics, might be one piece of the puzzle. Barrett also suggests that in the case of burglaries, the installment of modern security and surveillance equipment explains the drop in some crimes.

Another possible reason that will be discussed later was the rise of community organizations in the 1980s and 1990s that in a sense replaced the antipoverty groups that declined or were abolished after the fiscal crisis. These organizations helped to clear the streets of drug pushers in some communities and provided access to various services. I suspect, however, that the growth of the informal economy, particularly among the million or so immigrants who arrived in New York in the 1990s, is a bigger part of any explanation. This provided a self-made safety net for many immigrants and other poor people who might otherwise have turned to crime. It is significant in this regard that zero tolerance did not extend to the multitude of off-the-books jobs, sweatshops, outsourced homework, and illegal housing arrangements that underwrite the city's local and export economies. And it certainly didn't extend into well-off neighborhoods or the corporate suites of midtown and downtown.

It did extend to the homeless in Manhattan. In 1994, the

Human Resources Administration (HRA) cut the staff that helped the homeless from ninety-four to fifteen. At the same time, all borough emergency intake centers were closed except that in the Bronx, which became the sole place at which the homeless could apply for shelter. Application there was by an 800 number only. Operators were directed to discourage application, often telling applicants to report to an HRA office the next day. By 1995 HRA staff had been cut by three thousand. On the other hand, the mayor had the city hire five hundred "fraud detection" investigators.[59] The number of these poverty police would go up to 1,500. In July 1996, the Department of Homeless Services reported, "The NYPD has begun a quality of life initiative in Manhattan from Battery Park to 110th Street, river to river." This area was, of course, the two central business districts and the bailiwick of the well-off and white. At its center was Times Square. Prior to this, under both Dinkins and Giuliani, the police had broken up homeless encampments but had not done a "clean sweep" of the streets. The city also tightened eligibility for the shelters, no longer giving families "the benefit of the doubt." Some 2,400 families were rejected, though most won their appeals. The next year over 14,000 families were refused emergency shelter. By 1998, 57 percent of those who applied were rejected, and in the Bronx intake center it hit 90 percent in 1998. Most won appeals, but the message was clear.[60]

Punishment for being poor didn't end there. Naturally, the welfare rolls were purged well before the 2001 deadline in the national welfare reform act. Between 1995 and 1997, when the city program went into effect, 235,000 people were dropped from Home Relief, a temporary program, and AFDC/TANF. By 1999, the figure was said to be 550,000. The total numbers of those on public assistance fell from 1.1 million in 1995 to 493,000 in 2001. Even those in the city's new Work Experience Program were not safe. In 1997, for example, 69 percent of those in the program were "sanctioned" off the rolls. Even more astounding was the operation of the city's job centers, formerly welfare centers, allegedly changed to help welfare recipients find work. It turns out the primary goal of these centers, according to an employee manual, was not to find jobs. It was to divert people from applying for welfare and for food stamps, a program fully funded by the federal government. In the case of food stamps, people applying were told there were no applications, come back tomorrow. Half a million people lost out on food stamps as a result. This made a huge difference for many poor people since the food stamps lifted a family on public assistance from 50 percent of the federal poverty level to about 80 percent in 1999.[61]

All of this seemed like the resurrection of Roger Starr's planned shrinkage: drive the poor from the global city by making life miserable for them. As early as 1995, this sort of language came from city hall. One aide told the *New York Post*, "Making the city inhospitable to the poor is the best way to 'clean it up.' " Giuliani himself is reputed to have answered a question in a budget briefing in 1995 as to whether driving the poor from the city was his "unspoken strategy" by saying "That's not an unspoken strategy. That's the strategy."[62] If that was really its goal, the strategy didn't work. New York's population grew by over half a million and most of those were immigrants. They and the hundreds of thousands kicked off welfare and food stamps worked in the low-wage jobs the global city depended on. Most likely many carved out a place in the informal economy where they too held up the lifestyles of the rich and near-rich.

The reduction of street crime, the sweeping away of beggars and the homeless, and the implementation of zero tolerance in Manhattan all had another consequence. They helped clear the way for gentrification and "development" in poor and working-class communities such as Harlem, Hell's Kitchen, and the Lower East Side. Areas once considered dangerous appeared safe. Or, at minimum, the promise of police protection and the removal of nuisances from the area made some neighborhoods attractive to well-heeled people who would not have even thought of moving there in the past. The migration of middle-class people into an area, on the other hand, facilitated planned shrinkage.

Giuliani didn't always get his way. For example, his suggestion to eliminate fire alarm boxes in order to save money on false alarms didn't fly. Nor did his proposal to privatize the water system, which he estimated would bring the city $2 billion on the market. His plan to sell off hospitals and ultimately privatize the entire pubic hospital system, however, came all too close to happening. The city's Health and Hospital Corporation (HHC), a semi-autonomous public agency, ran eleven hospitals with total assets worth $2.9 billion by 2001. It was losing Medicaid patients to a new state-sponsored HMO, which required members to use affiliated private hospitals. They were also losing Medicaid patients to the private hospitals, who now wanted them to cover costs. Giuliani's strategy was classically neoliberal: starve it, complain of its budget deficits, sell off bits, then privatize the whole thing. So the mayor cut the amount the city was supposed to contribute for the examinations and care given to the city's prisoners, uniformed employees, and the uninsured. This "subsidy" fell from $350 million a year to $14 million in 1997. In 1994–95 the staff was cut by five thousand. The mayor proposed to start by selling three hospitals. The idea of selling public hospitals was credible because the big private, so-called voluntary, hospitals were merging and buying small ones in order to become more competitive. Obviously, they would want to buy the best of the HHC hospitals, leaving a shrunken, inferior system. Contrary to what many believed and Giuliani said, private hospitals are not required to provide more than emergency care and could and did turn sick and wounded people away. The public hospitals were the place of last resort for immigrants and the poor. But Giuliani was intent on going all the way and privatizing the whole HHC system. He set up a blue-ribbon panel to dispose of the matter. As one observer of the panel put it, "The Blue Ribbon Panel didn't *conclude* that the system ought to be privatized, it *assumed* that the system ought to be privatized." Many throughout the city opposed this idea. The city council took Giuliani to court to stop it and ultimately the sale of the three hospitals and the bigger plan were knocked down by the state supreme court in 1997.[63]

Rudy, it seemed, was not invincible. And he had problems as the 1997 election drew near.

Reelection and the Fall

By 1997, members of Giuliani's inner circle of advisers were squabbling. In February, the *Times* revealed that Liberal Party boss and close Giuliani supporter Ray Harding was lobbying city hall for Herman Badillo's lobbying firm. But the bombshells came in August. *Vanity Fair* magazine ran a story accusing the mayor of having an affair with Cristyne Lategano, his press aide. Then, in August 1997, police beat and sodomized Haitian immigrant Abner Louima at the 70th Precinct in Brooklyn. Giuliani reacted quickly, however, denouncing the incident, removing several officers from the precinct, and setting up a panel that included some credible people to investigate. His Democratic opponent, Ruth Messinger, at first backed the mayor's response, which was enough to neutralize the issue.[64] Rudy got a pass.

But he had a few things going for him as well. For one, a racially divided city. For another, a splintered Democratic Party in which some people thought maybe the mayor was on the right track. After all, crime was down, midtown was getting spruced up, the tourists were coming, the economy had improved, and the welfare rolls were dropping. So, if you had a decent job, a good place to live, and prospects for keeping both, things probably seemed to be getting better. In the Democratic primary, Manhattan borough president Ruth Messinger narrowly defeated Reverend Al Sharpton, while city councilman Sal Albanese ran a poor third. As the general election approached, a number of Democratic notables deserted for Giuliani, including Ed Koch and even a handful of black politicians. Sensitive to the conservative mood of the city and country— it had been only a couple of years since the Republicans swept Congress—Messinger delivered a muddled message.[65]

In the 1997 general election, Giuliani beat Messinger 57 to 41 percent. As Table 4-3 shows, he won with 76 percent of the white vote to Messinger's 21 percent. Messinger got 79 percent of the

TABLE 4-3
Percent of votes by race and political identification, 1997

	Giuliani	Messinger
Total	57	41
Non-Latino white	76	21
Black	20	79
Latino	43	57
Democrat	45	54
Independent	65	32
Republican	92	6

Source: Kaufman in Halle, ed., *New York and Los Angeles,* 2003.

black vote. The Latino vote, however, was somewhat more evenly split than in 1993, with Giuliani getting 43 percent and Messinger 57 percent. The turnout was low, at 38 percent. The black turnout had dropped by about 23 percent from 1993, with blacks composing 21 percent of the voters in 1997 as opposed to 28 percent in 1993. This meant that even though Messinger got the bulk of that vote, the numbers were not high enough to make a difference. The white vote also dropped by 21 percent, but given its size this was not enough to hurt Giuliani very much. The Latino vote numbers fell the least, making up 20 percent of the vote in 1997, up from 13 percent in 1993, so that the closer split in this vote in 1997 did make a difference. What is most striking is the shift in the Democratic vote, which went 45 percent for Giuliani in 1997 compared to 33 percent in 1993. The shift in the Latino vote explains some of this, but equally notable is the increase in Giuliani's Jewish vote from 68 percent in 1993 to 72 percent in 1997. What had emerged was a further decline in the meaning of being a Democrat when it came to mayoral elections, reflecting declining organization and further racial polarization. The defection, however, did not apply to the other citywide or council positions, which remained over-whelmingly Democratic. At the same time, the council was still dominated by Speaker Peter Vallone, a conservative Democrat. Vallone's Queens council district, which he held until term limits ended his council career, had voted overwhelmingly for Giuliani. In other words, the conservative shift was real, but it did not necessarily require people to shift party registrations, or even identities. The shift of the Democratic Party toward the right was, of course, a national trend as well.[66]

Another aspect of this shift, however, was the astounding fact that much of organized labor supported Giuliani, and not Ruth Messinger, in 1997. This included the Central Labor Council as well as DC 37 and other municipal unions. The first to endorse had been Charles Hughes of the seventeen-thousand-member Local 372. Giuliani had not taken the stance toward labor Koch had or the one expected of him. He had, in fact, courted union leaders, especially DC 37's Stanley Hill. Cordial relations did not buy DC 37 or other municipal unions good contracts, however. Quite the opposite. Hill had been persuaded in 1995 to negotiate the notorious "double zeros" contract, meaning that there were no wage increases in the first two years of the five-year contract.[67] Furthermore, when Giuliani started his war on welfare in early 1995, a year before President Clinton signed the federal welfare reform bill into law, he had convinced Hill to allow welfare clients in the city's new Work Experience Program to work in the city agencies his union represented. By the time of the 1997 election, the mayor had cut 250,000 people from the city welfare rolls. In the same period he cut the budget of the Department of Homeless Services by 22 percent despite a peak in the homeless shelter population.[68] Labor's passive tolerance of this indicated that for all its rhetoric, the city's broader social problems were not their concern. Pacifying the vengeful mayor was. In any case, it was likely that union endorsements helped shift some white votes to the Giuliani column.

Money also played a role, as it always does. During his political career, Giuliani raised a total of $50 million, spent on three mayoral races and one very unsuccessful race for a seat in the U.S. Senate against Hillary Clinton in 2000. He went into the 1997 mayoral race with a war chest of $10 million, almost the spending maximum allowed by law for those who take city matching funds. He raised this, as one biographer put it, "by schmoozing the realtors, developers, lobbyists, bankers, and corporate executives who made up New York's permanent government." Among these were "men named Trump, Rockefeller, Rudin, Speyer—an endless stream of fat cats and the people who worked for them, all of whom required access to City Hall."[69] One of Giuliani's biggest fund-raisers was once again developer Bruce Ratner. Since individuals and corporations can only give $7,700 under the city's campaign finance law, Ratner and others acted as "bundlers," collecting the donations from as many well-heeled donors as possible. For example, of the eighty-nine corporate contributions of $5,000 or more, Ratner was the intermediary in eleven cases. By late July, Ratner had reportedly put together $120,000, mostly in corporate contributions, for the mayor. Under the city's law, matching funds of up to $1,000 can be added to a city resident's contribution. Hence a $1,000 contribution gets an additional $1,000, while a maximum gift of $7,700 would return $8,700. So, Ratner's $120,000 would bring in roughly $15,000 extra. Giuliani's biggest contributor was William Koeppel, a real estate developer and landlord who had been caught trying to force his tenants to donate to the Giuliani campaign. The Giulani campaign was caught accepting $342,602 in illegal contributions, mostly from corporate donations over the $7,700 limit. The campaign was dutifully slapped on the wrist with a $220,000 fine. Messinger was able to raise only $3.75 million, not including matching funds. She received only five individual contributions of $5,000 or more, compared to seventy-seven for Giuliani.[70]

Giuliani was in the odd position of having a respectable election mandate while also being a lame-duck mayor. A 1993 referendum had limited elected city officials to two four-year terms. Called Proposal 4, it had passed by 59 percent on the same day Giuliani was elected to his first term.[71] Lame duck or not, Giuliani continued to exercise the strong mayor model, but this time he ran into more and more trouble, much of it of his own making. His affair with Cristyne Lategano ended and a reconciliation with his wife, Donna Hanover, seemed to be in the works. Then, in the spring of 1999, he started a new affair with Judi Nathan, a former nurse who worked for Bristol-Myers Squibb. They got spotted in an East Side restaurant and his reconciliation with Hanover collapsed. The mayor would later come clean. Then there was the attempt to cut the funds of the Brooklyn Museum of Art because of the irreligious painting by African artist Chris Ofili, which pictured the Virgin Mary smeared with elephant dung. Most New Yorkers saw the mayor's action as a violation of free speech rather than a defense of religion. Sixty percent of New Yorkers sided with the museum against the mayor.[72] His love life and authoritarian instincts, however, were not the worst of it.

Giuliani ran on and took credit for the drop in crime. He had merged the city's various police forces and enlarged the unified NYPD from 29,000 to 40,000. As we have seen, much of the activity of the NYPD was around the zero tolerance program of soaring misdemeanor arrests and detentions. But along with the falling crime rate and the swelling department came increased police shootings: from twenty-two in 1993 to twenty-nine in 1994, twenty-six in 1995, and thirty in 1996. Giuliani had not only ignored the report of the commission he set up after the Louima beating, he even ridiculed it. The shootings would later fall to twenty in 1997, nineteen in 1998, and eleven in 1999. After all, as we saw above, violent crime was dropping in New York. Zero tolerance enforcement, what today we might call pre-emptive enforcement, hadn't fallen. One of those 1999 shootings killed Amadou Diallo, a West African immigrant who made the mistake of reaching for his wallet. He had been killed by the notorious Street Crime Unit. This set off huge protests in which hundreds of people were arrested. Giuliani called the protests "silly." Then in March 2000, police from Operation Condor, a part of the zero tolerance program, tried to buy drugs from Patrick Dorismond, a Haitian immigrant who had no drugs. When Dorismond protested, he was shot. As Jack Newfield wrote, "If Patrick Dorismond were white, he would never have been asked for drugs by the police." The whole racist basis of zero tolerance was exposed for those who hadn't already gotten it. The mayor, however, went on TV to say that Dorismond "was no altar boy."[73]

As the end of his second term approached, Rudy Giuliani was

becoming very unpopular. Jimmy Breslin wrote of the mayor, "In all the years, of all the cheap politicians of this city, nobody in record or lore has ever gone lower or lousier than Giuliani." Many agreed. A poll revealed that 79 percent of New Yorkers thought his comments on the Dorismond shooting "made the situation worse." Even before the Dorismond shooting, 82 percent of New Yorkers thought police brutality was a "serious or somewhat serious" problem. His job approval rating fell to 32 percent. That was down from an already low 40 percent in April 1999. While he couldn't run for mayor again, his sinking popularity derailed his planned 2000 run for the U.S. Senate. Whether or not his decision to withdraw from the Senate race was, as he said, based on his diagnosis of prostate cancer, his political career seemed over.[74] Then came September 11, 2001.

From Ground Zero to America's Mayor

The terrorist attacks on the World Trade Center shook New York as few events ever had. Michael Sorkin and Sharon Zukin put it about as well as anyone in the introduction to their 2002 book, *After the World Trade Center*, when they wrote:

> Suddenly, New York's gorgeous mosaic was tiled in tombstones by this equal opportunity mass murder. The third-generation Irish, Italian, and Jewish stockbrokers, the women who had worked their way up to executive assistants and vice presidents, the Indian and Pakistani computer experts, the Caribbean security guards, and the Mexican cooks: of 50,000 who worked in the World Trade Center, nearly 3,000 died there. And they remain incredibly present—in moving daily obituaries in the *New York Times*, in the missing posters that still cover so many walls, in the lists of the fallen outside our firehouses.[75]

Most of the posters and little memorials are gone by now, cleared away by the parks department, but the memory of that day and the immediate aftermath for those of us who lived in the city at that time remains strong.

One of my most powerful memories was the immediate, instinctual response of so many working-class New Yorkers: construction workers, city nurses, ambulance drivers, taxi drivers, Transit Authority employees, those with the skills needed for a rescue operation, and long lines of blood donors, as well as the firefighters and police. Except for these last two groups, they were, for the most part, not dispatched by city authorities, but came as volunteers. Later it would all get organized, but in the beginning it was a spontaneous act of courage and mercy. The city's newspapers would be full of praise for the blue-collar heroes who came to save people they didn't know from the collapsed towers the rescuers had never worked in. They noted the outer-borough zip codes on the picture IDs of these volunteers. They noted too, in one *Times* op-ed, the absence of stockbrokers and bankers among the volunteers or blood donors. Those who came were, tragically, too late to save lives and soon it became the work of excavation and recovery. Throughout the city, there was a sense of collective destiny that crossed the usual lines of cleavage.[76] This tragedy and these working-class people saved Rudolph Giuliani's political career.

Some say the mayor, with just under four months left, put himself at the front of a monumental task; some say he just put himself in front of the cameras. Jack Newfield wrote, "Giuliani seized ownership of the atrocity, and the camera made him seem like a great man." I have heard both sides from police, firefighters, construction workers, and students who worked in the recovery and whom I know through my teaching work. Whatever the case, Giuliani was propelled from a collapsing career and a divisive and socially disastrous reign to "America's Mayor," even a possible presidential candidate after George W. Bush serves out his second term. Encouraged by his new celebrity, he tried to get the state legislature to let him run for another term. Failing that, he asked the other mayoral candidates to grant him an additional ninety days. Although they went along, the effort came to naught.[77]

New York's Economy at the End
of the Giuliani Era

What was the social and economic legacy of America's mayor after two terms in office? Despite eight years of economic growth in the country and an average annual increase of 4.2 percent in the real gross city product between 1994 and 1999, much of New York's population still lived in recession conditions. From 1994 through 2000, employment in the city increased by 399,000 jobs, but 35 percent of these went to commuters. While real wages in the United States had risen about 4 percent from 1996–97 to 1998–99, in New York in the same period they rose only 3 percent and much of this went to the top fifth of the population. The rise in U.S. wages by the pre-recession years of 1998–99 put them above their 1988–89 level, but in New York they remained 6.1 percent below those years. Only black and white women and college graduates saw real wage increases over that period. Every other group by race, education, and occupation saw a decline. Professionals and managers saw the smallest decline (−2.7 percent), while service workers, the city's new mass proletariat, saw the biggest decline (−14.7 percent) over those years. While the U.S. unemployment rate had fallen from 7.5 percent in 1992 to 4 percent in 2000, in New York City it fell from its 11 percent high in 1992 to 6 percent, 50 percent above the national rate.[78] In the 1990s more poor families with children had at least one person working, 82.6 percent compared to 77 percent in the 1980s. At the end of the 1980s, the city's poverty rate for families with children and at least one working person was only slightly higher than that of the country, just under 12 percent compared to 11 percent. By the mid-1990s, the nation's rate of poverty for these families was just under 10 percent, while New York's was just under 20 percent. Both rates fell in the late 1990s, but New York's remained about 60 percent higher than the U.S. rate and well above its late 1980s level.[79] In other words, New York continued creating a huge low-paid, increasingly poor workforce.

Housing for the poor became scarcer even as the homeless were turned away from shelters. This homeless population was, of course, not spread evenly across the city's racial and ethnic groups. Fifty-nine percent were black, and 32 percent Latino. Giuliani drastically reduced the city practice, pursued under Dinkins and Koch, of rehabbing properties seized by the city for nonpayment of taxes. Giuliani simply reduced the seizures from 44,033 in 1994 to 13,278 in 2001. From 1996 through 1998, the number of affordable housing units fell by 19 percent, or 1.3 million units. From 1996 to 1999 the number of vacant units that rented for $400 or less fell by 67 percent, while those renting for $400 to $599 fell by 38 percent Yet, during these years from 1994 through 1999 almost fifty thousand new units of housing were built at a cost of $3 billion, virtually none of it affordable. The lack of new *affordable* housing and the spread of gentrification was pushing existing affordable housing off the market.[80]

The city's tax and budget shifts during the Giuliani years also indicate that he followed business elite priorities religiously. So, for example, the real estate tax fell as a percentage of the city's tax levy from 42.9 percent in FY1994 to 35.5 percent in FY2001. The percentage of the total real estate tax paid by Class IV property, comprising office buildings and other commercial property, heavily located in Manhattan and by far the largest chunk of property value in the city, dropped from 49.6 percent in 1995 to 48.4 percent in 2001. The rate on this valuable, radically underassessed property also dropped from 10.38 percent in 1995 to 9.7 percent in 2001. The tax on Class I property, basically family homes and small apartment buildings located mostly in the outer boroughs, rose from 10.93 percent in 1995 to 11.33 percent in 2001. Tax abatements doubled, rising from a 2.2 percent equivalent of city tax levy in 1995 to 4.4 percent in 2001. These do not include ICIP, IDA, and other retention and incentive programs. Real estate taxes were kept down by keeping taxable assessed values below the growth of real values. From 1995 through 2001 the estimated full market value of taxable property rose by 21 percent, while the "taxable" assessed value rose by 18 percent hence reducing the real tax rate. The sales tax as a percent of total tax levy, which had accounted for 16.2 percent in 1990, rose from 15.8 percent in 1994 to 18.1 percent in 2001. The only slightly progressive personal income tax, which composed 17 percent of the total in 1990, rose from 20 percent to almost 25 percent of the total between 1994 and 2001.[81] Giuliani had accomplished a significant shift in the tax burden. He had also turned a budget surplus into a deficit estimated at $4 billion. To deal with this and the city's projected share of the cost of 9/11 cleanup, he proposed 15 percent cuts across most city agencies, fire and police exempted.[82]

We can see the same shift of resources away from most of those expenditures and costs the business elite always demands be held down or even reduced—the shift that began following the fiscal crisis. Table 4-4 shows the changes in the major elements of the expense budget between Giulian's first and last budgets, FY1994 and FY2001. Looked at by function, general governmental expenses were held steady. Public safety and the judicial system increased

TABLE 4-4
City expense budget by major functions,* 1994 and 2001 ($millions)

	1994	%	2001	%	% Change
General government	$874.8	2.7	$1,078	2.7	0.0
Public safety and judicial	3,846	12.3	5,875	14.6	53.0
Board of Education	7,561	24.1	11,545	28.7	53.0
CUNY	353	1.1	393	.097	−1.1
Social services	8,030	25.6	8,717	21.7	−0.9
Health (incl. HHC)	1,620	5.2	1,959	4.9	−21.0
Housing	590	1.9	478	1.2	−19.0
Total expenditures	31,348	100.0	40,227	100.0	28.0
Real total expenditures (1982–84=100)	21,152.5		22,714.3		7.4

* Functions listed represent 75 percent of total budget.
Source: *Report of the Comptroller*, 2001, 234–43.

from 12.3 percent of the budget to 14.6 percent over this period in line with his emphasis on law enforcement. The growth of Board of Education expenses is most likely due to the growth in population and the number of teachers and other school employees, which grew from almost 89,000 in 1995 to 102,320 in 2001. Health, housing, and social services all declined as a proportion of the budget, the latter due to the precipitous drop in people on public assistance. Giuliani's welfare reform had accomplished what the elite had long wanted, the stabilization of such costs and their relative reduction. On top of that he achieved the elite's greatest goal, the slowing of budget growth to a near stop. As the last line in Table 4-4 shows, he had restrained budget growth in real terms to 7.4 percent over seven years, a little over 1 percent a year—and that in a period of fairly rapid economic growth.[83]

Looked at from another angle, he had also achieved a slowing down of municipal labor costs. From 1997 through 2001, the municipal workforce grew by an average of less than 1 percent a year, with small ups and downs. In real terms, wages, benefits, and pensions combined grew by 3.3 percent a year from 1997 through 2001. This compared favorably with a 4.5 percent growth in real labor costs under Koch from 1983 to 1989. The category "other than personal services," which accounts for things like contractors, supplies, and equipment, grew by 5.4 percent a year adjusted for inflation from 1997 through 2001. Medicaid and welfare combined actually fell by an average of 1.5 percent a year.[84]

None of this, of course, improved the living standards of working-class New Yorkers of any race or ethnicity whether they worked for the city, cleaned parks as part of Work Experience Program, or worked in the ever lower-paying parts of the private economy. As Table 4-5 shows, employment trends continued those established earlier with manufacturing; transportation, warehousing, and utility; and wholesale trade employment all falling as more blue-collar jobs disappeared, while financial, retail, and service jobs grew. Among blue-collar jobs, only those in construction increased. Some of the drops in employment by 2001 were due to the recession that hit in 2000 and to September 11, 2001. But the

TABLE 4-5
Wage and salary employment in New York City, 1995 and 2001

	1995	2001
Services	1,481	1,818
Wholesale trade	158	156
Retail trade	243	272
Manufacturing	208	177
Financial	467	474
Transportation, warehousing and utilities	132	129
Construction	90	122
Government	560	565
Total	3,339	3,692

Source: *Comprehensive Annual Financial Report of the Comptroller*, FY 2004, 295.

growing number of low-income jobs in services and retail, on the one hand, and in high-income jobs in finances and business services, on the other, increased the extremes of income.

About half a million people rose above the official poverty rate from 1995 to 1999, while about 2.2 million remained below it. But the official poverty line hardly tells the whole story. The real wages of the city's low-income workers remained stuck where they were in 1992. The number of working poor in the city had grown by 80 percent from the late 1980s to the late 1990s, compared to about 25 percent for the country.[85] Not surprisingly, income inequality grew dramatically during this period. By the late 1990s, the average income of those in New York's top fifth of families was 20 times that in the lowest fifth, almost twice the U.S. rate of 10.6 times. Perhaps the symbol of the success of the elite's efforts since the fiscal crisis was that this multiple of 20 that separated New York's bottom fifth from its top had doubled from 9.5 times in the late 1970s. In terms of total family income, the top fifth of New Yorkers' share had gone from 43.2 percent in the late 1970s to 54.3 percent in the late 1990s.[86]

While Giuliani was not responsible for the enormous rise in

executive compensation that fueled some of this shift in income in the late 1990s, he had presided over a massive redistribution of income in favor of capital through his acceleration of tax incentives and subsidies, his shift in the tax burden, and the distribution of city expenditures. The ever deeper entrenchment of the city's economy in the process of globalization, which was both encouraged by and pushed the emphasis on central business district development and financial industries, skewed employment possibilities and income distribution toward business and the upper classes. Immigration, another feature of globalization, fed the army of low-wage workers on which so much of this structure of wealth and inequality depended. The global city's economy was based on global and local speculation. It was an unstable mix that called forth more of the same. In the early twenty-first century the city would embark on an unprecedented program of mega-projects that, if carried through, would transform the city once again from the West Side to downtown to the shores and heart of Brooklyn and Queens. It would be a gigantic upscaling of this most upscale of cities. A new mayor, fit for the task by wealth and business smarts, would preside and new elite organizations would form and fight. The transformation of city politics would reach a new low.

5

The Bloomberg Phenomenon

New York Elects a Stranger

Politicians come and go, but the development agenda and the grander global ambitions of New York's business elite continue. The style of politics and presentation, however, changes as do the political coalitions and voting configurations. With the departure of Rudy Giuliani, the city was ready for a moderation in leadership style. None of the candidates that fought to replace Giuliani was much like him, at least in style. New York politics was still a rough-and-tumble affair, with at least as much friction among Democrats as between them and any likely Republican. It turned out that the Republican was a Democrat who seemed to fit within the myth of New York liberalism—neither a Koch nor a Giuliani. Michael Bloomberg was an unknown. He would be judged not so much by the measure of the city's old and largely unused liberalism, let alone that "social democratic polity" we saw in the pre-1975 city, as by the fact that stylistically he was not Rudy Giuliani. This would cover a lot of shortcomings: for example, the new mayor's devotion to the greater neoliberal project that the nation and much of the world were acting out, as well as his loyalty to the narrower development agenda of the city's business elite, set during the fiscal crisis but expanding rapidly as the twenty-first century arrived.

On November 6, 2001, Michael Bloomberg was elected mayor of

New York. In his first run for any public office Bloomberg beat Democrat Mark Green by just 35,489 votes out of 1.5 million.[1] The easy explanation was that Bloomberg had spent a total of $74 million of his own money in the primary and general elections compared to Green's $16.2 million.[2] Bloomberg alone had refused to participate in the city's campaign finance program and, hence, faced no spending limits. No doubt this put the largely unknown Bloomberg ahead of the starting line. It also made a mockery of the city's campaign finance reform, designed precisely to limit the role of private money in city elections. His fortune, estimated at about $4 billion in 2001, bought him top political consultant David Garth, who previously charged $25,000 a month plus a 15 percent slice of any TV ads, and who had helped elect John Lindsay, Ed Koch, and Rudy Giuliani. His fortune and business success had also bought him a *Business Week* cover and articles full of praise in *Newsweek* and *Variety*.[3]

Running up to the Republican primary season Bloomberg had already spent $8 million. He then beat the better-known former Bronx borough president and congressman Herman Badillo by a 66 percent to 25 percent margin in the Republican primary at a total cost of $20 million—possibly the only Republican primary in city history in which both major candidates were former Democrats. Indeed, Bloomberg had switched parties only in October 2000, a month before announcing his candidacy, in order to avoid the crowded and predictably nasty Democratic primary the following year.[4] Despite all the money, a Bloomberg victory in the general election was anything but inevitable. In August, polls had Green beating Bloomberg by 25 points should the two match off in the general election. One usually savvy political journalist could write only a week or so before the election that Green's triumph was so assured that "it's hard to see what can change an outcome that seems increasingly foregone."[5] Something happened on the way to that election.

Four major candidates faced off in the Democratic primary, originally set for September 11, but postponed until September 25. These candidates were Mark Green, then public advocate; Fernando Ferrer, Bronx borough president; Alan Hevesi, the city comptroller; and Peter Vallone, speaker of the city council—all of whom faced term limits in their current office. The search for money was intense even though each was subject to a $5.5 million limit for the primary. The Real Estate Board of New York, hoping for "access" at city hall no matter what, contributed $250,000 to each of the four. Vallone and Hevesi engaged intermediaries to bundle individual contributions. Hevesi raised $7.2 million in contributions, while Vallone took in $4.7 million. Ferrer, who raised $5.4 million for the primary and subsequent runoff, ran on the theme of supporting "the other New York," meaning poor and minority working people. He came in first, beating Green by just over 36,000 votes. But this was only 35.6 percent of the total vote, less than the 40 percent required for a first-round win.[6] Ferrer had the backing of the big unions, DC 37, the United Federation of Teachers, and 1199. Green had the firefighters and the Policemen's Benevolent Association, an indication that he was going to run to the right in hopes of gaining some of the outer-borough white vote. There was something almost Koch-like in the voter coalition he sought. In the runoff, Green, in a pitch for white votes, attacked Ferrer's "two cites" theme as "borderline irresponsible" and raised the racially charged question, "Can we afford to take a chance?" In addition, Green implied that Ferrer was a stooge of the Reverend Al Sharpton, a sure way to garner white votes. It worked and Green won the runoff with just 51 percent of the vote.[7]

As it turned out, Green's narrow victory over Ferrer was a Pyrrhic one. Green may have gained white votes, but he lost black votes. The "Can we afford to take a chance?" ad infuriated many blacks as well as Latinos. Sharpton criticized Green, threatening a boycott of the election. The city's black radio stations attacked Green. They began to "court" Bloomberg, as the *Village Voice* put it. As black radio stations lined up with an anti-Green message and sometimes an overtly pro-Bloomberg position, people began to joke about "Radio Bloomberg." The airtime in the black community allowed Bloomberg to send a positive message that he was no Giuliani or even a Mark Green. Green got 75 percent of the black vote, 10 percentage points less than Democratic candidates tradi-tionally average. He also ran behind previous Democrats in the Latino communities, getting only 49 percent of that vote—less than Ruth Messinger's 57 percent in 1997 or Dinkins's 60 per-cent in 1993.[8] Bloomberg captured 25 percent of the black vote and 40 percent of the Latino vote. In addition, turnout was low, at around 38 percent, something that always hurts Democrats and which could also be attributed to the reaction to Green in the black and Latino communities.

Who Was the New Mayor?

Clearly, Bloomberg was no Rudy Giuliani. The ad hoc coalition that elected him was nothing like Giuliani's, nor did his rhetoric resemble the previous mayor's. Bloomberg may have been a liberal of sorts, but he was not a Lindsay either. What he was, was part of the city's business elite, a "corporate liberal" in the time of the neoliberal—a social liberal with a businessman's trust in the market and a bent for private-public partnerships over public pro-vision. Bloomberg would prove to be a master at presenting his rea-sonable, competent, in-charge, even caring image. But the reality was different from the image. He criticized tax abatements but used them extensively. He talked of affordable housing but pur-sued the post-crisis developmental agenda of more luxury housing than ever. In fact, he would back an unprecedented array of mega-projects far beyond what anyone might have envisioned in 1975. If successful, he would once again change the Manhattan skyline and, for the first time, convert much of Brooklyn into a high-rise city. He made grand gestures about education for all but created an ap-proach designed to advance some and not others. He talked of his humble origins but lived and worked among the city's elite.

As he never tired of explaining, Bloomberg was from a middle-class background. He had worked at Salomon Brothers from 1966, when he graduated from Harvard Business School. According to one of his friends, Bloomberg, a Massachusetts transplant, ac-quired his view of the city while at Salomon Brothers. "Michael learned more about the city from the trading desk of Salomon than he could have learned anywhere else," his fellow Johns Hopkins graduate and Salomon trader, Morris Offitt, told *New York* magazine. Thus, even before becoming a billionaire, Bloomberg began to view the city through financial-sector lenses. The impact of this angle of vision was well described by another self-made millionaire and friend of Bloomberg's, investment firm manager Steven Rattner. He told the same magazine, "It gets harder, frankly, to have perspective on what goes on in the real world because your life changes and you operate in a certain way where you're just not taking your dry cleaning to the cleaners anymore . . . you're trying to elect a guy you think has compassion and cares and really wants to be better, even if he can't possibly imagine how tough it would be to live in Bushwick in some five-story walkup."[9]

In 1981, Bloomberg was "fired" from Salomon after a failed power struggle. He used $4 million of his $10 million golden parachute to start the financial IT firm that became Bloomberg LP. His business had a major impact on the world financial industry and made him a key player in it. His newly acquired wealth allowed him to work his way into New York City's business, social, and cultural elites. By the time he ran for mayor, he was firmly implanted on some twenty boards of such prestigious institutions as Lincoln Center for the Performing Arts, the Metropolitan Museum of Art, the New York Public Library (which is a private institution), and the Spence School (an elite school from which one of his daughters graduated), among others. In addition, he was a popular member of the charity ball and dinner party circuit of New York's social elite. His philanthropic giving became legendary and, during his first term of office, a source of goodwill in many of the city's ethnic and racially based organizations, a topic we will return to later.[10]

Bloomberg is fond of saying he owes nobody any favors for his election and reelection because he paid his own way, so it is important to understand how hollow this argument truly is. Michael Bloomberg is a player in the city's, the nation's, and the world's business elite. He is the poster child for the new producer services that define a global city and that link the decentralized financial markets of the world. To see him in a pluralistic context as a lone player and "outsider," as he put it, would make it hard to understand his priorities and behavior as mayor.

Building a Governing Coalition

Bloomberg's 2001 election was hardly a mandate, and the mixture of those who cast their votes for him scarcely a stable coalition. The other citywide officials, comptroller, and public advocate; four of five borough presidents; and all but three city council members were Democrats, although as we have seen, that no longer defined their actual politics.[11] To turn his election victory into a viable administration would require a governing coalition with considerable clout and durability. However broad it might get, this meant starting at the top, where he knew people. Perhaps because his claim to not be a "career politician" was true at first, he included among his top appointed posts a number of aides to past mayors and politicians. But it also seems clear he intended to assemble a broad but loyal group of close aides who could reach out to the city's political and economic elites, i.e., its "permanent government," as that had shaped up by the beginning of the twenty-first century.

Among the loyalists was Patricia Harris who had worked for Koch on cultural affairs and in 1994 went to work for Bloomberg LP as manager of his philanthropic activities. She was made deputy mayor for administration, which included cultural matters. She was known for her persistence in getting what she wanted and her efficiency. In Bloomberg's second term she would be promoted to first deputy mayor.[12] Daniel Doctoroff, a millionaire investor and managing partner in Oak Hill Management, was chosen deputy mayor for economic development and rebuilding. Doctoroff had pushed for the 2012 Olympics and a stadium to house them during the Giulani years and was a booster of West Side development. In Bloomberg's second term he would shift his focus to downtown development as a new appointee to the Lower Manhattan Development Corporation. Amanda Burden, the socialite heir to the Standard Oil fortune said to have trusts and investments worth $45 million, friend and neighbor to Bloomberg, and an architect who had worked on Battery Park City under Koch, was named head of the Department of City Planning, which also made her chair of the City Planning Commission. This was a key position in the coming rush to mega-development that would characterize Bloomberg's reign. Kevin Sheekey, former chief of staff to Senator Daniel Patrick Moynihan and later director of intergovernmental affairs at Bloomberg LP, was made special adviser to the new mayor. Sheekey would eventually draw a $250,000 salary for that job, far more than mere deputy mayors, commissioners, or other advisers made. The mayor's press secretary, Ed Skyler, had been a deputy press secretary under Giuliani. Of his eight senior advisers, three were Republicans, two of whom had worked for Giuliani, and one was a former Koch aide. Of his eighteen junior advisers, five were Republicans, four of whom had served under Giuliani.[13] Ray Kelly, his new police commissioner, appeared to be the sole representative of the Dinkins administration. His top African American and Latino appointees, notably deputy mayors Dennis Walcott and Carol Robles-Roman, came from outside the political arena. In short, the new mayor gathered around him experienced professionals, several of whom had worked for him at Bloomberg LP before he became mayor, plus many from the two most polarizing and development-prone administrations of the twentieth century. Several of his top aides, including Harris, Burden, Sheekey, and deputy mayor for operations Marc Shaw, were Democrats. Yet missing were the clubhouse crowds and union supporters. It was neither a Republican administration in the Giuliani sense nor a traditional Democratic regime. It seemed to be a hybrid with a definite slant toward the priorities that had characterized all administrations since the fiscal crisis of the 1970s.

What Bloomberg was building was not so much a coalition as an administrative apparatus—something he understood well as an effective businessman. As a media mogul, he would, of course, use the media to promote his administration. But he would develop another channel to the city or at least to the opinion makers and cultural leaders of New York's many ethnic, racial, and cultural communities. This would be through his philanthropic activities. As we saw, Ed Koch had skillfully used city contracts with nonprofit social agencies to buy, not so much loyalty, as acceptance and lack of resistance to his economic policies. Bloomberg also appeared to employ city contracts as a way of gaining widespread goodwill. In fact, the number of city contracts exploded from 6,849 valued at $9.9 billion in FY2000 to 17,402 worth only $7.5 billion in FY2006. This would indicate that while Bloomberg was cutting back on spending, he was spreading the largesse far more broadly and in smaller amounts. As in the past the Board (now Department) of Education and the Administration for Children's Services awarded the largest contracts.[14] Bloomberg would take privatization even further, however, and use his own money to accomplish similar political goals.

Bloomberg has four channels for making personal donations: his company, Bloomberg LP; his personal trust, the Michael R. Bloomberg Family Foundation Trust; the Carnegie Corporation of New York; and the city's Mayor's Fund to Advance New York. The latter is a city agency, previously called Public/Private Initiatives, that the new mayor beefed up and renamed. By 2005 it had raised $52.9 million, $6 million from Bloomberg, and distributed much of this to various community programs and causes. Far more important are Bloomberg's private donations. Prior to becoming mayor, he had given generously to Johns Hopkins University, his alma mater, the private schools his two daughters attended, several of New York's cultural institutions on whose boards he sat, and a number of health-related institutions. No one doubts that he took these causes seriously or that he believes philanthropy is a duty of the wealthy. But his giving both grew and took a decided political turn after he became mayor. In 2000 he gave about $100 million to some 600 organizations; by 2004 this was up to about $150 million to 843 groups. Even his usual donations to the city's cultural institutions took on a political dimension as he cut the budget of the Met and others. In effect, he privately gave back some of what he publicly took away.

More important is the goodwill he bought in communities that were less visible in his pre-mayoral life. As Sam Roberts and Jim Rutenberg wrote in the *Times*:

> From 1997 to 2000, the number of groups that got donations from Mr. Bloomberg and had Harlem in their names grew from 2 to 6, then to 13 in 2003. The number whose names included Staten Island went from 2 in 1999 to 8 in 2003; the Bronx, from 0 to 6 in 2003, and Brooklyn, from 3 in 1997 to 13 in 2003.[15]

During his first term in office Bloomberg dispensed a total of $600 million of his money.[16] This money, of course, mostly goes to tax-exempt nonprofit organizations via his company or family trust. About $30 million of it was channeled through the Carnegie Corporation, run by his friend Vartan Gregorian. Some of the organizations receiving money through one or another of these channels include: the Abyssinian Development Corporation, a Harlem church-based nonprofit headed by the politically active Reverend Calvin Butts III; the Bedford-Styvesant Restoration Corporation; the Allianza Dominicana; Aspira, a Latino advocacy group; One Hundred Black Men, Inc.; the Haitian Centers Council; the Bronx Council of the Arts; the Asian American Arts Alliance; the Ballet Hispanico, and the Dance Theater of Harlem. This mixture of cultural and development-oriented organizations is meant to influence community leaders and opinion shapers. Mostly, there is no immediate quid pro quo, but the message is clear enough. Reverend Butts, for example, who supported Green in 2001, while insisting he is "not for sale," also says of Bloomberg that he is a "fairly generous man where poor people are concerned." The executive director of Ballet Hispanico said, "The money made it possible for us to keep our doors open." NaRhee Ahn, director of the Asian American Arts Alliance told the *Times*, "He knows exactly what he's doing about where he puts his money. He's doing the right thing for himself and for Chinatown."[17]

This is not so much about vote-buying as something more subtle, effective, and legal. As the *Times* reporters put it, "The right thing, many beneficiaries said, can be just as much about muting criticism as about building political support."[18] In terms of governing, as opposed to winning elections, the ability to silence criticism from community and cultural leaders of black, Latino, Asian, immigrant, and some outer-borough white groups is crucial. What is striking is that Bloomberg's donations go to a very broad sector of the city. The inclusion of Staten Island stems from his attempt to build support or lack of opposition from the right. Having taken Staten Island by four to one, he courted its conservative Republican borough president, James Molinaro, funneling more police and firefighters to the smallest borough as well as his personal donations. His most bizarre use of his own money to garner political support, however, was his buying the ballot line of the Independence Party, the political arm of the cult around Dr. Fred Newman and Lenora Fulani. This purchase got him 59,000 votes on the Independence line.[19]

We can't know how often the quid pro quo of silence has been demanded or simply given, but we have a glimpse of how it worked in one case. As the 2005 election season approached, Patricia Harris, still overseeing Bloomberg's philanthropic activities, called members of the board of the Metropolitan Museum of Art to rebuke them for buying $100 tickets to a Gifford Miller fundraiser. Miller was the Democratic speaker of the council and a potential mayoral candidate in 2005. Bloomberg's social connections also helped him head off money for the opposition. Toni Goodale, another socialite friend of his, whose daughter worked for Bloomberg's corporation counsel, her childhood friend Michael Cardozo, also stopped contributing to Miller.[20] Undermining real and potential opposition or criticism was important to Bloomberg because the new mayor faced a grim economic reality.

Recession, 9/11, and the Deficit

Mayor Bloomberg inherited a recession, a stock market slump, the devastation of 9/11, and a huge budget deficit. In the spring of 2000, U.S. gross domestic product hit its peak and then slumped, growing only intermittently for the next year.[21] Early in 2000, the dot-com bubble began to burst and the stock market slump commenced. As Robert Brenner described it:

E-commerce firms saw their share values collapse first, in spring 2000. From the end of the following summer, the broader markets began to drop alarmingly. By the winter 2001, the technology-and-Internet-dominated NASDAQ index, central site of the equity price run-up, had declined by 60 per cent from its peak in early 2000. The S&P 500 was in bear territory, having fallen by more than 20 per cent from its high point. Five trillion dollars in assets had gone up in smoke.[22]

It was the dot-coms and new media firms that populated New York's Silicon Alley who led the slump. Not surprisingly, New York City was hit hard. Real gross city product ($2000) fell from $441 billion in 2000 to $424 billion in 2001, and $408 billion in 2002. From mid-2000 to mid-2001 the city's working families lost $3.7 billion in wages and salaries, a drop of 4.1 percent. Wall Street accounted for more than 60 percent of that loss. Computer services, New York's Silicon Alley, saw 28 percent of its jobs disappear in this period. The value of the twenty top dot-coms, the "Alley 20" index, fell from over 200 at its peak in late 1999 to about 40 in March 2002. By September 2001, the city had lost over 52,000 jobs. Then came September 11, 2001, and matters got worse. In terms of the city's economy, the terrorist attacks of 9/11 destroyed six office towers, eliminating over 13 million square feet of space and damaging 17 million more. Over eighty thousand jobs were lost in the immediate wake of 9/11. One billion dollars in tourism were lost in 2001 alone. By late 2002, 159,000 jobs had been lost to recession, slump, and terrorism. It was an almost perfect storm for New York's financial, business services, and dot-com industries. But it wasn't just the well-heeled of downtown who lost out. As the *Times* noted, many of the jobs lost due to 9/11 were those of cooks, cabdrivers, sales clerks, and seamstresses. Altogether, the city comptroller estimated a loss of $100 billion, $60 billion in jobs and income, $34 billion in property damage.[23]

By the time he took office the new mayor faced a $4.8 billion budget shortfall in the upcoming FY2003 budget, the first he would control. The two-year loss in city revenues due to 9/11 was estimated at $2.1 billion. To cover this, Bloomberg's 2002–06 financial plan called for $1.5 billion in Transitional Finance Authority (TFA) bonds. The state legislature had expanded this 1997 program on September 13, 2001, to cover 9/11-produced costs. But the plan also proposed cuts across the board: youth and community services, 19 percent; children's services, 18 percent; homeless services, 17 percent; and public health by 11 percent, to mention a few. Even the police and fire departments were not spared initially with proposed cuts of 7 percent and 6 percent, respectively. These were to produce $1.9 billion in savings for FY2003. Early retirement, cuts in fringe benefits, and state and federal government aid were to close the rest of the gap, though huge deficits were still projected for future years.[24] In November, with the budget gap reaching about $5 billion, the mayor proposed further cuts: $200 million from education; $61 million from children's services; $29 million from social services; $29 million from health and hygiene; $24 million from libraries; and so on. Attrition was to pare the police by over 2,600 jobs and social services by almost 1,600. Altogether, a total of 8,241 jobs were to go and $655 million trimmed by June 30, 2004, the end of fiscal year 2003.[25]

What actually happened was somewhat different. Compared to actual spending in FY2002, there were some real cuts. In particular, the new mayor, who took a $1 salary, cut his office's expenses by 15 percent, from 2002 to 2003. Borough presidents took cuts in their operations, as did the public advocate, the Department of Investigation, Board of Elections, the Campaign Finance Board, and government in general. Parks and recreation, housing, police, fire, and corrections all saw some cuts. Despite all this the total expenditures rose by 8.5 percent from FY2002 to FY2003. The big gainers were debt service, which rose by 84 percent over that year and accounted for almost a third of the total increase; pension costs, up 17 percent; the Board of Education, 8.2 percent; and smaller gains in other agencies.[26] What would happen during Bloomberg's first term was not so much austerity as a shift in spending priorities that, with only a few exceptions, reflected the usual preferences of the business elite's developmental agenda. The heavy lifting in shifting budget priorities had already been done by Koch, Dinkins, and Giuliani. Bloomberg only had to fine-tune while attempting to close the budget gap.

As Table 5-1 shows, over the three Bloomberg expense budgets (FY2003–FY2005) for which modifications for actual spending have been reported, as opposed to the "adopted" budget or the five-year plan, redistributive functions along with other normal functions generally declined as a proportion of spending. There is no radical departure from the priorities set many years before. Rather, there is a proportional reduction of some essential services, including at least one of the mayor's spoken priorities, education, which grew at less than half the rate of total expenditures. In his first three budgets, Bloomberg succeeded in reducing total labor costs as a percentage of total spending. Notable is the rise of the debt service, partly a result of using TFA bonds as the primary means of reducing the annual shortfall. A growing portion of the budget was going directly to Wall Street as interest and less to city workers and working-class neighborhoods. Unable to eliminate the gap through borrowing, Bloomberg would turn to raising taxes in 2003. This would not be the exercise in redistribution some imagined, because the one place Bloomberg would not turn to save the city money was the annual tax giveaway business had learned to exploit and expand so well.

TABLE 5-1
Selected NYC expenses FY2003–FY2005
($millions & agency % of total)

	2003	%	2004	%	2005	%	Growth %
Total	$44,340		$47,292		$52,790		19.1
Education	12,673	28.6	13,061	27.6	13,776	26.1	8.7
Social services	9,321	21.0	9,650	20.4	10,329	19.6	10.8
Health (incl. HHC)	2,242	5.1	2,418	5.1	2,424	4.6	8.1
Housing	437	.09	449	1.0	512	.9	17.0
Debt service	2,535	5.7	4,173	8.8	4,333	8.2	71.0
Personal service*	23,608	53.2	24,410	51.6	26,924	50.9	14.0

* Includes wages, salaries, fringe benefits, and pension contributions.
Sources: Office of Management and Budget, *Expense, Revenue, Contract, FY 2006;* Office of the Comptroller, *Comprehensive Annual Financial Report of the Comptroller, FY 2005.*

Capital spending during Bloomberg's first term showed a pattern similar to the expense budget in most cases. Naturally, some of this spending is the result of projects authorized under Giuliani, but there is a notable change. First, capital spending slows down from an average annual increase of just over 6 percent from 1996 through 2001 to 1.3 percent a year from 2002 through 2005. Capital spending for the Department of Environmental Protection, which supplies important parts of the city's infrastructure, grew by 62 percent in those years, police by 49 percent, corrections by 25 percent, and juvenile justice by three and a half times. Fire department capital spending rose in 2003 and then slumped to 26 percent below its 2002 level. Parks declined by 10 percent, and the Department of Health and Mental Hygiene by 22 percent. The Department of Housing Preservation and Development saw an overall drop in the level of spending of 10 percent. The biggest decline in new investment was in the Department of Education, which saw a 45 percent decline is spending—a surprising fact given that education is supposed to be the mayor's single biggest priority and that so many schools are overcrowded wrecks. Another surprise was the big increase in spending that went to the Health and Hospitals Corporation.[27] This calls for a closer look.

Between 2002 and 2004 spending on HHC capital projects was cut by almost half to $34.7 million, a smaller outlay than almost any other city agency except the individual library systems and the City University. Then in FY2005 it jumped to 345.7 million. This leap, it turns out, was not to improve the city's public hospitals, but to build one of the Partnership for New York City's pet projects, the East River Science Park. This is being built on the Bellevue Hospital campus, hence the partnership with HHC. It is not a health care facility, nor is it even a public facility. Rather it is an industrial park for biotech firms, as the partnership put it in its press release, one of a number of a "business incubators." Its goals, as described by partnership CEO Kathryn Wylde, include recruiting and retaining "top talent," expanding job opportunities, and promoting a "growing entrepreneurial sector." The project will be built by Alexandria Real Estate Equities and cost $1.3 billion over five years. The partnership has contributed $10 million from its New York City Investment Fund.[28] In fact, a commercial science park on the East River appears as one of the four priorities to make New York competitive in the partnership's 2005 report on its overall priorities for development. As we will see later, the partnership's priorities are remarkably similar to Bloomberg's.[29]

New York City Taxes: The Write-off Rip-off

Evading taxes has long been a basic business art. Actually getting your hand in the tax till legally in order to reduce your tax burden is fairly new. Greg Leroy puts the takeoff point for the practice of getting tax abatements, incentives, subsidies, underassessments, cheap loans through bond sales, and other gifts from local and state governments somewhere in the 1970s. It is all part of the competition between states and cities for investment and jobs—or even just the retention of jobs. As discussed in Chapter 6, this competition includes that for the financial and producer services that define a global city and are so central to New York's economy. It is a competition driven not only by companies on the make and the states and cities that seek them out, but by location consultants who teach firms how to milk these governments. The new art of raiding the public till includes drumming up fake competition and threats of relocation. It is estimated to transfer $50 billion a year nationally from local and state treasuries to private businesses. Nowhere is this corporate con game more prevalent than in New York.[30]

Mayor Bloomberg began his first term with a positive gesture concerning tax giveaways. He had Bloomberg LP reject a $14 million tax abatement. At the time he said, "Any company that makes a decision as to where they are going to be based on the tax rate is a company that won't be around very long. . . . If you're down to that incremental margin you don't have a business." In fact, one of the nation's leading relocation consultants, Robert Ady, estimates that of all the factors in making a location decision taxes account for about 5 percent of relevant costs in the case of office-based work. Labor and rents are far more important.[31] But the tax scam is not about survival or location, it is about enhancing the bottom line. New York City offers fifty programs for doing just that, as well as other techniques, notably the property assessment system, for reducing taxes on business and the wealthy. As with so many things, the mayor's practice would not match his rhetoric. Despite his statement on retention deals, sixty-three new job-retention deals would be struck by the city's Economic Development Corporation and Industrial Development Agency in his first eighteen months in office. Several went to elite private schools, others to small businesses, and still others to firms such as Merrill Lynch, American Airlines, Met Life, Forest City Ratner, the *New York Post*, and the United States Tennis Association, to mention a few.[32]

In 1998, the city's tax expenditures were worth $1.7 billion. By the time Bloomberg took office in 2002, they had already risen to an annual value of $2.1 billion, about equal to the amount of revenue lost to 9/11 and the recession. To put it another way, it was the equivalent of about 44 percent of the $4.8 billion budget shortfall

Bloomberg faced when he took office. His administration would preside over a continuing increase in these expenditures. In FY2003 they would increase to $2.4 billion, then to $3.1 billion in FY2004 and $3.3 billion in FY2005.[33] Thus, during his first term, including 2002, tax expenditures rose by 57 percent, three times the increase of budget expenditures, and well ahead of the 42 percent increase in city tax-levy revenue.[34] Not all of this tax expenditure goes directly into the hands of developers, landlords, and businesses. For example, in FY2005 some $127 million went to senior homeowners and renters, veterans, and disabled persons. That is just under 4 percent of total expenditures. In that single year, all homeowners received a $400 tax rebate, which totaled another $257 million. So, together, the elderly, disabled, veterans, and homeowners, rich and poor, got about 12 percent of FY2005 tax expenditures. The leftover $259 million of individual aid went to co-op and condo tax abatements. But this is only the beginning of the program.

Housing development in the form of J-51 exemptions and abatements for renovation, 421a exemptions for new housing, with exemptions lasting for ten to twenty-five years, and several other smaller programs to promote housing totaled $617 million in tax breaks for FY2005. Of this, $25 million, or 4 percent of total housing development funds, went to low-income housing.[35] Most of the housing development exemptions and abatements are for New York's upscale housing market, with 60 percent in Manhattan. That year, Economic Development expenditures amounted to $397 million, of which $371 million went to businesses via the Industrial and Commercial Incentive Program (ICIP). This, of course, is a direct subsidy to business, and 44 percent of this total also ends up in Manhattan.

The lion's share of the tax expenditures programs, however, is in real estate property tax abatements and exemptions on existing property. In FY2005 this amounted to $2.8 billion or 85 percent of that year's tax expenditure program. A little over $800 million of this went to public agencies, which include state-sponsored authorities like Battery Park City Authority, an upscale housing and office

complex; Port Authority, owner of Ground Zero; three development agencies; and the Housing Authority, which gets about 40
percent of the $800 million. The other nearly $2 billion goes to
those lucky enough to get to the head of the line at the Tax Commission, which rules on who gets a property tax reduction, or to
be among the city's permanently tax-exempt institutions.[36] In addition to the public agencies, this includes "nonprofit" religious and
educational institutions, like major landlords Columbia University,
New York University, and the Catholic Church. Instead of property
taxes they make an annual payment in lieu of taxes (PILOT). In
FY2005, this amounted to $169.6 million for the public agencies
alone. The net loss of tax revenue for the public agencies was
$808 million for that fiscal year. The total PILOTs in 2005 came to
$210 million. In fact, 58 percent of properties were fully or par-
tially tax-exempt in FY2005, up 16 percent from 2004, well above
the 40 percent they composed at the time of the fiscal crisis. Altogether in 2005 they composed 60 percent of billable assessed value,
up 17.6 percent from the year before. The remaining 42 percent of
properties, of course, may still receive abatements or lowered assessments.[37]

Another way to reduce one's property tax bill is to get the assessment, the alleged value of your property, reduced. Property is not
taxed on its market value, but on an assessment made by the Department of Finance. These assessments can be appealed at the Tax
Commission. During Bloomberg's first three years in office the
number of applications for assessment reductions accepted by the
Tax Commission rose from 2,823, valued at $444 million in 2002, to
4,672, worth $2.4 billion in 2004, two-thirds of this value destined
for Manhattan properties. Thus applications accepted doubled
while their value in property taxes not paid grew by almost five
and a half times. The market value of property in those years rose
by 19 percent, not inconsiderable, but not enough to explain the
tidal wave of tax assessment breaks. Some of those high on the
2004 list include: the World Financial Center at $108.3 million;
Olympia & York for $72.5 million; Citibank for $17 million; and
the Millenium Hilton for a total of $32.7 million, to mention only

a few familiar names. In fact, many high on the list were buildings, structures that were not going anywhere. Others were city-based real estate firms.[38] These pointless giveaways simply rewarded businesses for things they had done or were in the process of doing with or without a tax break and well-to-do owners for doing nothing.

The property tax is the city's largest source of revenue, as it is for most cities. Although it is based on a 1981 state law, it is the only tax over which the city has the authority to raise or lower the rate. It also controls, with some limits set by the state law, the assessment of property for tax purposes, which is crucial to the actual tax paid. All other major taxes must be passed by the state legislature. In 2003, the mayor raised the property tax rate by 18.5 percent to address the continuing budget shortfalls. This raised the weighted average from 10.41 percent per $100 of assessed value to 12.36 percent. Since there is a growing number of requests for reduced assessments, the assessment on which the tax rate is figured also changes over time. On the other hand, the market value of New York City property grew at an accelerated rate during this period. It grew from $392.3 billion in 2002 to $540.4 billion in 2005. Billable assessed value as a percentage of market value, however, fell from 25.56 percent in 2001 to 20.4 percent in 2005.[39] Total revenue from the real estate tax grew from $10.1 billion in 2003 to $11.6 billion in 2004 and then leveled off at $11.6 billion in 2005. So, as a proportion of revenue the real property tax fell from 43.5 percent in 2003 to 37.5 percent in 2005 at a time when rising property values should have increased revenues significantly.[40] What the mayor taketh away, the Tax Commission restoreth to those with clout, under the watchful eye of the mayor.

City tax-levy revenues did rise by 42 percent over this period, almost 10 percent between 2004 and 2005 alone, but not as a result of the real property tax. Two property-related taxes rose significantly as hot property changed hands: the real property transfer tax and the mortgage-recording tax reportedly brought in $2.3 billion. Reflecting a general economic upturn, there were significant increases in the personal income tax, the general corporation tax, the financial corporation tax, and the general sales tax, which together brought in an additional $1.7 billion of the total increase in tax-levy revenues of $3.8 billion. These were enough to create a $1.5 billion surplus.[41] Had assessments not been placed so low for so long, the real property tax, too, would have brought in a windfall as a result of the city's skyrocketing real estate market.

On top of this, neither the rates nor the change in assessments were the same for all classes of real estate. The rate per $100 of assessed property value varies from class to class and over time. From FY2002 through FY2004, the rate on Class IV, which represents the central business district, dropped from 9.63 percent to 8.80 percent, while that on Class I, family residential property, rose from 11.95 percent to 14.55 percent. Residential property has always been assessed at a much lower rate than commercial property, but here the rate was rising for smaller family homes and falling for office and commercial property. It is also likely that business does better at reducing assessments than individuals, and big business better still. In any case, the result was that as a percentage of the total billable assessed valuation, Class IV fell from 48.4 percent in 2002 to 46.3 percent in 2005. Class I, on the other hand, rose slightly from 10.4 percent of the total to 11.3 percent in those same years.[42]

An analysis by Josh Barbanel of the *New York Times* revealed that the prewar Manhattan co-ops inhabited by some of the city's wealthiest people actually pay a lower rate on real market value than owners of small two- and three-family houses in the outer boroughs. Co-op owners of 720 Park Avenue, a classic prewar with twelve-room apartments, pay $3.20 per $1,000 of actual market value, while the owners of two-family homes on 148th Road in Rosedale, Queens, paid over $9 per $1,000 of market value. This difference, of course, stems from the fact that co-ops and condos are not assessed at market value, but are wildly underassessed. Prewar co-ops are assessed by comparing them to older rental buildings whose market value is much lower because they are rent-regulated. In fact, the co-op board of 720 Park Avenue, through its building manager's lawyers, has applied for reductions in the building's assessment every year since at least 1996. So, for example, in 2003 and

2004 its assessment was reduced by $1 million per year. At its most recent assessment, it was valued at $141 per square foot, or $141,000 for a 1,000-square-foot apartment. Such an apartment in that building, however, sold for $20 million in 2005. And, of course, the notion that the value of this Park Avenue co-op would have declined in that period is absurd. On average prewar co-ops are assessed at $94 per square foot, postwar co-ops at $111, and condos at $200. The owners of two-family homes in Queens, on the other hand, probably don't have tax lawyers. Furthermore, their property values are estimated by a computer program that follows increases in property values. So they will see an increase in their tax bill from time to time.[43]

Indeed, taxes have gone up for residential property in general, but not evenly. The tax bill on single-family homes went up 62 percent from 2002 through 2005, those on condos by 43 percent, and those on co-ops even less. The reason, of course, was the enormous boom in property values during those years. In other words, the market value was outrunning the lowered assessments on many residential properties. But, as we saw above, it did not actually result in much growth in total real property tax revenue, mainly because both assessments and taxes on these sorts of residences are fairly low. Since the values on upscale housing rose much faster than that in low-income neighborhoods, tax increases, as shown on a map compiled by the *New York Times*, tended to hit well-to-do areas harder. This was not a matter of policy but of the market punishing those who made out best on the value of their property.[44] Such punishment was abated for some, as we saw above, when they sold their hot property for a nice gain. Indeed, property sales were up almost 30 percent from 2000 and included just over 10 percent of all properties.[45]

On top of the assessment reductions, co-op and condo owners of less than three units have received a regular abatement that reduces their taxes by at least 17.5 percent below the regular rate. About 20 percent of condo and co-op owners receive breaks of 25 percent. This cost the city $277 million in 2005. The law granting these abatements, which cut some co-op rates 19–35 percent below

those on one- to three-family buildings by one estimate, was renewed in 2004, with no objections from city hall. Attempting to fix
the inequity would no doubt bring a taxpayers rebellion from the
well-heeled co-op denizens the Upper East and West Sides of Manhattan, who benefit the most from it. As one Democratic state assemblyman from the Upper East Side told the *Times*, "It has been
easier for the mayor and the city to live with the abatement and
give up hundreds of millions of dollars in city revenue, rather than
finding the political will to fix the entire system."[46] In the case of
Mayor Bloomberg, this would require a fight with his friends and
neighbors.

The Department of Finance did issue a report in January 2004
that called for several steps to eliminate corruption in the assessment process—usually a too cozy relationship between a property
owner and an assessor. The reforms would improve the process of
assessing and make it more transparent by sending annual "Notices of Value" to the owners of all 950,000 or so properties in the
five boroughs. The notices would explain the factors used to assess
value for tax purposes. The report even proposes a future study of
the impact of changes in the law, such as assessing co-ops and condos in the same way as small homes, having one standard for all
properties, and merging utilities (Class III) with other commercial
property (Class IV). These changes could produce a fairer system,
but they remain only on paper.[47] Even though the reforms might
bring in more revenue, it does not appear to be on the mayor's
agenda. What is clear is that during Bloomberg's first term several
billion dollars were lost to the city and gained by business, real estate interests, and well-off owners of condos and co-ops. It is unlikely that back in the mid-1970s even Felix Rohatyn, Richard
Shinn, or David Rockefeller could have imagined such a windfall.
When the January 2006 property tax bills went out, they continued
an unexpected drop of some magnitude for owners of condos and
co-ops in buildings with four to ten floors. This cut taxes on many
of these units by half. The average reduction was $1,800 citywide.
For the owners that qualified in Manhattan, the savings averaged
$2,800; in Brooklyn, $800. The purpose was to bring rates on these

smaller condo and co-op buildings in line with those on rental buildings.[48] This was a blessing for upper-middle-income people but failed to address the problem of housing costs for middle- and low-income residents.

Housing for Who?

If the newly elected mayor had inherited a potential fiscal crisis in 2002, he now faced a real housing crisis. Between 1990 and 2000, the city's population increased by 695,276 people, while its stock of low-rent housing, that with rents at or below $500 a month, had fallen by 517,345 apartments, more than half the total in 1990, to 490,799.[49] To make matters worse the city-owned stock of housing that had been rehabilitated and made into low-rent housing by Koch and Dinkins had dropped from 44,035 units in 1994 to 9,477 by 2002, as they were sold to private owners. Giuliani's Building Blocks program had sold off 18,166 units of in rem housing between 1996 and 2002. The Bloomberg administration would reduce the in rem stock by another 7,000 units by 2005, bringing the total down to about 2,400. The housing stock was growing, gaining almost 200,000 units between 1999 and 2002.[50] Nevertheless, housing was scarce. In 1996 there had been over 81,000 vacant units, but in 2002 there were only 61,265 for a much larger population.[51] In fact, the citywide vacancy rate went from 4 percent in 1994 to 2.9 percent in 2002. From 1990 to 2000 construction and rehabilitation had produced 195,726 units in the outer boroughs, but only 5 percent of these had a federal low-income tax credit. From 1995 to 2005, the city had lost over 9,000 units that accepted Section 8 vouchers, which provide public rent subsidies, with another 35,000 at risk. In 2002 only 3.4 percent of the city's housing units were covered by Section 8. The waiting list for a Section 8 voucher was already eight years and 200,000 people long. The Bloomberg administration did increase the number of Section 8 vouchers it issued from 2,700 in 2002 to 6,000 in 2003, but this did not even make up for those lost. Of all 61,000 vacant units in 2002, only 9,094 were publicly rent-supported in any way.[52]

Housing had become more expensive. The median contract rent in the city had risen from $595 in 2002 to $706 in 2002. Those figures included public housing and units with regulated rent. By 2005, an unregulated two-room apartment went for a "fairmarket" rent of $1,075.[53] Rents in rent-stabilized buildings had risen from about $1,000 a month for a one- or two-year lease to $1,200 for a one-year lease and $1,400 for a two-year lease in 2004.[54] An indication of the rising cost of housing, particularly in relation to stagnant incomes, was that the proportion of renters who paid 50 percent or more of their income on housing had risen from 18.9 percent in 1996 to 22.7 percent in 2002. It was even worse for homeowners, whose homes composed about 30 percent of the housing stock. Owners who paid more than 60 percent of their income for housing rose from 3.2 percent in 1996 to 14.3 percent in 2002. The percentage of income that the average homeowner paid rose from 36 percent in 1985 to 46 percent in 2005.[55] This was, no doubt, a result of rising home prices in the city's hot market. According to figures from the Independent Budget Office, the average sale price of a home in 2000 was $307,184. But by 2005 it was $571,938, a jump of 86 percent, or just over 14 percent a year. This, in turn, increased assessments on one- to three-family homes and hence taxes. The *New York Times* found that the highest percentage of small homeowners paying more than 35 percent of their income on housing lived in working-class census tracts in the Bronx, Queens, and Brooklyn.[56]

In 2004, the average price of an apartment in Manhattan hit $1.3 million, up 30 percent from a year earlier, while luxury apartments averaged over $5 million.[57] With land more or less finite, the soaring upscale market affected all housing prices to one degree or another. Even rent-regulated housing was not exempt. In 2004, Bloomberg's Rent Guidelines Board, over vigorous protests, raised the rents on the city's million-plus rent-stabilized apartments by 3.5–6.5 percent. Since 1999, the monthly rents on stabilized apartments had risen by 40 percent. Thus, many of these apartments moved closer to the $2,000 level at which they become deregulated. From 1999 to 2002, the city lost 73,271 regulated apartments, after losing 94,906 from 1981 to 1999. Although the 1999–2002 drop may be an overstatement due to sampling differences in the 1990s and 2000s, the direction of rent regulation is clear—it is declining at an accelerating rate as more apartments hit the $2,000 mark that deregulates the unit.[58]

Mayor Bloomberg got high praise from many of the city's housing advocacy groups, the *New York Times* noted just before the 2005 election. Victor Bach of the Community Service Society of New York, an advocacy group for the poor, told the *Times*, "The mayor's first five-year plan put housing back on the screen in public policy."[59] Here one senses another example of the "at least he's not Giuliani" syndrome so common among liberals. But not every one was buying it. The *Times* also reported working-class families in Queens in 2005 wondered about the mayor's real priorities. One Ozone Park resident told the *Times*, "I can't vote for Bloomberg again. He hasn't done anything to make it less expensive to live here." Another said, "Even Stevie Wonder can see that people are getting poorer, working people are really being squeezed, you can't buy a home. But you listen to the mayor and 'everything's fine.'" The mayor told Queens residents he would build one hundred thousand housing units.[60] While this was election-time talk, he did have a program.

The twin problems of a tight housing market and a recession brought the acceleration of homelessness. The average daily homeless shelter population rose from 5,029 in 2000 to 9,165 in 2003. Even Giuliani, whose draconian homeless policy we have already seen, was moved to create some ten thousand new affordable housing units in his final year in office. Bloomberg, who had made housing one of his major issues, would go further. In December 2002, he announced a new housing program called the New Housing Marketplace. The goal was to build 65,000 new units of affordable housing by 2008. The goal was later raised to 68,000: 39,500 through renovation and 28,500 by new construction. The program would be jointly run by the Department of Housing Preservation and Development (HPD) and the Housing Development Corporation (HDC). HDC provides low-interest mortgages, while the

HPD oversees programs in which the city participated. By 2005, the mayor could announce that over twelve thousand new units were under construction and another sixteen thousand under renovation.[61] As its name hinted, this was not a public housing program or a rent subsidy program similar to Section 8. In line with the mayor's general approach to development, this was another way to stimulate private development beyond the usual tax expenditures. The city's own capital budget for HPD was not increased, and in fact fell from $380 million in FY2002 to $343 million in FY2005.[62] The funds would go to developers or community nonprofit housing groups like the Enterprise Foundation and the New York City Housing Partnership. Indeed, much of the funding for the program came from outside the city's revenue stream. The Enterprise Foundation, for example, contributed $1 billion to the New Housing Marketplace. An additional $130 million would come from a newly created Battery Park City Housing Trust Fund. There was to be a smaller program of supportive housing with a goal of twelve thousand units known as Uniting for Solutions Beyond Shelters. The 68,000 units under the New Housing Marketplace were only partially funded by the city, were to be privately owned by landlords (some nonprofit), and were simply designated "affordable."[63]

Here was the problem. The HPD defined "affordable" as housing costs equal to 30 percent of the metropolitan statistical area's 2004 median family income of $62,800.[64] This would be an annual rent of $18,840 or a monthly rent of $1,570. The first problem with this definition is that the actual median family income in New York City as a whole was $44,131, or 70 percent of the metro median income. An $18,000-a-year rent would be 43 percent of the city's median income, well above the 30 percent upper limit on what a family should spend on housing. For those in the Bronx, Queens, and Brooklyn, where the median family income was below the citywide median, it would be even more unaffordable. The New Housing Marketplace program was divided into various income levels. According to HPD, 76 percent of the 28,550 new and preserved units already or soon to be under way would go to those with a median income of $50,240 or less. The breakdown was: 22 percent for those under $18,840 (5,728 rental units and 648 owner units); 29 percent for those from $18,840 to $31,400 (7,364 rentals and 971 owner units); and 25 percent for those from $31,400 to $50,240 (5,523 rentals and 1,781 owner units).[65] Assuming tenants would pay 30 percent of their income for rents or mortgages, the only units that would fall into the usual category of low-income housing would be the 6,376 units in the lowest income group. All the others would be paying more than the average contract rent for 2002 of $706 a month. This is not likely to make much of a dent in the bigger problems of people paying an outsized percentage of their rent, on the one hand, and of homelessness, on the other. Federal programs aimed at the city had the same problem. A 2003 HUD program that was to provide $50 million for three hundred units of "affordable" housing in lower Manhattan required a family to earn between $50,000 and $85,000.[66] A joint city-HUD program to rehabilitate 360 one- to three-family houses owned by the Federal Housing Administration and sell them to families with a maximum income of $72,000 was announced in late November 2005.[67] Not much help for the city's low-income population.

While Bloomberg's major housing initiative earned him the "better than Rudy" tag that helped keep him popular, some of his actions seemed almost Rudyesque and truly Republican. For example, year after year from 2003 through 2005 he requested that state senate majority leader Joseph Bruno (a Republican) block a bill in the state legislature that would expand the Senior Citizens Rent Increase Exemption Program (SCRIE), which protects seniors with disabilities from rent increases. The city's Independent Budget Office estimated it could help 36,000 additional disabled seniors and would only cost the city $14 million a year when at full implementation.[68] In 2005, he vetoed a city council bill that would protect tenants from losing Section 8 housing when a landlord tried to get out of the program. In buildings with a high proportion of Section 8 tenants, they would be allowed to buy the building and retain Section 8 vouchers. The council overrode Bloomberg's veto by a vote of 44–3, with the council's three Republicans siding with the mayor. The reason for the mayoral veto was that it would place too much of a burden on building owners. Yet, as one council member argued, the failure to pass the bill could lead to evictions and the loss of more affordable housing.[69] In both of these cases, it is the interests of the landlords that dominates. The Republican Bloomberg trumped the liberal Bloomberg so many of the voters in 2005 thought they knew.

Homelessness was another problem that Bloomberg had promised to address. His rhetoric on the subject was the opposite of Giuliani's. He did not threaten to punish the homeless, but take on the problem. During his first two years in office, the homeless shelter population soared from 8,071 families in 2002 to 9,203 in 2003, and then down slightly to 8,922 in 2004. According to city's Department of Homeless Services (DHS) shelter census reports, the total homeless population in shelters continued to rise from 34,576 in 2002 to 38,310 in 2003.[70] In 2004, it fell by almost a thousand to 37,319 and it fell again in 2005 to 34,080, according to the DHS. The drop was big enough, the mayor claimed, to justify the closing of the Carlton House shelter in Queens. The figure for 2005 was an improvement, but still far above the previous high of 28,000 in 1987. The mayor would claim that the homeless population was shrinking, eventually to disappear into all the "affordable" housing he was creating. In fact, the city claimed to have put over seven thousand families in permanent homes over the previous few years.[71] It probably didn't hurt that there was a drop in the city's unemployment rate from 8.4 percent in 2003 to 4.7 percent in August 2005.[72]

More controversial was the count of the street homeless. Here the city claimed a drop from 1,560 to 1,482 of Manhattan street homeless from 2003 to 2004. This was questioned by the Coalition for the Homeless, which accused the DHS of a flawed methodology in counting the street homeless, a group that is difficult to count accurately. The number on the street dropped slightly again in 2005, to 1,476 in Manhattan. The total for all boroughs came to 4,395. Previous surveys had not included all the boroughs and were not comparable.[73] What was clear was that the problem of homelessness in New York City had not gone away.

One of the most scandalous ways of providing "permanent homes" for the homeless, was the scatter-site program begun in 2000 by Giuliani. Under this program, the city began renting apartments from landlords with virtually no competitive bidding or oversight at rents of $2,500 to $3,000 or so a month—more than a two-bedroom rental in one of the city's better neighborhoods. But these rentals were often dilapidated, facing scores of violations, and, of course, not in high-income areas. In 2000 the program had some forty-nine families; by October 2002 it had 1,932. DHS commissioner Linda Gibbs told a March 2003 council hearing that she couldn't really cut back on the program "as long as the demand exceeds the supply." In fact, the city had increased the program by 22 percent since Gibbs took over.[74] No doubt, the glacial pace of building decent supportive housing has kept the city dependent on this scam.

As with housing in general, Bloomberg passed as reasonably liberal and sympathetic toward the homeless, i.e., not Rudy. But also as with housing, he seemed to have his mean side. For example, in June 2004 the DHS ordered the directors of fifty shelters to draw up a hit list of five shelter residents who could be evicted for one reason or another. Gibbs told the *Daily News*, "If we saw a case we thought was appropriate for sanction, we would raise that with the agency. The policy is in effect and every person in the shelters is potentially eligible." One shelter director said, "They are going over the cases with a fine-tooth comb."[75] Also in June 2004 Bloomberg ordered the Housing Authority to rigorously enforce a law passed under Giuliani that allows public housing tenants to be evicted if they or a guest have ever been convicted of a felony drug charge. Called Operation Safe Housing, it allows a family to face eviction if someone with a record visits them. Tenants' rights advocates say it's a program to reduce public housing in order to lower the budget deficit.[76] Later that year, the city decided to shift the distribution of Section 8 vouchers from the homeless to low-income workers—to rob Peter to pay Paul. Gibbs told the *Daily News* that people were applying to shelters to get to the front of the line for the vouchers.[77] This would stop that, but leave the homeless even more helpless.

The unspoken but often tolerated alternative to low-rent public housing is the city's illegal underground housing conversion market. This goes back at least to the 1970s. In Elmhurst, Queens, for example, what began as the legal conversion of one-family homes into two-family houses spurred illegal "infill" and subdivided occupancy units in similar homes.[78] This is where a one- or two-family house is divided into multiple single-room units, from basement to attic to garage, which are then rented out. Each room may be inhabited by several people. This is in violation of the housing code, produces overcrowding and stress on neighborhood resources, and is dangerous to the tenants. In December 2005, for example, three children and one adult died in a fire in Elmhurst because there was no proper exit from their unit in the converted building. Yet the demand for housing, especially among immigrants, is so great that it is estimated there are one hundred thousand such units in the city. The city councilman from the Elmhurst area where the fire took four lives calls the illegal housing a "financial reality" in a city where housing is both scarce and increasingly expensive. Black-market housing has also spilled over into areas zoned for industry. One study stated, "We found more than 30 buildings converted in the East Williamsburg Industrial Park." Not surprisingly, complaints were on the rise. Complaints were up in all boroughs, but Queens had the most, rising from about nine thousand a year in 2002 to fifteen thousand in 2005. Violations issued by the city from 2002 through 2005, however, were below those in the final Giuliani years.[79] A crackdown on such housing would no doubt cause the shelter population to rise dramatically. Clearly, the housing crisis remained just that as Mayor Bloomberg began his second term.

There are new low-rise two- and three-family buildings going up in Brooklyn and Queens. This private development, spurred by demand, tax breaks, and the rapid rise in value of one-, two-, and three-family buildings. Since 2001 the value of such houses has risen by well over 10 percent a year and was projected to rise by 22 percent in 2005.[80] These new buildings appear even in very poor neighborhoods like Bedford-Stuyvesant, but they are not cheap. Or, to put it another way, they are "affordable" only in comparison to Manhattan or gentrified Brooklyn. A look at ads in both local and citywide newspapers shows rents not far behind gentrified Park Slope or Cobble Hill. A new three-family house in Bedford-Stuyvesant sells for $690,000. Similar older, less subsidized buildings are advertised at over $900,000. Most likely these will be bought by prospective landlords and the apartments rented out. Rents listed in low-income areas of Brooklyn and Queens are advertised from $1,100 to $1,500 for one- or two-bedroom units, $13,000 to $18,000 year and scarcely affordable for the poor or near poor.[81]

Bloomberg's initiatives in housing exist within the context of the greater development agenda of New York's developers, real estate moguls, corporate interests, and the administration itself. It is a neoliberal agenda in which public money, in forms we have already seen and others we will examine later, combined with private funds, is used to foster private profit on a grand scale. This is a program in which the mayor's New Housing Marketplace and other programs are overwhelmed in scale and resources. Public provision shrinks within a sea of mega-projects pushed by the city's business elite and endorsed by the vast majority of politicians. New York's real housing policy is being fought out on Manhattan's West Side and downtown; in the so-called Atlantic Yards near downtown Brooklyn, and on that borough's waterfront from Coney Island to Red Hook to Williamsburg; as well as in parts of Queens and the Bronx. As we shall see in Chapter 6, almost the only limit to this development agenda is the clash among the developers themselves.

Education Reform

While Bloomberg had not run on the issue of education in 2001, by 2002 he had made reform of New York's failing public school system a priority. Like President George W. Bush with his No Child Left Behind program, Bloomberg would reorder the system's priorities and change the way it was run. Few denied that New York's public schools, like many across the country, were in deep trouble. Reforming the city's huge public school system, with 1.1 million children in over 1,300 schools, would be a daunting challenge. Giuliani's panacea had been vouchers, but even his appointed, and then fired, school chancellors wouldn't buy it. Bloomberg vowed to take over the school system from the elected Board of Education and reshape it.

In early 2004, Governor Pataki's Commission on Education Reform had called for a $4 billion *a year* increase in spending for New York City schools. Later that year, a "special masters" panel appointed by New York State supreme court justice Leland DeGrasse reported that it would take $5.6 billion in operating funds over four years above the current budget levels and an additional $9.2 billion to give students the "sound basic education" promised by the state's constitution.[82] No such increase in either operating expenses or capital spending was forthcoming or planned. The average annual increase in the education expense budget from 2003 through 2005 was $368 million, a little over a quarter of the $1.4 billion a year called for. The planned capital budget was $6.5 billion over five years, not $9.2 billion over four.[83] New York City spent half of the $20,000 per student that private schools and neighboring suburban public schools spent: money that bought smaller class sizes, better facilities, up-to-date books, computers, extracurricular programs that broaden one's outlook, and better-paid teachers. As Rebell and Wardenski of the Campaign for Fiscal Equality argue, "The wealthy know that money matters in providing opportunities for their children, and the nation's poor know quite well that the lack of resources that only money can buy has denied them access to these same opportunities."[84] Nevertheless, there would be no attempt to double resources or even spend significantly more than in the past. As a percentage of the expense budget, spending on education actually fell during Bloomberg's first term, as we saw above.

Instead, Bloomberg and his new chancellor opted for the latest in neoliberal education policy. The neoliberal education agenda involved a set of goals and policy proposals that centralize authority, remove influence from parents despite occasional rhetoric to the contrary, standardize and limit the scope of education for working-class students, and introduce managerial norms and corporate money and influence. Results would be by solely quantitative measures produced by frequent standardized tests. It had been developed not only by domestic right-wing think tanks like the Heritage Foundation, but expressed globally by the World Bank in its 2004 *World Development Report* and by the Organization for Economic Cooperation and Development, the organization of the twenty-nine richest countries.[85]

The object of this new theory of education reform was to create a flexible workforce, not a smart one. Testing and standard curriculum were central to measure quantitative results of the kind that business executives understood. In its effort to create a "universal" test, the OECD called for "reading to perform a task," as opposed to "reading to be informed." Where privatization was possible it should be pursued. Where it was too controversial, steps such as vouchers, charter schools, or academies, publicly funded but privately run, should be taken. Both students and funds would be gradually transferred out of the old public schools and into the new semi-private, often corporate-run systems. The whole idea was to strip down public education to what was needed to produce a viable workforce.[86] George W. Bush's 2001 No Child Left Behind initiative was a version of this. Bloomberg had to build on Bush's program.

The dismal state of a majority of New York's schools made it easy for the new mayor to argue for reform, and reform meant direct mayoral control of the schools. Despite some resistance and opposition, in June 2002 the state legislature gave him that control. In July, he appointed Joel Klein schools chancellor.[87] Klein was not an educator. He was a lawyer, a Washington insider in the 1990s who had prosecuted Microsoft on antitrust charges. Before becoming chancellor he had run the U.S. operations of the big German publisher Bertelsmann. The lack of experience in education was not seen as a weakness but as a strength, for another feature of the neoliberal education agenda is running things like a business. And, indeed, across the country public school systems were being run by former corporate executives, generals, and the like. Klein, who liked the mayor's managerial methods, said, "Mike and I are similar in our analytical approach. We look for management solutions."[88]

The Bloomberg/Klein program, known as Children First, built on the No Child Left Behind program. It included a core curriculum for all but two hundred schools, standardized testing already in place, charter schools, "small schools" inside older large schools to help problem students, a Leadership Academy to train principals, and Impact Schools, where discipline and crime were problems. What was in the making was a sort of three-tier education system. At the top, where they had always been, were the two hundred schools thought to be good and usually populated by students from middle- or upper-middle-class areas. These schools were exempt from the core curriculum, presumably free to learn more than "reading to perform a task," and their students mostly college-bound.[89] This tier was not new, but now it was enshrined in the ' Children First hierarchy. A complicated mechanism for transferring into one of the better of the city's 318 high schools replaced the old haphazard method. Both student and school list their choices, and if they match, you get in. Then there were the charter schools. Here was an even more pronounced element of choice and potentially a halfway house to privatization, since they were run by private firms or nonprofit organizations. They were exempted from many of the state regulations, freeing them to follow the neoliberal agenda. The track record on charter schools around the country, however, was mixed at best. Studies by both the American Federation of Teachers and the U.S. Department of Education found that children in charter schools did no better on average than those in traditional public schools across the country.[90] The original plan was to create fifty, but Klein has asked for more. At the bottom are the bulk of the 1,350 schools. Some of these have "small schools" inside to help underperforming students, but for the rest there are just more tests. For those deemed unsuited for college there is the Learning to Work track to low-wage service employment.[91]

Klein and Bloomberg have been quick to claim success because state and city tests showed progress. The results were the highest since standards-based testing was introduced in 1999. Yet, even these results were uneven. For example, the 2005 state math tests showed significant progress among fourth graders, but a slight drop among eighth graders. Then, too, the results were not much different from those around New York State. Robert Tobias of New York University, who sat on the Board of Education for thirty-three years and was in charge of testing for thirteen of those, questions the reliability of the test scores, saying, "These scores in particular don't prove what they claim."[92] More important was the question of just what was really being measured by these tests. When reading tests were flat in 2004, more test prep time and regulations were imposed. Teachers complained they were doing five hours of test prep per week, the near equivalent of a day's teaching time. Among the subjects reportedly suffering were science and social studies, which are not tested like reading and basic math. Randi Weingarten of the UFT said of these new regulations on test prep, "It's drill, drill, drill, cram, cram, cram without the real basics. And kids forget the information as soon as the test is taken."[93] At best, the students are learning how to take tests. What they are not likely to learn in the bulk of the city's standardized school is critical thinking.

Another neoliberal feature of Children First and a Bloomberg favorite is the public-private partnership. In this case, it is more like the invasion of the wealthy and the corporate-minded. For one thing, management skills seem to be the emphasis of the Leadership Academy, which is to train school principals. Its chair is Jack Welch, the former CEO of General Electric who made $123 million in his last full year there. Welch was famous for his antiunion, tough-guy stance, something the new principals would presumably learn from him. The vice chair of the academy is Richard Parsons, CEO of Time Warner. Jill Levy, president of the principals' union, said she feared the academy was designed to turn out "brainwashed" anti-union principals. For another, the Academic Intervention Services, meant to prep those who didn't do well in their tests, are outsourced to for-profit outfits like Kaplan and Sylvan

Learning. Then there is the deal with Snapple to supply sugary drinks for the students.[94]

Another feature of the public-private partnership approach is the new emphasis on fund-raising among the wealthy. It was with much fanfare that the mayor and chancellor announced in November 2005 recent gifts of $24 million, $18 million of it from the Bill and Melinda Gates Foundation.[95] By December 2005, they had raised $311 million from wealthy individuals and their foundations. Money has come from what Merryl Tish, a member of the state Board of Regents, which administers one standard test, described as "the club of people in New York that support just about everything"—in other words, New York's business elite of which she is a member in good standing. The advantage of this private money is that it is not subject to the many regulations that public funds face. So, much of this money was destined to support the "small schools" ($117 million), charter schools ($41 million), and the Leadership Academy ($70 million)—the core pieces of the neoliberal aspects of the new plan.[96] The obvious advantage of this is that the mayor and chancellor are free—and funded—to push the managerial side of the Children First program.

Almost everyone, including city officials, pays lip service to the notion that parents must be involved directly if schools are to be improved and their children better educated. Yet Children First is consciously structured to keep the parents away from the schools themselves. The old community school boards were abolished and replaced by community education councils. In truth, the old community boards were not usually dominated by parents but by members of the teachers union, representatives of the Catholic Church, and others with an interest in the direction of public education, but the new councils are powerless. An indication of just how powerless was that voter turnout for their elections plunged even where there was a history of parent activism. Each school would also have a full-time, paid "parent coordinator," another layer of administration.[97] If the coordinator can't deflect parent anger, the thirteen new Regional Support Offices created as part of the program, where parents can voice their concerns, will keep even those more aggressive parents well away from the schools themselves. If your image of school administration is that of a Jack Welch or other corporate-minded managers, you don't want emotional parents interfering with things. That parents are concerned is indicated by the DOE's statistics that the support offices received over 1 million phone calls and 631,700 walk-in visits in 2004–5. There is also the fact that over one hundred thousand people still belong to parent-teacher associations.[98]

Not surprisingly, the Partnership for New York City is enthusiastic about Children First. Its *Progress Report*, conducted by the Steinhardt School of Education at New York University, says, "there is good reason to be pleased by the progress of New York City's public school system and optimistic about the future." It cites as "most important" a decline in the number of "low-performing" schools, higher test scores, and increased graduation rates. It also cites drops in overcrowding among elementary and middle schools, from 45.9 percent in 2002 to 26 percent in 2005. In high schools, however, 70 percent of schools remained overcrowded.[99] Whether all these quantitative measures will really produce the sort of minimally literate and numerate workforce the neoliberals seek remains to be seen. What seems certain is that the city's class and race structures will not be altered by this approach, even if test scores continue to equal out some more. The majority of students will still be headed for the low-wage, dead-end jobs. Furthermore, any approach to learning that ignores the surrounding social conditions that produce "low-performing" students and schools is bound to fail. The interesting thing here is how much the neoliberals share the old, largely discredited liberal assumption that education alone can pull people up out of poverty. A labor market such as New York City's, along with racial segregation by neighborhood and school, will continue to thwart the hopes of the 20–40 percent of those who are stuck in or near poverty. Individuals will escape, as they always have, but the structure will not go away because the schools are run like corporations where the bottom line is all that truly matters.

Reelection Victory

The 2005 mayoral election was reportedly the first in the city's history in which non-Hispanic whites were a minority. As recently as the 2004 presidential election, whites still composed 51 percent of registered voters. But as the children of immigrants grew of age and others became citizens, the balance finally changed. By that time the most common name on the registration list was Rodriguez, according to John Mollenkopf of the City University Graduate Center.[100] This would seem to help Fernando Ferrer, who had won the Democratic primary in September and faced Bloomberg in November. But it was not to be. Perhaps a sign that demographics alone would not bring victory was that Ferrer won the primary only by the grace of the other Democrats. Ferrer got 39.9 percent of the vote, just 250 votes short of the 40 percent he needed to avoid a runoff. In a most unusual move, the other Democratic contenders decided to avoid the sort of nasty runoff that hurt them in the past. As Table 5-2 shows, the primary itself was very racially polarized. The two white candidates, Congressman Anthony Weiner and council speaker Gifford Miller, both got most of their votes from whites. C. Virginia Fields, the African American borough president of Manhattan, got 71 percent of her votes from blacks. Ferrer also got the bulk of his votes from Latinos, but the percentage was lower than the comparable percentages of the other candidates' racial votes. Latinos, divided between Puerto Ricans, Dominicans, Mexicans, and Central and South Americans, were less of a block vote than blacks, who were similarly divided between African Americans, West Indians, and a growing number of Africans. Asians, another new factor, spread their votes among the four major candidates, with a slight preference for whites, indicating the lack of a block vote in the absence of an Asian candidate.[101] What all of this seems to indicate is that while racial polarization is alive and well in New York politics, there is enough uncertainty in the Latino and Asian votes to allow a white candi-

TABLE 5-2
Democratic primary 2005:
share of vote by race (%)

Candidate	Share of Total Vote (%)	Vote by Race (%)			
		White	Black	Latino	Asian
Ferrer	39.9	2	32	62	1
Weiner	29.0	76	2	8	12
Fields	16.0	4	71	17	3
Miller	10.0	77	6	10	4
Others	5.0	–	–	–	–

Source: *New York Times*, September 15, 2005.

date to become mayor in spite of the current demographics of the city. As it turned out, even the black vote was uncertain.

Bloomberg won 59 percent of the vote to Ferrer's 39 percent. Bloomberg got 70 percent of the white vote and 49 percent of the black vote, both higher than his 2001 returns among these groups. He got 35 percent of the Latino vote, which was less than in 2001, but this time he was running against a Latino. In other words, Ferrer did not hold enough of the Latino vote or get enough of the white vote to even come close to winning.[102] Several factors undermined Ferrer's chances. One was money. Bloomberg spent $77.9 million of his own money compared to $9 million spent by Ferrer, according to the Campaign Finance Board.[103] And Ferrer had to fund a primary as well as the general election. Additionally, Ferrer did not get the sort of labor support a Democrat would expect and that limited his fund-raising capacities. Bloomberg, on the other hand, was endorsed by District Council 37 of AFSCME, Local 32B/J of the Service Employees International Union, UNITE HERE, Local 3 of the IBEW, and the AFL-CIO Central Labor Council. Other unions, such as those of the teachers, police, and firefighters, did not endorse either candidate.[104] No doubt all that money Bloomberg had spread around the city for the last four years helped convince recipients that he was concerned about their projects and their communities. But it was also that Ferrer's campaign just never seemed to gel or excite. He tried the "two New Yorks" and then abandoned it. The *Times* characterized his campaign as "faintly populist."[105] Part of it was also that Bloomberg had won many over with his competent management of the city, and his un-Rudy-like behavior. He had brought the city through a great tragedy and a recession and things seemed to be looking up for many. Restaurant and bar traffic, retail trade, and above all tourism were all up from their post-9/11 lows, and the mayor was quick to take credit.[106] But those who didn't see a better life than before didn't vote in large numbers or couldn't vote.

A total of 1,235,998 New Yorkers voted in the 2005 general election for mayor. In March of that year the New York State Board of Elections showed that 3,903,852 people were registered to vote in the city. Assuming registration did not slip by November, only 32 percent of the electorate bothered to go to the polls.[107] This is fairly low for New York City. In absolute numbers it was almost 300,000 fewer than had voted in 2001, when Bloomberg won by a much narrower margin, and a whopping 1,755,142 fewer than voted in the 2005 Democratic primary.[108] Obviously, there was a sense that Bloomberg was going to win and people stayed home in droves. Given that low-income people generally don't vote in as great a proportion as those with higher incomes and better education, it is almost certain that the middle and upper classes elected the mayor.

Ferrer carried the Bronx, his base and the only borough he won, by 58 percent; turnout was slightly below average, 31 percent compared to 32 percent. Staten Island, which voted 77 percent for Bloomberg, had an above-average turnout of 36 percent and contributed 9 percent of the votes that reelected him. Brooklyn, which gave Ferrer the largest number of votes, 28 percent of his total, had a turnout of only 29.6 percent. A higher turnout in Brooklyn and the Bronx might have made a difference. But there was no Jesse Jackson effect of the sort that had put Dinkins in office, despite an appearance by Jackson in October.[109] There was no "movement" to bring the missing thousands to the polls. Insofar as those unions whose members were largely people of color mobilized, it was mainly for Bloomberg. The county organizations could barely make a difference at the level of citywide elections. The old Democratic Party voting coalition, long in disarray, seemed to have vanished. The fact that one of Ferrer's major fund-raisers was an out-of-town businessman said a great deal, not only about Ferrer as a candidate, but about the state of the Democratic Party, locally and nationally. Ideologically, the New York Democrats, like their national counterparts, lacked a clear or unified message.

With such a majority and little organized opposition on the horizon, Bloomberg took office with an air of confidence. He moved quickly to reorganize his leadership team. All four of the new deputy mayors had been part of the first administration and three had worked for Bloomberg LP. Patricia Harris moved from overseer of the mayor's charity operations to first deputy mayor. Kevin Sheekey, said to be the strategist of the 2005 campaign, became deputy mayor for government relations, and communications director Edward Skyler, deputy mayor for administration. Linda Gibbs, former director of Homeless Services and the only non–Bloomberg LP person of the four, became deputy mayor for health and human services. As one political consultant told the *Times*, "They are all people who will carry out exactly what he wants to carry out."[110] What he wanted was what elite New York wanted—more and more development.

6

Behind the Skyline:
New York's Elite Remakes
the City and Itself

On June 7, 2005, in the garden of the Museum of Modern Art among a crowd of celebrities, business moguls, and the mayor of New York, David Rockefeller celebrated his ninetieth birthday.[1] David Rockefeller symbolized the financial leadership of the city, but also of the nation and, arguably, of the developed capitalist nations. He was a man of imperial vision. As a young man of thirty-four in 1949 he was elected to the board of the prestigious Council on Foreign Relations. In 1970 he became its chair. Shortly after this he helped form the Trilateral Commission, an organization of business and political leaders from North America, Europe, and Japan that sought to promote globalization and open markets. He was, as he wrote, a "proud internationalist." In other words, he was a man whose business interests and political vision were, like the city he attempted to shape, global in scale. He and Chase played a key role in the recycling of petrodollars and greatly expanded his interests in the Middle East, adding to those already around the world.[2] For David Rockefeller the transformation of New York, both physically and fiscally, was the key to managing a global empire. As in global city theory, New York was the nerve center of the world economy, and it required the oversight of the elite to keep it on focus.

This was the man who for almost five decades had been the activist leader of New York's business elite. His footprints were all over Manhattan. In 1956 he commissioned the designing and building of 1 Chase Plaza, his bank's new headquarters in downtown Manhattan, which opened in 1961. In the same year he founded the Downtown–Lower Manhattan Association (DLMA), an organization of powerful downtown business leaders dedicated to pushing the development of lower Manhattan. It has about ninety members, all big businesses downtown, and still operates. The new DLMA recommended clearing the docks, markets, and tenements of much of downtown to make way "to create an expanded financial services industry." It also called for an "around-the-clock" Wall Street community and "affordable housing." The latter became Battery Park City, a scarcely affordable project of brother Nelson. When Nelson Rockefeller became governor in 1958, David, through the DLMA, revived an old idea for a world trade center at the foot of Manhattan and convinced the new governor to make it a state project in order to insulate it from public pressure and city rules. By 1960 planning for such a center commenced under the control of the Port Authority of New York and New Jersey, the country's oldest "public benefit" agency. Founded in 1921 to oversee the port, it possessed the power to bypass city land-use rules and zoning regulations, and to use eminent domain, which it did to demolish 164 buildings on 14.6 acres in 1961 to make way for the World Trade Center.³ This set an important precedent by which key members of the business elite recruit the state government and its various unaccountable authorities to do what the city, with its complicated rules and zoning patterns, its county machines, and, prior to the fiscal crisis, its generally decentered government could not do effectively. In one sense, the manner in which the World Trade Center was planned and executed was an unconscious rehearsal for the fiscal crisis regime. This pattern would be repeated in the reconstruction at Ground Zero and the redevelopment of lower Manhattan after 9/11 and, indeed, the reshaping of much of the city.

The Rockefeller fingerprints, if not quite their footprints, could be seen later on Manhattan's West Side, where the value of Rockefeller Center (the old footprint) was in danger. To promote Westway, David along with fiscal crisis regulars Richard Shinn, William Ellinghaus, and Walter Wriston formed what became the New York City Partnership in 1979 and later the Partnership for New York City. Westway went down to defeat in 1985, but the partnership became an important player in shaping the city's skyline. David, himself, called it the most "effective private sector organization in New York City's history." In 2002, the partnership merged with the Chamber of Commerce and Industry, thus becoming a much broader representative of New York business.[4] On the West Side, the Rockefeller Brothers Fund also played a significant role in planning the development of Times Square, Clinton (Hell's Kitchen), and other parts of the West Side in the 1970s and 1980s. Unlike the other Rockefeller foundations, the Brothers Fund had remained tightly controlled by family members and focused on real estate development.[5] David had retired as chairman and CEO of Chase in 1981, and from the Family Office, which manages much of the family fortune, in 1992, but as he wrote in his *Memoirs* he remained active in business and world affairs.[6] Along with aging fiscal crisis veterans like Wriston, Rohatyn, and Shinn, Rockefeller became an emeritus member of the city's permanent government. Like America's capitalist class as a whole, New York's business elite and the permanent government it presided over had changed. The generation of the fiscal crisis nevertheless left an important legacy to a reshaped business elite in organizations such as the Alliance for Downtown New York and the New York City Partnership and in a method that allowed them to largely circumvent city politics when that seemed advantageous.

The Business Elite and the Permanent Government in the Early Twenty-first Century

New York City remains the nation's most dense and wealthiest corporate headquarters complex. Forty-three of the Standard & Poor 500 are still headquartered in the city, about the same as twenty years earlier. If this were expanded to the S&P 1500, the number of headquarters would rise to ninety-two. Thirty-six of these are in

FIRE industries and thirty-one in manufacturing. The city's FIRE businesses account for about 40 percent of the nation's market valuation of firms in that industry.[7] But much has changed. There were the mergers of banks and financial firms of recent years. Rockefeller's Chase, for example, had been acquired by the Chemical Bank in 1996, though it kept the Chase name. Along the way, it acquired Manufacturers Hanover and the National Bank of Detroit. Then in 2000, it merged with JP Morgan to become JP Morgan Chase. In 2004 it bought Chicago-based Bank One. In the service field what had been the New York Telephone Company subsidiary of AT&T was now Verizon, the result of mergers with New England Telephone upon the breakup of AT&T, and then with Bell Atlantic in 1997, GTE in 2000, and MCI in 2005.[8]

Indeed, the merger movement from the second half of the 1990s through 2005 altered the U.S. business landscape once again, with important consequences for the New York business elite. From 1995 to 2000 the value of all mergers and acquisitions (M&As) soared from $896 billion to $3.4 trillion. With the recession the value of M&As sank to $1.3 trillion. In 2004, the total value rose to $2 trillion, and then to $2.7 trillion in 2005 in announced mergers or buyouts. Although energy firms would pull ahead in 2004 and 2005, taken together FIRE and business services were leaders in the field as of 2003. Financial firms would be second in 2004 and 2005.[9]

This escalation in the concentration of capital not only affected New York by increasing the size and global reach of many of its firms, but also produced an increase in income for the financial outfits that advised, financed, and conducted many of these mergers. The fees earned for their role in M&As by investment bankers brought $31 billion worldwide in 2005, up from $23.9 billion in 2004. Five New York firms were among the six worldwide who earned over $1 billion in fees. Table 6-1 shows their earnings for 2004 and 2005. Goldman Sachs led the pack, with almost $2 billion in fees in 2005. Not far behind was Morgan Stanley, with nearly $1.6 billion, pulling ahead of JP Morgan in 2005. The largest source of fees for these financial giants was the financial industry

TABLE 6-1
Fees earned by the top five New York financial advisers
in M&As, 2004 and 2005
($millions)

	2004	2005
Goldman Sachs	$ 1,372.8	$ 1,987.3
Morgan Stanley	977.6	1,575.2
JP Morgan	1,1,041.8	1,293.7
Citigroup	981.9	1,216.5
Merrill Lynch	585.3	1,116.1

Source: Thomson Financial, *Mergers & Acquisitions Review*, Fourth Quarter 2005.

itself.[10] The significance of these fees, of course, is that they bring a great deal of money into the city, much of it to a small group of people. And the fees, of course, are only one piece of the revenues and profits the city's financial firms bring in.

It is worth noting how this helps create the enormous income inequality that characterizes New York in a more extreme way than the country as a whole. Unlike most industrial, service, and retail firms, Wall Street devotes half its revenues to compensation for its managers, traders, analysts, etc.—not including clerical or cleaning staff. As one Wall Street veteran told *New York* magazine, "Wall Street is just a compensation scheme. They literally exist to pay out half their revenue as compensation."[11] Bonuses alone were $15.9 billion for Wall Street as a whole in 2004 and hit $21.5 billion in 2005. Goldman Sachs provides a good example of how this largesse is distributed. In the first three quarters of 2005, Goldman Sachs drew in $18.5 billion in revenues. Half of this, $9.25 billion, was set aside for compensation. It was expected that the year's total revenue would be about $22 billion, with $11 billion going toward compensation. If divided evenly this would amount to $500,000 per employee. Of course, it was not. Although the company had gone public, the partners still controlled the distribution of this booty, a disproportionate amount of which went to them in the form of salaries, direct compensation, and/or bonuses. At Goldman Sachs, the 250 partners, now called partner managing directors, sliced off 15 percent of the $11 billion for themselves. That's $1.65 billion for 250 people. If divided evenly that would be $6.6 million a piece. But it's not. The senior partner/managers determine who gets what. In 2004, CEO Henry Paulson earned $29.8 million (up to $38 million in 2005), President Lloyd Blankfein got $29.5 million, Chief Financial Officer David Viniar got $19 million, and Vice Chairs Robert Kaplan and Suzanne Nora Johnson each made $17.5 million. Traders can be among the best paid according to what they bring in. Traders who use the firm's money can make $15–20 million. One crude-oil trader took home an estimated $20–25 million in 2004. A derivatives trader in their London office made $25–30 million. None are well-known like the CEO, but they make almost as much, occasionally more. The next layer down makes from $1.75 million to $3 million. Below that the remaining 35 percent of the $11 billion goes, according to performance and what it takes to keep them from going, to the rest—about $1.25 million apiece. Further down the line, newly hired analysts make $70,000, and associates with MBAs about $90,000.[12] Presumably, these upper-middle-income newcomers are on their way, or think they are on their way, up to the high levels of compensation and wealth.

Although Goldman Sachs is the leader in many ways, it is not the most generous to its top executives. Stanley O'Neal of Merrill Lynch, the first African American to become CEO of a major investment firm, took in just over $32 million in 2004, while Richard Fuld of Lehman Brothers made $35.3 million that year. The big winners on Wall Street, however, were the hedge fund managers. Edward Lambert of ESL Investments made just over $1 billion, while James Simons of Renaissance Technologies pulled in $670 million and Bruce Kovner of Caxton Associates made $550 million.[13] Industry consolidation, the income from mergers in other industries, and pure speculation had created a new generation of superrich individuals as well as a trail of well-paid newcomers

with their eyes on the big compensation packages. Neither recession, nor stock market slump, nor 9/11 ended the excesses of the
late 1990s or moderated this trend.

Another trend that brought changes to the nation's capitalist
class and hence to New York's business elite was the fusion of management and ownership. Since the rise of the giant corporations in
the late nineteenth century, management and ownership had become separate and distinct aspects of capitalist organization. In
1990, however, two academics sparked a new trend. That year
Michael Jensen of the Harvard Business School and Kevin Murphy
of Rochester University wrote a paper bemoaning the fact that
high-level managers had become bureaucrats, overseeing the
growth of company revenues, but ignoring profits and dividends.
They proposed to make stocks and stock options a major portion of
executive compensation in order to align the interests of managers
and shareholders. If managers were owners, they argued, they
would pay more attention to profits, dividends, and share value.
Stock ownership would "tie managers tighter to the mast," as
Jensen put it years later.[14] In fact, it worked. Beginning in the 1990s
dividends surpassed "retained profits," those to be reinvested in the
company, year after year even during the recession and stock market slump.[15] The practice also produced a new mode of thinking
and behaving, though not exactly what Jensen and Murphy had
foreseen. They did lead to an eye on earnings, but also to any path
or tactic that would increase or inflate earnings. For one thing, the
law prevents holders of options, as opposed to fully owned stocks,
from collecting dividends. Hence these executives developed an interest in share buybacks that would retire shares, thus increasing
the value of the remaining shares, including their own. Between
1994 and 1998, nonfinancial corporations spent $509 billion on
stock purchases. This accounted for half of the more than $1 tril-
lion these corporations borrowed in those years. But it did drive
up the value of shares and hence, the wealth of these executives
and their fellow shareholders.[16] David Harvey describes the consequence of this trend:

The first is for the privileges of ownership and management of capitalist enterprises—traditionally separated—to fuse by paying CEOs (managers) in stock options (ownership titles). Stock values rather than production then become the guiding light of economic activity and, as later became apparent with the collapse of companies such as Enron, the speculative temptations that resulted from this could become overwhelming.[17]

The extent of accumulated wealth due to stock ownership by CEOs can be seen in Table 6-2, which shows the total stock, including all stock incentives paid in 2004 as well as stock options, total compensation, and accumulated equity of several top New York CEOs. Note that the accumulated equity shown here is only for their stake in their own company and does not necessarily represent their total fortune. In the case of the investment firms, the base salary is in the mere six figures, so the bulk of their income comes from stocks and bonuses presumably based on performance but usually controlled by the senior executives.

TABLE 6-2
CEO stock, total compensation & accumulated equity 2004 ($millions)

Company	CEO	Stock Comp.	Total Comp.	Accum. Equity
Bear Stearns	J. Cayne	$14.2	$30.9	$637.9
Citigroup	C. Prince	9.6	20.4	69.5
Goldman Sachs	H. Paulson Jr.	29.1	29.8	421.7
Lehman Bros.	R. Fuld	17	27.9	459
Loews	J. Tish	.3	2.7	214
McGraw-Hill	H. McGraw III	6.6	9.8	76.3
Merrill Lynch	S. O'Neal	31.3	32	102
Morgan	Stanley P. Purcell	13.8	22.5	195.9
Verizon	I. Seidenberg	10	16.8	43.5

Source: *New York Times*, April 3, 2005.

One of the consequences of this style of compensation is that it has become possible to accumulate considerable wealth in a relatively short time. Among other things, this has meant that New York's capitalist class has expanded rapidly and is no longer based primarily on "old" money, i.e., robber baron–era money. As one writer pointed out, the old familiar names that decorate so many city institutions appear less and less in the press or on TV. The names of the more recently rich are generally not well known, except for a few characters of the Donald Trump type. Nevertheless, this expansion has vastly increased inequality in the city, and in the nation. David Harvey cites a growth in the ratio of CEO income to the median income nationally from thirty to one in 1970 to five hundred to one in 2000.[18] Paul Krugman has argued that the gap between a CEO and the average worker was one thousand to one by the end of the 1990s. This has also meant an increasing concentration of wealth at the top. Whereas in 1991 the top 1 percent of households owned 38.7 percent of corporate wealth, by 2002 they owned 53.4 percent and by 2003, 57.3 percent. Tax cuts on dividends and capital gains have aided the accumulation of such wealth. Krugman points to a new Gilded Age in which inequality and conspicuous consumption are back in style. He notes, as have others, that management ideology and practice have shifted from what some would see as essentially that of an efficient bureaucrat to an entrepreneur in hasty pursuit of wealth and none too careful about how to accumulate it. This is, of course, a different type of person than a David Rockefeller or even a Walter Wriston, not to mention Felix Rohatyn. They were out to make and preserve fortunes and were happy to exploit any and all, here and abroad, but also wanted to preside over the orderly development of the city as they saw it. They had a largely positive view of government.[19] They did not leave development to the market any more than they left their family fortunes or corporate businesses to such vagaries. It seems likely that a significant portion of the newer generation of finance capitalists resident in or around New York have a narrower view of things.

Indeed, through their simple desire to live the life of the Gilded

Age, the new superrich are changing the face of the city by their own consumption. At least some of the city's estimated (some say underestimated) 168 billionaires are looking for mansions à la Gilded Age, with dire consequences for the distribution of space in the city. Bruce Kovner, the hedge fund billlionaire we met above, bought the old Fifth Avenue mansion that housed the International Center of Photography and turned it into his residence. Similarly, the Town Club and Lycée Français properties on the Upper East Side have been turned into Gilded Age–style residences. The conversion of the Plaza Hotel into pricey condos is another example of how the superrich or developers hoping to attract them have "privatized" spaces that were once open to the public, even if privately owned. So, step-by-step the city's street life is closed in and the price of land and housing goes up even more.[20]

All of this new wealth has been made possible by financial deregulation. Economic neoliberalism, however, is often combined with a sort of passive liberalism on social issues such as race, gender, reproductive choice, sexual preference, lifestyle, etc. This is the legacy of a generation close to the 1960s and early 1970s, for we are not talking, yet, about the twentysomething Wall Street analysts and traders who are still taking in five- or six-figure salaries. New York City is praised for its diversity, while those who represent that diversity in their vast numbers are mostly left to their own devices economically. Indeed, they are freed of their "dependency" by cutting back on welfare and other social provisions. They will appreciate higher education at CUNY more because they have to pay more and more for it, just like those from more privileged strata—or so the argument goes. One difference is that today, a handful of African Americans, like Merrill Lynch's Stanley O'Neal or Deborah Wright of Carver Bancorp, find themselves seated as part of the city's business elite on the board of the Partnership for New York City and/or the Alliance for Downtown New York.[21] This combination of economic neoliberalism and social liberalism might be called the New York difference. Not that it is found only in New York, but that its density among the still predominantly white upper and upper middle classes seems greater than in much of the rest of the country. It is part of what gives New York its largely undeserved liberal reputation. It is this combination that is the key to understanding Mayor Bloomberg. In a very real sense, the rising generation of soon-to-be or already superrich have elected one of their own.

Because accumulating fortunes rapidly in the market is so central to the rising business elite, development is not only as central as it was in the first decades of the post-crisis era, but more so and on a different scale. As in the stock market, so in New York's real estate market, the scale of money involved is monumental. Here we see not only the old aristocracy of real estate development and construction, the Rudins, Tishmans, Speyers, Dursts, etc., but the brash "newcomers" who grab the headlines, like Donald Trump or Bruce Ratner, and who are not found on the boards of Real Estate Board of New York or the Partnership for New York City, although they are likely to be members and overlap is considerable. Ratner's firm, Forest City Ratner, for example, is a member of the Alliance for a Better New York, a three-hundred-member coalition founded by developer Lew Rudin and now led by his son William Rudin, who also sits on the Lower Manhattan Development Corporation (LMDC) board. But Ratner is an individualist with little time to sit on boards.[22] It is often these more brash types who have moved development around the city in recent years. But it is not simply the developers and big landlords who drive the process. The mega-projects of the early twenty-first century are also driven by the demand created by the rising rich and those close on their heels. Not just good housing, but luxury housing, if not in Manhattan then in a transformed Brooklyn or Queens area. Not just office space, but prime office space in one of the two prime locations, midtown and downtown.

The permanent government described by Jack Newfield and Paul Du Brul back in the 1970s was composed of the activist core of the business elite: finance, real estate, and corporate. They identified what they called the "Golden Triangle of politics–real estate–banking." This included the political machines, the county Democratic organizations, their leaders, and their clubhouses, as key players.[23] The elected officials come and go, but the county leaders and their clubhouses live on. Queens County Democratic leader Thomas Manton has held that position since 1986 and Herman "Denny" Ferrell has been New York County (Manhattan) chair since 1981. Clarence Norman of Brooklyn went back almost as long. His reign, however, was cut short in 2005 when he was convicted of various campaign finance violations and sentenced to two to six years in prison. Since term limits were imposed on elected city officials in 1993, the longevity of county leaders is even more significant. But do the county organizations and clubhouses wield even as much power as they did back in the 1970s? The most common answer is no. Much of their power, as we have seen, was lost well before the fiscal crisis: patronage greatly diminished by media politics, civil service, New Deal and Great Society programs, and the city's own unique public provision—housing, hospitals, CUNY. Patronage shrank, but more recently so has both nationally provided social programs and the city's own public sector—by starving it or charging increasing fees to use it. The county leaders shifted the emphasis of their patronage in contracts that produce money and jobs from the city's treasury to the state's some time ago. The leaders, when they don't get convicted of crimes, as did Norman, sit in the state assembly or senate or, in the case of long-time survivor Thomas Manton, in Congress.[24] There are funds and contracts to be found in Albany and "earmarks" in Washington on a scale big enough to buy some loyalties locally but small enough to avoid big political fights in those capitals.

A recent glimmer of the influence of the county organizations appeared in the fight over who would become speaker of the city council. Within the council, this is a powerful position since the speaker sets the agenda. After the 2005 election, a six-way power struggle over who would be speaker developed, with the leading candidates Christine Quinn of Manhattan and Bill de Blasio of Brooklyn. Apparently, the practice of giving campaign contributions to fellow council members to get their votes in the speaker race did not assure victory. Five of the candidates did it and spent more than Quinn, but she won.[25] She won with the backing of the county leaders from Brooklyn, Queens, and the Bronx. This was brokered in back rooms as in the old days. As the *Times* put it, "Democratic leaders in Queens, the Bronx and Brooklyn helped engineer the near-unanimous vote."[26] Only Brooklyn's Charles Barron, famous for being a former Black Panther, abstained "because of the process." The new leader of the Brooklyn organization, Vito Lopez, swung his weight to Quinn even though de Blasio was from Brooklyn. He said he wanted his organization to be "a player."[27] So the county leaders and their organizations still count at one level of city politics. But it is only one level—the local level. With the Board of Estimate long gone, they have little say over citywide candidates, policies, or development issues. Indeed, they have little ability to elect the mayor. But the clubhouses still circulate petitions for candidates in council, assembly, state senate, or congressional districts and challenge those of opponents in the primaries. So they have an effect on the council's composition. The council often takes on the mayor, and Quinn, like her predecessor, Gifford Miller, has often been involved in resisting cuts in social programs as well as fighting the West Side Stadium. It is said she plans to be a check on the mayor, although she also says she will cooperate with him. But the mayor has much power and his base has no reliance or dependence on the county organizations. As described in Chapter 5, his power and governing coalition rest on his own networks and money as well as the sweeping powers the city charter grants the office. The county organizations are, at best, on the periphery of power. Perhaps another symbol of how things have changed, including how some of the outer-borough county leaders think, is that Quinn, who represents Greenwich Village, SoHo, Chelsea, and part of Hell's Kitchen, is the first woman speaker and is openly gay.[28]

One group that seems to have increased its influence is the lobbyists who swarm around city hall and the Municipal Building. They are not something new, but there are more of them and they take in and presumably hand out more money. In 2000, there were 148 registered lobbyists representing 728 clients, who paid a total of $14.5 million for their efforts. By 2004, the number of registered lobbyists had increased to 225 representing 1,195 clients and making $22.6 million.[29] This looks like peanuts compared to the 34,000 plus lobbyists registered with the U.S. Congress in 2005, billing around $3 billion.[30] But they have to be considered part of the city's permanent government because they do influence the city government. The growth in their numbers and influence, ironically, stems in part from the term limits imposed in 1993. The turnover means that interest groups are more likely to hire lobbyists to keep track of the changing personnel at city hall. It also makes the politicians more dependent on the lobbyists because they barely have time to learn the ropes, and the lobbyists, as permanent representatives of sections of the permanent government, are more than happy to explain things. On the one hand, term limits undermine the sort of "iron triangle" or "subgovernment" arrangement that corrupts Congress and the federal bureaucracy. On the other, it makes the politicians more vulnerable when they're new. As one *New York Times* columnist put it, "Lobbyists know more about city government than most newcomers do."[31] It is probably an indication of the future that when Christine Quinn was sworn in as speaker, "the Council chamber couldn't hold all the lobbyists who turned up," reported *Times* columnist Joyce Purnick.[32]

The council, however, is only one of many city entities targeted by lobbyists. The mayor's office is a frequent target, but also high among the objects of lobbying is the City Planning Commission, which deals with land use, zoning, and what is euphemistically called demapping, i.e., the elimination of a street. The Landmarks and Preservation Commission is another frequent target, as it too deals with limits on construction and land use. Some of the biggest lobbying firms that specialize in this area are: Greenberg Traurig, Fishbein Badillo Wagner & Harding, and Strook, Strook & Lavin. Greenberg Traurig is actually an international multiservice law firm, with 1,500 lawyers worldwide. It once employed Jack Abramoff, who was at the center of a whirlwind of scandal and corruption in 2005–6. Not surprisingly, there is a revolving-door effect. Herman Badillo, former Bronx borough president and congressman, is an active lobbyist both on his own and for Fishbein Badillo Wagner & Harding. The Wagner is son of the former mayor and a former council member himself. The Harding in that outfit is Liberal Party leader Ray Harding. He became a Giuliani supporter, in return for which Liberal Party members got twenty-three posts in the Giuliani administration. One of those was Ray's son, Robert, who became a deputy mayor under Giuliani. He was also appointed to the LMDC by Giuliani, where he still sits. Robert also remains an active lobbyist for Greenberg Taurig, which employs four lawyers on its New York "government relations team," all of whom formerly worked in city government. Then there is former council speaker Peter F. Vallone Sr., who is a lobbyist for Constantinople Consulting, another major lobby organization. One of his jobs at Constantinople in 2003 was to represent Waste Management Inc. before the council he had led not so long before. Another politician to pass through the revolving door is Guy Molinaro, Republican Party bigwig and former Staten Island borough president, who took in $622,800 in lobbying compensation in 2003–5. Among the city officials he lobbied was his son, James Molinaro, the current borough president of Staten Island.[33]

Lobbying plays an important if not always decisive role in the great land use and development struggles of the early twenty-first century. For example, in the fight over the West Side Stadium, to be discussed later, opponent and potential competitor to a West Side Stadium, Madison Square Garden, spent $866,624 over three years to defeat the new stadium. In this it was aided by state assembly speaker Sheldon Silver, who killed it. New York, as a global financial and business service center, is also important to the nation's major corporations, who lobby the city and its various agencies whether or not they are headquartered there. New York–based Pfizer, for example, spent $271,000 over three years on city "health issues." Phoenix-based copper giant Phelps Dodge spent $408,000 in that period lobbying the mayor's office and city council for unspecified consideration. Elite groups like the Partnership for New York City and the Alliance for Downtown New York, whose president, Carl Weisbrod, was also its lobbyist as well as a member of the LMDC, also lobby. They spend relatively little, however, as their influence flows through other visible and not so visible channels.[34]

One other group of people worth mentioning in connection with political influence are the bundlers we met in Chapter 4. They are few in numbers, but illustrate some things about New York politics. These are well-connected people who collect campaign contributions from others. In the New York City Campaign Finance Board reports they are called "intermediaries." This is a new practice, first developed nationally in the wake of the federal campaign finance laws of the 1970s. As we saw in the context of the 1997 Giuliani campaign, one of the biggest was Bruce Ratner, who specialized in corporate donations. A Giuliani bundler who focused on individuals in that election was Kenneth Langone, a founder of Home Depot. He pulled in fifteen out of seventy-seven donations of $5,000 or more. Home Depot and Ratner's outfit, Forest City, are competitors. Yet in politics they work together with a certain division of labor. In fact, they also collaborate in business. In 2004, Ratner joined in developing the languishing East River Plaza, a suburban-like mall in which Home Depot is one of the anchor stores. In 2005, Langone was raising money to defeat New York State's outspoken attorney general, Eliot Spitzer, in his run for governor. Spitzer, a Democrat, had sued Langone and New York Stock Exchange chair Richard Grasso. Langone was chair of the NYSE compensation committee when it gave Grasso $139 million in compensation over several years. Clearly, Langone did not want to see Spitzer in the governor's mansion. By late December 2005, Langone had raised $1 million, not for a Republican opponent, but for Thomas Suozzi, who faced Spitzer in the Democratic primary in 2006.[35] Members of the permanent government are frequently bipartisan when the situation calls for it. The Democrats also have bundlers. For example, during the 2005 mayoral race, there were at least three people who actively solicited contributions for Ferrer. By far the most active at the $1,000 or more level was Leo J. Hindery. Hindery is a wheeler and dealer in the telecommunications industry, whose various and serial CEO-ships are too numerous to mention, although he was with Global Crossing for a while just before the scandal. He is not a New Yorker, but in 2001 he became CEO of the Yankees Entertainment and Sports Network, which broadcasts Yankees games over cable and gives him a direct stake in the city. He is also a big fund-raiser for the national Democratic Party. He was responsible for 34 out of the 104 donations to the Ferrer campaign of $1,000 or more. As with Greenberg Traurig, Hindery's involvement reminds us that political money in New York elections comes not only from New Yorkers or nearby suburbanites but from all over the country.[36] New York is too important to too many business interests and well-heeled people to be left to New Yorkers alone.

If in the late 1970s Newfield and Du Brul spoke of the "Golden Triangle of politics–real estate–banking," we would have to say that today it is a Platinum Star of politics-lobbying–real estate–banking–corporate power. The permanent government as of 2005 was different in some respects from that of the 1970s. The machines were less important, while lobbyists had increased their presence and influence; a new generation of extremely wealthy business leaders in real estate, banking, but also industry and business services, was taking shape; and the ideology of neoliberalism had taken root in the economic thinking of much of the business elite. Another important difference is that as of 2005 there was no clear leader of the sort that David Rockefeller, Walter Wriston, Richard Shinn, or Felix Rohatyn were during the fiscal crisis. Perhaps another crisis in city governance or finances would produce such leaders, but for now the emphasis is on making money. The developmental agenda that captured city government as a result of the fiscal crisis was still in place, but driven by somewhat different and occasionally contradictory forces. Elite organizations such as the Partnership for New York City continued to push development. They were joined by state-created entities, above all the Lower Manhattan Development Corporation; its parent, the Empire State Development Corporation; and the Port Authority, themselves composed of elite elements. In addition, there were the footloose entrepreneurs of the real estate world, notably Donald Trump, Bruce Ratner, and Larry Silverstein, the leaseholder of Ground Zero. Sometimes these elements came together and sometimes they seemed to work at cross-purposes. Together or not, they all pushed to alter the skyline of New York City.

Perhaps one way to look at the agenda held by much of the business elite and most of the political establishment is to cite the Partnership for New York's economic development priorities. In their *2005 Priorities* they named four:

- Redevelopment of the World Trade Center site in Lower Manhattan and upgrading the transportation infrastructure in order to reinforce the Downtown Business District;
- Rezoning the Far West Side to encourage residential and commercial development, in conjunction with the expansion of the Jacob K. Javits Center;
- Construction of a commercial science park on the East River in order to anchor a biosciences industry cluster in the City.
- Rezoning and public investment to encourage private development projects that strengthen secondary business districts, reclaim neglected waterfront land and produce more affordable housing across the five boroughs.[37]

Two things are notable here. The first and most important is that the development vision of much of the business elite had moved far beyond the Manhattan central business districts. It had now come to encompass large tracts of the outer boroughs, not simply the downtown Brooklyn and Long Island City projects of the 1980s and 1990s, and not, as the document says for "affordable housing," if by that we mean housing that low- or even middle-income people can afford. The geographic scope was far greater than during the years of the fiscal crisis. The second is the absence of any mention of sports arenas or stadiums in Manhattan, Brooklyn, or Queens. These projects were important to the sports franchises and the developers involved, but not to the business elite as a whole and, in particular, its downtown component. Most likely, the conflicts within the broader real estate–banking complex over the West Side Stadium precluded a unified position. Here was a fissure, not only within the business community but between elements of the political establishment and the lobbyists who took up one or another side. Obviously, the projects to be discussed had their origins well before the partnership published its 2005 "advocacy agenda," so there is no implication that that organization was guiding the process singlehandedly. As broad as its constituency was, it was only one of a number of conflicting economic and political forces pushing development beyond where it had dared to go before. Far from a conspiracy, market forces, capitalist competition, and to some extent local resistance all played key roles in what became the messy process behind the changing skyline.

The Mega-Projects

In 2003, the New York Building Congress, a construction industry group, took a number of city officials, presidents of Empire State Development Corporation subsidiaries, and real estate and construction industry leaders on a tugboat tour of the East River waterfronts. The tour included the Queens waterfront; the waterfront of Brooklyn from the Brooklyn Navy Yard to DUMBO, just under the Manhattan Bridge; Governor's Island; and lower Manhattan. Daniel Tishman, CEO of Tishman Realty and Construction, told the hundred opinion shapers and decision makers, "New York's waterfronts are indeed a new frontier, and the East River contains many of the best locations [for development] left in the city." City planning commission chair Amanda Burden called the development plans for the Greenpoint-Williamsburg waterfront "one of the most ambitious rezoning plans in the City's history."[58] But the speakers were preaching to the choir. Projects were already on the drawing board or in the works that would touch not only the East River waterfront, but the Hudson River waterfront and a good deal of inland territory all around the city. It was the era of the mega-projects and New York was in for some big changes.

Before looking at some of the major projects in detail, let us lay out altogether the total sweep of the development plans already on the books. To start, according to the mayor, in 2005 there were sixty-five development projects in the works and thirty-five rezoning decisions covering three thousand city blocks to clear the way.[39] Requests for rezoning come both from developers and from neighborhoods experiencing rapid change, taller buildings, etc. Not all of the Bloomberg rezonings are meant to allow for high-rises or the sort of mega-project discussed here. Some are down-zonings that prevent or limit such development. Most of the down-zonings, particularly those that restrict density, are in established white areas. By far the largest territory covered by down-zoning is on Staten Island. Also included are white middle-class Riverdale in Manhattan, gentrified regions of Brooklyn, and traditionally white middle- and working-class areas like Bay Ridge and Bensonhurst in Brooklyn and Bayside in Queens. A lot of the rezonings meant to encourage mega-projects are in waterfront and former industrial areas, but some are in well established residential areas like Prospect Heights in Brooklyn.[40]

The plans on the books or in progress are not just another spurt of high-rise offices, although there are plenty of those. Nor are most of them about single skyscrapers. Most of all, as noted above, they go far beyond the central business districts of Manhattan to bring Manhattan-style structures to more than just the business districts of the outer boroughs. They will transform downtown Manhattan and the West Side, but also a good deal of Brooklyn and smaller parts of Queens and the Bronx. The city is facing, or rather is in the midst of, a major makeover of the built environment. Here is a list of the major projects as of late 2005.

The Mega-Project Makeover
- Downtown/Ground Zero rebuilding and expansion: Freedom Tower, memorial, transit center, 7 World Trade Center, Goldman Sachs headquarters, extension of Battery Park City, fifteen-plus upscale apartment towers, and Hudson River Park, connecting downtown to the West Side.

- West Side: High Line (an abandoned elevated track) upscale commercial and residential development from Fourteenth Street to Thirtieth Street; Javits Convention Center expansion; Hudson Yards high-rise office and housing development; Hell's Kitchen/Clinton development; Harlem gentrification, high-rise, and commercial development.
- East Side: Governor's Island "tourist mecca" connected to both lower Manhattan and Red Hook in Brooklyn by an aerial tramway; luxury housing at South Street Seaport; downtown commercial science park; Randall's Island water park; East River Plaza shopping mall in East Harlem.
- Brooklyn: Brooklyn Navy Yard development; Williamsburg high-rise waterfront development; DUMBO waterfront development; 1.3-mile Brooklyn Bridge Park waterfront commercial and high-rise housing development; Red Hook commercial waterfront development and cruise ship pier; Gowanus housing development; Fourth Avenue high-rise housing; Atlantic Yards sports arena and high-rise housing; Coney Island makeover.
- The Bronx: new $800 million Yankee Stadium; the new $85 million fish market (moved from downtown's Fulton Market); development by Related Companies on sites of Bronx Terminal Market and House of Detention.
- Queens: seventy-four acres of Queens West housing and office waterfront development at Hunters Point; $600 million Shea/Mets Stadium revitalization; Long Island City office development.

To avoid political conflict with citizens and city politicians, most of these projects will have the land on which they are built taken by, and the project cleared and/or overseen by, the state of New York through the Empire State Development Corporation (ESDC) and its many subsidiaries. To give you an idea of the extent of ESDC involvement in the projects listed above, here is a list of its subsidiaries operating in the city and where they are or have been involved.

Empire State Development Corporation Subsidiaries

Subsidiary	Area
Lower Manhattan Development Corporation	Ground Zero/Downtown
42nd Street Redevelopment Corporation	Times Square
Times Square Hudson River Park Trust	West Side waterfront
Pennsylvania Station Redevelopment Corporation	West Side midtown
Harlem Community Development Corporation	Harlem
Governor's Island Preservation & Education Corp.	Governor's Island
Brooklyn Bridge Park Development Corporation	Brooklyn waterfront
Atlantic Yards Area Redevelopment Project	Downtown Brooklyn
Queens West Development Corporation	Queens East River waterfront

Source: Empire State Development Corporation, www.nylovesbiz.com.

Those familiar with the map of New York City will recognize that these projects, were they all to go through, would transform much of the waterfront of Manhattan, Brooklyn, and Queens. To be sure, there will be green spaces or strips, but there will also be rows of tightly lined high-rise structures all along the waterfronts of these boroughs. The format of Queens West, for example, is remarkably like that of Battery Park City, a tight double row of high-rise buildings with a thin green strip in front on the water and the city cut off from behind.[41] In addition, several "inland" neighborhoods in Manhattan and Brooklyn will become upscale "projects," tall housing blocks in tight formation. Many of both the waterfront and inland projects have been or will be designed by the same prestigious architect, Frank Gehry. The transformation will be greatest for Brooklyn, which has up until now been a place of low-rise neighborhoods with distinct characteristics. While it is common to say that the era of Robert Moses, the bulldozer, and urban renewal is long past, there is a sense in which what is occurring in many parts of the city is a new type of urban renewal for the well-to-do. There is no single force like a Robert Moses behind this transformation of the skyline. Indeed, there is no central urban planning behind all this development. The traditional powers of the city's Department of City Planning and City Planning Commission have, like the city's budgetary powers in the 1970s, been hijacked by the state in the service of private development. Nor is there anything like a proven market for all of this high-priced real estate. Whether or not the market for this expensive development holds up in the end, billions will be spent and made in the process of building. The long line of interests who stand to profit from such construction will be enough to drive this development unless or until some other force, a movement of resistance or a real estate slump, slows it, stops it, or redirects it. On January 18, 2006, in a two-hour meeting, the seven-member board of the ESDC approved the new Yankee Stadium, the improved Shea Stadium, the Brooklyn Bridge Park, and commercial development on Governor's Island.[42] The rest of this chapter will focus on development in Manhattan and Brooklyn.

Downtown Development: The State Moves In

When the terrorist attacks brought down the twin towers, it was the city that took charge of the rescue and cleanup. FEMA, which is supposed to respond directly, played no role other than providing funds. Furthermore, both Giuliani and Bloomberg resisted pressure from the Bush administration to give total control of the cleanup to Bechtel, although in the end it got a contract for some of the work. With the help of many volunteers and city workers, it was the city's Department of Design and Construction, created earlier by Giuliani, that presided over that massive task, completing it ahead of schedule in May 2002. But when it came to rebuilding at Ground Zero and the surrounding area, it was a different matter. Even as the recovery work commenced, the Real Estate Board of New York (REBNY), the Partnership for New York City, and the

Alliance for Downtown New York, apparently fearful that a Democrat, Mark Green or Fernando Ferrer, would soon be mayor and dead set on keeping the city council away from decision making, implored the governor to put some state entity in charge. Thirty real estate and business leaders met with Governor Pataki only two days after 9/11. In October, REBNY called for a "reconstruction authority with private sector representation to handle the funds and rebuilding efforts for Lower Manhattan."[43] Pataki was more than willing to grant their request for much the same political reasons.

The state was already deeply involved in lower Manhattan through the Port Authority, which owned Ground Zero; the Metropolitan Transit Authority, which owned the subway stations destroyed during the collapse of the twin towers; and the Battery Park City Authority, which housed many downtown residents. It also had the Empire State Development Corporation, which had already played a part in various city projects, notably Times Square. To bypass Democratic assembly speaker Sheldon Silver, who represented the downtown district in the state legislature, as well as any Democratic mayor and the city council, on November 2 the ESDC created the Lower Manhattan Development Corporation as its subsidiary. LMDC was to draw up the plans and lead the implementation not only of rebuilding at Ground Zero, but of developing the surrounding area as well. It would be funded by an initial $2.7 billion federal community development block grant, which was later supplemented to bring the total to $3.5 billion.[44] As in the fiscal crisis, the state intervened to do the bidding of the business community and to exclude as much as possible the local government, not to mention the citizenry, from any say over the redevelopment process.

At first, the governor gave himself a majority of the board members, allowing the mayor only four out of eleven. By April, with Republican Bloomberg in office, the governor expanded the board giving the new mayor half the sixteen appointees. Two Giuliani and two Pataki appointees left, while Bloomberg allowed the reappointment of both lobbyist Robert Harding and Verizon executive Paul Crotty, actually taking only six positions. In effect, Pataki had a majority. In any case, the composition of the LMDC board was predominantly elite in its membership and heavily Republican. Table 6-3 does not include the original Giuliani and Pataki appointees who were removed with the expansion of the board, nor does it include those appointed in 2005, when Bloomberg made an effort to gain some control of a badly stalled process. They will be discussed later.

TABLE 6-3
LMDC as elite hub in a dense network, 2001–5
("P" indicates Pataki appointment, "G" Giuliani, "B" Bloomberg)

Name		Business	Other *
Robert Balachandran	P	Bear Stearns	Pataki
Roland Betts	P	Chelsea Piers/films	Rangers w/Bush
Paul Crotty	G	Verizon	Koch and Giuliani
Lewis Eisenberg	P	Granite Capital	Port Authority, Bush funder
Richard Grasso	G	NYSE	
Robert Harding	G	Greenberg Traurig	Giuliani
Sally Hernandez-Piñero	B	Related Cos. (RE)	Koch and Dinkins
Thomas Johnson	P	Greenpoint Bank	Chemical, Manhattan Hanover
Edward Lewis	B	Essence Magazine	PNYC, Times Sq.
Ed Malloy	P	Building Trades	NYS AFL-CIO
Stanley Shuman	B	Allen & Co./ News Corp	(E)FCB
John Whitehead	P	Goldman Sachs	Reagan admin.
Madelyn Wils	P	Tribeca Film Inst., CB1	ADNY
Howard Wilson	G	Proskauer Rose	CBC, Giuliani
Carl Weisbrod	B	Trinity Real Estate	ADNY, Giuliani
Frank Zarb	P	NASDAQ/Smith Barney	Ford admin.

* Name of mayor indicates LMDC member involvement in that administration.
Sources: Lower Manhattan Development Corporation; Good Jobs New York; Partnership for New York City; Alliance for Downtown New York.

The LMDC board allocated money, lots of it. Some of it went to the organizations represented on the board. The Tribeca Film Festival of which Madelyn Wils was the CEO got $3 million in 2004. The New York Stock Exchange, which Richard Grasso chaired at the time, got a more modest $160,000 in 2002. Con Edison and Verizon stood to gain much from a $750,000 grant for utility restoration, despite the presence of Crotty from Verizon and Sally Hernandez-Piñero, who sat on the Con Edison board. The Alliance for Downtown New York got $4,320,000 in three separate grants, even though both Carl Weisbrod and Madelyn Wils were affiliated with it. In all these cases, these related members recused themselves from the vote. Of the twenty-seven recusals from December 2001 through July 2004, Weisbrod and Wils accounted for half. But this seemed like a ritual in which it was understood that the rest would approve the funding in any case. Howard Wilson, on the other hand, left because of a conflict of interest—his law firm represented WTC leaseholder Larry Silverstein.[45] The LMDC, however, faced a bigger set of problems than the appearance of corruption: the Port Authority, Larry Silverstein, and the lack of a clear plan.

Downtown Development: Port Authority Problems

The Port Authority owned the sixteen acres now called Ground Zero. In July 2001, it leased the office space of the twin towers to Larry Silverstein and the underground retail mall to Westfield America, a nationwide mall operator. This pleased the neoliberal bent of Governor Pataki, who said, when the deal was closed: "We have worked hard to put those developments in the hands of the private sector experts who pay taxes."[46] But it wasn't quite that simple. First, theoretically the governor controls the Port Authority by his power of appointment, but he shares this power with the governor of New Jersey, which tends to diminish his power. Second, and more important, the Port Authority (PA) may be a public institution, but it is financed like a private corporation. It is funded by the sale of bonds and legally it has a fiduciary responsibility to its bondholders that trumps any legislative or political mandates. The PA must do what is necessary in the view of its executives to pay its bondholders. This gives it enormous independence from government, but also requires an income stream. When the PA was owner and landlord of the World Trade Center, it collected that money itself. Since July 2001, it was Larry Silverstein who collected rents. By the terms of his lease he paid $120 million a year to the PA. After 9/11 Silverstein's insurers paid the annual lease fee, but it was drawing down the total value he could recover when a settlement was finally reached with the insurers. Thus, both the PA and Silverstein had a vested interest in rebuilding revenue-creating office space. From the beginning, both insisted that whatever was built on Ground Zero had to include at least 10 million square feet of office space. They never budged from this position. At one point, the LMDC announced a reduction in office space, but rapidly abandoned that idea.[47] Despite some differences over what should be built at Ground Zero, the LMDC never challenged this demand, nor did Governor Pataki. It was the bedrock of rebuilding that limited everything else.[48]

There would be a long, complicated duel between the PA and the LMDC over the plan and design of Ground Zero and what was to go on it. After a show of six designs in the summer of 2002 was universally rejected, a second competition was held. In 2003, Daniel Libeskind was chosen to do the overall plan of the sixteen acres and presumably design the tower that would replace the World Trade Center. But Silverstein, backed most of the time by the PA, retained his own architect, David Childs of Skidmore, Owings & Merrill. He had designed Silverstein's new 7 World Trade Center, the Time Warner Center at Columbus Circle, and the new Bear Stearns headquarters in midtown. In the end Libeskind's master plan was twisted beyond recognition and Childs was given authority over the final design of the tower, although the pretense of a collaboration with Libeskind was maintained publicly. This was the result of an agreement negotiated by Louis Tomson, first president of the LMDC, and Joseph Seymour, executive director of the PA. Both were Pataki appointees and loyalists.[49]

Members of the LMDC felt that some opportunity for public input was needed to legitimize the process. They had consulted regularly with a coalition of architects and planners calling itself New York New Visions, but this was pro forma.[50] The most visible effort to solicit broad public input came in July 2002. Earlier in the year the Regional Plan Association had taken the lead in forming a broad coalition of people and groups, with Battery Park City and Tribeca heavily represented. Called the Civic Alliance to Rebuild Downtown New York (Civic Alliance), its members expressed doubts and even opposition to the office space straightjacket Silverstein and the PA had wrapped the planning process in. In July 2002, they held a massive event called Listening to the City that drew 4,500 participants. It was a well-run, high-tech open forum. Speaker after speaker called for things that were not on the agendas of the PA or the LMDC. They called for job training for those who had lost jobs, childcare centers, and schools. The top priority was affordable housing. According to the Civic Alliance, "55 percent of the July 20 participants identified housing for all income levels and ages as most important." But according to Columbia University urban planning professor Susan Fainstein, when the PA reacted to these criticisms and demands, "The call for affordable housing received no attention."[51]

There was to be housing off of Ground Zero. The conversion of old office buildings to residential use had gone on for some time. After 9/11 the Real Estate Board of New York convinced the city to offer cash incentives to retain or attract residents to lower Manhattan. The program worked. Vacancy rates in the area dropped from 10 percent just after 9/11 to 5.4 percent by mid-2003. The federal government contributed $1.65 billion in tax-free Liberty Bonds to encourage new building downtown. These are distributed by the city's Housing Development Corporation and the state's Housing Finance Agency. Some of the developers to be involved included: Related Companies, the Durst Organization, Rockrose, Forest City Ratner, and the Albanese Organization. By May 2004 about fifteen residential buildings funded by Liberty Bonds were in the works. The state put up $675.8 million to finance three new apartment buildings.[52] But as the Regional Plan Association and the Fiscal Policy Institute pointed out, "low- and middle-income households cannot afford most of the new housing downtown."[53] Indeed, one of the three new buildings was 10 Liberty Street, where rents start at $2,400 for a one-bedroom apartment and go to $3,870 for a two-bedroom unit. For an 80-20 deal, where 20 percent of the units are supposedly affordable, builders get a big tax break. But the units don't have to be downtown. So four new buildings are providing 390 units of "affordable" housing—all in the Bronx. In any case, the definition of "affordable" downtown is even worse than that in the mayor's housing program. If you earn $66,000 or less, you might qualify for a $1,650-a-month studio. If you are a family of three, the limit is $84,750 for a $2,119-a-month two-bedroom apartment. The rent on the two-bedroom apartment amounts to 30 percent of the upper income limit, which means that the upper limit is also the lower limit if one is to stick with the 30 percent limit considered the most a family should pay. Actually, only 5 percent of downtown units will be set aside for these incomes. To complaints that the Liberty Bond program is driving out low-income people, "housing officials respond that Liberty Bonds were not "intended to create affordable housing, but to rebuild an area that was still staggering when the program began in 2002," wrote the *Times*.[54]

Then there was Battery Park City. After 9/11 it was evacuated completely for a week. About 45 percent of its residents did not return. They were replaced by newcomers attracted by the incentives. One 2005 study concluded that the newcomers were somewhat less wealthy than the old tenants, but that they "only came because of the cheap rents and will leave as soon as the subsidies run out." It also says the post-9/11 residents they interviewed "were ethnically similar to the population demographics reported in the 2000 census: 73 percent were white, 15 percent Asian, 7 percent Latino, 3 percent African American, and 2 percent West Indian."[55] Whatever happened downtown, it would not be truly affordable housing, nor would it come close to reflecting the demographics of the city.

The Partnership for New York City's prioritization of transportation for downtown was, of course, key to the area's development as a vital financial and business center. The Port Authority understood this as well and went ahead with its own plan for a transport center for the PATH, the New Jersey to New York lightrail system it ran. This was to connect with a nearby subway station rebuilt by the MTA. In 2003 on their own initiative the PA hired Santiago Calatrava, a highly respected Spanish architect, to design the transit center, and by 2005 ground was broken on the project. Also taking his own initiative was Larry Silverstein, who began construction of the Childs-designed 7 World Trade Center, which was completed in 2005. In December 2004, he got a favorable jury decision on his insurance claim that the attacks on the twin towers accounted for two events. While he didn't get the full $7 billion he was after, he got $4.5 billion, enough to proceed with his projects.[56] In September 2005, Governor Pataki signed into law a bill extending tax breaks and incentives to downtown businesses, not housing, which included 7 World Trade Center.[57] Yet another tower was planned by Goldman Sachs across the street from the proposed Freedom Tower in Battery Park City. For this forty-story office building they would receive $1.65 billion in Liberty Bonds, plus another $230 million in tax breaks and grants. James Parrott of the Fiscal Policy Institute said that Goldman Sachs "took advantage of the city and state's desperation." He also noted, "This trend toward giving tax incentives and tax breaks is verging out of hand."[58] While some, including Mayor Bloomberg, worried that there might be too much office space downtown, the office towers rose one after the other.

Then in May 2005, in one of the stranger events of a very contentious process, Goldman Sachs told the police that the current design and location of the yet-to-be Freedom Tower were security risks. They showed the police a simulation of what a car bomb on West Street could do to the tower if built as proposed. The tower was postponed and redesigned by Childs to include a bunker-like concrete base that met police concerns. It would still be the full 1,776 feet tall Silverstein had insisted on.[59] Whether or not it was part of Goldman's motive, the postponement gave Goldman a head start in the competition for tenants.

During his campaign, Mayor Bloomberg voiced criticisms of the whole Ground Zero plan. He suggested that Silverstein was a problem and should be removed from the process—though he acknowledged "nobody can figure out how to do it." He also questioned the need for so much office space as opposed to residential space. "There is a question of how much demand there is for office space and how much demand there is for residential, and I think it's time to see what the marketplace really wants," he said while campaigning in October.[60] With all the institutional behemoths, bureaucrats, and billionaires on the scene, there wasn't much room for the marketplace, but the mayor had taken a stance. Shortly after taking office for the second time, he also took action.

Only a week or so after the election, Bloomberg appointed six new members to the LMDC board. These were: deputy mayor Daniel Doctoroff; deputy mayor Marc Shaw; finance commissioner Martha Stark; city planning commission chair Amanda Burden; ABNY chair William Rudin; and Verizon president and vice chair Lawrence Babbio. Robert Harding and Carl Weisbrod were reappointed. Rudin represented old-line real estate, while Babbio replaced Crotty as Verizon representative. What was really new was the inclusion of his top political team. Doctoroff and Burden, in particular, represented his key development officials. In announcing his appointments Bloomberg said, "Lower Manhattan, both on and off of the World Trade Center site, is and will continue to be a top priority of mine. To that end, I am appointing a mixture of top members of my Administration as well as civic and business leaders to further our efforts."[61] Obviously, the mayor's intent was to gain a measure of control over a process from which he had been almost totally excluded. The appointments make it clear that this was still a developer's agenda and was not about democratizing the process but about simply giving the city input. He spoke of more housing and fewer office towers, and of more street life and less concrete, steel, and glass. He held a tiny lever in the fact that the city owned the streets around Ground Zero and, as it turned out, some space from streets "demapped" when the WTC was built.[62] As of this writing it is too soon to say what he will do with this new team or, given the institutional barriers, what he can do. One thing to note is that this represented a shift from his and Doctoroff's previous focus on the West Side. No doubt the defeat of the West Side Stadium he and Doctoroff had so vigorously promoted had something to do with it.

West Side War

We will look at the West Side from the northern end of Battery Park City through Harlem. The first of the many recent West Side projects to be implemented was the Hudson River Park, a thin strip of green running from Battery Park City to Fifty-ninth Street along the West Side, with sizable commercial interruptions. Work began in 1999 under the guidance of the ESDC's Hudson River Park Trust. Like all of these "green" projects, the park is to be self-supporting. This means that it must include commercial properties that lease land from the trust. While the idea of a green strip along the waterfront is a good idea, critics argue that there isn't much green and it isn't really park at all. Greenwich Village opponents of the project as designed described it as "the Develo-park: a large commercial development with a tiny park tucked somewhere inside." In any case, with an initial budget of $330 million for construction, Hudson River Park pales when compared to most other West Side development plans.[63] But it brings in its wake a string of high-rise apartment buildings. In Greenwich Village the glass towers are rising along West Street, the boundary of the park, blocking and threatening the historic buildings in the area. One resident resister said, "We are an island of historical significance drowning in a sea of development—development that is now lapping at our doors." Another called the string of glass towers at West and Perry Streets, "Miami-on-the-Hudson."[64]

Just above Greenwich Village is Chelsea, where entertainment complexes inhabit the old docks and the green strip is not to be found. Just inland, Chelsea is an area of galleries, boutiques, and restaurants, as well as the low-rise, largely gentrified old housing that gives the neighborhood its charm. From Fourteenth Street along Eighth Avenue to Thirtieth Street, a railroad runs through it. Known as the High Line because it is elevated, it was built in the 1930s to deliver freight to businesses and docks along the West Side. It has long been abandoned and overgrown with weeds. It is a neighborhood curiosity, even a tourist attraction, and part of the funky charm of the area. But with the city's no-real-estate-deal-left-behind policy, it is to be cleaned up at a cost of $130 million. Not refurbished as a railroad, but as a strolling mall surrounded by luxury condos and rentals, pricey restaurants, and yet more galleries. The ever-present and well-connected Related Companies will be building high-rises in cooperation with other developers. The Related Companies is the largest developer in New York. Its CEO, Steven Ross, is on the board of governors of REBNY. Sally Hernandez-Piñero of the LMDC sits on Related's board. In a building they built in the area in 2001, the rents for a two-bedroom apartment range from $2,300 to $6,500 a month. The cost of buying a two-bedroom apartment already exceeds $1 million in the area. Altogether, the plan is, the *Times* reported, for "5,500 units of housing, all but 1,100 of them for the fabulously well heeled." Predictably the area will be transformed both physically and financially. As for the avant-garde artists who began transforming the area years ago and the smaller galleries they show in, one gallery owner told the *Times*, "The radical work which guides art and makes progress will get priced out."[65]

In the news, the focus on West Side development in 2005 was the Jets stadium, which was also meant to serve the 2012 Olympics if New York got the franchise. As we saw earlier, the project was the brainstorm of Daniel Doctoroff in the mid-1990s. It was enthusiastically picked up by Mayor Bloomberg, who promoted the city's bid for the 2012 Olympics and made Doctoroff deputy mayor for development. The stadium, which would bring the Jets football team back from New Jersey, was expected to cost from $1.6 billion to $2.4 billion, and the related expansion of the Javits Center another $1.4 billion.[66] But, as with so many other big-ticket projects, the state had something to say about it since its money would be involved. The key figure in this was not the usual suspect, the Empire State Development Corporation, but state assembly speaker Sheldon Silver. Silver represented downtown Manhattan and was up front about defending the interests of those who build and inhabit those office towers. Reporting on a conversation he had with the mayor in May, Silver told *New York* magazine:

> I told him that 24 million square feet of new commercial space on the West Side doesn't make sense. Forget the stadium for a moment. Downtown you've got 7 World Trade Center. There is not a foot of office space that's leased. There are at least three undesigned buildings on Ground Zero still to come. They haven't been designed because they say there's no demand. And the only response from both the governor and the mayor is 24 million square feet of office space on the West Side to compete with downtown? Madison Square Garden let me know that their plan [for the West Side] is purely housing.[67]

In other words, Silver, in alliance with Madison Square Garden, which as we saw spent a lot of money lobbying on this and which could be hurt by a competing stadium, would kill the stadium in hopes of heading off some of the office development on the West Side and possibly directing more state and city money downtown. As one of the three members of the state's Public Authorities Control Board he had the power to veto a $300 million state matching grant for the stadium.[68] And so he did in early June, just before the International Olympics Committee rejected New York as a site.[69] West Side development, however, never depended on the stadium deal. Madison Square Garden, for example, already had a $10 million tax break from the city for its housing plans. James Parrott of the Fiscal Policy Institute estimated that the annual tax breaks for announced West Side projects would come to $1.3 billion, "more than the city spends on mass transit, parks, youth programs, libraries, and the arts," he argued.[70]

The giant of West Side development was the Hudson Yards project, estimated to cost $3 billion. This is overseen by the MTA, a New York State agency that owns the working rail yards on the West Side over which the development would be built. The project's financing was described by Daniel Doctoroff in February 2004. The deck over the rails will cost an estimated $400 million. All of this money is to be raised through bonds valued at $2.77 billion over ten years issued by yet another authority, the Hudson Yards Infrastructure Corporation. The money to pay bondholders back is to come from payments in lieu of taxes, the money paid to the city by tax-exempt organizations and properties at rates far below what they would pay in taxes. Once the deck over the railroad tracks is finished it will be sold to private developers, who will build the office and housing towers using the bond-raised money. The Related Companies and Vornado Realty, whose CEO is on the board of the Partnership for New York City, will oversee the development. It will be called Midtown West, a name that may or may not stick. The Hudson Yards project also includes the extension of the number 7 subway line to Eleventh Avenue, another partnership priority; the 7 train currently runs east and west between Queens and Manhattan, as far as Seventh Avenue. This would connect the Queens West project directly with midtown and the Hudson Yards. Also, the old Farley Post Office, a two-block structure built in imposing neoclassical style, will be converted to a rail station under the direction of the ESDC's Pennsylvania Station Redevelopment Corporation. It will replace the underground Penn Station at a cost of $818 million. It will include retail and entertainment facilities much like Grand Central Terminal on the East Side.[71] One of the complaints about the Hudson Yards project, taken as a whole, is that it will eliminate the sort of street life so characteristic of New York, replacing it with towers and indoor malls. Another, common to most of the mega-projects, is that it will overload the infrastructure, parking, schools, and other facilities of the area. Yet another objection is that public money is being used to further private wealth by building upscale housing.

A little farther up the West Side, past a rapidly gentrifying Hell's Kitchen, one finds Trump Place, a long row of garish high-rises standing guard over the Hudson River. The problem is they begin where the Hudson River Park stops, so these pricey buildings overlook the West Side Highway with no green strip in sight. Trump wanted to bury the highway, taking it underground from Sixty-first Street to Seventy-second, where Riverside Park begins. Over the highway would be a green strip and, of course, more Trump buildings. The steel frame over the sunken highway on which the new buildings and park would be built received initial funding of $2.5 million from the U.S. Congress via an "earmark" in the federal highway bill, the nation's largest pork barrel after the defense budget. No senator or representative has taken credit for this gift. The project has supporters beyond Trump, however. Philip Howard, chairman of the Municipal Arts Society, likes it because it would extend Riverside Park, which starts at Seventy-second Street, all the way to Sixty-first. The total cost of the project would run from $120 million to $300 million.[72] What seems to be the case is that small edges of green have become the common bribe for unbounded high-rise development.

Finally, just past the Upper West Side is Harlem. There is no single mega-project set for Harlem yet. But gentrification, which began in the 1990s, is well under way. The Empire State Development Corporation's Harlem Community Development Corporation is pushing well past the refurbishing of Harlem's old brownstones, encouraging commercial development and the building of new low-rise and high-rise housing, most of which will be out of the reach of long-time Harlemites. This traditional center of black culture in America may be the first victim of white in-flight.[73] Between the lightning pace of gentrification in some areas and the rabbit-like proliferation of mega-projects, it has become difficult to take a snapshot of the city, either physically or socially, and hope that it will stand up for a while. For example, in a study of the changing demographics of Los Angeles and New York published in 2003, the authors could write of a map they had constructed from 2000 census data:

> A careful look shows that there are only a few high-income areas left in New York City. These include the upper east and west sides (the latter at least up to Eightieth Street), Brooklyn Heights, Battery Park, and some "gentrifying areas," such as Soho and Park Slope.[74]

Five years later the picture was very different. The same study, however, does point to the rapid rise of income from 1990 to 2000 in areas such as SoHo, Tribeca, and Harlem in Manhattan and the gentrified areas of Brooklyn. By 2005, income in most of these areas was up even more. The new mega-projects, along with rapidly rising housing costs, will continue to change the picture as high-income areas expand.[75]

In 2006, another massive blow to middle-income housing came when Met Life announced it would sell the giant Stuyvesant Town and Peter Cooper Village housing complex for $5 billion. Located near the East River just north of Fourteenth Street and housing 25,000 people, this eighty-acre complex has been a fortress of rent-stabilized, middle-income housing for generations. For years, Met Life has been chiseling away at the controlled rents, but two-thirds of the units still remain below the $2,000-per-month limit that protects the tenants.[76] Whoever buys this housing giant is sure to push rents up as fast as the law allows, taking one more giant piece of Manhattan out of reach of civil servants, schoolteachers, and other middle-class families.

The Battle for Brooklyn

When most people hear "New York" they think of Manhattan. Brooklyn is something else. When people outside of New York think of Brooklyn they might think of "da Dodgers," Coney Island, stickball in the streets, Ralph Kramden, *The Lords of Flat-*

bush, Saturday Night Fever, or the Bed-Stuy of *Do the Right Thing.*
Except for the Dodgers, those things are still around, but they are
not quite the same and not what characterizes Brooklyn in the early
twenty-first century. Brooklyn's population grew by 10 percent
from 1980 to 2000 to reach 2,472,523. As of the 2000 census the
largest immigrant group in Brooklyn was West Indians at 283,749,
or 11.5 percent of the borough's people. Blacks as a whole were up
from 32 percent in 1980 to 36 percent, most of that growth due to
the West Indians. The West Indian Day parade down Brooklyn's
Eastern Parkway each Labor Day weekend is one of the city's
biggest events. Groups that have lost population since 1980 include
the Irish, Italians, and Puerto Ricans. Groups that have grown include West Indians, Russians and Ukrainians, Mexicans, and
Africans. Orthodox and Hasidic Jews remain a significant part of
the borough. Whites as a group have declined from 56 percent of
the population in 1980 to 41 percent in 2000. The borough's average household income was $32,135 in 2002, the city's second low-
est, just ahead of the Bronx. Yet the number of households that
earn more than $100,000 a year has grown from 4 percent in 1980
to 10 percent in 2003. Those who make between $75,000 and
$100,000 have increased from 6 percent to 10 percent. Still, almost
two-thirds of Brooklyn households make less than $50,000 and 36
percent make less than $25,000.[77] Brooklyn is polarized by income,
race, and class.

This polarization has had a definite spatial form. Since the
1960s, professionals have moved to Brooklyn for the attractive
housing stock and lower prices. The result, of course, was massive
gentrification spreading out from Brooklyn Heights into Cobble
Hill and Carroll Gardens to the south and Boerum Hill to the
southeast. In Park Slope, further east and down Flatbush Avenue,
gentrification spread from Prospect Park down to Fifth Avenue and
beyond. Most of the displaced in these cases were white or Latino
working-class families who could no longer afford the rents or
taxes as land values rose. Caught in between these gentrified
neighborhoods and the soon to be created Atlantic Yards project,
with its arena and seventeen high-rise apartment buildings, is

Gowanus, a neighborhood named for the industrial canal that runs through it. It is a gaping hole of factories and dowdy working-class homes in the midst of pricey land and housing. The canal, which used to be a smelly sewer, is clean today and even has striped bass swimming in it. The area is, in fact, one of the last successful manufacturing districts in the city. As of 2004 it had five hundred industrial firms, up 25 percent since 1997, employing three thousand workers. Only 3 percent of the industrial space in the area was vacant. Altogether 14,500 people live in the residential part of Gowanus.[78] If this area were converted to upscale residences, the whole of northwest Brooklyn would become a largely white upper-income district facing off against an overwhelmingly lower-income black central Brooklyn.

The case of Gowanus is instructive because it is not an instance of gentrification but of predatory development. It is not the usual vanguard of artists and young professionals but of well-financed developers, including a diamond billionaire, who want to build high-rise and loft apartment buildings. Emblematic of the times, the vanguard in this case is Whole Foods, which is clearing a big space in the middle of Gowanus for a superstore. Many of the blue-collar residents oppose this development since it will price them out of their homes. They have resisted some rezonings that would allow such development. As of late 2005, the balance of forces appeared to be against the residents, since Fourth Avenue, the border between Gowanus and Park Slope, was set for high-rise residential development. This was part of a bigger rezoning, announced by city planning commissioner Amanda Burden in 2003, that would protect the brownstones in Park Slope but open up Fourth Avenue and the side streets to high-rise development. In some cases this would replace rent-stabilized buildings with taller market-rate ones. It would also drive out the remaining black and Latino residents. As David Yassky, city councilman for the area, put it, "There's no question that some of the folks who have lived around Fourth Avenue for years are going to have to move."[79] The fight over Gowanus and Fourth Avenue was hardly noticed, however, hidden as it was beneath the shadow cast by the much bigger development only a few blocks away.

The Atlantic Yards are the rail yards of the Long Island Railroad, which is owned by the MTA. So important is the development of this area that the Empire State Development Corporation created the Atlantic Yards Development Corporation to take, by eminent domain when necessary, surrounding properties that didn't belong to the MTA. The developer was Bruce Ratner of Forest City Ratner. While there was supposed to be open bidding and, in fact, another developer made a lower bid, it was clear from the start that the land would be given to Ratner. The project was centered on a sports arena for the Nets, but included 8,500 housing units in seventeen high-rise buildings and 4.5 million square feet of office space. The original design by Frank Gehry had the usual double rows of buildings with some trees. Amanda Burden waxed eloquent about Gehry, "Having a Frank Gehry–designed arena in Downtown Brooklyn will put Brooklyn on the map globally." Even Gehry called his first design "horrible," however, and Ratner told him to do another.[80] Famous for his wavy off-center designs, Gehry seemed to have the contracts to design almost everything of any size going up in Brooklyn. Atlantic Yards, at the corner of Flatbush and Atlantic Avenues, was at the edge of downtown Brooklyn and the project would overlap into Prospect Heights, a majority black neighborhood. Housing would have to be torn down. Land values around the project would rise—good for those who could afford to hang on to theirs, not so good for those who couldn't or had to pay higher rents. At first resistance was determined and strong.[81] But Ratner was no ordinary developer.

Mayor Bloomberg strongly favored the development. Most of the area's elected representatives, however, opposed the Atlantic Yards development, at least as it was projected. Congressman Major Owens, state senator Velmanette Montgomery, and city councilmember Letitia James all spoke out against the "mixed-use" project. So did two organizations, the largely white Develop—Don't Destroy Brooklyn and the Downtown Brooklyn Leadership

Coalition, an organization of black clergy. The objections included the loss of existing low-income housing and local businesses, the alteration of the character of the neighborhood from low-rise to high-rise, the exacerbation of serious traffic jams that are already a problem at Atlantic and Flatbush Avenues, and the overloading of schools and other facilities. But Bruce Ratner had a strategy designed to appeal to many in the community. In this he was supported by Roger Green, the black assemblyman for the area. The first part was to offer a Community Benefit Agreement (CBA). This is a device already used in other cities whereby the developer agrees to provide certain amenities, often low-income housing, in return for support of the project. The CBA that Ratner eventually agreed to went beyond the usual 80-20 deal. It said that Atlantic Yards would include 30 percent middle-income and 20 percent lower-income rental units. It became known as the 50-50 agreement.[82]

For the second part of the strategy, Ratner and his executives vigorously campaigned for the project in the black community, hiring a local PR firm. They were able to split the Downtown Brooklyn Leadership Coalition, drawing the well-know Reverend Herbert Daughtry to Ratner's side even as the CBA was being negotiated. ACORN, a nationwide community-based organization, also supported and pushed for the 50-50 agreement. Some of this support appears to have been bought by Forest City Ratner. On the eve of the agreement, with Assemblman Green's support, a group of African American activists formed Brooklyn United for Innovative Local Development (BUILD), ostensibly to do job training, although none of the officers had any experience in that. The *Daily News* leaked an IRS statement that said BUILD expected $5 million over two years from Forest City Ratner. This did not seem to materialize, but Forest City Ratner did contribute $100,000 and provide free office space and equipment for BUILD. BUILD strongly supported the Atlantic Yards and was supposed to do job training for it. At the same time, a piece of the initial site preparation was given to McKissack & McKissack, a long-established, black-owned construction firm. The CBA was signed in June. But the Reverend Mark Taylor of the Downtown Brooklyn Leadership Council made it clear that not all African Americans in the area approved of the CBA. Its opponents point out that there is no specification of what low or even middle income is. As we have seen above, the city's idea of "affordable" is quite high. They also point out that the CBA is a memorandum of understanding and not a binding contract. Furthermore, the CBA contains an escape clause that allows Forest City Ratner to get out of the agreement by paying BUILD $500,000. The eight groups that signed the CBA are bound to publicly support the Atlantic Yards development and have enthusiastically done so. While opposition continues, there wasn't much doubt that the Atlantic Yards will rise above Brooklyn.[83] Nor is there much doubt that the Brooklyn waterfront from Greenpoint across the border from Hunters Point, Queens, to Atlantic Avenue will be transformed by a similar process.

Glass and steel high-rises will rise along Brooklyn's coastline as well. Residents of Williamsburg and Greenpoint also tried to stop or get concessions over the row of forty-story luxury apartment buildings that will cover their waterfront. The Williamsburg Warriors, complete with headbands, joined with hipsters to fight the "Manhattanization" of the area. But the deal that ultimately cleared the way for developers was brokered by the new Brooklyn party boss, Vito Lopez. As chair of the state assembly's housing committee, Lopez got the committee to extend a Manhattan rule requiring new housing to devote 20 percent of its units to "affordable" housing in order to get a 421a tax break. The new rules also require this low-income housing to be located in the high-rise—not far away in a low-income neighborhood. In addition, all building service workers would be union and get the prevailing SEIU Local 32BJ rate. And 30 percent of the units will be for middle- and low-income people. The rezoning of the area was approved by the city council in May and praised by both Mayor Bloomberg and borough president Marty Markowitz.[84] It had now become routine to negotiate some of the terms of the "Manhattanization" of Brooklyn, but stopping it seemed impossible.

A little bit down the Brooklyn coast is the newly gentrified and developed community of DUMBO (Down Under the Manhattan Bridge Overpass). While its attraction has been its loft-style apartments in old warehouses, a two-building hotel and a sixteen-story apartment building are planned for this small area. The proposed Brooklyn Bridge Park would begin at the west end of DUMBO and run around the waterfront to Atlantic Avenue, 1.3 miles away. This would encompass Brooklyn Heights. This plan, overseen by ESDC's Brooklyn Bridge Park Development Corporation, was backed by Democratic city councilmember David Yassky, who urged an even larger rezoning. The park itself will contain 1,240 mostly luxury condominium units, a 225-room hotel, 400,000 square feet of retail space, 95,000 square feet of office space, and 1,183 parking spaces along the waterfront to provide sufficient income for this "self-supporting" park. The Sierra Club opposed this "park" and the idea of parks that are not publicly funded. The 2005 plan was the second one, and worse by most accounts. The first one was actually a park with no housing. The new plan was more like the others with all manner of buildings in addition to the condos. Strong objections got some modifications. For example, a thirty-story building was trimmed to twenty stories, and an entrance to the park considered unwelcoming was widened. As Sandy Balboza of the Atlantic Avenue Betterment Association put it, "Shorter here, taller there—residential development on Atlantic just isn't going to benefit the avenue." There would be hearings before Community Board 6, but the ESDC and its Brooklyn Bridge Park Development Corporation were in charge and approved the "park" on January 18, 2006.[85]

The upscale high-rises weren't just going up on the waterfront. They were appearing around the older gentrified historic areas as well. In Fort Greene, a thirteen-story condo building went up on a block of brownstones. The Brooklyn Academy of Music (BAM) was planning a new theater and music library that few objected to, but the Clarett Group, a development firm that had built four upscale apartment towers in Manhattan since 2003, bought up several properties near BAM with a plan to build thirty stories of condos in this low-rise area.[86] In Carroll Gardens, which will soon be surrounded by developments in the Atlantic Yards, downtown Brooklyn, and the BAM area, saw the first multistory condominium buildings go up in 2005. This is an area of two- and three-story houses. The new condos are not skyscrapers, but at six or more floors and made of steel and glass, they are changing the character of the neighborhood. These areas are not "downzoned," so there are no limits on this type of development. Furthermore, the condos sell as fast as they go up.[87]

Next door, just across the noisy Brooklyn-Queens Expressway, is Red Hook, an old waterfront neighborhood that contains Brooklyn's last working container dock and is still home to many working-class residents. It also contains abandoned docks, factories, and warehouses. The residential part, which is most of the area, appears run-down, but is, in fact, in the throes of early gentrification—with its not-so-well-off artists, writers, etc. The reasonably priced bars, restaurants, and stores are evidence of the trend. But this will change. The working port is to be replaced by a cruise ship terminal, another waterfront space will host an Ikea store, and the main "low-rise Civil War–era commercial strip could be converted to a mixed-use space with a maritime museum, a public school, a café or brew-pub run by a relocated Brooklyn Brewery," according to a local newspaper.[88] In fact, the city turned away an offer by a German shipping line to operate on the piers, which would have brought $1.6 billion in business, because they were already committed to the cruise line option and the more upscale, tourist-friendly ambiance it would bring.[89] Whether the current artists, writers, and remaining working-class residents will be able to afford the rents that follow remains to be seen. Resistance to closing the working freight docks has come from Teamsters Local 805, which represents a number of workers on the docks. Local 805 president Sandy Pope told a rally in March 2006 that the city seemed more interested in "condominiums for the rich" than jobs for regular New Yorkers. The Local 805 members won a brief reprieve when the city allowed them to unload a ship carrying cocoa beans, but Andrew Alper of the Economic Development Corporation said the city was not interested in longshore work.[90]

We end our tour of Brooklyn at Coney Island. It's still a good and much-used beach, a place where working-class people of all races take in the sun in the summer months and the Polar Bear Club members still swim in the dead of winter. Nathan's still dispenses its famous hot dogs to locals and tourists alike. It is easily accessible by subway. But the old amusement park and much of the immediate area is run down, with few rides still operating. It is, in fact, a mystery as to why this oceanfront property has gone undeveloped for so long. In September 2005, the city announced a development plan. The first plan was big, garish, and mostly indoors to make it commercially viable year-round. It would include the inevitable condo tower, this one nineteen stories. Neighbors called it "Las Vegas by the Sea" and were not happy with it as planned. At the end of 2005, there was talk of scaling it down. The plan was still up in the air, but with city and state planning agencies that have seldom met a development they don't like, it seems likely something of the sort will go up.[91]

The areas we have described as gentrified or in the process of development compose only a relatively small part of Brooklyn's land mass, perhaps 10 percent as of 2005. Most of the borough remains working- or lower-middle-class. In those areas there is also a lot of construction going on. A drive around working-class Brooklyn reveals lots of new one-, two-, and three-family structures. Building permits in Brooklyn as well as in Queens have soared in recent years. In Brooklyn they went from 2,339 in 2000 to 12,369 in 2004. In Queens, from 1,826 to 13,452 in those years.[92] Some of these permits, of course, are for the upscale towers and developments already discussed, while others are for commercial development. Many, however, go to the smaller structures that now dot even slum areas. But housing prices have gone up throughout Brooklyn and elsewhere. In working-class Sunset Park, already under some development pressures, houses go for $725,000, one resident told the *Times*, "and that's on a bad block."[93] Few residents of Sunset Park or other areas of working-class Brooklyn can afford that. Most of the new houses popping up will be bought by investors who will then rent the apartments to working families. Rents in working-class Brooklyn and Queens have, however, gone up much faster than incomes. In fact, real wages in the outer boroughs fell by 2.9 percent from 2002 to 2005. Housing prices in the city as a whole, however, rose 14.7 percent from 1996 through 2005 compared to 8.4 percent for the country. An apartment in working-class Crown Heights went from $850 a month to $950 from 2004 to 2005. The person who experienced this increase told the *Times* he felt "priced out of Brooklyn, where I was born and bred."[94] The new housing isn't bringing rents down because of the pressures on land value caused by gentrification and, now, relentless development. The gentrifiers are already buying up brownstones in Bed-Stuy, just as they did in Harlem several years ago. While the better-off people in northern Brownstone Brooklyn can object to too many towers in the mega-projects and condos invading their neighborhoods, it is much more difficult for working and middle-class people in the rest of Brooklyn to resist the largely invisible forces of the market brought on by the mega-projects and condos.

Space is a class issue. The development agenda of New York City's business elite, the large returns on high-rise development, and the enabling actions of New York State, largely through the ESDC, have shrunken the space available to working-class New York. Globalization has made the city's upper classes wealthier in absolute and relative terms than at any time since the Gilded Age. Today's robber barons are financial speculators and real estate moguls who shape the city's economy and built environment both through their investments and their outsized demand for luxury living. They have molded an economy resting almost entirely on the vagaries of international finance and the services it and its practitioners require. Their influence on city politics has grown, focused since the fiscal crisis on the office of the mayor, replacing the influence of the old machines, union get-out-the-vote efforts, and racial block votes with community charity, campaign contributions, and lobbying, much as it has nationally. New York State government, too, has become their instrument for reshaping the city in their expensive image. What of working-class New York? This force, which once shaped many of the social institutions that made New York different and gave it a "social democratic polity," as Freeman put it, appears disunited and weaker than during the years before the fiscal crisis of the 1970s. Often out of sight beneath New York's rising skyline, it nevertheless makes itself heard from time to time.

7

Beneath the Skyline

On December 20, 2005, just after three in the morning, 33,700 New York City bus and subway workers began walking off the job. It was the first time in a quarter century their union, Local 100 of the Transport Workers Union, had struck. The issues on the table were health care payments and a two-tier pension scheme that would have required new hires to pay more into the pension fund than current employees—issues that impacted union negotiations all across the country. Furthermore, the pension issue had been raised only moments before the contract had expired on December 15, as if to provoke the union.[1] But beneath these issues and the provocation were deeper grievances over the way the Metropolitan Transit Authority (MTA), the big state-run outfit that controlled both city transit and commuter railroads in the region, treated its workers. There was the issue of "broadbanding," having previously special- ized workers perform many different jobs, i.e., job loading. Above all, however, was the draconian disciplinary regime. In 2004 the MTA filed 15,200 disciplinary citations, one for almost every two workers. That was up from 10,000 in 2002, the last time the union negotiated a contract. Although the union leadership did nothing to prepare for a strike and much to avoid one, there were many who believed a strike was in the cards sooner or later, given the pent-up anger of the workers. The transit strike was illegal and the members knew well that they would be fined two days' pay for each day on strike. Yet they were willing to face that certainty in order to make themselves heard by both state and city administrations who had not listened or, worse, believed that the regime they backed was justified. When a tentative agreement was worked out shortly after the three-day strike, the members rejected it, albeit by a thin margin of seven votes. In April 2006, state supreme court judge Theodore Jones sentenced union leader Roger Toussaint to ten days in jail, of which he served five days; fined the union $2.5 million; and suspended the union's dues checkoff indefinitely.[2] The contract, virtually unchanged, was finally approved in April.[3]

The strike was a reminder that New York's organized working class was still alive and kicking. Its unions still claimed a million members, as they had in 1945, and a density of about 26 to 29 percent, almost two and a half times that of the nation.[4] The unions, occupations, and industries were, of course, very different from those of 1945 or 1955. Public-sector and health care unions had taken the place of manufacturing and longshore unions. Although union household members made up 37.6 percent of those who voted in the 2004 presidential election in New York City, compared to about 24 percent nationally, the optimistic and politically assertive character of organized labor in the city, as in the nation, was severely diminished.[5] The force that had expanded the limits of New York's unique welfare state from the early to mid-twentieth century now fought a rearguard action to preserve what remained of it in the early twenty-first century. Still, some unions like the TWU, 1199, and the Communications Workers fought visible battles. Inside many of the city's public- and private-sector unions rebellion sprang from the ranks, anxious to reassert some power and defend their embattled living and working conditions. In addition, many low-income working-class New Yorkers not represented by recognized unions joined or created organizations to influence pay and working conditions. Some were unions in fact if not in official affiliation; others were community-based. In either case, they made up a significant part of the city's broader labor movement.

While New York's workforce faced the same issues as workers elsewhere in the country, many also had to deal with the impact of 9/11 on top of an ongoing recession.

Recession, 9/11, and the New York Working Class

The impact of disasters, whether natural or manmade, tend to follow the social terrain of the area they hit. The September 11 attacks on and collapse of the World Trade Center towers were no exception. While the impact was felt across the country, the economic and human impact were most dramatic in New York and the surrounding area. In terms of where the victims lived in the city, the collapse of this dense financial center saw the greatest number of dead concentrated in Manhattan's Upper East Side, home to many well-to-do brokers, traders, and bankers who worked in the twin towers. The second highest death count was registered on Staten Island, where many firefighters and police lived. Not far behind was the oceanfront community of Belle Harbor in the Rockaways, Queens, where seventy victims lived, mostly firefighters. The lower-paid clerical, hotel, restaurant, and delivery workers who perished lived throughout the city and had little traceable geographic impact. The communities closest to Ground Zero were affected economically according to their social composition. So Battery Park City and Tribeca, closest to Ground Zero, both well-heeled communities, recovered relatively fast, each in precise order of wealth, Tribeca first, Battery Park City second. Slightly removed but much poorer, Chinatown felt the economic impact for years as its businesses were cut off from the usual flow of tourists and visitors and its garment industry crippled.[6]

Economically, the impact of 9/11 reached far beyond the concentrated communities of financiers and firefighters to touch many of the city's working-class occupations and neighborhoods. In the immediate aftermath of 9/11 some 3,500 workers who cleaned hotels and buildings in downtown Manhattan lost their jobs and income, while "black car" drivers who catered to Wall

Street reported their business was down by 80 percent.[7] Between August 2001 and January 2002, the city's industries lost about 124,000 jobs, of which at least 75,000 were directly related to 9/11. In other words, the attacks increased the job loss already under way due to the recession and/or restructuring related to globalization. In some cases, however, a booming industry was hurt, leading to layoffs. This was the case with many of the occupations dependent on the city's previously booming tourism and entertainment industries. While time would replace many of the lost jobs, the income lost to those workers affected would not be recovered. Among disadvantaged workers, those groups who experienced greater losses of jobs, hours worked, and income in comparison to the same groups in other U.S. cities from April 2000 through December 2003 included women high school graduates, black men, Latino women, and recently arrived immigrant women. But the effects did not stop there. In most cases, the legacy of September 11 exacerbated trends already under way—trends that were already hurting many of the city's workers and whose impact was likely to be very long run.[8]

The differential impact of recession, on the one hand, and 9/11, on the other, can be gathered by looking at job loss among low-, middle-, and high-income groups by occupation in three periods: pre-9/11 recession; immediate 9/11 impact; and post-9/11 recession. As Table 7-1 shows, job losses began before 9/11 but increased significantly as a result of the attacks, and then continued at a more modest pace as the recession continued in New York. Given that the attacks hit the heart of the financial industry, it is not surprising that in terms of job loss it was mid- and high-wage jobs that suffered most. The clustering of jobs by wage level, however, obscures to some extent the class impact, in that many of the mid-level jobs are, in fact, working-class jobs.

TABLE 7-1
Recession and 9/11 impact on low-, mid-,
and high-wage occupations, NYC
Jobs lost per period

	Pre-9/11 (12/00–8/01)	9/11 (8/01–1/02)	Post-9/11 (1/02–8/03)
Low-wage	17,200	31,700	8,500
Mid-wage	19,600	52,800	35,200
High-wage	13,600	39,200	25,300
Total	50,400	123,300	69,000

Source: Parrott and Cooke in Chernick, ed., *Resilient City*, 2005.

In the low/middle/high scheme, low-wage workers composed only 25.7 percent of the city's workforce in 2000, while mid-wage workers made up the largest group at 46.3 percent in the way that Parrot and Cooke have divided things. If we include such major mid-wage occupational groups as construction (129,000); installation, maintenance, and repair (132,000); transportation and material moving (221,000); and office and administrative support (823,000) as working-class occupations, the class distribution of occupations and of the impact of both recession and 9/11 looks very different. First of all, working-class occupations amounted to 2,269,000, or 60.5 percent of the city's 3,751,000-strong workforce in 2000.

As Table 7-2 shows, working-class job loss from the immediate impact of 9/11 was 62.5 percent of the total and 65.5 percent for

TABLE 7-2
Job loss in immediate 9/11 period and overall recession

	Immediate 9/11	Overall Recession (12/00-8/03)
Working-class job loss	77,000	159,000
Total job loss	123,300	242,700
Working class as % of total	62.5%	65.5%

Calculated from Parrot and Oliver in Chernick, *Resilient City*, 2005.

the entire period up to August 2003. Thus, the impact on working-class jobs is somewhat greater than on middle- or upper-class jobs, both in terms of the immediate impact of 9/11 and of the recession as a whole. The effects on the industries that employed these low- and middle-income workers was, however, very uneven. The impact of recession and 9/11 on the financial sector was obviously great, explaining the loss of many high-income jobs. In terms of working-class jobs particularly hard-hit, however, three industries saw things go from bad to worse for their employees: airlines, garment manufacturing, and the taxi industry. Each of these industries had been reshaped by restructuring related to globalization and the neoliberal policies meant to enable it.

Since deregulation in 1978 the airline industry had been in a state of turmoil and reorganization. Airlines, of course, are to the movement of business executives, financiers, and even immigrant workers what telecommunications are to the movement of information in the global economy. The growth of competition with the carriers of other nations and the entry of low-cost, nonunion domestic and international carriers in the 1980s led to intensified competition and pressures on costs. By 2001 most of the old-line major carriers were in or near bankruptcy, while several of the low-cost upstarts had gone bust as well. The major airlines demanded concessions by unionized workers in an industry that was 80 percent unionized. There were strikes, of which the 1989 Eastern Airlines strike was the most dramatic. That strike ended with the collapse of the airline and the banning of its owner, Frank Lorenzo, from the industry.[9] Even for an industry in turmoil, the impact of 9/11 was drastic and rapid. In the first three months after the attacks 140,000 airline workers were laid off. In New York, the workforce went from 54,700 in August 2001 to 45,700 a year later. Of the jobs lost from the immediate impact of 9/11, only 2.4 percent were management jobs. Ninety percent of the jobs lost were among reservation and ticket agents; pilots and cargo handlers; parking attendants and taxi drivers; flight attendants and baggage porters; and mechanics. Most of these workers lived in Brooklyn, Queens, or nearby Nassau County on Long Island, all areas near the two major airports: JFK and LaGuardia.[10] Thus, the geographic impact was somewhat concentrated on these largely working-class communities.

The Bush administration and Congress moved rapidly to aid the "industry," meaning the corporations, with a $15 billion bailout, but not a penny was allocated for the thousands of workers and their families hit by this catastrophe. New York airline workers were barred from the emergency aid available to downtown Manhattan residents because they lived outside that area. Furthermore, their unemployment insurance lapsed in July 2002. Medical benefits also stopped, although those who could afford to, about 47 percent, kept them at their own expense under COBRA. House majority leader Dick Armey, who had supported aid to the companies, opposed action by Congress to aid these workers, telling members of the House, "the model of thought that says we need to go out and extend unemployment benefits and health insurance benefits and so forth is not, I think, one that is commensurate with the American spirit here." In the end they did receive some mortgage and rent aid from FEMA. The hope of finding jobs in other air lines, even outside of New York, however, proved futile for most.[11]

The International Association of Machinists (IAM), which represents the mechanics and baggage handlers, set up one-stop centers across the country through its Center for Administering Rehabilitation and Employment Services (IAM CARES). These were meant to help displaced workers of all crafts and unions find jobs and get other help. In New York centers were set up in Manhattan and Queens; the latter, being close to JFK and LaGuardia, was the busiest. But there wasn't much these centers could do to change the dire situation in the labor market or the limits of government aid. Psychological problems among these airline workers became widespread.[12] The problems of airline workers were compounded with the launching of the war in Iraq in 2003. Airlines used the crisis of war to extract new concessions and cut their workforces nationwide. United Airlines furloughed 2,000 flight attendants and 1,148 mechanics, along with thousands of nonunion workers only days after the war began in March. Northwest laid off

4,900 soon after, while US Airways and American extracted wage concessions from their workers.[13] New Yorkers took their share of cuts and concessions.

Unlike Tribeca or Battery Park City, Manhattan's Chinatown is a business, tourist, and manufacturing center, as well as a residential area. Its residents, and those in the other Chinese population centers in the city—Sunset Park, Brooklyn, and Elmhurst and Jackson Heights, Queens—are dependent on its businesses and industries for employment. While Chinatown is about ten blocks from Ground Zero, everything below Fourteenth Street, and later Houston Street, both above Chinatown, was cut off from normal traffic for a number of weeks. For security reasons, a couple of the main streets into Chinatown were closed for much longer. This not only killed tourism for a long time, but it crippled the area's garment manufacturing industry. In the immediate aftermath of 9/11, 23 percent of Chinatown's workforce was laid off. Fully 80 percent of restaurant workers lost their jobs for a period, while 46 percent of garment workers were laid off, most permanently.[14]

Prior to 9/11, Chinatown's garment industry employed some fourteen thousand workers in 250 factories. These small, low-cost operations arose as Chinatown expanded north of Canal Street, replacing many of the older apparel shops in midtown. They were mostly tied to the fashion district, formerly the city's traditional garment district, in midtown for which they produced batch orders for companies like Ann Taylor, Brooks Brothers, Prada, Neiman Marcus, and Bergdorf Goodman. About half the workforce lived outside of Chinatown in Brooklyn or Queens and thus were unable to get to work when lower Manhattan was closed off. A year after 9/11, seventy-five shops employing 3,500 workers were still closed. To make matters worse, most of the shops and workers were ineligible for government aid for six months after the attacks because 80 percent of the shops were north of Canal Street—the initial cutoff point for aid. Even when workers could get to work, it remained difficult to make deliveries to midtown as Park Row, a major entry and exit point, was closed for security reasons, a fact that hurt an industry already in trouble.[15]

The Chinese-owned section of the garment industry in New York represented a holdout for manufacturing jobs in the city. Prior to 9/11 it employed 56,000 workers throughout the city, a majority Chinese and most women. Much of this industry was characterized by sweatshops, particularly in the outer boroughs. In Chinatown's piece of the industry 86 percent of its fourteen thousand workers belonged to UNITE, the union of garment and textile workers. UNITE, and before it the ILGWU, had long pursued a job retention strategy that allowed low wages, long hours, and substandard conditions. The major difference between workers in Chinatown and the nonunion shops was that the union workers got health insurance, no small thing for these exploited workers. Most of Chinatown's apparel workers were documented immigrants. The industry, however, was under extreme pressure from overseas competition, as well as from lower-cost producers in the outer boroughs. It survived largely due to its proximity to the fashion district in midtown, which was now limited. Another problem in the pre-recession era was that the booming dot-com start-ups of the 1990s were gobbling up Chinatown space, pricing many small apparel companies out of the area—and out of the union. The aftermath of 9/11 permanently wounded the Chinatown apparel industry. The plight of the garment workers went from bad prior to 9/11 to worse after. As of 2004, only 150 shops employing six thousand workers remained in business. The eight thousand who lost their jobs permanently would have difficulty finding almost any job, as few spoke English.[16]

The taxi industry has long been a central part of the city's transportation network, but like the city's airline and garment industries, it experienced a profound transformation during the 1980s and 1990s. As we have seen, the city's economy became more and more dependent on financial and business services, on the one hand, and tourism and entertainment, on the other. As Biju Mathew has explained, the taxi industry was restructured in at least two important ways to meet this change. First, the payment system by which employers and employees split "the meter" and the workers received a commission was replaced with one in which workers became independent contractors required to lease their cabs. This meant the workers assumed the risk, since the lease payment had to be up front and the bulk of fares went to paying that and fuel costs before the driver earned anything. This change was in line with similar practices associated with "lean production" and contracting out across the world economy. Second, the industry was divided into three parts: the yellow cabs working the streets, the black cars (or limos) working under contract to corporations, and the livery cars serving various neighborhoods, the latter largely replacing the "gypsy cabs" of the 1960s and 1970s. The black car companies served Wall Street and other corporate businesses with upscale cars more in line with the elevated lifestyle of its global executives and financiers. The black cars, like taxis, were also leased by the workers. This took business from the yellow cabs, who formerly trolled this lucrative market. The yellow cabs carried the largely white middle layer of corporate New York, along with the growing legions of tourists. This restructuring was accompanied by a draconian regime of control put in place by Mayor Giuliani and administered by the Taxi and Limousine Commission.[17]

While some 40,000 commercially licensed drivers revolve through the different parts of the industry, there are about 24,000 yellow cab drivers, around 2,000 of whom are owner-operators. The rest work under the lease system. As the industry changed in the 1980s, so did the workforce. The older white ethnic and African American drivers retired or moved on to be replaced by new immigrant groups, typically displaced from their homelands by the forces of globalization. Ninety-five percent of the drivers are immigrants. South Asians from India, Pakistan, and Bangladesh made up about 60 percent of the workforce, with others coming from the Middle East, Haiti, Africa, and the Caribbean. As many as 85 percent are Muslims.[18]

September 11 brought an economic and social catastrophe for New York taxi drivers. Wall Street closed, tourism dropped, and airline flights evaporated. Income plunged, while operating costs, the lease plus gas, remained high, even where owners gave the drivers a small break. According to one survey, during the first week after

9/11, the number of trips with passengers dropped from just over twenty-seven to ten per day while lucrative airport runs virtually disappeared. By late 2002, income had not even recovered its pre-9/11 level of about $88 a day for the usual twelve-hour shift put in by drivers: taxi drivers surveyed were taking in an average of only $62, a little over $5 an hour or just about the minimum wage. Drivers reported deep debt and considerable distress. Like the airline and garment workers, they were denied relief or emergency aid because they didn't live in downtown Manhattan. Some, like the airline workers, got mortgage and rent, i.e., lease, aid from FEMA, but many were afraid to apply.[19]

If the Chinatown garment workers were largely invisible, just faces in the busy streets of New York's three major Chinatowns, the taxi drivers could hardly have been more visible. As Asians, Middle Easterners, and Muslims, yellow cab drivers rapidly became the object of insults, violence, and official harassment in the aftermath of 9/11. Like other working-class New Yorkers, taxi drivers had pitched in on and after 9/11, giving free rides to Ground Zero volunteers, rescue and excavation workers, and grief-stricken relatives of victims. Already losing money, they had sacrificed time and income to help out. But few were repaid with kindness. The notion of a city pulled together in one community was not true for people with their complexion, national origin, or religion. Caught between a homeland they could not make a living in and a new country that rejected them, some left the industry and the city.[20] More might have left, but they had an organization that would stand by them, the New York Taxi Workers Alliance—to be discussed later.

From the end of 2000 through the spring of 2005, the impact of the recession, which in New York bottomed out in the summer of 2003, brought another shift toward low-wage jobs. Over half of the 191,975 net decline in employment is accounted for by the loss of over 88,000 blue-collar jobs, a majority of them in the middle-income range. The higher-paid financial, professional services, and information industries also saw big drops in employment. Some of this was due to the rapid consolidations in the banking and investment sectors, while some was the result of relocations in the wake of

9/11. As Table 7-3 shows, the big gains in this period were almost all in low-wage sectors: entertainment and tourism, hotels and restaurants, hospitals and private social services, the latter, in part due to the enormous increase in the contracting out of these services during Bloomberg's first administration. During the partial recovery from August 2003 through March 2005, finances, professional services, and information made gains (together 11,860), indicating a positive future for these sectors. Blue-collar jobs, on the other hand, continued their decline (−13,079), albeit at a slower rate, following the long-term trend. Low-wage sectors in entertainment and tourism; education, health and social services; and "other" services made gains (together 33,613). The trend toward greater inequality of income continued, giving New York City and hence New York State, the greatest level of inequality in the country.[21]

TABLE 7-3
NYC employment by industry, December 2000 and March 2005*

	Dec. 2000	March 2005	Net gain/ loss
Total	3,754,435	3,562,460	−191,975
Manuf., trans. & utilities	429,417	341,402	−88,015
Wholesale	154,732	147,186	−7,546
Retail	284,438	278,274	−6,164
Information	193,038	164,231	−28,807
Financial activity/FIRE	491,195	438,074	−53,121
Professional services	330,257	290,056	−40,201
Management of companies	52,469	55,590	3,121
Administrative & support	210,427	187,487	−22,940
Edu., health & social services	631,233	673,520	42,287
Entertainment, tourism & hospitality	262,422	276,287	13,865
Other services	149,290	151,509	2,219
Government	564,353	553,026	−11,327
City employees*	264,061	250,856	−13,205

*Figures for FY2000 and FY2005 (FY = July 1–June 30)
Sources: James Parrott, "Hearing Before the New York City Rent Guidelines Board," Fiscal Policy Institute, May 2, 2005; *New York City Comptroller's Report for Fiscal 2005.*

The Unions: Falling and Stagnating Incomes and Rebellion in the Ranks

Real weekly household wages fell for all New Yorkers by an average of 4.6 percent from the first quarter of 2000 through the fourth quarter of 2003, i.e, from the peak to the trough of the recession. These are *wages* and do not include other types of income, like the bonuses and stock awards, dividends, and interest paid to the high rollers discussed in Chapter 6. The impact of 9/11 differed from one income level to another. Low-income households saw their weekly wage fall from $588 in the third quarter of 2001 to $540 in the fourth quarter. Middle-income households, on the other hand, saw theirs rise from $909 to $921 in that period, while high-income households went from $1,524 to $1,614. Over the whole 2000–2003 period all groups of wage and salary workers lost buying power, but the rate at which they fell varied from high-, middle-, and low-income groups. High-wage earners lost 4.7 percent over the 2000 through 2003 period, middle-income households lost 5.7 percent, and those with low incomes lost 9.8 percent. Parrott and Cooke suggest that periods of unemployment explain the drop and the differences.[22] But incomes in the outer boroughs continued their decline, dropping by 2.9 percent from 2002 to 2005. Much of the general loss in real wages can be explained by the squeeze play of inflation and slow wage growth. As Michael Dolfman of the regional Bureau of Labor Statistics office told the *Times,* "You had in all boroughs except Manhattan, increases in wages and salaries that were less than in the rest of the country but inflation being greater."[23] It is also explained by the relative growth of low-wage jobs evident in Table 7-3.

Some New York workers covered by major union contracts negotiated in the late 1990s and early 2000s managed to keep up with or even a little ahead of inflation as they headed into the new century. In 1998, the Communications Workers of America negotiated a two-year contract with Bell Atlantic (later to become Verizon) with 3.8 percent and 4 percent raises. In 2000, after a three-week strike,

workers at Verizon got 12.9 percent over three years. Following con-
cessionary trends in the private sector nationally, however, a settlement in 2003 without a strike netted only a lump-sum payment of
3 percent in the first year and 2 percent hourly increases in the following two years.[24] In 1999 a four-year agreement between TV network ABC and 2,400 members of the CWA-affiliated National
Association of Broadcasting Employees & Technicians (NABET)
won increases of 3 percent for two years and 3.5 percent for the
next two years, although at a cost of considerable concessions in
other areas.[25] New York City transit workers got an average of 4
percent a year over three years, also at the cost of some givebacks.[26]
Members of AFSCME District Council 37, emerging from the
"double-zeros" contract negotiated in 1995, scandals surfacing in
1998, and a trusteeship in that year, nevertheless got 4 percent a
year for two years beginning in 2000.[27] Police, corrections officers,
and other uniformed city employees formed a Uniformed Forces
Coalition in 2000 and won two-and-a-half-year contracts with
raises of 4.6 percent a year.[28] Teamsters at UPS would get over 3
percent a year if they were full-timers and from 8 to 10 percent a
year if they were part-timers.[29] FedEx workers got an average of
3.4 percent a year in their 1999 five-year agreement.[30] But not
everyone was so fortunate.

At least 10,000 airline workers in the New York area, as we
saw, faced concessions before and after 9/11, while some 24,000
taxi drivers lost income badly in the wake of 9/11. Twelve thousand New York postal workers got 2 percent in the first year and 1.4
percent in the second year of their 1999 two-year contract.[31] A
twenty-month strike at the Domino Sugar refinery in Brooklyn
ended in defeat in the spring of 2001.[32] The 1997 contract, the last
one negotiated by Gus Bevona, the crooked president of SEIU
Local 32BJ, which represented 29,000 doormen and building
maintenance workers in the city, brought only 8.3 percent over
three years, roughly half a percentage point per year ahead of inflation.[33]

The rounds of bargaining that took place in the last Giuliani
years and first year or so of the Bloomberg administration were af-

fected not only by recession and 9/11, but by internal crises in a number of unions. Two major unions saw reform efforts end in leadership changes imposed by their international unions. SEIU Local 32BJ, mentioned above, saw a dramatic change in leadership. A small reform movement led by rank-and-file building workers Carlos Guzman and Dominic Bentivegna drew the intervention of the national union, headed at that time by Andy Stern. Bevona, famous for his half-million-dollar salary, his penthouse suite atop the union headquarters, and the practice of selling jobs to members for thousands of dollars, was "retired" after eighteen years in office with a $1.5 million golden parachute. A trusteeship was imposed first under Tom Balanoff from Chicago and then under Michael Fishman from the SEIU staff, who would go on to become local president.[34]

Only two months prior to Bevona's downfall, DC 37 executive director Stanley Hill left office in the wake of widespread scandal. Some locals in the district council had seen officers embezzle as much as $4.5 million. The revelation of the embezzlements led to reprisals against whistleblowers and reform officers.[35] In the ensuing fight it was soon revealed that the vote that had approved the 1995 double-zeros contract had been stolen. One of the chief vote manipulators was Al Diop, president of Local 1549, one of the largest in the district council, who produced five thousand extra ballots in case things went the "wrong" way. They did, and he deployed unused ballots to turn things around. Diop was found guilty of stealing $1 million from the local treasury and, in the manner of Gus Bevona, possessed an elegant penthouse atop the DC 37 headquarters in downtown Manhattan. The union once considered the epitome of social democratic unionism had become a cesspool of corruption.[36] DC 37 was put in trusteeship by AFSCME under Lee Saunders, a staffer for the national union. At the same time, a reform movement calling itself the Committee for Real Change was formed by a coalition of local officials to push for democratic reforms, including the direct election of the district council's top officers. The reformers, led by Roy Commer, president of Local 375, Mark Rosenthal, president of Local 983; Charles Ensley of 371, who had blown the whistle on ballot-stuffing, and Ray Markey of Local 1930, were generally supportive of Saunders despite differences and clashes. Saunders went on in 2000 to negotiate the two-year contract with 4 percent increases each year. In February 2002, Lillian Roberts, a former leader of Hospital Workers Local 420, was unanimously elected executive director of DC 37 by the executive board, at the urging of Saunders. But Roberts had been away from the union for twenty years and opposition to her leadership, considered too timid by many, would emerge later.[37]

Rebellion from below succeeded in two other major New York City unions: the postal workers and the transport workers. The postal workers' contract, mentioned above, was a national contract, but as with so many agreements in recent years, issues of working conditions were also at stake. This was part of what led to a rebellion in the twelve-thousand-member New York Metro Area Postal Workers Union, the union that represents inside workers. Also at issue was the old leadership's practice of using expense accounts for personal expenses and of granting themselves secret annual bonuses. In the March 1999 local election a slate of seven reformers, headed by William Smith, defeated the old guard led by former president Josie McMillian. The old guard, however, still held most of the executive board seats, which would make change difficult.[38] In the 36,000-member Transport Workers Union Local 100, the eleven-year-old opposition New Directions caucus's presidential candidate Roger Toussaint beat the incumbent Willie Smith with 60 percent of the vote. New Directions also swept the other top offices and the executive board. This was New Directions' fourth run for power, improving on the incremental gains of the previous three. In the 1998 election its candidate, train driver Tim Schermerhorn, had won 49.5 percent of the vote and the caucus had taken twenty-one of the forty-six executive board seats. The origins of this rank-and-file-based revolt went all the way back to 1984, with the founding of the newsletter *Hell on Wheels* by a coalition of socialists and union militants. New Directions had played a major part in the 1999 contract fight, calling a demonstration that brought ten thousand people to the streets.[39] Toussaint, however, would not fulfill the expectations of many Local 100 members and internal conflict would reemerge.

Insurgency and reform were not limited to these more high-profile unions. In 2000, the rank-and-file-based New Caucus overturned the old leadership of the Professional Staff Congress, an AFT affiliate representing sixteen thousand faculty and professional staff at the City University of New York (CUNY). The New Caucus leadership opened the union to full membership for part-time teachers for the first time.[40] In 2002, DC 37 Local 420, representing 7,500 public hospital workers, saw its longtime president James Butler defeated by an insurgent slate headed by Carmen Charles, a medical technician. Both candidates were black and Butler had a reputation as a strong civil rights advocate, but Charles and her slate reflected the growing proportion of immigrant workers. The voter turnout had been low, and the margin of victory small, and Butler challenged the outcome. In the end Charles and her slate took office.[41] In 2003, longtime member of the Teamsters for a Democratic Union (TDU) Sandy Pope was elected secretary-treasurer of Queens-based Teamster Local 805. She would later become president of 805.[42] Members of Utility Workers Local 1-2, representing Con Edison workers, also saw a successful insurgency in 2005.[43] In the United Federation of Teachers (UFT), dissidents captured six executive board seats in 2005. This small inroad was quite an accomplishment since the UFT boasts one of the most effective internal political machines of any union, in place since the 1960s and running from top office down to the schools.[44] Bus drivers who transport the elderly and disabled began organizing the Drivers Coalition in Amalgamated Transit Union (ATU) Local 1181 as early as 2001. ATU Local 1181 is a huge catchall local with 14,000 members. The thousand or so bus drivers, mostly immigrants, felt ignored by the local and organized to pressure for a decent contract and representation. In response the local called its first general membership meeting and put coalition leader Patrick Lorquet on the negotiating committee. In April and May 2004, the coalition itself led a two-week strike that produced a better-than-average contract, with 4 percent pay increases each year, a $700 signing bonus, and additional sick and vacation days.[45] Despite widespread rebellion from below and the rise of new leaders, whether from above or below, not all were as successful as the Drivers Coalition. Overall, the impact on public-sector bargaining for the rest of Bloomberg's first term was negligible.

For one thing, the system of public-employee bargaining that had been thrown off-center during the fiscal crisis of the 1970s continued to malfunction. Typically, contract settlements lagged over two years beyond their expiration date: the city and/or the state would drag their feet in hopes of gaining more concessions as such resistance as there was worn down. The mayor, despite calling city workers part of his team, made it clear that "productivity" gains, i.e., concessions, would be required in every new contract.[46] So, for example, after two and a half years in "negotiations," in late 2005 the UFT settled the contract that had expired in 2003 with retroactive pay raises of only 3.4 percent a year—slightly behind the average metropolitan New York inflation rate of 3.6 percent a year for that period. Furthermore, the price for even this was a longer workweek, loss of control over nonteaching assignments, and the loss of the right to file grievances over disciplinary letters placed in their files. Despite the concessions, the contract was ratified in November 2005 by 73 percent.[47] The police, also lagging two years, won a binding arbitration that gave them 10.25 percent over two years, an above-average settlement that would impact other uniformed services. This decision also contained "cost-saving and productivity" concessions including lower starting salaries for new hires. The starting salary for police dropped from $34,514 to $25,100.[48] City doctors got 10 percent over three years, but had to add thirty minutes to their workday. The Uniformed Sanitationmen got 4 percent a year, but had to produce productivity gains that would allow a cut of two hundred workers and would introduce one-man trucks for the first time.[49]

The DC 37 contract settled in April 2004, well over a year after the last contract expired, offered a $1,000 signing bonus in the first year in lieu of any pay increase, 3 percent in the second year, and 2 percent in 2006, the third and last year of that contract. The average pay of DC 37 members just before the settlement was $28,000, so the new percentage rate increases would not even bring the average to $30,000, well below the average income in the outer boroughs. Furthermore, it was deeply concessionary, with new hires to get 15 percent less pay than current employees and fewer vacation and sick days. There was the promise of an additional 1 percent in the final year based on productivity gains. In fact, the 1 percent would be granted by Bloomberg as a way to get DC 37's endorsement in the 2005 election, although, of course, it was not officially presented that way.[50] In July 2006, DC 37 reached another agreement with the city, also a year overdue. This contract would deliver a 10 percent wage increase over thirty-two months, possibly a little ahead of inflation.[51] The Professional Staff Congress, without a contract for three years, finally pried a settlement out of the triumvirate of city, state, and CUNY, with whom they had to bargain in late April 2006.[52] In June 2006, twenty municipal unions representing 175,000 city workers joined together to engage in coalition bargaining for the next round of contracts. Harry Nespoli of the Uniformed Sanitationmen said, "We're joining together in solidarity because none of us wants to go years and years without a contract again."[53] Although it included most city unions, DC 37 was not among them, a fact that could undermine the new coalition.

The other public-sector unions were not happy with the DC 37 settlement since it traditionally set the pattern for other nonuniformed unions. Just after Bloomberg was reelected, Randi Weingarten of the UFT told the independent weekly civil service paper, *The Chief*, "When Lillian did the deal for DC 37, it worked for her members but it certainly didn't work well for the rest of us." Weingarten said of Bloomberg's strategy in the last round of city worker negotiations, "The Mayor was very effective in having the unions bid against each other. It used to be said that the unions whip-sawed the city; this mayor whip-sawed the unions."[54] What might have been added was how willing the unions had been to be whip-sawed and how ineffective the Municipal Labor Committee, which Weingarten chaired, had been in resisting this. What had become clear was that the mayor was willing to grant wage in-

creases slightly above inflation if he could extract cost-saving concessions on productivity or two-tier wage schemes. The historian
Joshua Freeman described Bloomberg's bargaining stance as "non-
belligerent" but "very hard line." Charles Brecher of the Citizens
Budget Commission, which had always argued that wage increases
should be based on real productivity increases, told the *Times*,
"People used to look at us like we're crazy for saying that. Now, it's
accepted that that's how it's going to be."[55] Another piece of the
business elite's developmentalist agenda had become the norm,
with the result that public-sector wages and, hence, working-class
incomes throughout the city remained depressed. While both the
size of the city workforce and its cost had risen, they had done so
more slowly than the city budget as a whole, so total labor costs had
fallen from 53.2 percent of the budget in FY2003 to 50.9 percent in
FY2005, as we saw in Chapter 5.[56]

The Failure of Union Reform in New York's Public-Sector Unions

Rank-and-file insurgency and union reform movements are an in-
tegral part of American labor history and politics. It's hard to say
when this began, but the ousting of Samuel Gompers as president
of the AFL at the 1894 convention, albeit for only one year, might
do.[57] In any case, from the formation of the Trade Union Educational League in the early 1920s, built at the start on rank-and-file
insurgencies in several unions, through the victory of the Miners
for Democracy in 1972, on to the election of Ron Carey as general
president of the Teamsters with the backing of the Teamsters for a
Democratic Union in 1991, union reform movements have helped
to shape many U.S. unions.[58] At the national level, where union bureaucracy is most stubborn, total victory is rare and setbacks frequent. But across the country's fifty thousand or so union locals,
leadership turnover is common, often the result of insurgency
rather than simply a normal changing of the guard. Old guard
leaders seldom go peacefully, and when they have let wages and
conditions deteriorate, rebellion often breaks out sooner or later.

Another feature of rank-and-file rebellion is that it tends to come in waves. Sometimes, as following World War I, during the 1930s, or during the years from 1966 through the late 1970s, these insurgencies occur in the context of a bigger labor upheaval. It is generally under those circumstances that they are most successful in leaving their mark. Indeed, the rise of public-sector unionism in the 1960s and 1970s had occurred in the context of both the general social upheaval and a significant labor insurgency in those years. Within the major public employees unions, notably AFSCME, the AFT, and both postal workers unions, a new generation of leaders had broken their way through the lethargy, bureaucracy, and failed strategies of their respective old guards.[59]

The wave of union insurgencies that hit New York in the late 1990s and early 2000s took place in the context of the general retreat of organized labor in the United States as well as in the city. It was, of course, this very retreat that motivated the insurgencies. But it was also this context that explained some of its limits and failures in union after union. How were new leaders to turn things around and make significant gains if they could not change the underlying power relations? These power relations were the result of numerous trends, including the impact of globalization, the general rightward drift of the country, and the employers' offensive in industry after industry in the long run, and the recession in the short term. For public employees in general, the fiscal crunch imposed by national and state neoliberal policies—and for those in New York City, the power shift and the neoliberal agenda that had long been successfully imposed on the city by its rampant business elite—created more barriers. To break through such a convergence would no doubt have required a social upheaval, not only in the city, but nationally as well. This was not forthcoming by mid-decade.

To alter the balance of forces in New York City's unions even slightly would have required changes in two other relationships: that between the members and leaders, on the one hand, and that between the leaders and the employers, on the other. These two relationships are themselves interrelated. Bureaucratic business unionism maintains a close "business-like" relation with the em-

ployer, public or private, in inverse relation to the leader's relation
to the union's members. Bureaucracy, unaccountability, and pro-
scription of criticism insulate leaders from members and free them
to cut deals. Sometimes actual corruption follows. To end the cozy
relationship of union leader to boss that is often the object of insurgency, the balance of these two relationships must be shifted.
Changing the faces of officers is not enough. Reforms need to be
put in place that solidify the power and influence of members and
the accountability of leaders. Structures and norms of member
participation and leader accountability are needed and, ultimately,
a new democratic culture has to be shaped.[60] Too often insurgent
groups think only in terms of putting better leaders in office, with
the result that the basic relationship of the union to the employer is
soon or eventually replicated, the new leaders "tamed," and the
top-down culture left to justify and reproduce the lack of change.

While most local unions are fairly democratic, larger ones, like
TWU Local 100, or districts containing many locals, like DC 37,
tend to evolve structures designed to insulate leaders from members. District Council 37, with its 120,000 members in fifty-six
local unions of various sizes, elects its top officers by a system of
weighted voting that favors the officers of a few big locals. There is
no direct vote by the members of the officers who negotiate the
conditions covering all its locals. In the case of TWU Local 100, top
officers are elected directly, but there are no local-wide meetings.
Members meet by division, of which there are twelve. Until 1999,
the local's vice presidents were not elected by division, but at-large;
thus there was no direct accountability to the members in the fragmented divisions. In fact, vice presidents supposedly representing
certain workers were elected and reelected on the leadership slate
even when a majority of votes in the division went against them. In
1999 the New Directions movement forced one reform on the old
leadership: election of vice presidents by division instead of at
large. There were still, however, no local wide meetings in which
members, particularly when organized, could confront the leadership on a more regular basis that the triennial local elections.[61] But

such structural changes are hard to come by and by themselves seldom enough to alter the old internal power relations.

These old relations are further cemented by the huge amounts
of money available to the top leaders to dispense in jobs, perks, and
higher salaries for officers. In DC 37, for example, the executive director makes $250,000 a year, and so, too, do some of the officers of
the larger of its fifty-six locals. On top of this are the expense accounts and union credit cards.[62] This kind of money is likely to
make holding on to office the priority, as well as making it unlikely
that officers' salaries will be reduced to something even close to the
best-paid members' earnings. In a union where the average member makes about $29,000, such salaries underline the distance of
leaders from members. An example was the falling-out among reform officers newly elected in DC 37 Local 420. Even where officers are scrupulously honest, this sort of money is bound to have a
corrupting effect on their relationship with their members and a
soothing one on their relationship with similarly paid city officials.
The vast amounts in the treasury controlled by the top officers also
provides a sort of patronage system that tends to create a loyal cadre
of staff. This type of patronage is evident in DC 37, TWU Local
100, the UFT, and other large unions. In TWU Local 100, it became
an explicit means by which the incumbent leadership bought
off some New Directions leaders, leading to a split in that caucus in
the 1990s.[63]

In DC 37, officers are elected by a block-vote system whereby
the two largest of the council's fifty-six locals, 1549 and 372, control 40 percent of the votes. The vote of the local is controlled by its
officers. So, to get elected or reelected, the executive director, who
really has the power, along with other top officers, only needs to
round up these two locals plus one or two more. The patronage,
perks, and mutual support of reelection make this easy. The huge
salaries, in turn, make local reelection common. Thus, an attempt
in 2005 by Roberts's opposition to unseat her failed even though
the reformers won a majority on the executive board, indicating
that a direct vote on top positions might have meant a victory for

the reformers. Similarly, an attempt by the reformers to change the rules and have the top officers elected directly by all members of DC 37 failed because a constitutional change requires a two-thirds vote, which gives the officers of the large and loyal locals the advantage.[64]

The failure of union reform in this wave of opposition was also in part due to the limited views of the reformers themselves in many cases. Most of the insurgencies described above were mounted by local officials or small groups of activists. The vast majority of members remained on the sidelines or simply voted their preference. To buck the structural barriers would require a greater and deeper upheaval, one in which deeper layers of the ranks were players. Apathy, or at least inaction and caution, as well as hierarchical attitudes are ingrained in most of us from childhood. To overcome these requires a strategy more focused on rank-and-file activation and involvement than is often the case. Partly, too, it is easier for dissident activists to just do it themselves. Mobilizing and motivating the members is more difficult, so too often the path of least resistance is taken, hierarchical attitudes inadvertently reinforced, and the reformers are unable to change things dramatically. Finally, even among activists and reformers the motivation is often instrumental: elect new, more honest, militant, crafty leaders and they will deliver the goods. TWU Local 100 is an example of some of these problems.

The core that founded *Hell on Wheels* in 1984 was composed of veterans of the social movements on the 1960s and 1970s, including a few socialists. As two of the leaders of what would become the New Directions caucus in 1988 put it, "We were convinced that the key to the changes we wanted to make in the union was organizing the rank and file, or at least a sizable minority of them, to act on their own behalf, regardless of who was in office."[65] This they pursued through various contract campaigns and direct actions, including slowdowns on the subway system. Faced with frustration as the incumbent leaders delivered one substandard contract after another, more New Directions members began to push for a greater or even sole emphasis on taking power. By the late 1990s, New Directions had a majority of the executive board but still could not control the top officers. As noted above, the incumbent president, Willie James, offered some New Directions members staff positions. A few members took these in the belief they would have more impact on union policy. In fact, they were absorbed into the administration. There were splits, but most importantly New Directions became an organization with two souls: rank-and-file activism, on the one hand, and electoralism, on the other. There is no logical reason for such a separation. No one opposed the idea of taking power in the local, but the issues of timing and circumstance, namely, the need for a larger body of rank-and-file activists and leaders, divided the group.

When New Directions won office in 2000, it was the electoralist wing that dominated. The new president, Roger Toussaint, eventually abolished New Directions. The reform movement that took office fragmented. As is often the case with reform movements that fail, things did not totally return to the bad old days. Had that been the case, the 2005 strike would almost certainly not have happened, but the vision of a democratic local united in resistance to the MTA bosses was lost, at least for the time being. One indication that the urge for reform and democracy was not completely dead was that the contract rejection vote was led by former New Directions activists.[66]

Although this wave of union reform did not succeed in transforming New York's large public-sector unions, the urge for change never completely disappears. Three organizations in New York City encourage and help union reformers keep the spark alive and develop better organization: the Association for Union Democracy (AUD), *Labor Notes,* and the Teamsters for a Democratic Union (TDU). All three are national in scope. AUD has its headquarters in Brooklyn and *Labor Notes* and TDU, while headquartered in Detroit, both maintain offices in the same building as AUD. AUD is the country's oldest union democracy advocacy group, tracing its origins back to the 1960s and Herman Benson's newsletter *Union Democracy in Action.* AUD was set up in 1969, and in 1972 it became an organization with a staff, board of directors, and a little bit of money. TDU was founded in 1976 and *Labor Notes* in 1979. While TDU focuses on Teamster locals, AUD and *Labor Notes* provide education and aid to a variety of reform movements in the New York area. AUD played a role in supporting the successful struggle of the bus drivers in ATU Local 1181, discussed above, while *Labor Notes* staff has worked with reformers in the International Longshoremen's Association, among others. *Labor Notes* publishes a monthly magazine and holds workshops, "schools," and biennial national conferences, attracting about a thousand union activists as well as working with specific reform groups. AUD works directly with reform groups and maintains a national network of union democracy lawyers. It also conducts workshops and holds occasional conferences. As centers of education, advice, and support, neither AUD nor *Labor Notes* can substitute for rank-and-file organization, but they continue to play an important role both nationally and in New York.[67]

If union reform could not turn the balance of forces more to labor's side, neither did electoral politics. As we have seen, the unions in general, even the public-sector unions, seldom if ever presented anything like a united front in city politics. By the late 1990s, the politics of the deal and/or the endorsement from fear dominated the political practice of most of the major public-sector unions. DC 37's endorsement of Bloomberg in exchange for the 1 percent pay increase in 2005 was only the most obvious example.[68] The futility of this approach could be seen not only in the round of public-sector bargaining that dragged into 2006, but in the mayor's tough postelection stance on issues like health care costs and pensions—despite a predicted $3.3 billion surplus by the end of fiscal year 2006.[69] The likelihood of advances through electoral politics are also limited by the general retreat of the Democrats, the disorganization of that party in the city, and the top-down nature of the manner in which most unions intervene in elections. Just as their bureaucratic structures limit leverage in bargaining and render reform efforts by local officials inadequate, so endorsements by top official and executive committees with no reference to the members limit union political functions to giving money to politicians over whom they have no authority. This, of course, is not unique to New York City, but it simply reinforces the passivity of the members and wastes this huge potential force for change.

The only breath of innovation in labor's approach to politics was the formation of the Working Families Party (WFP) in 1998. Several unions, including regions of the CWA, UAW, Steelworkers, and Amalgamated Transit Workers, and locals of UNITE, HERE, and the Teamsters, along with community-based ACORN launched the statewide party "to inject issues important to New York State's working people more forcefully into the statewide political debate," according to CWA District 1 political director Bob Master.[70] New York State is one of the few states whose election laws allows "fusion." This is where a third party is allowed to put a major party candidate on their ballot line. On the one hand, this allows a candidate to receive an endorsement from more than one party. As we have seen, La Guardia, Lindsay, Koch, and Giuliani all used this tactic. On the other hand, it allows a minor party to gain ballot status by the votes it gets from the major party candidate on its line. In New York State, a third party must get fifty thousand votes in a gubernatorial election to get regular ballot status. In most cases, it does this by endorsing a major party candidate for governor. This makes third parties viable pressure groups in New York State. The Working Families Party seldom runs its own candidates and is clearly meant to influence Democratic Party policy and/or pressure for progressive legislation. Its organizers claim that it was central to getting the state legislature to raise the state minimum wage to $7.15 over two years. It did this by putting a high-ranking Republican on its ballot line and helping him win in return for a pledge to work for an increase in the minimum wage. What makes the WFP different from the major parties is that it actually mobilizes union and community activists to go door-to-door campaigning for issues as well as candidates.[71]

So far, however, the WFP has largely stayed clear of New York City, concentrating on suburban and upstate counties and state politics. The major exception to this was WFP's intervention in 2003 in both the judicial and city council elections in Brooklyn.

A scandal involving Brooklyn Democratic boss Clarence Norman led the WFP to run an independent slate of judges in that borough, getting about a third of the votes. In an even more unusual situation involving the council election to replace the murdered councilman, James Davis, Letitia James ran on the WFP and won handily against Davis's brother, a thoroughly incompetent campaigner. WFP also claims a role in some city legislation and in defeating Bloomberg's attempt to do away with partisan elections in a 2003 referendum. So far, however, WFP maintains only one volunteer organizer in all of New York City and has not attempted to become a force in electoral politics there.[72] In any case, with its strategy of endorsing major party candidates, it is hard to see how it can alter the fragmented nature of labor politics in the city or, working primarily as a pressure group representing only a small piece of organized labor, how it can affect the balance of power in the face of business organization and unity.

In 2005, five unions left the AFL-CIO to set up a new federation known as the Change to Win Coalition, later Federation. Led by the SEIU, it included the Carpenters Union, which had already left the AFL-CIO, the merged UNITE-HERE, the Laborers, the Teamsters, the United Food and Commercial Workers, and the United Farm Workers, who joined a little later. It held its founding convention in St. Louis in September 2005.[73] The ostensible reason for the split was the AFL-CIO's undeniable failure to stop its decline by more aggressive organizing. Whatever the national issues, all of the Change to Win (CTW) unions are important in New York City. A split among the unions could lead to raiding one another for members. In any case, the split certainly would not help the problem of disunity that so affected the city's unions. As of April 2006, however, the locals of the CTW unions remained affiliated with the Central Labor Council.[74]

In New York City, in this period, there was a certain amount of new labor organizing, particularly among immigrant workers. Taxi and black car drivers, retail workers, garment workers, and others took the initiative in creating unions where none had existed— ever or for many years. One of the biggest and most successful of these efforts was the New York Taxi Workers Alliance. A model of self-organization, the alliance began as an Asian American advocacy group known as the Lease Drivers Coalition. In early 1998, it became an independent mass-membership organization open to all yellow cab drivers. Barely four months old, on May 13, 1998, it called a strike that brought 24,000 cabbies out for twenty-four hours. The alliance grew to 5,500 dues-paying members, doing much of their recruiting at airport holding pens, but was clearly capable of rousing far more to action. Though it is not affiliated with any official union or with the Central Labor Council, its leaders and members regard it as a union. As we saw earlier, its members are treated as independent contractors and, as a result, have no legal collective bargaining rights or contracts. It has a paid staff of one. Yet it has had a number of successful campaigns. In the wake of 9/11 it got FEMA to grant its members mortgage and rent loans. Its biggest victory came in 2004, when it finally negotiated a fare increase of 26 percent, with 70 percent of the increase going to the drivers.[75]

The twelve thousand drivers of the black cars that serve corporations on a contract basis also organized themselves. Like the yellow cab drivers, they were independent contractors who leased or owned their cars. Most are South Asians, but others come from the Middle East, East Asia, and Central America. Like the yellow cab drivers they are harassed by the Taxi and Limousine Commission. They make between $4 and $6 per hour, working long hours. They began organizing in 1995. Unlike the taxi drivers, however, they approached a union, District 15 of the Machinists. In 1996, they organized their own local, Machinists Lodge 340, with the encouragement of the district. In 1997, the Machinists won an NLRB case declaring the drivers employees. In 1999, they won their first collective bargaining agreement at one of the bigger car services. Nevertheless, the new union faced enormous resistance from the employers and, because so many were Muslims, from the federal government. By 2005, Lodge 340 had about a thousand dues-paying members and an ongoing organizing drive.[76] Other organizing drives initiated in the late 1990s included Mexican workers at greengrocers, first by UNITE Local 169 and then UFCW Local 1500; African grocery store delivery men by United Food and Commercial Workers (UFCW) Local 338; and welfare recipients working in the city's Work Experience Program by ACORN. The Mexican and African immigrants working in and around the grocery stores initiated these drives themselves. The unions came along later and, in the case of the UFCW, locals were not always attentive to the needs of these workers.[77] One of the more ambitious organizing drives was that by SEIU Local 32BJ to organize some sixty thousand security guards across New York State. The drive was kicked off with a rally featuring mostly representatives of other organizations that promised community support for the effort. This was pulled together largely by ACORN. So far, Local 32BJ claims to have two thousand guards as union members.[78] There is even a concerted effort by the IWW to organize Starbucks's countless stores in New York.[79]

Where Community Meets Work

The unions are not the only working-class organizations in the city. Indeed, the city is strewn with organizations of various sorts, many of which touch the lives of working-class residents. The number of ethnic and national organizations is huge, for example. So are the number of private service and advocacy agencies aiding immigrants and other low-wage workers. Of those who voted in the 2004 presidential election, over 10 percent belong to a neighborhood organization, 7.3 percent to a parent-teacher association, and 4.6 percent to a tenants group. The percentages may sound small, but they represent almost a quarter of a million of those voters in neighborhood organizations, well over a hundred thousand in tenant groups. Because these percentages count only voters and, hence, citizens, they exclude the many immigrants active in such groups. Almost three-quarters of these voters lived in the more working-class outer boroughs.[80] To understand the breadth of organization of immigrants in the city a little better, we turn to those groups based in various communities that focus much of their work in the workplaces of their residents. Many of these organizations are called worker centers, either by themselves or by others.

Janice Fine, the leading expert on worker centers, writes:

> Worker centers are defined as community-based and community-led organizations that engage in a combination of service, advocacy, and organizing to provide support to low-wage workers. The vast majority of them have grown up to serve predominantly or exclusively immigrant populations.[81]

These organizations are yet another response to the pressures of globalization, which has sent tens of thousands of new immigrants to New York, and to the industrial shifts that reshaped the city's economy, creating anew a vast low-wage workforce. Much of this restructured workforce was considered either beyond the reach of traditional unionism or beneath the cost-benefit calculations of union leaders. Some of this labor force, however, sought organization to deal with the intolerable terms and conditions of their work. The worker centers were based in communities where these workers tended to both live and work and so organizations with a definite geographic and ethnic reach that dealt with both conditions of life and work made sense. The objects of their activities that are most characteristic of workers centers are housing and work itself.

The oldest of the centers date back to the late 1970s and early 1980s, but most are more recent. Nationally, one count found that in 1992 there were five such organizations. By 2005 they numbered at least 139, more if the definition is broadened somewhat. The New York metropolitan area encompasses at least twenty-three of them; the city alone has sixteen.[82] The oldest existing worker center in New York City is, by most accounts, the Chinese Staff and Workers' Association (CSWA). Founded in 1979, it came out of an effort by waiters in Chinatown restaurants to organize themselves into HERE Local 69 in 1978. Local 69, however, ignored the waiters, who eventually turned to the new Chinese Staff and Workers' Association. Perhaps ironically, the CSWA went on to organize an independent union at the New Silver Palace, one of Chinatown's largest restaurants. In 1980, they won a contract and soon workers at other restaurants were organizing independent unions with the help of the CSWA.[83]

Most of the workplaces that worker centers focus on are not large or prosperous enough to make unionization feasible—at least on a shop-by-shop basis. Nor do the centers have the resources to take on these industries—retail, garment, and entertainment—on a city-wide basis. The most typical activity in relation to the workplace is winning unpaid back wages and overtime pay. CSWA did this at garment shops in Chinatown. Make the Road by Walking, a worker center in the largely Latino Bushwick section of Brooklyn, helped Latina garment workers in the neighborhood's tiny sweatshops build their own organization, Trabajadores en Acción. Its members were not concentrated in any particular shops and could not function as a union. If they had tried, the shop would no doubt have closed down and relocated elsewhere in the city. What Make the Road and Trabajadores en Acción did was pressure various agencies or go to court to enforce state and national wages and hours legislation and win back wages and overtime pay. In this they were very successful, winning over $200,000 in unpaid wages by late 2002.[84]

In the newer immigrant communities work and housing are intimately related and almost always substandard. Thus, housing is another issue taken up by worker centers like CSWA, Make the Road, and others. In the Bronx, the Northwest Bronx Community and Clergy Coalition took on the problem of scatter-site housing for the homeless. The scatter-site program, discussed in Chapter 5, not only cost the city hundreds of millions, but provided seriously substandard housing for homeless families. The coalition worked with both homeless and long-term residents to draw the city's attention to this scandal.[85] It is quite likely that this campaign led the city to finally begin cutting back on this program.

While most worker centers are based in specific ethnic neighborhoods, the Restaurant Opportunities Center was based on that industry and specifically the experience of 9/11. When the twin towers came down, 70 workers at the Windows on the World restaurant were killed and 250 displaced. They had been members of HERE Local 100, but their jobs were gone. With help from Local 100, they set up the Restaurant Opportunities Center (ROC) as a temporary self-help project. Instead, it turned into a permanent workers center doing for restaurant workers outside the union what worker centers do elsewhere—win back pay, get displaced workers jobs, etc. They reached well beyond former Windows on the World workers, working with other workers centers and groups to improve conditions in the nonunion part of the industry. After a number of years acting as a cooperative caterer, the center succeeded in setting up its own cooperative restaurant, Colors.[86]

Worker centers are an important addition to working-class organization in New York, but like the unions they have their limits and structural problems. First, they are small. Most of those that are membership groups have five hundred or fewer members. Perhaps more important is the matter of social power. Steve Jenkins, who was an organizer for Make the Road, argued that shared injustice does not necessarily mean shared social power. Unlike unions, the centers cannot stop production. They can exercise social power through rent strikes or civil disobedience, but their power over workplace issues, which is a major focus and purpose, is limited to appealing to governmental units or agencies and other elite institutions. Whether lobbying city hall for housing improvements or going to the courts or state agencies for back pay, there is a strong tendency for the workers to be dependent on professionals—organizers, lawyers, etc. Most of these centers are also dependent on foundation grants, which means dependency on the priorities of foundation officials and boards and on those who are best at writing grant proposals. Thus, community-based groups tend to be dependent on staffers who are frequently, though not exclusively, drawn from the educated middle class. Biju Mathew of the Taxi Workers Alliance holds an even harsher critique of these organizations. He writes, " 'Communities' in the CBO [community-based organization] world are not organized communities, but at worst tokens for the self-perpetuation of the activist class, and at best occasionally mobilized groups of people."[87] While this seems overly negative, it points to the problem of who really directs these organizations when skill often substitutes for mass social power.

Viewed only in the terms in which worker centers and similar community-based groups define themselves and act today, these limits are real. But it is possible that in a period of more general social upsurge they can become a source of broader mobilization. The power of the poor, as most past upheavals show, lies in three areas: the disruption of business as usual; organization into and/or alliance with other working-class organizations, notably unions; and political action by virtue of numbers. The first is the traditional recourse of the poor, whether in the form of urban disorder, concerted civil disobedience, rent strikes, even mass workplace strikes. The 1960s provide many examples of this. The second, unionization or alliances with unions, is trickier. There is a history of tension between many worker centers and unions they have tried to work with. As one ROC leader put it in terms of the HERE, the union "seems to have trouble letting go."[88] Bureaucratic unions don't like sharing power with risky or unfamiliar groups. Yet there are also many examples of cooperation between the two. And while many unions prefer to ignore low-wage workers, many of the recent gains have in fact been among low-wage workers with no central workplace, such as home health care workers in New York as well as in California. Once again, the context is crucial and periods of more general resistance and upsurge offer greater possibilities. We are, after all, talking about a situation in which the unions themselves go through some major changes.

Finally, in terms of political action, worker centers would seem to have exactly what is needed to reintroduce grassroots politics, this time on a class basis, namely a geographic base and a core of activists. If, indeed, most have around five hundred members and insofar as these members are really a core of community/workplace activists, they can compose a potentially significant force—city-wide, taken together, this would be about seven thousand activists. In a city where as much as 30 percent of the electorate are foreign-born, immigrants have considerable potential to exercise power.

The main problem has been that this 30 percent represents many different groups with distinct identities, as do the worker centers.[89] But it is precisely the potential of the centers for coalescing these identities that makes them a potential class political force—if we understand that class is not a monochrome phenomenon. As it stands, most worker centers have nonprofit 501(c)3 status for funding purposes, which prevents them from engaging directly in electoral work. The simple separation of the workers organizations, for example, Tabajadores en Acción from Make the Road, could get around this. In any case, it is usually the stated goal of most worker centers to create independent worker organizations. Sensing the power of coalition and the potential for rapid growth under changed circumstances, a struggle for more independence is likely to arise anyway. There is also, of course, a matter of just what sort of politics would allow for such changes. Certainly not the essentially corrupted, money-driven, fragmented city politics as is. Certainly not the politics of endorsement and deal currently practiced by the unions. Two things should be noted concerning political organization among immigrants. While there are immigrant political associations connected to the Democratic Party, there is not the sort of neighborhood level clientelist organization that the old machines provided and that tied earlier immigrants to the Democratic Party. Second, as Lorraine Minnite found from voting surveys, "Noteworthy is the weaker connection to partisanship among immigrants compared to native-born voters."[90] Weaker still are such partisan ties, we can assume, among the newest immigrants, who tend to be the base of the worker centers. The potential for some form of independent politics down the road seems real if not inevitable.

To the worker centers we would have to add the countless organizations, some permanent, some temporary, that have focused on housing, either by resisting gentrification or development; pressuring for low-cost housing, rent control, and other issues of housing affordability; or dealing with specific landlords. The Metropolitan Council on Housing, for example, is the oldest of the advocacy groups for affordable housing. There are homeless advocacy groups, notably the Coalition for the Homeless. More activist in ori-entation are the many neighborhood groups that arise in working-class areas to resist gentrification, upscale development, or the destruction of cheap housing. The Lower East Side of Manhattan provides some examples of such organizations. Groups like the Met Council and Good Old Lower East Side organized rent strikes and other actions meant to keep housing in that rapidly gentrifying area within the range of the still large lower-income population. In the 1980s and beyond, there were squatter movements in the Lower East Side and South Bronx. Other groups arose more re-cently, some mentioned in Chapter 6, to fight the destruction of neighborhoods and affordable housing as development reached areas like Williamsburg in Brooklyn or Hell's Kitchen in Manhat-tan. Typically, as we saw in the case of the Atlantic Yards develop-ment project in the previous chapter, local groups are able to win some concessions from the city, state, and/or developer, but are not able to stop the transformation of their area, much less of the city as a whole. As William Sites put it, "In New York alone, there was a surge of neighborhood-based organizing in many areas of Manhat-tan, the Bronx, and Brooklyn, much of it (as in the Lower East Side) producing certain useful community-based housing initia-tives without registering strong impacts on development policies or the larger transformation of the city."[91] Still, as we saw above, over one hundred thousand New Yorkers belong to some sort of tenants organization.

Because nearly half of the city's workforce is foreign-born, im-migrants play a special role in recent developments in many unions and communities. But their potential as leaders of upheaval must also be seen at both the global and the national context. As many writers on the role of immigrants in unionization drives, such as the famous Justice for Janitors victory in California in the early 1990s, immigrant activists often come with more political back-ground, training, and experience than native-born workers. They come from troubled nations where they have played a part in polit-ical events and organizations. Their view is often more global. The current activists among them are often connected to national networks dealing with immigrant rights. The AFL-CIO and most of its affiliates, including those now in the Change to Win Federation, adopted a more positive attitude toward immigrant rights in 1999 and in 2003 supported the Immigrant Workers Freedom Ride. This was a national effort actively supported by several unions, consciously taking the name of the heroic actions of the civil rights era. It was not by accident that this national march ended in New York with a rally of thousands in Queens.[92]

But the events that showed the power and potential of immigrant workers in New York came on April 1 and April 10, 2006. On April 1 tens of thousands of mostly Latino immigrants marched across the Brooklyn Bridge to rally in opposition to proposed national legislation to criminalize undocumented workers and build a two-thousand-mile wall along the U.S.-Mexico border. This was part of a nationwide outpouring of millions of immigrants in rallies, marches, and work stoppages that ran from March 25 through April 10—half a million in Los Angeles, three hundred thousand in Chicago, one hundred thousand in Phoenix, and many more. On April 10, a second demonstration in New York attracted 125,000 according to its organizers. This march drew together many immigrant groups. *Village Voice* writer Sarah Ferguson described the scene: "The streets of downtown were a United Nations of Central and South Americans, Caribbeans, Filipinos, Koreans, Somalians, Senegalese, Pakastanis, Bangladeshis, and a smattering of Europeans—all rallying to the cry of 'legalization not criminalization.' "[93] Clearly, immigrants showed themselves to be a political force with considerable mobilizing power in New York and around the nation.

The New York City Working Class Today

The city's working class presents a picture of fragmentation and weakness. It is tempting to compare this state of affairs unfavorably to that which prevailed from the 1940s through the early

1970s. In 2005 the only strike with disruptive power was the three-day transit strike in December. In 1945 and 1946 a series of strikes disrupted the city for almost two years. The groups of workers who conducted those speak much about what has changed. First, the elevator operators brought the central business districts to a halt in September 1945. Next came a wildcat strike by the longshoremen. Then came the tugboat operators. Each of these strikes had enormous disruptive power.[94] Then there were the mass rallies for progressive causes, one after another, at Madison Square Garden, described by Joshua Freeman in his *Working-Class New York*. Also in 1945 there was a twenty-three-member city council with two members from the American Labor Party, two from the rival Liberal Party, two Communists, five Republicans, and twelve Democrats; this was possible not only because of the extent of left-wing labor organization, but because of the proportional representation electoral setup that prevailed from 1936 through the 1945 election. In that last year, the candidate with the most votes was Mike Quill, the president of the Transport Workers Union, running on the American Labor Party line.[95] This was the moment when the city hit its peak as the largest industrial center in the country, but it was also the dawn of the Cold War, which would wipe away much of the radical political culture of the city.

In any case, such a comparison misses the larger point that social classes change in composition and outlook as the economy that shapes them changes. So, if the elevator operators, longshoremen, and tugboat operators are mostly gone, other groups of organized workers, on a scale hardly imaginable then, have arisen. The 1960s was the moment of transition in which the new workers of color who were becoming a majority of the city's public and private workforce got organized. From that era came new giants like 1199, DC 37, and Teamsters Local 237, while others, like TWU Local 100, experienced a transition from their old white ethnic base to one of black and Latino workers. Today's 1 million union members are far more diverse and representative of the direction of the country than New York's older ethnic groups. The 1940s, which seemed to be the pinnacle of working-class culture and radicalism in the United States, was in fact the end of a period. The 1960s would revive in different forms the struggle to make New York a social democratic polity, expanding access to some of the old public institutions and creating a new, though highly imperfect, set of community-based institutions. Today, new community-based institutions arise where the old ones atrophied or were abolished. And despite their limitations, the worker centers, tenants groups, and neighborhood organizations, involving more than three hundred thousand people, are more independent than the publicly funded and dependent community groups of the 1960s. So a simple comparison with the past fails to tell us much about the potential of the city's working class to reverse the course set by the business elite and permanent government since the mid-1970s. One aspect of assessing such potential is to look more closely at the conditions that working-class people in New York face after thirty years of developmentalism.

For all the differences in income and circumstance, all groups of working-class people in New York City saw their real hourly wages fall from 2000 to 2005. As Table 7-4 shows, women did worse than men, blacks and Latinos worse than whites. Only employees with a college degree or more made gains, indicating that what we can broadly take to be middle- and upper-middle-class employees were able to ride the tide of rising incomes in financial and business services. Women, blacks, and Latinos not only did worse, but the ratio of their wages to those of whites fell in this period: women, from 88 percent of male wages in 2000 to 86 percent in 2005; blacks, from 73 percent to 71 percent of whites in those years; and Latinos, from 61 percent to 55 percent. Looking at the five-year average of the same period, the wage premium of native-born workers over immigrants was $4.23 an hour or 34.9 percent—and immigrants composed 48 percent of the workforce by 2005.[96] These figures reflect both the shift of work toward low-wage service sector jobs and the fact the huge immigrant workforce, along with many native-born people of color, were trapped in these growing sectors. To this

TABLE 7-4
Real median hourly wages, 2000–5

Demographic	First Half 2000	First Half 2005	% Change
All NYC resident workers	$15.13	$14.40	−4.8
Males	$16.59	$15.42	−7.1
Female	$14.55	$13.23	−9.1
White	$19.16	$18.16	−5.2
Black (non-Latino)	$13.97	$12.85	−8.0
Latino	$11.64	$10.00	−14.1
High school	$13.30	$12.00	−9.8
College degree or higher	$23.28	$23.85	2.4

Source: Fiscal Policy Institute, *New York City's Labor Market Outlook, with a Special Emphasis on Immigrant Workers*, December 9, 2005, 6.

must be added the growing share of this declining income that must go to pay for housing, as we saw in earlier chapters.

Declining living standards in a city of vast wealth are bound to bring some sort of reaction. If, in fact, the city's working-class majority, including the now huge proportion of immigrants, were simply a disorganized mass of competing individuals, the prospects might be grim. But, in fact, there is a great deal of organization beneath the skyline of the city. Most have problems and leadership is still weak and in retreat. But recurring efforts from below, in both unions and communities, reveal a potential for greater changes and resistance. Furthermore, U.S. history is marked by upsurges that change the political agenda. There is a sort of debate over how, not if or when, another period of social upheaval might emerge. In his book *The Next Upsurge: Labor and the New Social Movements*, Dan Clawson argues for some combination of new types of organizing coming out of the (now not so new) social movements, community-based worker groups, and changes within the unions that converge at some point in time. Immanuel Ness doubts this and roots a possible upsurge more in rank-and-file rebellion and self-activity, particularly among immigrant workers.[97] The incredible immigrant worker demonstrations of March and April 2006 lend credibility to that possibility. No one knows when, or even if, such an upsurge will come, but if American history is a reliable guide, a major challenge to the neoliberal agenda on a national scale seems likely. If that happens, no matter where it starts, it will sweep over the islands that compose the global city.

Conclusion:
Neoliberal Triumph

In the three decades since the fiscal crisis, New York has been transformed politically, industrially, economically, demographically, and physically. The city could boast of increased tourism, a larger population with greater diversity, a rising skyline, falling crime rates, and a cultural life that was the glittering jewel in the global crown. But New York was not only the global city, it was now the neoliberal city, the city that the business elite had pushed for in earnest since 1975. Perhaps a symbol of the changing atmosphere of the city was the crisis faced by that long-standing critic of political corruption and excessive wealth, the *Village Voice*. As if to imitate the larger business world, the *Voice*'s parent company, Village Voice Media, merged with the more mainstream New Times Media in early 2006. Almost immediately, the change in editorial policy became clear when investigative reporter Jim Ridgeway was fired. The new boss, Michael Lacey, made it clear that there had been enough Bush-bashing and political opinion. Twenty *Voice* employees signed a letter demanding Ridgeway's return. Seventeen employees eventually quit to protest what they saw as the watering-down of the *Voice*'s traditionally dissident stance. By mid-2006 it appeared that New York would lose its one militant voice against the neoliberal direction of the city.[1] In the meantime, the new political and economic agenda rolled along.

Concentrated executive power has always been a goal of New

York's business elite and by and large it has been solidified since the crisis regime of 1975. Political power rests overwhelmingly with the mayor, providing a clearer focal point for the organizations of the elite, their lobbyists, their money, and themselves both during election time and throughout the year. The centrality of the mayor's office in turn limited the influence of working- and lower-middle-class communities over the allocation of resources, land use, and all the policies that affected jobs, incomes, and housing. Mayoral candidates were not dependent on whatever remained of the Democratic Party, one reason for twenty years of Republican mayors. Money drove mayoral elections just as it did those for other high offices. The Democrats no longer had a central place, such as the old Board of Estimate, where the borough presidents served as representatives of the county organizations and could cut deals. The city council was, in fact if not in the wording of the charter, weaker than ever. Some of this was due to the terms limits introduced in 1993, much of it to the permanent alliance of the mayor, regardless of party, with the business elite, its policy/pressure organizations, and the hangers-on that composed the new permanent government. So there was seldom any political barrier to the developmental agenda.

Economically the city looked more like what the leaders and backers of the crisis regime had wanted thirty years ago, the Rockefellers half a century ago, and the Regional Plan Association as far back as 1929.[2] Some of these changes, to be sure, were the result of larger national and worldwide trends, but much of what made New York so strikingly different from the rest the country was the outcome of elite pressure, city politics, and an incredibly wealthy capitalist class able to direct the development of the city's built environment. The number of persons on public assistance, a major elite *bête noir*, had fallen from over 1 million in 1996 to just over 400,000 in 2005. While this would have happened as a result of national legislation passed in 1996, the Giuliani administration had introduced its own workfare program, the Work Experience Program, in 1995. In fact, the welfare rolls dropped by about sixty thousand people before the national welfare reform act would have been in effect.[3] The city's labor market was also transformed. Whereas in 1969 there had been 1.4 million blue-collar jobs in manufacturing, construction, transportation, and utilities, making up 40 percent of the workforce, in 2005 there were only 341,402, less than 10 percent of all jobs. The labor market was now dominated by low-wage service jobs, many supporting the lifestyles of the old and new rich, on the one hand, and very high paying professional and executive jobs, on the other. Wall Street "produced" far more wealth with almost the same number of employees. In real terms, Manhattan, the heart of the city's export economy, produced almost twice the gross product it had in 1983 and two and a half times what the outer boroughs produced.[4]

Fiscally, the city conformed to the 1975–79 recommendations of the MAC, TCCF, and various elite policy groups. For one thing, in 2005 and 2006, it showed a budget surplus, although this was always shaky.[5] On the tax front, the real estate tax had fallen from 50 percent of the city tax levy in the 1970s and over 40 percent in the 1980s to just over 30 percent by fiscal year 2005. Taxes of all business income, which had risen during the 1980s from about 11 percent of total tax-levy revenues in the early 1970s to 17 percent by 1990, were back down to 11 percent in 2005. Even the commercial occupancy tax had fallen as a proportion of the total, from just over 3 percent in the 1970s and 4 percent in the 1980s to little more than 1 percent of city revenues in 2005. The personal income tax, which rose as a percentage during the 1980s to 17 percent in 1990 was down to 16 percent by the time Michael Bloomberg was reelected mayor.[6] All of this despite the phenomenal rise in property values and high incomes over this long period. On top of this, of course, the city's big businesses, developers, and wealthy property owners receive the lion's share of the more than $3 billion in annual tax expenditures, a practice that didn't really take off until the 1970s but which has become a fixture of urban policy across the country.[7]

The expenditure side of the city's annual budgets was, if anything, even better from the developmentalist point of view. The redistributive functions (welfare, social services, health, and housing) had dropped from a high of 35.8 percent of both expense and capital budget spending (minus debt service) in 1969 and 30 percent by 1989 to just 22 percent in fiscal year 2005. Spending for developmental functions (infrastructure and transportation) had been 11.2 percent of the total in 1975 and fell after that, but by 2005 it was up to an average of 12 percent or more during Bloomberg's first term. Spending on education fell from 29 percent of expenditures in the late 1960s through 1975 to 24 percent in 2005, despite all the rhetoric about the need for improved education. Much of the decline was accounted for by the drop in spending on higher education, i.e., CUNY, which fell from 4.5 percent of the total in 1975 to less than 1 percent in 2005. In part this was because the state had assumed staff costs at the four-year colleges, but also because of the introduction of tuition and its constant rise in recent years—a longtime demand of the business elite and an increased burden on the working class.[8] The city's total labor costs, next to welfare the biggest target of business pressure, had also fallen as a percentage of total spending from about 53 percent in 1975 to 45 percent in 2005.[9]

Over the three decades since the fiscal crisis, the city's upper classes had done extremely well. To be sure, they took a hit during the recession that stretched from 2000 into 2003, when total salaries paid in the securities industry fell from $46.1 billion to $37.8 billion and bonuses slumped from $19.5 billion to $8.6 billion.[10] But bonuses were already rising in 2003, and as we saw in Chapter 6, incomes and bonuses were up again in 2004. We also saw that by 2005, the top 20 percent of Manhattan earners made fifty-two times what the bottom 20 percent earned and, of course, the top 1 percent made many times more. To put that in context, in 1980 the top fifth made twenty-one times that of the lowest fifth.[11] So, in the borough that housed much of the financial and business service elite, income inequality had grown by two and a half times in twenty-five years. As we saw, property values grew through bust and boom. Rents on commercial property in all Manhattan central business districts did drop from late 2000 to the third quarter of 2003, but then began to rise again. The cost of buying a one-, two-, or three-family home was projected to rise by 95.6 percent from

2000 through 2005, despite the construction of such units in Brooklyn and Queens. Residential rents, as we also saw, just rose and rose. The annual inflation rate for housing in New York City (4.1 percent) was almost twice that of the nation (2.2 percent) in 2003 and 2004, pushed as it was by rapid upscale development.[12] While all of this was bad news for most New Yorkers, it was obviously good news for landlords, developers, speculators, bankers, and the others who profit from rising property values.

The neoliberal triumph was not complete. The city still had a public health care delivery system unlike any other American city. It had not been sold off to the private hospitals as some had advocated, Giuliani among them. Though tuition at CUNY continued to rise and drive away lower-income students, it remained the largest urban university system in the country. The huge 24/7 transit system was still public and the MTA producing a surplus, though often denying it. Also, the city's million-member unions had not disappeared or even shrunk as a proportion of the workforce as they had elsewhere. Indeed, they could still show the potential power they had from time to time, as in the 2005 transit strike or the threatened April 2006 strike of 28,000 doormen serving a million well-to-do New Yorkers in 3,500 buildings. So palpable was that threat that it led the Realty Advisory Board on Labor Relations, the industry's bargaining arm, to concede to a major union demand for a raise.[13] And, from time to time, the city's giant labor movement could also wrangle some political victories. These included the living wage law of 2001, covering about one hundred thousand workers, and the sizable increase in the state minimum wage to $7.15 by 2007.[14]

Nevertheless, the victory of real estate over welfare state was great enough to make the problem of poverty more severe in New York than in the country as a whole (see Table C-1). In 1975, in the depth of a worldwide recession and the city's fiscal crisis, 15 percent, or a little more than a million New Yorkers, were poor by the official measure. In 2005, after two or three years of economic growth, about 1.8 million people in New York were officially poor.

TABLE C-1
Poverty rates, United States and New York City, 2003–4

	U.S.	NYC
White (non-Latino)	8.5%	12.9%
Black (non-Latino)	24.8%	28.8%
Latino (any race)	22.5%	29.4%
Citizen	12.2%	23.1%
Not a citizen	21.8%	23.9%

Source: Community Service Society of New York, September 2005.

That is a poverty rate of 22 percent, about twice the national rate and well above that of 1975.

One dubious explanation is that New York has more of the kinds of persons who are likely to be poor in America—blacks, Latinos, immigrants. But even this doesn't explain the extent of poverty in the neoliberal city because all of these groups also have higher poverty rates in New York than nationally. Even the rate among whites is 50 percent above the national level.

Nor was this disparity simply a consequence of the city's higher-than-average unemployment rate and percentage of those no longer in the labor market. Fully 86 percent of poor households surveyed for the Community Service Society of New York in 2005 had a working member.[15] The basic problem, as we have argued elsewhere, is that the labor market that had developed as a result of the intersection of broader national and global trends with local policies simply paid too little to bring people out of poverty even when the economy grew and jobs were created. Poverty is now embedded in the structure of the city's economy. Even the passage of a city living wage law and the increase in the state minimum wage, though helping many, cannot change the dismal reality of the city's low-wage labor market. The result goes beyond the official poverty rate: another 1.6 million New Yorkers live near poverty, with incomes under twice the official level. Some 42 percent of the population live in or on the edge of poverty—in one of the richest cities in the world—and they pay a higher proportion of those poverty wages on housing than people in the rest of the country.[16]

Power, Not Program

What, then, is to be done? What could challenge, much less over-come, the enormous power of New York's business elite and its mayoral alliance? In their 1977 book about the roots and realities of the fiscal crisis, Jack Newfield and Paul Du Brul concluded with an elaborate program for turning the city around in such a way as to favor the majority over the "permanent government." It was a fine program, and while some of it is dated, much is still relevant. It is similar to more recent proposals for turning things around, for ex-ample, from historian Mike Wallace in *A New Deal for New York*.[17] The problem was that Newfield and Du Brul, like Wallace, could not offer much in the way of strategy or even concrete organiza-tional steps toward winning such a program. Programs, no matter how good, do not attract a mass following by themselves. Knowing this, Newfield and Du Brul offered the following glimmer of hope:

> The most important lesson we have learned, as political citi-zens, is this: Reform—change for the better—comes only when movements of common people rally around an idea and create new leaders from the bottom up. Movements of ordinary people, acting out of self-interest, can write law. The moral authority of exemplary action can change lives.[18]

The movement they hoped for didn't arrive or arise in the decades since they wrote. There have been exemplary actions, resistance all along, and even moments of great social outpouring. But a move-ment with the power to "write law" or make "change for the better" on a scale big enough to reverse the neoliberal agenda has yet to burst on the scene. Yet, as we have seen, there are the ele-ments of such a movement gathering beneath the city's skyline: from neighborhood real estate resisters to immigrant-based worker centers, from union dissidents to dissident unions, new leaders learn and the flammable stuff of a working-class social movement accumulates.

Social movements can make the costs of peace for one or another sector of the mayoral-business alliance high enough to win concessions: To put it on the defensive, force it to retreat, and wring concessions from it, much less break it up somewhere down the line, however, will require the sort of disruptive mass movement we haven't seen for some time. Mass self-activity changes lives and consciousnesses. What seems unthinkable today becomes common sense tomorrow. If and when this process accelerates, for it is always there in embryo, it just might change the face of New York once again. And it may not stop there.

NOTES

Introduction: The Neoliberal Transformation of New York City

1. George Lankevich, *American Metropolis: A History of New York City* (New York: New York University Press, 1998), 259.

2. Ira Katznelson, *City Trenches: Urban Politics and the Patterning of Class in the United States* (Chicago: University of Chicago Press, 1981), 45–49; Thomas Bender, *The Unfinished City: New York and the Metropolitan Idea* (New York: The New Press, 2001), *passim*; Lankevich, *American Metropolis*, 259.

3. Martin Shefter, *Political Crisis/Fiscal Crisis: The Collapse and Revival of New York City* (New York: Columbia University Press, 1992), 13–37.

4. Ibid., 20.

5. Joshua Freeman, *Working-Class New York: Life and Labor Since World War II* (New York: The New Press, 2000), 55–71.

6. See ibid., 179–255; Shefter, *Political Crisis/Fiscal Crisis*, 41–81; François Weil, *A History of New York* (New York: Columbia University Press, 2004), 259–85 for progressive accounts; Roger Starr, *The Rise and Fall of New York City* (New York: Basic Books, 1985), *passim*, for a conservative interpretation; Robert Fitch, *The Assassination of New York* (London: Verso, 1993), *passim*, for an account of how the city's elite pushed manufacturing out.

7. *New York Times*, September 4, 2005, www.nytimes.com; Lawrence Mishel, Jared Bernstein, and Sylvia Allegretto, *The State of Working America 2004/2005* (Ithaca, NY: ILR Press, 2005), 67.

1: The Crisis in Context

1. Organization for Economic Cooperation and Development, *Historical Statistics, 1995 Edition* (Paris: OECD, 1995), 154, 176; Ernest Mandel, *The Second Slump* (London: NLB, 1978), 14–21, 68–77.

2. Council of Economic Advisers, *Economic Report of the President, 2002* (Washington, DC: U.S. Government Printing Office, 2002), 333, 380, 381, 370, 372, 426.

3. Asher Arian, Arthur Goldberg, John Mollenkopf, and Edward Rogowsky, *Changing New York City Politics* (New York: Routledge, 1991), 2; Roger Sanjek, *The Future of Us All: Race and Neighborhood Politics in New York City* (Ithaca, NY: Cornell University Press, 1998), 142–43.

4. Martin Mayer, *The Bankers* (New York: Weybright and Talley, 1974), 3–21.

5. Ibid., 531.

6. Jerry Markham, *A Financial History of the United States*, vol. III (Armonk, NY: M.E. Sharpe, 2002), 18.

7. David Harvey, *A Brief History of Neoliberalism* (New York: Oxford University Press, 2005), 27.

8. Eric Darton, *Divided We Stand: A Biography of New York's World Trade Center* (New York: Basic Books, 1999), 174.

9. Council of Economic Advisers, *Economic Report of the President, 2002*, 430.

10. Phillip Zweig, *Wriston: Walter Wriston, Citibank, and the Rise and Fall of American Financial Supremacy* (New York, Crown Publishers, 1995), 476; Mayer, *Bankers*, 325.

11. Saskia Sassen, *The Global City: New York, London, Tokyo* (Princeton, NJ: Princeton University Press, 1991).

12. P.J. Taylor, G. Catalano, and D.R.F. Walker, "Measurement of the World City Network," *Urban Studies* 39, no. 13 (2002): 2367–72.

13. Matthew Drennan, "The Local Economy and Local Revenues," in *Setting Municipal Priorities: American Cities and the New York Experience*, ed. Charles Brecher and Raymond D. Horton (New York: New York University Press, 1984), 44–58.

14. Weil, *History of New York*, 262 (see intro., n. 6).

15. Darton, *Divided We Stand*, 20.

16. Jean-Paul Rodrigue, "The Port Authority of New York and New Jersey: Global Changes, Regional Gains, and Local Challenges in Port Development," *Les Cahiers scientifiques du transport* (Paris), February 2004, 6–7.

17. Temporary Commission on City Finances, *The City in Transition: Prospects and Policies for New York: The Final Report of the TCCF*, New York, June 1977, 148 (henceforth TCCF, *Final Report*).

18. Fitch, *Assassination of New York*, 280 (see intro., n. 6).

19. TCCF, *Final Report*, 58–59.

20. Drennan, "Local Economy," 47, 54, 56.

21. Matthew Drennan, "The Local Economy and Local Revenues," in *Setting Municipal Priorities, 1981*, ed. Charles Brecher and Raymond D. Horton (Montclair, NJ: Allanheld Osmun, 1980), 33.

22. Charles Brecher and Raymond D. Horton, with Robert A. Cropf, *Power*

Failure: New York City Politics and Policy Since 1960 (New York: Oxford University Press, 1993), 7; Drennan, "Local Economy" (1984), 56–58.

23. TCCF, *Final Report*, 148.

24. Weil, *History of New York*, 262–63.

25. Robert Brenner, *The Boom and the Bubble: The U.S. in the World Economy* (London: Verso, 2002), 7–49.

26. Kim Moody, *Workers in a Lean World: Unions in the International Economy* (London: Verso, 1997), 119–23.

27. Sidney M. Milkis and Michael Nelson, *The American Presidency: Origins and Development, 1776–2002*, 4th ed. (Washington, DC: CQ Press, 2003), 326–29.

28. Thomas Byrne Edsall, *The New Politics of Inequality* (New York: W.W. Norton, 1984), 128–29.

29. Thomas Ferguson and Joel Rogers, *Right Turn: The Decline of the Democrats and the Future of American Politics* (New York: Hill and Wang, 1986), 100–113; Kim Moody, *An Injury to All: The Decline of American Unionism* (London: Verso, 1988), 127–35; Edsall, *New Politics of Inequality*, 120–29.

30. Robert Pecorella, *Community Power in a Postmodern City: Politics in New York City* (Armonk, NY: M.E. Sharpe, 1994), 54–55; Robert Caro, *The Power Broker: Robert Moses and the Fall of New York* (New York: Vintage Books, 1975), 361–63, 345–46, 451–54, *passim*.

31. Freeman, *Working-Class New York*, 55–71, 104–42 (see intro., n. 5).

32. Dan Clawson, *The Next Upsurge: Labor and the New Social Movements* (Ithaca, NY: ILR Press, 2003), 38.

33. Harvey, *Brief History of Neoliberalism*, 44–48.

34. Wallace S. Sayre and Herbert Kaufman, *Governing New York City: Politics in the Metropolis* (New York: W.W. Norton, 1965).

35. Ester R. Fuchs, *Mayors and Money: Fiscal Policy in New York and Chicago* (Chicago: University of Chicago Press, 1992), 214–25.

36. Richard Wade, "The Withering Away of the Party System," in *Urban Politics, New York Style*, ed. Jewel Bellush and Dick Netzer (Armonk, NY: M.E. Sharpe, 1990), 271–94; John H. Mollenkopf, *A Phoenix in the Ashes: The Rise and Fall of the Koch Coalition in New York City Politics* (Princeton, NJ: Princeton University Press, 1992), 80; Pecorella, *Community Power*, 32–34.

37. Mollenkopf, *Phoenix in the Ashes*, 76–80.

38. Shefter, *Political Crisis/Fiscal Crisis*, 99.

39. Jack Newfield and Paul Du Brul, *The Abuse of Power: The Permanent Government and the Fall of New York* (New York: Viking Press, 1977), 206.

40. Fuchs, *Mayors and Money*, 242–43; Jewell Bellush, "Clusters of Power: Interest Groups," in *Urban Politics*, 296–334.

41. Fuchs, *Mayors and Money*, 242.

42. Charles V. Hamilton, "Needed, More Foxes: The Black Experience," in *Urban Politics*, 359–83.

43. Mollenkopf, *Phoenix in the Ashes*, 72–92.

44. Freeman, *Working-Class New York*, 179–200.

45. Frances Fox Piven and Richard Cloward, *Poor People's Movements: Why They Succeed, How They Fail* (New York: Vintage Books, 1979), 288–308.

46. Katznelson, *City Trenches*, 143 (see intro., n. 2).

47. Robert W. Bailey, *The Crisis Regime: The MAC, the EFCB, and the Political Impact of the New York City Financial Crisis* (Albany: State University of New York Press, 1984), 40–41, 110–11.

48. Freeman, *Working-Class New York*, 255.

49. Joan Weitzman, *City Workers and Fiscal Crisis: Cutbacks, Givebacks, and Survival* (New Brunswick, NJ: Institute of Management and Labor Relation, Rutgers, 1979), 26–31, 53–58; Jewel Bellush and Bernard Bellush, *Union Power and New York: Victor Gotbaum and District Council 37* (New York: Praeger, 1984), 227; Mark H. Maier, *City Unions: Managing Discontent in New York City* (New Brunswick, NJ: Rutgers University Press, 1987), 112.

50. Bellush and Bellush, *Union Power*, 239–67.

51. Freeman, *Working-Class New York*, 225.

52. Bellush and Bellush, *Union Power*, 266–68, 438–46.

53. Freeman, *Working-Class New York*, 206–98; Bellush and Bellush, *Union Power*, 225–34.

54. Sassen, *Global City*, 90–125; Manuel Castells, *The Information City: Information Technology, Economic Restructuring, and the Urban Regional Process* (Oxford: Blackwell, 1989), 343.

55. Drennan, "Local Economy" (1984), 48.

56. Sanjek, *Future of Us All*, 31–35.

57. Sayre and Kaufman, *Governing New York City*, 503–8; Bellush, "Clusters of Power," 297–99.

58. Shefter, *Political Crisis/Fiscal Crisis*, 24.

59. Mollenkopf, *Phoenix in the Ashes*, 92–94; Bellush, "Clusters of Power," 296–334.

60. Drennan, "Local Economy" (1984), 45.

61. Ibid., 44–58.

62. Castells, *Information City*, 343.

63. Sassen, *Global City*, 90–110; Castells, *Information City*, 338–47. Producer services include finances and telecommunication as well as legal, engineering, accounting, architectural, advertising, etc.

64. Sassen, *Global City*, 109. The very technology that encouraged "agglomerations" would later make possible the decentralization of some of these producer services, but in the 1970s their centralization was the trend.

65. Paul N. Balchin, David Issac, and Jean Chen, *Urban Economics: A Global Perspective* (New York: Palgrave, 2000), 81.

66. Darton, *Divided We Stand*, 29–31.

67. Drennan, "Local Economy" (1984), 53–54.

68. Darton, *Divided We Stand*, 140.

69. Sassen, *Global City*, 44–45; Darton, *Divided We Stand*, 159; Steven Peter Vallas, *Power in the Workplace: The Politics of Production at AT&T* (Albany: State University of New York Press, 1993), 117; Peter Dicken, *Global Shift: The Internationalization of Economic Activity* (London: Paul Chapman Publishing, 1992), 360–64.

70. Brecher and Horton, *Power Failure*, 186.

71. *Report of the Comptroller of the City of New York, FY1982*, 184 (henceforth *Report of the Comptroller*).

72. *Report of the Comptroller, 1975–1976*, 153.

73. Sayre and Kaufman, *Governing New York City*, 505–8; Bellush, "Clusters of Power," 296–99.

74. *Public Employee Press*, June 6, 1975, 4; *New York Times*, February 16, 1975, IV-6; *New York Times*, February 18, 1975, 1; *New York Times*, May 17, 1975, 12.

75. *Public Employee Press*, June 6, 1975, 4.

76. Brecher and Horton, *Setting Municipal Priorities, 1981*, 1.

77. Newfield and Du Brul, *Abuse of Power*, 177; Bailey, *Crisis Regime*, 8–9.

78. Bailey, *Crisis Regime*, 39.

79. Shefter, *Political Crisis/Fiscal Crisis*, 25–29.

80. Jack Bigel and Ed Rogowsky, "Dale Horowitz," interview in *CUNY-TV Oral History of New York City Fiscal Crisis of 1970's*, 1996, available at http://newman.baruch.cuny.edu/DIGITAL/2003/amfl/oral_histories.htm. Bailey, *Crisis Regime*, 17–18; Freeman, *Working-Class New York*, 258; Zweig, *Wriston*, 473–78.

81. Horowitz, *CUNY-TV Oral History;* Bailey, *Crisis Regime*, 17–18.

82. Bailey, *Crisis Regime*, 20–23.

83. Fuchs, *Mayors and Money*, 18.

84. Markham, *Financial History*, 6–7, 48–49; Darton, *Divided We Stand*, 44; Zweig, *Wriston*, 82–86.

85. Robert Lamb and Stephen Rappaport, *Municipal Bonds: The Comprehensive Review of Tax-Exempt Securities and Public Finance* (New York: McGraw-Hill, 1980), 281–82; Mayer, *Bankers*, 521–24.

86. Zweig, *Wriston*, 478.

87. Mayer, *Bankers*, 8–19.

88. Newfield and Du Brul, *Abuse of Power*, 178.

89. Charles Morris, *The Cost of Good Intentions: New York City and the Liberal Experiment, 1960–1975* (New York: W.W. Norton, 1980), 232; Municipal Assistance Corporation (MAC), *Annual Report of the Municipal Assistance Corporation to the City of New York, 1976*, 11.

90. MAC, *Annual Report, 1976*, 11.

91. Bailey, *Crisis Regime*, 27; Newfield and Du Brul, *Abuse of Power*, 179–81; *Who's Who in America, 1980–81*, 41st ed., 988.

92. MAC *Annual Report, 1976*, 12.

93. MAC, "Minutes of the Reconvened Meeting of the Board of Directors," July 18, 1975, 2–6; MAC, "Minutes," July 22, 1975, 3.

94. Bailey, *Crisis Regime*, 31; Newfield and Du Brul, *Abuse of Power*, 180.

95. Bailey, *Crisis Regime*, 31.

96. MAC, *Annual Report, 1976*, 12.

97. Bailey, *Crisis Regime*, 39–40; *Public Employee Press*, September 12, 1975, 1.

98. Bailey, *Crisis Regime*, 41–43, 91–94; *New York Times*, September 12, 1975, 1; *New York Times*, December 12, 1975, 56.

99. Bailey, *Crisis Regime*, 94–100, 104–11.

100. Ibid., 115.

101. *Public Employee Press*, June 6, 1975, 4; *Public Employee Press*, June 20, 1975, 11–14.

102. Zweig, *Wriston*, 503.

103. Dennis R. Judd and Todd Swanstrom, *City Politics: Private Power and Public Policy*, 4th ed. (New York: Pearson/Longman, 2004), 332; Zweig, *Wriston*, 502–10.

104. Newfield and Du Brul, *Abuse of Power*, 69.

105. MAC, *Annual Report of the Municipal Assistance Corporation for the City of New York, 1978*, 1; *New York Times*, November 27, 1975, 1; *New York Times*, December 10, 1975, 1; Shefter, *Political Crisis/Fiscal Crisis*, 137–39.

106. *New York Times*, January 30, 1975, 1; *Public Employee Press*, February 14, 1975, 12.

107. *Public Employee Press*, January 17, 1975, 2; *Public Employee Press*, February 28, 1975, 3; *Public Employee Press*, March 14, 1975, 1, 4; *Public Employee Press*, March 20, 1975, 1, 3; *Public Employee Press*, April 11, 1975, 3; *Public Employee Press*, May 9, 1975, 3.

108. Freeman, *Working-Class New York*, 261–62; Bellush and Bellush, *Union Power*, 391–93; Ray Markey, then president of DC 37 Local 1930 and a delegate to the DC 37 assembly, interview by author; *New York Times*, May 21, 1975, 48.

109. *New York Times*, July 21, 1975, 1.

110. Bellush and Bellush, *Union Power*, 384–88; Maier, *City Unions*, 172–73.

111. Bellush and Bellush, *Union Power*, 387.

112. Victor Gotbaum, *CUNY-TV Oral History*.

113. Fuchs, *Mayors and Money*, 18; Horowitz, *CUNY-TV Oral History*; Lamb and Rappaport, *Municipal Bonds*, 283.

114. *Public Employee Press*, October 8, 1976, 4.

115. Zweig, *Wriston*, 510–11; Walter Wriston, Victor Gotbaum, and Herman Badillo, interviews, *CUNY-TV Oral History*; Bill Schleicher, currently editor of the DC 37's *Public Employee Press* and a reporter for it in 1975, interview by author, September 13, 2004.

116. H. Ron Davidson, "Harry Van Arsdale and the New York City Fiscal Crisis, " research paper, University of Chicago, August 1999, 20–28; Freeman, *Working-Class New York*, 277–79; *New York Times*, October 30, 1975, 1.

117. Weitzman, *City Workers*, 36–37; Bellush and Bellush, *Union Power*, 397; Bailey, *Crisis Regime*, 72; Bill Schleicher, interview by author, September 13, 2004.

118. Weitzman, *City Workers*, 63–65

119. MAC, "Minutes of Special Meeting of the Board of Directors, " July 29, 1975, 6; Bellush and Bellush, *Union Power*, 401; Freeman, *Working-Class New York*, 267–69; Wriston, *CUNY-TV Oral History; New York Times*, October 30, 1975, 1.

120. MAC, *Annual Report, 1976*, 15; MAC, *Annual Report, 1977*, 4.

121. Freeman, *Working-Class New York*, 268–69; Wriston, *CUNY-TV Oral History*.

122. Weitzman, *City Workers*, 42–45.

123. Bellush and Bellush, *Union Power*, 408–9; Freeman, *Working-Class New York*, 280; Weitzman, *City Workers*, 46–47; *Public Employee Press*, September 10, 1976.

124. Freeman, *Working-Class New York*, 269; Horowitz, *CUNY-TV Oral History*.

125. MAC, *Annual Report, 1978*, 8; Shefter, *Political Crisis/Fiscal Crisis*, 165; Bailey, *Crisis Regime*, 48–49.

126. Bellush and Bellush, *Union Power*, 266–68.

127. Shefter, *Political Crisis/Fiscal Crisis*, 163–64.

128. Freeman, *Working-Class New York*, 277–79.

129. David Gordon, "Capitalism and the Roots of Urban Crisis, " in *The Fiscal Crisis of American Cities*, ed. Roger Alcaly and David Mermelstein (New York: Vintage Books, 1977), 108–12.

130. TCCF, *Final Report*, 93; Council of Economic Advisers, *Economic Report of the President, 2003* (Washington, DC: U.S. Government Printing Office, 2003), 417.

131. Terry Clark, Irene Sharpe Rubin, Lynne Pettler, and Erwin Zimmerman, *How Many New Yorks? The New York Fiscal Crisis in Comparative Perspective*, Research Report no. 72, Comparative Study of Community Decision-Making (Chicago: University of Chicago, 1976), 4a, 4b, 7a; Shefter, *Political Crisis/Fiscal Crisis*, 120; Fuchs, *Mayors and Money*, 257; David Halle, ed., *New York and Los Angeles: Politics, Society, and Culture—a Comparative View* (Chicago: University of Chicago Press, 2003), 11–13; Judd and Swanstrom, *City Politics*, 325, 337–40.

132. TCCF, June 1977, 124; Fuchs, *Mayors and Money*, 25; Shefter, *Political Crisis/Fiscal Crisis*, 116; Freeman, *Working-Class New York*, 214.

133. Maier, *City Unions*, 137–69.

134. Morris, *Cost of Good Intentions*, 185–88; Clark et al., *How Many New Yorks?*, 6b–7a.

135. Brecher and Horton, *Power Failure*, 35.

136. Shefter, *Political Crisis/Fiscal Crisis*, 114.

137. Ibid., 116–17; Sanjek, *Future of Us All*, 84; TCCF, *Final Report*, 85, 86; *Report of the Comptroller, 1974–75*, 155.

138. *Report of the Comptroller, 1960–1961*, 13, 38; *Report of the Comptroller, 1970–71*, 13, 38; *Report of the Comptroller, 1974–1975*, 13, 38; Shefter, *Political Crisis/Fiscal Crisis*, 88–89, 116.

139. TCCF, *Final Report*, 107.

140. *Report of the Comptroller, 1974–1975*, 13.

141. Morris, *Cost of Good Intentions*, 129.

142. *Report of the Comptroller, 1970–1971*, 188; *Report of the Comptroller, 1974–1975*, 218.

143. Morris, *Cost of Good Intentions*, 135–36.

144. George E. Peterson, "Capital Spending and Capital Obsolescence," in *The Fiscal Outlook for Cities: Implications of a National Urban Policy*, ed. Roy Bahl (Syracuse, NY: Syracuse University Press, 1978), 51–54; Sanjek, *Future of Us All*, 167–68.

145. TCCF, *Final Report*, 103, 105.

146. *Report of the Comptroller, FY 1970 and FY 1974*, 13.

147. TCCF, *Final Report*, 103, 107.

148. Ibid., 97.

149. Ibid., 62–63.

150. Brecher and Horton, *Power Failure*, 205.

151. TCCF, *The Role of Intergovernmental Fiscal Relations in New York City: The Fourteenth Interim Report*, New York, May 1977, 19.

152. TCCF, *Final Report*, 79.

153. Ibid., 97.

154. Morris, *Cost of Good Intentions*, 132; *Report of the Comptroller, FY1982*, 184.

155. *Public Employee Press*, June 20, 1975, 7.

156. Regina Armstrong, "Real Property Exemptions and Abatements," in Graduate School of Public Affairs, *Real Property Tax Policy for New York City* (New York: New York University, 1980), IV-12–IV-15.

157. Ibid., IV-7.

158. Brecher and Horton, *Power Failure*, 202.

159. Sanjek, *Future of Us All*, 87–89; Armstrong, "Real Property Exemptions," IV-12–IV-15.

160. Brecher and Horton, *Power Failure*, 193.

161. Darton, *Divided We Stand*, 140.

162. Drennan, "Local Economy" (1984), 49–62.

2: From Crisis Regime to Mayoral-Business Coalition

1. Richard C. Wade, "The Withering Away of the Party System," in *Urban Politics* (see chap. 1, n. 36), 281–82; Jack Newfield and Wayne Barrett, *City for Sale: Ed Koch and the Betrayal of New York* (New York: Harper & Row, 1988), 140–41; Brecher and Horton, *Power Failure*, 99 (see chap. 1, n. 22).

2. Bailey, *Crisis Regime*, 138–44 (see chap. 1, n. 47).

3. Mollenkopf, *Phoenix in the Ashes* 92–95 (see chap. 1, n. 36); Brecher and Horton, *Power Failure*, 126–31.

4. Newfield and Barrett, *City for Sale*, 3, 12.

5. Mollenkopf, *Phoenix in the Ashes*, 63–80.

6. Brecher and Horton, *Power Failure*, 99–108; Mollenkopf, *Phoenix in the Ashes*, 159.

7. Mollenkopf, *Phoenix in the Ashes*, 19, 125–26; Brecher and Horton, *Power Failure*, 126–34.

8. Mollenkopf, *Phoenix in the Ashes*, 156.

9. Bailey, *Crisis Regime*, 140–41.

10. TCCF, *Final Report*, 200–277.

11. MAC, *Annual Report, 1978*, 1.

12. Shefter, *Political Crisis/Fiscal Crisis*, 155 (see intro., n. 3); William Sites, *Remaking New York: Primitive Globalization and the Politics of Urban Community* (Minneapolis: University of Minnesota Press, 2003), 54.

13. *Setting Municipal Priorities*, 246 (see chap. 1, n. 13); MAC, *Annual Report, 1978*, 1.

14. Raymond D. Horton and John Palmer Smith, "Expenditures and Services," in *Setting Municipal Priorities, 1983*, ed. Charles Brecher and Raymond D. Horton (New York: New York University Press, 1982), 82–83; David Grossman, "Debt and Capital Management," in *Setting Municipal Priorities, 1982*, ed. Charles Brecher and Raymond D. Horton (New York: Russell Sage Foundation, 1981), 130.

15. *Setting Municipal Priorities, 1981*, 2; Brecher and Horton, *Power Failure*, 20, 21, 168.

16. Dennis Judd and Todd Swanstrom, *City Politics: The Political Economy of Urban America*, 5th ed. (New York: Pearson/Longman, 2006), 177.

17. Carol O'Cleireacain, "The Private Economy and the Public Budget of New York City," in *The City and the World: New York's Global Future*, ed. Margaret Crahan and Alberto Vourvoulias-Bush (New York: Council on Foreign Relations, 1997), 30.

18. Sites, *Remaking New York*, 45–46.

19. Brecher and Horton, *Power Failure*, 201–3; *Report of the Comptroller, 1992*, 245; Citizens Budget Commission, "The Hidden Billions: Tax Expenditures in New York City," New York, November 1981, i.

20. Brecher and Horton, *Power Failure*, 210–14.

21. Ibid., 192, 213; Sanjek, *Future of Us All*, 95, 167 (see chap. 1, n. 3); *Report of the Comptroller, 1992*, 245.

22. Newfield and Barrett, *City for Sale*, 3–4.

23. Mollenkopf, *Phoenix in the Ashes*, 142–43.

24. Sanjek, *Future of Us All*, 93–94.

25. Mollenkopf, *Phoenix in the Ashes*, 61.

26. *Setting Municipal Priorities, 1981*, 2–3.

27. Newfield and Barrett, *City for Sale*, 3–4; Brecher and Horton, *Power Failure*, 35; Gordon Berlin, "Redesigning the Safety Net for the Working Poor, the Hard to Employ, and Those at Risk," in *Rethinking the Urban Agenda: Reinvigorating the Liberal Tradition in New York City and Urban America*, ed. John Mollenkopf and Ken Emerson (New York: Century Foundation Press, 2001), 107–9; John Mollenkopf and Manuel Castells, "Introduction," in *Dual City: Restructuring New York*, ed. Mollenkopf and Castells (New York: Russell Sage Foundation, 1991), 12.

28. Maier, *City Unions*, 181–82 (see chap. 1, n. 49); Brecher and Horton, *Power Failure*, 158–60, 249.

29. Weil, *History of New York*, 37–42, 54 (see intro., n. 6); Katznelson, *City Trenches*, 35 (see intro., n. 2).

30. Katznelson, *City Trenches*, 35–36; Bender, *Unfinished City*, 5–10 (see intro., n. 2); Weil, *History of New York*, 50.

31. Bender, *Unfinished City*, 3–6; Weil, *History of New York*, 44.

32. Bender, *Unfinished City*, 82–83.

33. Frank DeGiovanni and Lorraine Minnite, "Patterns of Neighborhood Change," in *Dual City*, 267; Neil Smith, Betsy Duncan, and Laura Reid, "From Disinvestment to Reinvestment: Mapping the Urban 'Frontier' in the Lower East Side," in *From Urban Village to East Village: The Battle for New York's Lower East Side*, ed. Janet Abu-Lughod (Cambridge, MA: Blackwell, 1994), 155; Brecher and Horton, *Power Failure*, 6; Freeman, *Working-Class New York*, 275–76 (see intro., n. 5).

34. Sites, *Remaking New York*, 39; Fitch, *Assassination of New York*, viii (see intro., n. 6).

35. Sanjek, *Future of Us All*, 283–84.

36. DeGiovanni and Minnite, "Patterns of Neighborhood Change," 269.

37. Ibid., 293–94.

38. Christopher Mele, "Neighborhood 'Burn-out': Puerto Ricans at the End of the Queue," in *From Urban Village*, 235–38.

39. Sites, *Remaking New York*, 76.

40. Martha Stark and Doug Turetsky, "Homeward Bound: A Twenty-first Century Affordable Housing Agenda for New York," in *Rethinking the Urban Agenda*, 145–46.

41. Brecher and Horton, *Power Failure*, 143–45; Newfield and Barrett, *City for Sale*, 5.

42. Raphael Sonenshein, "Gotham on Our Minds: New York City in the Los Angeles Charter Reform of 1996–1999," in *New York and Los Angeles* (see chap. 1, n. 131), 301–3.

43. Joseph P. Viteritti, "The New Charter: Will It Make a Difference?" in *Urban Politics* (see chap. 1, n. 36), 417–24; Sanjek, *Future of Us All*, 170–73; *New York Times*, April 26, 1989, sec. II, p. 1; *New York Times*, May 2, 1989, sec. II, p. 1; *New York Times*, May 12, 1989, sec. II, p. 1; *New York Times*, May 14, 1989, sec. I, p. 29; *The 2003–04 Green Book: Official Directory of the City of New York* (New York: NYC Department of Citywide Administrative Services, 2003), 68–69.

44. Freeman, *Working-Class New York*, 306–8; Brecher and Horton, *Power Failure*, 100–101.

45. Maier, *City Unions*, 186.

46. Bellush and Bellush, *Union Power*, 440–42 (see chap. 1, n. 49).

47. Maier, *City Unions*, 30–31.

48. Freeman, *Working-Class New York*, 284–85; Brecher and Horton, *Power Failure*, 244–50.

49. Maier, *City Unions*, 171; Freeman, *Working-Class New York*, 312–13; Jewel Bellush, "Room at the Top: Black Women in District Council 37," in "In Search of New York," special issue, *Dissent* (Fall 1987): 488–89.

50. Michael Oreskes, "Is It Still a Union Town?," in "In Search of New York," special issue, *Dissent* (Fall 1987): 490–91; Maier, *City Unions*, 171.

51. Leon Fink and Brian Greenberg, *Upheaval in the Quiet Zone: A History of Hospital Workers' Union, Local 1199* (Urbana: University of Illinois Press, 1989), 209–43; Freeman, *Working-Class New York*, 313–17.

52. Herman Benson, *Rebels, Reformers, and Racketeers: How Insurgents Transformed the Labor Movement* (Bloomington, IN: 1st Books, 2005), 36–56.

53. Freeman, *Working-Class New York*, 310.

54. *Labor Notes* no. 121, April 1989, 1, 14; *Labor Notes* no. 130, January 1990, 11.

55. *Labor Notes* no. 126, September 1989, 14; Freeman, *Working-Class New York*, 316–17.

56. *Labor Notes* no. 129, December 1989, 3, 12; Steve Early, *Holding the Line in '89: Lessons of the NYNEX Strike* (Somerville, MA: Labor Resource Center, 1990), 4–10, 14–19, 27–29.

57. Newfield and Barrett, *City for Sale*, passim; Brecher and Horton, *Power Failure*, 103–4.

58. Nicholaus Mills, "Howard Beach—Anatomy of a Lynching," in "In Search of New York," special issue, *Dissent* (Fall 1987): 479–85.

59. Brenner, *Boom and the Bubble*, 84–85 (see chap. 1, n. 25); O'Cleireacain, "Private Economy," 27; Mollenkopf, *Phoenix in the Ashes*, 62–63; Fitch, *Assassination of New York*, 145–46.

60. Mollenkopf, *Phoenix in the Ashes*, 174–75.

61. Ibid., 86–87, 117.

62. *Analysis of Demographic Changes Since 1980* (New York: NYC Department of City Planning, 1990), www.nyc.gov/htm/dcp.

63. Adrienne Kivelson, *What Makes New York City Run?* (New York: League of Women Voters of the City of New York Education Fund, 2001), 37–42; Martin Shefter, *Political Parties and the State: The American Historical Experience* (Princeton, NJ: Princeton University Press, 1994), 226–31; Simon Gerson, *Pete: The Story of Peter V. Cacchione, New York's First Communist Councilman* (New York: International Publishers, 1976), 61–66, 148–52; www.BlackPressUSA.com, September 18, 2005.

64. Martin Kilson, "The Weakness of Black Politics: Cursed by Factions and Feuds," in "In Search of New York," special issue, *Dissent* (Fall 1987): 523–29.

65. Arian et al., *Changing New York City Politics*, 73 (see chap. 1, n. 2).

66. Mollenkopf, *Phoenix in the Ashes*, 204.

67. Ibid., 84–85, 115, 179–83, 211; Hamilton, "Needed, More Foxes," 375–78 (see chap. 1, n. 42); Brecher and Horton, *Power Failure*, 102–8.

3: Globalization and the Underdevelopment of New York

1. United Nations Conference on Trade and Development (UNCTAD), *World Investment Report* (New York: United Nations, 1993), xx; UNCTAD, *World Investment Report* (New York: United Nations, 1995), 1; UNCTAD, *World Investment Report* (New York: United Nations, 2004), xvii, 9; Edward Mozley Roche, "Cyberopolis: The Cybernetic City Faces the Global Economy," in *City and the World* (see chap. 2, n. 17), 51.

2. UNCTAD, *World Investment Report*, 2004, 9.

3. Michael Yates, *Naming the System: Inequality and Work in the Global Economy* (New York: Monthly Review Press, 2003), 36–48; Joseph Stiglitz, *Globalization and Its Discontents* (New York: W.W. Norton, 2003), 53–73.

4. UNCTAD, *World Investment Report*, 2004, xx–xxi, 318.

5. U.S. Census Bureau, *Statistical Abstract of the United States, 2001*, 814; U.S. Census Bureau, *Statistical Abstract of the United States, 2004–2005*, 800, 802, 811.

6. Brenner, *Boom and the Bubble*, 81–83 (see chap. 1, n. 25).

7. U.S. Census Bureau, *Statistical Abstract of the United States, 1995*, 384; U.S. Census Bureau, *Statistical Abstract of the United States, 2004–2005*, 391, 427; Council of Economic Advisers, *Economic Report of the President, 2005*, 224–25.

8. Judd and Swanstrom, *City Politics*, 5th ed., 364 (see chap. 2, n. 16).

9. James Parrott, "The Tentative Recovery Is Still a Long Way from Restoring Jobs, Wages and Incomes to Pre-recession Levels for New York City's Low- and Moderate-Income Househoulds," testimony before the New

York City Rent Guidelines Board, May 2, 2005, 6, figure 1, http://www.fiscalpolicy.org/research_07.stm; James A. Parrott, "Bolstering and Diversifying New York City's Economy," in *Rethinking the Urban Agenda* (see chap. 2, n. 27), 44–48; Rae Rosen and Reagan Murray, "Opening Doors: Access to the Global Markets for Financial Sectors," in *City and the World* (see chap. 2, n. 17), 42–43.

10. H.V. Savitch and Paul Kantor, *Cities in the International Marketplace: The Political Economy of Urban Development in North America and Western Europe* (Princeton, NJ: Princeton University Press, 2002), 201.

11. Brenner, *Boom and the Bubble*, 175–76.

12. Parrott, "Bolstering and Diversifying," 47–48.

13. James Parrott and Oliver Cooke, "Tale of Two Recessions: The Current Slowdown in NYC Compared to the Early 1990s," Fiscal Policy Institute, New York, December 3, 2002, 8; Barney Warf, "Financial Services and Inequality in New York," *International Geographer* 2, no. 1 (2004): 110–12.

14. Warf, "Financial Services," 12.

15. Peter Newman and Andy Thornley, eds., *Planning World Cities: Globalization and Urban Politics*, New York: Palgrave Macmillan, 2005, 82–83.

16. Parrott and Cooke, "Tale of Two Recessions," 6.

17. Alan Altshuler and David Luberoff, *Mega-Projects: The Changing Politics of Urban Public Investment* (Washington, DC: Brookings Institution Press, 2003), 248–69, *passim*.

18. Greg LeRoy, *The Great American Jobs Scam: Corporate Tax Dodging and the Myth of Job Creation* (San Francisco: Berrett-Koehler, 2005), 2; NYC Department of Finance, *Annual Report on Tax Expenditures Fiscal Year 2004*, (New York, 2004), i, www.nyc.gov.

19. Savitch and Kantor, *Cities in the International Marketplace*, 3–4, 94; Mike Wallace, *A New Deal for New York* (New York: Bell & Weiland Publishers, 2002), 45–46.

20. Citizens Budget Commission, "The Media and Communications Industries in New York City," December 1998, 4–9.

21. Roche, "Cyberopolis," 56–58.

22. Citizens Budget Commission, "Telecommunications Infrastructure and New York's Competitiveness," November 1998, 1–3.

23. Rosen and Murray, "Opening Doors," 42–43.

24. Sites, *Remaking New York*, 54 (see chap. 2, n. 12).

25. Rosen and Murray, "Opening Doors," 41.

26. Edward Hill and Iryna Lendel, "Did 9/11 Change Manhattan and the New York Region as Places to Conduct Business?" in *Resilient City: The Economic Impact of 9/11*, ed. Howard Chernick (New York: Russell Sage Foundation, 2005), 35–52.

27. Judd and Swanstrom, *City Politics*, 5th ed., 362–86; Altshuler and Luberoff, *Mega-Projects*, 20, 32.

28. Savitch and Kantor, *Cities in the International Marketplace*, 90; Mark Levitan and Robin Gluck, "Who Needs a Living Wage?" Community Service Society of New York, April 1, 2002, 8; Parrott, "Bolstering and Diversifying," 45.

29. Fiscal Policy Institute, *The State of Working New York 2003* (New York: Fiscal Policy Institute, 2004), 68.

30. Parrott, "Bolstering and Diversifying," 49–54; *New York Times*, September 4, 2005, www.nytimes.com.

31. Parrott, "Bolstering and Diversifying," 48–54.

32. United Nations, *Human Development Report 1999* (New York: UN Human Development Program, 1999), 32; Barbara Ehrenreich and Arlie Russell Hochschild, eds., *Global Woman: Nannies, Maids, and Sex Workers in the New Economy* (New York: Henry Holt and Company, 2002), 18.

33. World Bank, *World Development Report 2006* (New York: Oxford University Press, 2005), 299.

34. Oscar Handlin, *Immigration as a Factor in American History* (Englewood Cliffs, NJ: Prentice-Hall, Inc., 1959), 5.

35. Jacqueline Jones et al., *Created Equal: A Social and Political History of the United States: From 1885*, vol. II (New York: Longman, 2003), 550; *Statistical Abstract 2004–2005*, 8.

36. Roger Waldinger, *Still the Promised City? African Americans and New Immigrants in Postindustrial New York* (Cambridge, MA: Harvard University Press, 1996), 42–43; Walter Thabit, *How East New York Became a Ghetto* (New York: New York University Press, 2003), 23–29.

37. Immanuel Ness, *Immigrants, Unions, and the New U.S. Labor Market* (Philadelphia: Temple University Press, 2005), 15–17; *Statistical Abstract 2004–2005*, 9–10.

38. Ness, *Immigrants*, 16.

39. Ellen Percy Kraly and Ines Miyares, "Immigration to New York: Policy, Population, and Patterns," in *New Immigration in New York*, ed. Nancy Foner (New York: Columbia University Press, 2001), 33–74.

40. Andrew Beveridge and Susan Weber, "Race and Class in the Developing New York and Los Angeles Metropolises, 1940–2000," in *New York and Los Angeles* (see chap. 1, n. 131), 63–73.

41. Ness, *Immigrants*, 17, 24.

42. Waldinger, *Still the Promised City?*, 158–60.

43. Richard Wright and Mark Ellis, "Immigrants, the Native-Born, and the Changing Division of Labor in New York City," in *New Immigration in New York*, 101–3.

44. *Green Book*, 647.

45. Ness, *Immigrants*, 20–21.

46. Ibid., 20; Gus Tyler, "A Tale of Three Cities: Upper Economy, Lower—and Under," in "In Search of New York," special issue, *Dissent* (Fall 1987): 470.

47. Saskia Sassen, "The Informal Economy," in *Dual City* (see chap. 2, n. 27), 87–92.

48. Levitan and Gluck, "Who Needs a Living Wage?," 4–9.

4: Politics in the 1990s

1. Sanjek, *Future of Us All*, 170 (see chap. 1, n. 3).

2. Arian et al., *Changing New York City Politics*, 124 (see chap. 1, n. 2); Mollenkopf, *Phoenix in the Ashes*, 180–85 (see chap. 1, n. 36).

3. *New York Times*, November 4, 1989, 29.

4. Freeman, *Working-Class New York*, 322–23 (see intro., n. 5).

5. Doug Henwood, *Left Business Observer* no. 58, April 1993, 2–3; *New York Times*, May 23, 1991, 1; August 20, 1991, B6; Mollenkopf, *Phoenix in the Ashes*, 207.

6. *New York Times*, July 1, 1991, B1; *New York Times*, August 20, 1991, B6.

7. Brecher and Horton, *Power Failure*, 105 (see chap. 1, n. 22).

8. Arian et al., *Changing New York City Politics*, 34–38;

9. Ibid., 142; Jim Sleeper, *The Closest of Strangers: Liberalism and the Politics of Race in New York* (New York: W.W. Norton, 1990), 276–84.

10. Sleeper, *Closest of Strangers*, 277.

11. Ibid., 267–73.

12. *New York Times*, September 26, 1989, B1–2.

13. *New York Times*, April 3, 1992, B3.

14. Sleeper, *Closest of Strangers*, 299; Sanjek, *Future of Us All*, 170.

15. *New York Times*, November 4, 1989, 29.

16. *New York Times*, December 6, 1989, 1.

17. *New York Times*, December 14, 1989, B1.

18. William Sites, "Public Action: City Policy and the Gentrification of the Lower East Side," in *From Urban Village* (see chap. 2, n. 33), 205–6.

19. Parrott and Cooke, "Tale of Two Recessions," 6–9 (see chap. 3, n. 13); City of New York, *Monthly Report on Current Economic Conditions*, Office of Management and Budget, July 30, 2001, Annual Historical Data NYC, n.p.

20. Sanjek, *Future of Us All*, 170

21. Fred Siegel, *The Prince of the City: Giuliani, New York, and the Genius of American Life* (San Francisco: Encounter Books, 2005), 47–51.

22. Judd and Swanstrom, *City Politics*, 5th ed., 177, 193 (see chap. 2, n. 16).

23. Brecher and Horton, *Power Failure*, 258; Sites, *Remaking New York*, 52 (see chap. 2, n. 12).

24. Sanjek, *Future of Us All*, 173–74.

25. Sites, *Remaking New York*, 52–54.

26. Fitch, *Assassination of New York*, 281 (see intro., n. 6); Sites, *Remaking New York*, 52

27. *New York Times*, March 24, 1992, p.1; Sanjek, *Future of Us All*, 171–72.

28. Sanjek, *Future of Us All*, 174–76.

29. Fitch, *Assassination of New York*, 282.

30. Sanjek, *Future of Us All*, 172–73.

31. Wayne Barrett, *Rudy!: An Investigative Biography of Rudolph Giuliani* (New York: Basic Books, 2000), 6–7.

32. *Planning World Cities*, 78–79 (see chap. 3, n. 15); Wayne Barrett, "Giuliani's Legacy: Taking Credit for Things He Didn't Do," GothamGazette.com.

33. Sites, "Public Action," 205.

34. Sanjek, *Future of Us All*, 152–53.

35. Thabit, *How East New York*, 1 (see chap. 3, n. 36).

36. Sanjek, *Future of Us All*, 153–54; Andrew Kirtzman, *Rudy Giuliani: Emperor of the City* (New York: HarperCollins, 2000), 32–35.

37. Siegel, *Prince of the City*, 60–63.

38. Kirtzman, *Rudy Giuliani*, 42–49, 57; Sanjek, *Future of Us All*, 154.

39. Evan Mandery, *The Campaign: Rudy Giuliani, Ruth Messenger, Al Sharpton, and the Race to Be Mayor of New York City* (Boulder, CO: Westview Press, 1999), 20.

40. Karen M. Kaufmann, "The Mayoral Politics of New York and Los Angeles," in *New York and Los Angeles* (see chap. 1, n. 131), 319; Mollenkopf, *Phoenix in the Ashes*, 209–13; *New York Times*, December 11, 1993, 27.

41. *New York Times*, December 11, 1993, 27.

42. Barrett, *Rudy!*, 265–67.

43. Kaufmann, "Mayoral Politics," 320.

44. Mollenkopf, *Phoenix in the Ashes*, 217–19.

45. Ibid., 214–19.

46. Fitch, *Assassination of New York*, 12–14; Sites, *Remaking New York*, 54.

47. Kirtzman, *Rudy Giuliani*, 74–78; Barrett, *Rudy!*, 289; Sanjek, *Future of Us All*, 179–80; Jack Newfield, *The Full Rudy: The Man, the Myth, the Mania* (New York: Nation Books, 2002), 37–60.

48. Sanjek, *Future of Us All*, 176–78.

49. Barrett, *Rudy!*, 7–9; Savitch and Kantor, *Cities in the International Marketplace*, 204–7 (see chap. 3, n. 10).

50. *Planning World Cities*, 80–82; Barrett, *Rudy!*, 8–10.

51. Barrett, *Rudy!*, 345.

52. Ibid., 68–69.

53. Michael Jacobson, "From the 'Back' to the 'Front': The Changing Character of Punishment in New York City," in *Rethinking the Urban Agenda* (see chap. 2, n. 27), 174–79.

54. Barrett, *Rudy!*, 341–42.

55. Jacobson, "From the 'Back,' " 172–78.

56. Barrett, *Rudy!*, 346.

57. J. Phillip Thompson, "One Step Forward, Two Steps Back: Liberalism, Race, and Local Democracy," in *Rethinking the Urban Agenda*, 195–97; Barrett, *Rudy!*, 333–35.

58. Barrett, *Rudy!*, 350–64.

59. Sanjek, *Future of Us All*, 183–84.

60. Ralph da Costa Nunez, *A Shelter Is Not a Home, or Is It?* (New York: White Tiger Press, 2004), 46–47; Barrett, *Rudy!*, 315–16.

61. Da Costa Nunez, *Shelter Is Not a Home*, 43–46; Barrett, *Rudy!*, 316–20; Sanjek, *Future of Us All*, 183–84; Community Service Society of New York, *Building a Ladder to Higher Wages: A Report by the Working Group on New York City's Low-Wage Labor Market* (New York: Community Service Society, 2000), 171 (henceforth *Building a Ladder*); *Report of the Comptroller, 2004*, 296.

62. Sanjek, *Future of Us All*, 184.

63. Sandra Opdycke, *No One Was Turned Away: The Role of Public Hospitals in New York City Since 1900* (New York: Oxford University Press, 1999), 178–89; *Report of the Comptroller, 2001*, 40; Sanjek, *Future of Us All*, 180–82.

64. Kirtzman, *Rudy Giuliani*, 192–215; Barrett, *Rudy!*, 411–17; Newfield, *Full Rudy*, 89.

65. Kirtzman, *Rudy Giuliani*, 196–97.

66. Kaufmann, "Mayoral Politics," 320, 331–32; *New York Times*, November 5, 1997, B3, B5; Kirtzman, *Rudy Giuliani*, 80–81.

67. Freeman, *Working-Class New York*, 324–25; Mandery, *Campaign*, 150.

68. Kirtzman, *Rudy Giuliani*, 172–74; Barrett, *Rudy!*, 313.

69. Kirtzman, *Rudy Giuliani*, 209; Barrett, *Rudy!*, 447–48.

70. Mandery, 186–87, 260–61; Kirtzman, *Rudy Giuliani*, 209; Barrett, *Rudy!*, 450, 456; *New York Times*, September 19, 1997, 30; *New York Times*, September 20, 1997, B2; NYC Campaign Finance Board, Searchable Campaign Finance Database, Election Cycle 1997, Candidate Giuliani, Rudolph, Contribution/Donation Public Disclosure Report, Individual, 1–7, Corporation, 1–7; Candidate, Messinger, Ruth, 1.

71. *New York Times*, November 3, 1993, B1.

72. Newfield, *Full Rudy*, 26–32; Barrett, *Rudy!*, 428–44.

73. Newfield, *Full Rudy*, 96–115; Barrett, *Rudy!*, 335.

74. Newfield, *Full Rudy*, 2–3, 116; Kirtzman, *Rudy Giuliani*, 275.

75. Michael Sorkin and Sharon Zukin, eds., *After the World Trade Center: Rethinking New York City* (New York: Routledge, 2002), vii–viii.

76. Tom Robbins, "Working Class Heroes," *Village Voice*, October 2, 2001, 22; *Daily News*, September 13, 2001, 17.

77. Newfield, *Full Rudy*, 1–2, 145–58.

78. *Building a Ladder*, 24, 25, 35–37; City of New York, *Monthly Report on Current Economic Conditions*, Office of Management and Budget, July 30, 2001, Annual Historical Data.

79. Mark Levitan, "It Did Happen Here: The Rise in Working Poverty in New York City," in *New York and Los Angeles*, 252–68.

80. da Costa Nunez, *Shelter Is Not a Home*, 66–68, 77; *Report of the Comptroller, 2001*, 272.

81. *Report of the Comptroller 2001*, 227–28; *Report of the Comptroller, 2004*, 274–80.

82. *New York Times*, October 9, 2001, D1.

83. *Report of the Comptroller, 2004*, 310; Brecher and Horton, *Power Failure*, 20, 25.

84. *Report of the Comptroller, 2001*, iii; Brecher and Horton, *Power Failure*, 36.

85. Levitan, "It Did Happen Here," 252–59; *Report of the Comptroller, 2004*, 294, 300; Parrott, Bolstering and Diversifying," 53–55.

86. Fiscal Policy Institute, "Family Income by Quintiles, New York City PSMA," October 31, 2005, www.fiscalpolicy.org.

5: The Bloomberg Phenomenon

1. New York City Board of Elections, "Statement and Return of the Votes for the Office of Mayor on the City of New York," 2001 general election, November 28, 2001, 1.

2. New York City Campaign Finance Board, "Campaign Finance Summary 2001 Citywide Elections," July 25, 2005 (henceforth Campaign Finance Board, "2001 Primary"); Kaufmann, "Mayoral Politics," 338 (see chap. 4, n. 40).

3. Tom Robbins, "The Ego Candidates," *Village Voice*, April 30, 2001, www.villagevoice.com.

4. *New York Times*, November 12, 2000, sec. 3, p. 2; *New York Times*, July 17, 2001, 1; Sara Kugler, Associated Press, *Yahoo News*, November 9, 2005.

5. Michael Tomasky, "The Domino Theory," *New York*, November 5, 2001, www.newyorkmetro.com; Kaufmann, "Mayoral Politics," 337.

6. *New York Times*, June 9, 2001, 1; *New York Times*, June 21, 2001, B1; New York City Board of Elections, "2001 Primary Election Statement and Return of the Votes for the Office of Mayor of the City of New York," October 11, 2001; Campaign Finance Board, "2001 Primary," 1–2.

7. New York City Board of Election, "2001 Primary Election Statement and Return of the Votes for the Office of Mayor of the City of New York," October 24, 2001, 1–5; Michael Tomasky, "The Union Label," *New York*, October 22, 2001, www.newyorkmetro.com; Kaufmann, "Mayoral Politics," 337–38.

8. Peter Noel, "Bloomberg Radio: How Black Talk Jocks Sold 'We Like Mike' to African Americans," *Village Voice*, November 14–20, 2001, www.villagevoice.com; Kaufmann, "Mayoral Politics," 320.

9. Chris Smith, "The Mayor and His Money," *New York*, October 3, 2005, 45–47.

10. *New York Times*, July 1, 2001, www.nytimes.com; Smith, "Mayor and His Money," 47.

11. *New York Times*, November 8, 2000, D5; League of Women Voters of

the City of New York Education Fund, *They Represent You 2003: Directory of Elected Officials*, New York, February 2003, 5, 9, 13, 17, 20.

12. *New York Times*, December 6, 2005, A1, B6.

13. Meryl Gordon, "The Winner's Circle," *New York*, November 12, 2001, www.newyorkmetro.com; Ralph Gardner Jr., "Social Planner," *New York*, May 13, 2002, www.newyorkmetro.com; *New York Times*, Mayor Bloomberg's Appointments, 2001, www.nytimes.com; Office of the Mayor, "Kevin Sheekey," 2005, www.nyc.gov; *Green Book, 2003–2004*, 5–7; *New York Times*, December 1, 2005, B3; Kirsten Danis, "Bloomy Bossing Around an Expensive Cabinet," *New York Post*, June 29, 2002, www.nytenants-online.

14. Office of the Comptroller, *Report on New York City Contracts, Fiscal Year 2000*, 10; Office of Management and Budget, *Adopted Budget Fiscal Year 2006: Expense, Revenue, Contract, 2005*, 13c–15c (henceforth *Expense, Revenue, Contract*); *Report of the Comptroller, 2001*, 10;

15. *New York Times*, May 23, 2005, www.nytimes.com.

16. Curtis Brainard et al., "Mayor Finances More Than His Own Campaign," *Columbia Journalist*, November 7, 2005, www.columbiajournalist.org.

17. *New York Times*, May 23, 2005.

18. Ibid.

19. Tom Robbins, "Bloomy's Hypocritical Oath," *Village Voice*, November 1, 2005, www.villagevoice.com.

20. Smith, "Mayor and His Money," 47; *New York Times*, May 23, 2005.

21. *Economic Report of the President 2005*, 221.

22. Brenner, *Boom and the Bubble*, 244–47 (see chap. 1, n. 25).

23. *New York Times*, November 6, 2001, B1; *New York Times*, November 19, 2001, 1; Office of Management and Budget, *Monthly Report on Current Economic Conditions*, October 12, 2005, "Annual Historical Data"; Office of the Comptroller, *Economic Notes*, May 2002, 3; Parrott and Cooke, "Tale of Two Recessions," 1–3 (see chap. 3, n. 13); *Planning World Cities*, 87–88 (see chap. 3, n. 15).

24. City of New York Office of Management and Budget, *Financial Plan Fiscal Years 2002–2006, Summary Book*, February 13, 2002, 3, 20.

25. *New York Times*, November 21, 2002.

26. City of New York, *Comprehensive Annual Financial Report of the Comptroller for the Fiscal Year Ended June 30, 2005*, William C. Thompson Jr., Comptroller, 2005, 257–67 (henceforth *Comptroller's Financial Report FY2005*).

27. *Comptroller's Financial Report FY2005*, 270–71.

28. Partnership for New York City, "Testimony on Behalf of the Partnership for New York City and the New York City Investment Fund by Kathryn Wylde," November 2, 2005, 1–3.

29. Partnership for New York City, *2005 Priorities*, 2.

30. LeRoy, *Great American Jobs Scam*, 1–18 (see chap. 3, n. 18).

31. Ibid., 43, 51–52.

32. City of New York Department of Finance, *Annual Report on Tax Expenditures Fiscal Year 2005*, i (henceforth *Tax Expenditures*); Good Jobs New York, "EDC and IDA Job Retention Deals Reported Between July 2002 and June 2003," www.goodjobsny.org.

33. *Tax Expenditures FY2003*, i; *Tax Expenditures FY2004*, i; *Tax Expenditures FY2005*, i.

34. *Comprehensive Annual Financial Report FY2005*, 253; *Expense, Revenue, Contract 2006*, ii.

35. *Tax Expenditures FY2005*, i, 12.

36. Ibid., i, 13–15, 58–59.

37. Ibid., 58.

38. New York City Tax Commission, *2004 Annual Report*, A2–3; New York City Tax Commission, "Actions on Applications in 2004 Reducing Assessments or Reclassifying Property," www.nyc.gov.

39. New York City Department of Finance, *Annual Report on the NYC Real Property Tax Fiscal Year 2005*, Office of Tax Policy, August 2005, 1 (henceforth *Real Property Tax Report FY 2005*); *Comptroller's Financial Report FY2005*, 274.

40. *Comptroller's Financial Report FY 2005*, 252–56, 274; *Expense, Revenue, Contract 2006*, ii; *Real Property Tax Report FY 2005*, 1.

41. *Comptroller's Financial Report FY 2005*, 252–53; Independent Budget Office, *Inside the Budget*, no. 144, December 13, 2005, 1–2.

42. *Comptroller's Financial Report FY 2005*, 276–77; *Real Property Tax Report FY 2005*, 1.

43. *New York Times*, December 11, 2005, sec. 11, pp. 1, 9.

44. *New York Times*, September 18, 2005, sec. 11, pp. 1, 8.

45. *Inside the Budget*, December 13, 2005, 3; *Real Property Tax Report FY2005*, i

46. *New York Times*, December 11, 2005, 9; *Real Property Tax Report FY2005*, 35.

47. Department of Finance, press release on Final Report on Assessor Reform, January 16, 2004, 1–5.

48. *New York Times*, January 27, 2006, B1, B8.

49. Coalition for the Homeless, "Loss of Affordable Apartments in New York City, 1990–2000," *Housing in New York City*, September 2002, Chart 1; *Comptroller's Financial Report FY 2005*, 294.

50. da Costa Nunez, *Shelter Is Not a Home*, 47–49, 65–68 (see chap. 4, n. 60); Furman Center for Real Estate and Urban Policy, *State of New York City's Housing and Neighborhoods 2003*, New York University, 2003, 4 (henceforth *Housing and Neighborhoods 2003*); City of New York, *Progress Report 2005: The New Housing Marketplace*, New York, 2005, 2 (henceforth *Progress Report*).

51. New York City Department of Housing Preservation and Development, *Selected Findings of the 2002 New York City Housing and Vacancy Sur-*

vey, 2003 (henceforth *Selected Findings*); Michael Shill and Benjamin Scafidi, *Housing Conditions and Problems in New York City: An Analysis of the 1996 Housing and Vacancy Survey* (New York: New York University School of Law Center for Real Estate and Urban Policy, 1997), Table 6 (henceforth *Housing Conditions*).

52. da Costa Nunez, *Shelter Is Not a Home*, 66; *Caribbean Life*, November 1, 2005, 1; *New York Times*, April 10, 2005, RE7; *New York Times*, August 28, 2005, 11; *New York Times Magazine*, March 24, 2002, 35.

53. *Selected Findings*, Tables 5, 7, 11; *Housing Conditions*, Table 4; *New York Times*, August 28, 2005, 11.

54. *New York Post*, June 18, 2004, 2.

55. Caroline Bhalla et al., *State of New York City Housing and Neighborhoods 2004* (New York: Furman Center for Real Estate and Urban Policy, New York University, 2004), 115; *Housing Conditions*, Table 11; *New York Times*, December 29, 2005, Al, C9.

56. *New York Times*, December 10, 2002; *Inside the Budget*, December 13, 2005.

57. *New York Post*, July 1, 2005, 15.

58. *New York Post*, June 18, 2004, 2; *New York Times*, April 10, 2005, 7.

59. *New York Times*, November 4, 2005, B1, B5.

60. *New York Times*, October 26, 2005, B1, B5.

61. Partnership for New York City, *Progress Report on the New York City School Reform*, September 2005, 1–13; *Green Book*, 196, 198.

62. *Comptroller's Financial Report FY2005*, 271.

63. *Progress Report*, 2, 3.

64. New York City Department of Housing Preservation and Development, *Housing Snapshot: A Summary of New York City's Housing Market*, April 2005, 1.

65. *Progress Report*, 24; Parrott, "The Tentative Recovery," 4, 9 (see chap. 3, n. 9).

66. da Costa Nunez, *Shelter Is Not a Home*, 58.

67. Office of the Mayor, "Mayor Bloomberg and HUD Secretary Jackson Announce Agreement to Restore Vacant Properties," November 22, 2005, www.nyc.gov.

68. Coalition for the Homeless, "Spotlight: Preventing Homelessness for Low-Income Tenants Living with Disabilities," 2005, 1.

69. Metropolitan Council on Housing, *Tenant/Inquilino*, September 2005, 2.

70. New York City Department of Homeless Services, *Statistics, Historic Data*, www.nyc.gov/dhs; Coalition for the Homeless, *Research: Basic Facts About Homelessness*, 2005, www.coalitionforthehomeless.org, 1–3.

71. Department of Homeless Services, press release, June 30, 2005, 1; Department of Homeless Services, *Historic Data; Newsday*, July 1, 2005, A22.

72. New York City Office of Management and Budget, *Monthly Report on*

Current Economic Conditions, October 12, 2005, "Resident Employment and Unemployment," "Annual Historical Data," n.p.

73. Department of Homeless Services, *HOPE 2005: The NYC Street Survey*, 2005, n.p.

74. Public Advocate Betsy Gotbaum, *Scatter Site Housing = Scatter Brain Housing*, report, no date, 1.

75. *Daily News*, June 14, 2004, www.nydailynews.com.

76. *The Indypendent*, August 26, 2004, 4.

77. *Daily News*, October 20, 2005, www.nydailynews.com.

78. Sanjek, *Future of Us All*, 97 (see chap. 1, n. 3).

79. *New York Times*, December 13, 2005, B3; *Metro New York*, June 27, 2005, 6.

80. Alan Hevesi, "Current Trends in the New York City Economy," Office of the State Comptroller, New York, September 2004, 11.

81. *Brooklyn Downtown Star*, January 26, 2006, 33, 34; *amNew York*, January 27–29, 2006, 32, 33.

82. Campaign for Fiscal Equity, press release, November 30, 2004, www.cfequity.org; *New York Times*, February 5, 2004, B1, B4; *New York Times*, December 2, 2004, 38.

83. Partnership for NYC, *Progress Report*, 10; *Report of the Comptroller FY 2005*, 270–71.

84. Michael Rebell and Joseph Wardenski, "Of Course Money Matters: Why the Arguments to the Contrary Never Added Up," Campaign for Fiscal Equity, January 2004, 5–6.

85. Lois Weiner, "Neoliberalism, Teacher Unionism, and the Future of Public Education," *New Politics* 10, no. 2 (Winter 2005), 105–7.

86. Ibid., 101–7.

87. *Progress Report*, 40–41.

88. John Heilemann, "The Chancellor's Midterm Exam," *New York*, October 31, 2005, 33.

89. Chris Smith, "Joel Klein's 200 Club," *New York*, February 17, 2003, www.nymag.com.

90. *New York Times*, January 22, 2006, sec. 14, p. 11.

91. Partnership for NYC, *Progress Report*, 5.

92. NYC Department of Education, press releases, September 22, 2005, 1; Heilemann, "Chancellor's Midterm Exam," 35.

93. *The Chief*, March 18, 2005, 1, 9.

94. Zahraa Abante-Hayes, "How New York City Is Failing Black Kids," *Black Commentator*, no. 136 (April 28, 2005), www.blackcommentator.com.

95. Office of the Mayor, "For Immediate Release," PR–432–05, November 17, 2005, www.nyc.gov.

96. *New York Times*, December 30, 2005, Al, B6.

97. *New York Times*, January 12, 2006, B4; *New York Times*, December 12, 2005, B3.

98. Partnership for NYC, *Progress Report*, 28; Lorraine C. Minnite, "Outside the Circle: The Impact of 9/11 Responses on Immigrant Communities in New York City," in *Contentious City: The Politics of Recovery in New York City*, ed. John Mollenkopf (New York: Russell Sage Foundation, 2005), 177.

99. Partnership for NYC, *Progress Report*, 4, 12, 13.

100. *New York Times*, September 13, 2005, B1.

101. *New York Times*, September 15, 2005, 1, B8.

102. *New York Times*, November 9, 2005, 1, B8, B9; *New York Times*, November 10, 2005, 1, B6, B7.

103. NYC Campaign Finance Board, "Campaign Finance Summary 2005 Citywide Elections," January 17, 2006, www.nyccb.info/public.

104. *The Chief*, September 23, 2005, 1; *The Chief*, November 18, 2005, 18.

105. *New York Times*, November 9, 2005, B8.

106. *New York Times*, October 9, 2005, 37, 40.

107. New York State Board of Elections, "Registration Totals by County," March 3, 2005, www.nys.gov; *New York Times*, November 10, 2005, B6.

108. *New York Times*, September 15, 2005, B8.

109. *Metro New York*, October 19, 2005, 2.

110. *New York Times*, January 11, 2006, B1, B5.

6: Behind the Skyline

1. *New York*, June 20, 2005, 14.

2. David Rockefeller, *Memoirs* (New York: Random House, 2003), 285–87; 406–18.

3. Ibid., 387–92; Susan Fainstein, "Ground Zero's Landlord," in *Contentious City* (see chap. 5, n. 98), 74; Mitchell Moss, "The Redevelopment of Lower Manhattan: The Role of the City," in *Contentious City*, 96; Lynne Sagalyn, "The Politics of Planning the World's Most Visible Urban Redevelopment Project," in *Contentious City*, 27; Darton, *Divided We Stand*, 14–16, 58–59 (see chap. 1, n. 8).

4. Rockefeller, *Memoirs*, 401; Partnership for New York City, "History," www.pfnyc.org.

5. Fitch, *Assassination of New York*, 212–20 (see intro., n. 6).

6. Rockefeller, *Memoirs*, 209, 495–96.

7. Sanders Korenman, "The Effects of 9/11 on New York's Publicly Traded Companies: A Brief Look at Financial Market Data," in *Resilient City* (see chap. 3, n. 26), 135, 152.

8. JP Morgan Chase, "The History of the Firm," Archives, www.jpmorganchase.com; Bell Atlantic, May 24, 2000, "Bell Atlantic on the Verge of 'Next Great Transformation,' " http://newscenter.verizon.com.

9. *Statistical Abstract 2004–2005*, 449; Thomson Financial, *Mergers and Acquisitions Review*, Fourth Quarter 2005, 1.

10. Thomson Financial, *Mergers and Acquisitions Review*, 2.

11. Duff McDonald, "How Goldman Sachs Is Carving Up Its $11 Billion Money Pie," *New York*, December 5, 2005, 49.

12. Ibid., 51–53, 121; *New York Times*, January 12, 2006, C3.

13. Kate Pickert, ed., "Who Makes How Much," *New York*, September 26, 2005, 40.

14. *New York Times*, April 3, 2005, sec. 3, p. 9.

15. *Economic Report of the President*, 2005, 315.

16. Brenner, *Boom and the Bubble*, 150–51 (see chap. 1, n. 25).

17. Harvey, *Brief History of Neoliberalism*, 32 (see chap. 1, n. 7).

18. Ibid., 16.

19. Paul Krugman, "For Richer," *New York Times Magazine*, October 20, 2002, www.nytimes.com; *New York Times*, January 29, 2006, www.nytimes.com.

20. Daniel Gross, "Don't Hate Them Because They're Rich," *New York*, April 18, 2005, 30.

21. Partnership for New York City, "Board of Directors," www.nycp.org; Downtown Alliance, "Board of Directors," www.downtownny.com.

22. Alliance for a Better New York, "History," www.abny.org; LMDC, "LMDC Board of Directors," www.renewnyc.com.

23. Newfield and Du Brul, *Abuse of Power*, 82 (see chap. 1, n. 39).

24. *New York Times*, January 8, 2006, 23; *New York Times*, January 12, 2006, B5; *Park Slope Paper*, January 14, 2006, 1; New York State Democratic Committee, "Assemblyman Herman D. Ferrell, Jr."; New York State Democratic Committee, "Thomas Manton," www.nydems.org.

25. *New York*, December 5, 2005, 20.

26. *New York Times*, January 8, 2006, 13.

27. *New York Times*, January 8, 2006, 23.

28. *amNewYork*, January 4, 2006, 3; *amNewYork*, January 5, 2006, 6; *Metro New York*, January 4, 2006, 4.

29. *New York Times*, January 12, 2006, B1.

30. Roger Davidson and Walter Oleszek, *Congress and Its Members*, 10th ed. (Washington, DC: CQ Press, 2006), 395, 415.

31. *New York Times*, January 12, 2006, B1.

32. Ibid.

33. *NYC Lobbyist Directory*, NYC Lobbyist Search, Year 2005, www.nyc.gov; Barrett, *Rudy!*, 447–48 (see chap. 4, n. 31); "Editorials," *The Nation*, January 30, 2006, 3–4; *Green Book 2003–04,*, 241; *City Limits Monthly*, July/August 2003, www.citylimits.org; Greenberg Traurig, "Greenberg Traurig New York," press release, May 27, 2005, 1.

34. *NYC Lobbyist Directory* 2005, www.nyc.gov.

35. NYC Campaign Finance Board, "Contribution/Donation Public Disclosure Report, Candidate: Giuliani, Rudolph, Election Cycle 1997," www.nyc.gov; *New York Times*, January 11, 2006, B3; *New York Times*, January 17, 2006, B8; *New York Times*, January 24, 2005, C4.

36. NYC Campaign Finance Board, "Contributions/Donations Public Disclosure Report, Candidate: Fernando Ferrer, Election Cycle 2005," www .nyc.gov; *Mother Jones,*, "The Mother Jones 400: Leo J. Hindery, Jr. (with Deborah)," March 5, 2001, www.motherjones.com.

37. Partnership for New York City, *2005 Priorities*, New York, 2005, 2.

38. New York Building Congress, *Newsletter*, Winter 2003, www.building-congress.com.

39. *Progress Report 2005*, "Mayor's Message."

40. *New York Times*, January 18, 2004, sec. 11, pp. 1, 4; *New York Times*, October 10, 2005, B4.

41. Empire State Development Corporation, "Site Plan," www.queens west.org.

42. *Downtown Brooklyn Star*, January 26, 2006, 1, 20.

43. Moss, "Redevelopment of Lower Manhattan," 99–100.

44. John Mollenkopf, "How 9/11 Reshaped the Political Environment in New York," in *Contentious City*, 210–11; Moss, "Redevelopment of Lower Manhattan," 101–3; Good Jobs New York, *Reconstruction Watch*, "The LMDC: They're in the Money; We're in the Dark," August 2004, 8.

45. *Reconstruction Watch*, "The LMDC," 12–14.

46. Fainstein, "Ground Zero's Landlord," 76.

47. Sagalyn, "Politics of Planning," 43–44; Fainstein, "Ground Zero's Landlord," 74.

48. Paul Goldberger, *Up from Zero: Politics, Architecture, and the Rebuilding of New York* (New York: Random House, 2004), 88–89.

49. Ibid., 112–15, 185–200.

50. Sagalyn, "Politics of Planning," 42.

51. Fainstein, "Ground Zero's Landlord," 78–79, 93; Moss, "Redevelopment of Lower Manhattan," 100.

52. *New York Times*, May 30, 2004, sec. 11, pp. 1, 4.

53. Moss, "Redevelopment of Lower Manhattan," 108.

54. *New York Times*, May 30, 2004, sec. 11, p. 1.

55. Setha Low, Dana Taplin, and Mike Lamb, "Battery Park City: An Ethnographic Field Study of the Community Impact of 9/11," *Urban Affairs Review* 40, no. 5 (May 2005), 662–68.

56. Goldberger, *Up from Zero*, 181–82; Sagalyn, "Politics of Planning," 61; *amNewYork*, September 9–11, 2005, 11.

57. *Metro New York*, September 1, 2005, 4.

58. *Metro New York*, August 18, 2005, 3; *Bond Buyer*, "Liberty Board OKs $1.65B for Goldman," August 15, 2005, www.bondbuyer.com.

59. *New York Times*, May 1, 2005, www.nytimes.com; *Curbed*, "How Goldman Sachs Exploded Freedom Tower Plans," May 2, 2004, www.curbed.com.

60. *amNewYork*, October 24, 2005, 3.

61. *Crain's*, "Mayor Names Six New LMDC Board Members," November 16, 2005, www.newyorkbusiness.com.

62. *New York Times*, November 9, 2005, B3; Sagalyn, "Politics of Planning," 30–31.

63. *Planning World Cities*, 85–87 (see chap. 3, n. 15).

64. *Metro New York*, October 19, 2005, 3.

65. *New York Times*, December 18, 2005, sec. 11, pp. 1, 9; *Metro New York*, August 4, 2005, 2.

66. Fiscal Policy Institute, *New York City 2005–2006 Budget Outlook*, February 2, 2005, 11; Tom Robbins, "The Hucksters," *Village Voice*, June 15–21, 2005, 20.

67. Chris Smith, "The Stadium Catbird Seat," *New York*, May 16, 2005, www.newyorkmetro.com/nymetro/news/politics/columns/citypolitic/1897/.

68. Ibid.

69. *amNewYork*, June 7, 2005, 6.

70. *Daily News*, January 19, 2005, www.nydailynews.com.

71. *amNewYork*, December 6, 2005, 6; *Metro New York*, July 19, 2005, 1; Good Jobs New York, "City's Proposal for Financing Development of Manhattan's Far West Side," www.goodjobsny.org; Empire State Development Corporation, "Farley—Penn Station Project," June 20, 2002, www.nyloves biz.com.

72. *amNewYork*, March 15, 2005, 1, 6.

73. Empire State Development Corporation, www.nylovesbiz.com.

74. Andrew Beveridge and Susan Weber, "Race and Class in the Developing New York and Los Angeles Metropolises, 1940–2000," in *New York and Los Angeles* (see chap. 1, n. 131), 58–59.

75. Ibid., 57–58.

76. *The Guardian*, August 31, 2006, 23.

77. *New York Times*, June 19, 2005, sec. 14, p. 12; *Park Slope Courier*, August 8, 2005, 4.

78. *New York Times*, November 28, 2005, B1, B4.

79. Paul Moses, "Poor Excuse," *Village Voice*, July 5, 2005, www.village voice.com.; *BKLYN*, summer 2005, 19–21.

80. Wired New York, *vBulletin*, "New Improved Brooklyn," April 28, 2004, www.wirednewyork.com; *Brooklyn Papers*, November 26, 2005, 3; *Fort Greene–Clinton Hill Paper*, November 19, 2005, 1, 16.

81. *Brooklyn Downtown Star*, October 6, 2005, 46; *Brooklyn Downtown Star*, November 17, 2005, 1; *amNewYork*, July 6, 2005, 3.

82. *Park Slope Paper*, May 28, 2005, 1, 12.

83. *New York Times*, October 14, 2005, B8; *Park Slope Paper*, May 28, 2005, 12; *Downtown Brooklyn Star*, September 1, 2005, 1, 25, 27; Good Jobs New York, "Comments of Bettina Damiani," testimony before the New York City Council, May 26, 2005, 1–5.

84. Paul Moses, "A New Colony," *Village Voice*, May 17, 2005, www.village voice.com; *Metro New York*, May 3, 2005, 1.

85. *Park Slope Paper*, July 23, 2005, 17; *Park Slope Paper*, August 13, 2005, 1, 14; *Park Slope Paper*, September 17, 2005, 1, 2; *Park Slope Paper*, December 10, 2005, 1; *Park Slope Paper*, January 26, 2006, 1, 15; *Downtown Brooklyn Star*, January 26, 2006, 2, 20.

86. *Park Slope Paper*, August 13, 2005, 1.

87. *Park Slope Paper*, January 14, 2006, 1, 5.

88. *Park Slope Paper*, December 3, 2005, 1, 6.

89. *Park Slope Paper*, April 9, 2005, 1, 2.

90. *Labor Notes* no. 325, April 2006, 7.

91. *Park Slope Paper*, September 24, 2005, 1; *Park Slope Paper*, December 10, 2005, 1, 12.

92. City of New York Department of Finance, *Annual Report on the NYC Real Property Tax*, August 2005, Part VII, 39.

93. *New York Times*, June 19, 2005, sec. 14, p. 6.

94. *New York Times*, January 26, 2006, A1, B6.

7: Beneath the Skyline

1. *The Chief*, December 30, 2005, 1, 7.

2. *Houston Chronicle*, April 17, 2006, www.chron.com; *New York Press*, April 19, 2006, www.nypress.com.

3. *Union Democracy Review*, no. 160 (January/February 2006), 1, 2; presentation to Empire State College class by TWU Local 100 member Tim Schermerhorn, December 14, 2005; *Labor Notes* no. 325, April 2006, 4; *Labor Notes* no. 327, June 2006, 14.

4. Freeman, *Working-Class New York*, 41 (see intro., n. 5); New York City Central Labor Council Web site, 2005; *Union Membership*, BLS, 2005.

5. Minnite, "Outside the Circle," 177 (see chap. 5, n. 98); Larry Sabato, "The Election That Broke the Rules," in *Divided States of America: The Slash and Burn Politics of the 2004 Presidential Election*, ed. Sabato (New York: Pearson/Longman, 2006), 107.

6. Nancy Foner, "The Social Effects of 9/11 on New York City: An Introduction," in *Wounded City: The Social Impact of 9/11*, ed. Nancy Foner (New York: Russell Sage Foundation, 2005), 3–19; Melanie Hildebrandt, "Double Trauma in Belle Harbor: The Aftermath of September 11 and November 12 in the Rockaways," in *Wounded City*, 106–7.

7. Editorial, *New York Times*, September 23, 2001, www.nytimes.com.

8. James Parrott and Oliver Cooke, "The Economic Impact of 9/11 on New York City's Low-Wage Workers and Households," in *Resilient City* (see chap. 3, n. 26), 190–200; Cordelia Reimers, "The Impact of 9/11 on Low-Skilled, Minority, and Immigrant Workers in New York City," in *Resilient City*, 241.

9. Andy Pollack, "The Airline Industry and Airline Unionism in the 1970s

and 1980s," in *Trade Union Politics: American Unions and Economic Change 1960s–1990s*, ed. Glenn Perusek and Kent Worcester (New Jersey: Humanities Press, 1995), 188–202.

10. William Kornblum and Steven Lang, "The Impact of 9/11 on the New York City Airline Industry," in *Wounded City*, 163–66, 175; Parrott and Cooke, "Economic Impact of 9/11," 200–201.

11. Kornblum and Lang, "Impact of 9/11," 174–77.

12. Ibid., 171–78.

13. *Labor Notes* no. 290, May 2003, 1, 14.

14. Parrott and Cooke, "Economic Impact of 9/11," 223.

15. Margaret Chin, "Moving On: Chinese Garment Workers After 9/11," in *Wounded City*, 180–90.

16. Ibid., 188–204; Vanessa Tait, *Poor Workers' Unions: Rebuilding Labor from Below*, (Cambridge, MA: South End Press, 2005), 170–71.

17. Biju Mathew, *Taxi! Cabs and Capitalism in New York City* (New York: The New Press, 2005), 49–106.

18. Monisha Das Gupta, "Of Hardship and Hostility: The Impact of 9/11 on New York City Taxi Drivers," in *Wounded City*, 209, 213; Mathew, *Taxi!*, 69.

19. Das Gupta, "Of Hardship and Hostility," 213–20, 223.

20. Ibid., 226–30.

21. Parrott, "Tentative Recovery," 6 (see chap. 3, n. 9); *New York Times*, January 27, 2006, B4.

22. Parrott and Cooke, "Economic Impact of 9/11," 216, 218.

23. *New York Times*, January 26, 2006, A1, B6.

24. *Labor Notes* no. 235, October 1998; *Labor Notes* no. 258, September 2000, 7; *Labor Notes* no. 296, November 2003, 3.

25. *Labor Notes* no. 239, February 1998, 6.

26. *Labor Notes* no. 250, January 2000, 1, 14; *Labor Notes* no. 252, March 2000, 10.

27. Lynn Taylor, president of AFSCME DC 37 Local 1930, interview by author, March 21, 2006.

28. *The Chief*, September 30, 2005, 1.

29. *Labor Notes* no. 222, September 1997, 14.

30. *Labor Notes* no. 239, February 1999, 4.

31. *Labor Notes* no. 238, January 1999, 3; *Labor Notes* no. 245, August 1999, 16.

32. *New York Times*, February 15, 2000, B1, B6; *Labor Notes* no. 265, April 2001, 4.

33. *New York Times*, March 9, 2000, B4; U.S. Department of Labor, Bureau of Labor Statistics, "Consumer Price Index—All Urban Consumers," www.bls.gov, March 30, 2006.

34. *Labor Notes* no. 240, March 2000, 6; *Labor Notes* no. 261, December 2000, 4; *New York Times*, March 9, 2000, B4.

35. *Labor Notes* no. 236, November 1998, 3; *Labor Notes* no. 237, December 1998, 2; *Labor Notes* no. 238, January 1999, 6.

36. Robert Fitch, *Solidarity for Sale: How Corruption Destroyed the Labor Movement and Undermined America's Promise* (New York: Public Affairs, 2006), 162–65.

37. *Labor Notes* no. 340, March 2000, 11; *Labor Notes* no. 341, April 2000, 2; Freeman, *Working-Class New York*, 324–25; *The Chief*, March 8, 2002, 1, 7.

38. *Labor Notes* no. 245, August 1999, 15, 16.

39. *Labor Notes* no. 263, February 2001, 1, 14.

40. *Labor Notes* no. 259, October 2000, 2.

41. *The Chief*, March 8, 2002, 1, 6; *New York Times*, May 15, 2002, B4.

42. *Labor Notes* no. 297, December 2003, 8; *Labor Notes* no. 325, April 2006, 7.

43. Discussions with members of Utility Workers Union Local 1–2 throughout 2005 at Cornell ILR School, New York.

44. Discussions with members of UFT Teachers for a Decent Contract slate throughout 2004–5.

45. *Labor Notes* no. 303, June 2004, 16, 14.

46. *The Chief*, December 20, 2002, 1, 12.

47. *The Chief*, October 7, 2005, 1; *The Chief*, November 11, 2005, 1; *Labor Notes* no. 320, November 2005, 6.

48. *New York Times*, June 29, 2005, B4.

49. *New York Times*, October 19, 2005, B1; *New York Times*, October 21, 2005, 1.

50. *The Chief*, February 27, 2004, 1; *The Chief*, May 7, 2004, 1, 7; *The Chief*, July 22, 2005, 1, 7; *The Chief*, October 29, 2004, 1, 12.

51. United Federation of Teachers, "Mayor Announces DC 37 Agreement," July 17, 2006, www.uft.org.

52. Professional Staff Congress, "Contract Settled," e-mail to PSC members from President Barbara Bowen, April 26, 2006.

53. United Federation of Teachers, "20 Unions, Including UFT, Form Bargaining Coalition," June 23, 2006, www.uft.org.

54. *The Chief*, November 18, 2005, 1, 18.

55. *New York Times*, October 16, 2005, B1, B5.

56. See Table 5-1 in chapter 5.

57. Philip Foner, *History of the Labor Movement in the United States*, svol. 2 (New York: International Publishers, 1955), 290–93.

58. Ray Tillman, "Reform Movement in the Teamsters and the United Auto Workers," in *The Transformation of U.S. Unions: Voices, Visions, and Strategies from the Grassroots*, ed. Ray Tillman and Michael Cummings (Boulder, CO: Lynne Rienner Publishers, 1999), 144–48; Anna Zajicek and Bradley Mash Jr., "Lessons from the UMWA," in *Transformation of U.S. Unions*, 221–28; for overview of recent reform movements see *Transforma-*

tion of U.S. Unions; Moody, *Injury to All* (see chap. 1, n. 29); and Benson, *Rebels* (see chap. 2, n. 52).

59. Bellush and Bellush, *Union Power*, 108–9 (see chap. 1, n. 49); Nelson Lichtenstein, *State of the Unions: A Century of American Labor* (Princeton, NJ: Princeton University Press, 2002), 181–85.

60. For more on this see Mike Parker and Martha Gruelle, *Democracy Is Power: Rebuilding Unions from the Bottom Up* (Detroit: Labor Notes, 1999), *passim*.

61. *Labor Notes* no. 263, February 2001, 14; Steve Downs and Tim Schermerhorn, *"Hell on Wheels*: Organizing Among New York City's Subway and Bus Workers," in *Transformation of U.S. Unions*, 169–73.

62. Fitch, *Solidarity for Sale*, 163–78; *The Chief*, February 20, 2004, 1.

63. Downs and Schermerhorn, *"Hell on Wheels,"* 182–84.

64. *The Chief*, February 20, 2006, 1, 12; *Labor Notes* no. 312, March 2005, 5; *Union Democracy Review*, no. 159 (November/December 2005), 5.

65. Downs and Schermerhorn, *"Hell on Wheels,"* 171.

66. Ibid., 177–88; *Labor Notes* no. 263, February 2001, 14; discussions with Steve Downs, Tim Schermerhorn, and other TWU Local 100 activists, December 2005.

67. For more information on these organizations see: www.tdu.org, www.labornotes.org, and www.uniondemocracy.org. The founding and much of the past work of AUD is described in Benson, *Rebels*.

68. *The Chief*, July 22, 2005, 1.

69. *The Chief*, November 18, 2005, 1, 18; William Thompson Jr., NYC Comptroller, press release, March 6, 2006, 1, www.comptroller.nyc.gov.

70. *Labor Notes* no. 234, September 1998, 3.

71. Discussions with Working Families Party leaders and activists, 2004–5.

72. Alyssa Katz, "The Power of Fusion Politics," *The Nation*, September 12, 2005, www.thenation.com; Working Families Party, "Working Families Party timeline, 1998–Present," www.workingfamiliesparty.org, January 26, 2006.

73. *Labor Notes* no. 320, November 2005, 3, 11.

74. New York Central Labor Council, "Local Unions," www.nycclc.org.

75. Mathew, *Taxi!*, 1–7,196–97.

76. Ness, *Immigrants*, 150–61.

77. Ibid., 58–129; Tait, *Poor Workers' Unions*, 205–16.

78. *Union Democracy Review*, no. 159 (November/December 2005), 1; *New York Times*, November 15, 2005, B5.

79. Anya Kamenetz, "Baristas of the World, Unite!: You Have Nothing to Lose But Your Company-Mandated Cheerfulness," *New York*, May 20, 2005, 38, 39, 105.

80. Minnite, "Outside the Circle," 177.

81. Janice Fine, "Worker Centers: Organizing Communities at the Edge of

the Dream," Economic Policy Institute Briefing Paper no. 159, December 14, 2004, 3.

82. Ibid., 1, plus my addition of two groups not on her list: Make the Road by Walking in Brooklyn and the Northwest Bronx Community and Clergy Coalition. Fine includes the Taxi Workers Alliance on her list, but I have put it with unions as it defines itself that way.

83. Tait, *Poor Workers' Unions*, 162–69.

84. Steve Jenkins, "Organizing, Advocacy, and Member Power," *Working USA: The Journal of Labor and Society* 6, no. 2 (Fall 2002): 56–66.

85. Community Development Project of the Urban Justice Center and the Northwest Bronx Community and Clergy Coalition, *Scattered Dreams: How the Scattered Site Shelter Program Exacerbates the Affordable Housing Crisis in Low-Income Neighborhoods in the Northwest Bronx*, December 2004, 5–19; also exposed in a TV video called *The City of Rich and Poor: Jack Newfield's New York* (Lefthanded Films, 2005).

86. Saru Jayaraman, "In the Wake of September 11: New York Restaurant Workers Explore New Strategies," *Labor Notes* no. 293, August 2003, www.labornotes.org.

87. Jenkins, "Organizing," 77–82; Mathew, *Taxi!*, 193–96.

88. Jayaraman, "In the Wake of September 11."

89. Minnite, "Outside the Circle," 171.

90. Ibid., 171.

91. Sites, *Remaking New York*, 119–33; also *From Urban Village* (see chap. 2, n. 33), 233–307.

92. Ness, *Immigrants*, 42–43.

93. *New York Times*, April 17, 2006, April 11, 2006, www.nytimes.com; Sarah Ferguson, "This Is the Time to Rise," *Village Voice*, April 11, 2006, www.villagevoice.com.

94. Freeman, *Working-Class New York*, 3–6.

95. Ibid., 58–60; Gerson, *Pete*, 61–72, 162–65 (see chap. 2, n. 63).

96. Fiscal Policy Institute, *New York City's Labor Market Outlook with a Special Emphasis on Immigrant Workers*, December 9, 2005, 6, 8, 15.

97. Clawson, *Next Upsurge*, 194–205; Ness, *Immigrants*, 189–90.

Conclusion: Neoliberal Triumph

1. Mark Jurkowitz, "NYC's Alternative Crisis," *The Phoenix*, February 16, 2006, www.thephoenix.com; *Democracy Now*, "The Village Voice Shakeup," April 13, 2006, www.democracynow.org; *New York Times*, June 12, 2006, www.nytimes.com.

2. Fitch, *Assassination of New York*, 37–53 (see intro., n. 6).

3. *Report of the Comptroller FY2005*, 296; Siegel, *Prince of the City*, 161–62 (see chap. 4, n. 21).

4. Parrott, "Tentative Recovery," 6, figure 1 (see chap. 3, n. 9); Brecher and

Horton, *Power Failure*, 194 (see chap. 1, n. 22); Hill and Lendel, "Did 9/11 Change Manhattan?" 40 (see chap. 3, n. 26).

5. NYC Comptroller, press releases, March 6, 2006, 1.

6. Brecher and Horton, *Power Failure*, 25; *Expense, Revenue, Contract, FY2006*, i, ii.

7. *Annual Report on Tax Expenditures, FY2005*, i; LeRoy, *Great American Jobs Scam*, 2 (see chap. 3, n. 18).

8. Brecher and Horton, *Power Failure*, 21; *Report of the Comptroller FY2005*, 264–67, 270–71.

9. Shefter, *Political Crisis/Fiscal Crisis*, 116 (see intro., n. 3); *Report of the Comptroller FY2005*, 267, 271; *Expense, Revenue, Contract, FY2006*, i. The comparison of labor costs to spending differs from that in the last chapter because it includes the capital budget in the total following Brecher and Horton, *Power Failure*, and Shefter, *Political Crisis/Fiscal Crisis*.

10. Office of the State Comptroller, *The Impact of Wall Street on Jobs and Tax Revenues*, Report 1–2005, April 2004, 13.

11. *New York Times*, September 4, 2005, www.nytimes.com.

12. OSC, *Current Trends*, 8–11.

13. *New York Times*, April 21, 2006, www.nytimes.com.

14. *Working Families Party Timeline*, 1–2.

15. Nancy Raskin, "Testimony Before New York City Council Joint Hearing: Select Committee on Community Development," Community Service Society of New York, November 15, 2005, 1, 2; Mark Levitan, *Poverty in New York City, 2004: Recovery?*, Community Service Society of New York, September 2005, 1, 13, 14.

16. *Working Families Party Timeline*, 1, 2; Raskin, "Testimony," 1.

17. Wallace, *New Deal, passim* (see chap. 3, n. 19).

18. Newfield and DuBrul, *Abuse of Power*, 240 (see chap. 1, n. 39).

INDEX

Abramoff, Jack, 209
Abzug, Bella, 63
Academic Intervention Services,
    189–90
ACORN, 272
Adler, Norman, 23
Ady, Robert, 170
African Americans: Atlantic Yards
    opposition, 235–37; Bloomberg
    appointments, 161; borough
    presidents, 89, 90, 117; CEOs,
    financial sector, 201, 205; on city
    council, 90; coalitions (1960s–70s),
    21–22; in crisis regime, 36; Dinkins
    appointments, 120; displacement, 75;
    first union leaders, 24, 83–84; free
    black communities, 74–75; internal
    migration, 108; Koch-era violence, 87;
    mayor (*see* Dinkins, David); under
    representation and Democratic Party,
    88–91; voter registration, 91, 114
Ahn, NaRhee, 163
airline industry: decline, 101–2; federal
    aid, inequity of, 249; post-9/11 losses,
    248–50; strikes, 85, 248
Albanese Organization, 223
Albanese, Sal, 142
Alexandria Real Estate Equities, 169
Alliance for a Better New York, 206
Alliance for Downtown New York, 198,
    210, 219
Alper, Andrew, 239
Alter, Susan, 128

Amalgamated Transit Union (ATU),
    269; Drivers Coalition gains, 259–60
American Federation of State, County,
    and Municipal Employees (DC 37),
    22–23; contract (2004–6), 260–61;
    corruption, 257; double zeros contract,
    144, 257; Koch era, 73, 82–84;
    protests/strike, 42, 47; reform (2000),
    257–58; wage increase (2000), 256
Anderson, Arvid, 81
Armey, Dick, 249
assessment reductions, property tax,
    172–76
Association for Union Democracy
    (AUD), 267–68
Astor, John Jacob, 74
Atlantic Yards, 185, 235–37; Community
    Benefit Agreement (CBA), 236–37;
    features of, 235; opposition to, 235–36
Atlantic Yards Area Redevelopment
    Project, 217, 235
Axelson, Kenneth, 40

Babbio, Lawrence, 226
Bach, Victor, 179
Badillo, Herman, 44, 62–63, 89, 128, 156,
    209–10
Bailey, Robert, 31, 32
bailout: business elite favored by, 40, 49,
    66–70; and crisis regime, 30–42;
    federal seasonal loans, 40–41, 48;
    Koch budget items during, 68–69;
    municipal union, cuts to, 37, 42–49;

bailout (*cont.*)
union pension fund bond purchase, 38, 43, 46–47
Balachandran, Robert, 220
Balanoff, Tom, 257
Balboza, Sandy, 238
banking industry: and recession of 1974–75, 11. *See also* financial sector
Barbanel, Josh, 174
Barbero, Frank, 81
Barrett, Wayne, 129, 137–38
Barron, Charles, 208
Barry, Francis, 36, 40
Battery Park City: development of, 197; post-9/11 residents, 224; tax-exempt status, 59, 72
Battery Park City Authority, 171
Battery Park City Housing Trust Fund, 180
Bay Ridge, down-zoning, 215
Bayside, down-zoning, 215
Beame, Abe: and fiscal crisis, 32, 44, 45, 55; Koch defeats, 62–63
Beatty, Vander, 119
Bedford-Stuyvesant, home sales figures, 185
Benson, Herman, 267
Bensonhurst, down-zoning, 215
Bentivenga, Dominic, 257
Betts, Roland, 220
Bevona, Gus, 256–57
Bigel, Jack, 43–44, 46, 48
Bishop, Jimmy, 84
Blankfein, Lloyd, 201
Bloomberg, Michael, 155–95; appointments of, 160–61, 195; budget deficit, 166, 170–71; budget items, 167–69; as business elite, 159–60, 206; and business elite, 176–77, 189–90; city contracts awarded by, 162; education reform, 185–91; election of 2001, 155–58; election of 2005, 192–95; and Ground Zero development, 219–20, 226–27; and homeless, 179, 182–83; housing, 171, 177–82; and municipal unions, 193, 255–62; philanthropy of, 159, 162–64; positions before mayor, 158–59; privatization, 162, 187; programs/services/jobs cuts, 166–68; real estate development under, 169;

September 11, economic impact, 165–66, 245–54; stock market slump (2000), 165; tax breaks under, 170–76; taxes, raising, 167; votes by race/party, 158, 192–93
Board of Estimate: abolition of, 79–80; and business elite, 64; mayor power position, 63; members of, 18–19
Boerum Hill, 233
Boesky, Ivan, 79
bonds. *See* municipal bonds
borough presidents: African American, 89, 90, 117–19; Latino, 89; as political machine, 18–19
boroughs: economic development goals (2005), 213–14; gentrified neighborhoods, 77; immigrant residents, 109; Koch-era taxation, 71; Manhattanization of, 7, 237; megaprojects (*see* individual boroughs); population by race (1988), 89; real estate values, rise in, 76–77; working-class population, 7, 74–75
Botnik, Victor, 87
Bratton, William, 134–37
Brecher, Charles, 30, 262
Brenner, Robert, 165
Breslin, Jimmy, 147
broadbanding, 243
broken-window thesis, 134–35, 138
Bronx: Bronx Terminal Market/House of Detention area development, 216; fish market plans, 216; Yankee Stadium, new, 216, 218
Brooklyn: Atlantic Yards, 235–37; Brooklyn Academy of Music (BAM) area development, 238; Brooklyn Bridge Park, 238; Coney Island makeover, 240; down-zoned areas, 215; DUMBO waterfront development, 238; Fourth Avenue high-rise housing, 216, 234; gentrified areas, 77, 233–34; Gowanas development dispute, 234–35; Navy Yard development, 216; population diversity, 233; real estate values increase, 240; Red Hook development/cruise ship plans, 216, 239; rents (2004–5), 241; Williamsburg/Greenpoint high-rises, 237

Brooklyn Academy of Music (BAM), area development, 238
Brooklyn Bridge Park, 218; features of, 238
Brooklyn Bridge Park Development Project, 217
Brooklyn Heights, 233, 238
Brooklyn Museum, 146
Brooklyn Navy Yard development, 216
Brooklyn Nets arena, 105. *See also* Atlantic Yards
Brooklyn United for Innovative Local Development (BUILD), 236–37
Bruno, Joseph, 181
Building Blocks, 177
bundlers, political influence, 211–12
Burden, Amanda, 160–61, 214, 226, 234, 235
business elite, 24–30; and bailout (*see* crisis regime); and Bloomberg, 176–77, 189–90; Bloomberg as member, 159–60, 206; Business Roundtable, 15–16; campaign contributions, 26, 64, 145; city government advisory groups, 67; conspicuous consumption, new superrich, 204–5; deregulation, benefits to, 205–6; and Dinkins, 118–20, 123–25; and gentrification, 78; and Giuliani, 144–45, 150–52, 220–21; Golden Triangle (politics/real estate/banking), 206–7; and Koch, 63–64, 67–70; management/ownership fusion, 201–4; and mergers and acquisitions, 199; as permanent government, 206–14; political influencers (1970s–2000s), 206–13; power organizations of, 25, 30; tax breaks (*see* tax exemptions/breaks)
Business/Labor Working Group, 45, 49
Business Roundtable: development of, 15–16; political influence, 16; business services, decline (1990s), 103
Butler, James, 259
Butts III, Calvin, 163

Calatrava, Santiago, 225
campaign financing. *See* mayoral elections; *specific mayors*
Campaign for Fiscal Equality, 186
capitalist class. *See* business elite

Cardozo, Michael, 164
Carey, Hugh: and fiscal crisis, 33, 35–38; and MAC Act, 35–38
Carey, Ron, 262
Carroll Gardens, 233, 238–39
Carter, Jimmy, 48
Carver Club, 90, 118
Casey, Albert, 39
Castells, Manuel, 26, 27
Center for Administering Rehabilitation and Employment Services (IAM CARES), 249
central business district (CBD), 28–30; business elite advocates, 30; location of, 24, 28
Central Labor Council, 23, 44, 63, 81, 83, 144, 270, 271
Chamber of Commerce and Industry, 67
Change to Win (CTW) unions, 270, 279
Charles, Carmen, 259
charter schools, 187, 188, 190
Chase, tax breaks, 124
Chelsea, High Line transformation plans, 228
Children First, 188–91
Childs, David, 222, 225
Chinatown, garment industry, post-9/11 losses, 250–51
Chinese Staff and Workers' Association (CSWA), 273–74
Chisholm, Shirley, 90
Citizens Budget Commission (CBC), 25, 30, 262
Citizens Union, 25
City Club, 25, 30
city council: African Americans on, 90; county leaders, influence of, 207–8; minority leadership under representation, 89–90
The City in Transition: Prospects and Policies for New York, 66–67
City Journal, 127
City Planning Commission: appointment method, 80; limited powers of, 218; and lobbyists, 209
City University of New York (CUNY): costs and crisis, 52; New Caucus gains, 259; open admissions, 21; tuition, 39–40, 72, 133
Civic Alliance to Rebuild Downtown New York, 223

Clarett Group, 238
Clawson, Dan, 282
Clearing House, 32
Clinton, Hillary, 144
coalition bargaining, 48
Coalition for a Just New York, 91, 118
Coalitions, NYC groups (1960s–70s), 21–22
Cobble Hill, 233
Coleman, John, 36, 66
Commerce and Industry Association, 25
Commer, Roy, 257
Commissioners' Plan (1811), 75
Committee for Real Change, 257
Communications Workers of America (CWA), 83, 255–56
Community Benefit Agreement (CBA), 236–37
community boards, 21
community education councils, 190
community policing, 121, 135
COMPSTAT program, 135
computer-related industries, NYC position, 102
Con Edison, 28–29
Coney Island, development plans, 240
Consolidated Metropolitan Statistical Area (CMSA), Manhattan status (1883–2004), 103–4
conspicuous consumption, new superrich, 204–5
Consumer Issues Working Group, 16
contract award system: and Bloomberg, 162; centralization of, 19–20; and county organizations, 19, 207; and EFCB review, 39; and Koch, 65; and Lindsay, 53
cooperative/condo apartments: assessment of, 174–75; tax abatement, 70, 78, 123, 175–76
corporate headquarters complex: business elite network, 26–30; central business district (CBD), 24, 28–30
corruption: Koch era, 86–87; municipal unions, 84–85
Cortines, Ramon, 132
Council Against Poverty, 65
county organizations: and contract awards, 19, 207; Koch relationship with, 65; political influence of, 19, 207–8

crime control: broken-window thesis, 134–35, 138; and community organizations, 138; Dinkins era, 136; Giuliani approach, 134–38, 146
crisis regime, 30–42; benefits from bailout actions, 40, 49, 66–70; *The City in Transition* proposals, 66–67; as coup of business elite, 31, 38, 49; defined, 18; Emergency Financial Control Board (EFCB) actions, 38–41; end of (1986), 79; formation/development of, 35–41; goals of, 30–31, 37; Koch favoritism, 63–64, 67–70; Mayor's Management Advisory Committee (MMAC), 37, 45; Municipal Assistance Corporation (MAC) Act (1975), 35–38; municipal union support of, 31; NYC economic prelude to, 16–18, 30–35; watchdog role, 79; working class, impact on, 72–74. *See also* bailout
Crotty, Paul, 220, 221
Cuomo, Mario, 62–63

Daily News strike, 116
Darton, Eric, 12
Daughtry, Herbert, 236
Davidoff, Sid, 119, 123
Davis, Ben, 90
Davis, James, 270
Davis, Leon, 84
DC 37. *See* American Federation of State, County, and Municipal Employees (DC 37)
De Blasio, Bill, 207
DeGrasse, Leland, 186
Democratic Party: bundlers of, 211–12; and racial under representation, 88–91
Department of City Planning, 218
Department of Design and Construction, 218
deputy comptroller, 38
deregulation: airline industry, 248; benefits to business elite, 205–6
desk appearance tickets (DATs), 136
DeVincezzo, Joe, 87
Diallo, Amadou, 137, 146
Dinkins, David, 114–30; appointments of, 120; as borough president, 90, 117–19; business elite favoritism,

118–20, 122–25; city council elections, 116–17; crime control, 136; defeats Koch, 65, 91–92, 118; and federal aid, 121–22; job loss under, 121–22; and municipal unions, 115–16; race relations, 125–27; real estate development under, 122–26; recession during term, 121–22; supporters of, 115–16, 119–20; tax breaks under, 123–24; votes by race/party, 129–30
Diop, Al, 257
Doctoroff, Daniel, 160, 226, 227, 228, 230
Dolfman, Michael, 255
Dorismond, Patrick, 137, 146–47
dot.com. *See* new media
double zeros contract, 144, 257
Downtown-Lower Manhattan Association, 25, 30, 132, 197
Drennan, Matthew, 24–25
Drivers Coalition, 259–60
Du Brul, Paul, 31, 206, 290
DUMBO, waterfront development, 238
Durst, Douglas, 134
Durst Organization, 223

Eastern Airlines, mechanics strike, 85, 248
East New York, ghetto, making of, 126
East River Plaza, 211, 216
East River Science Park, 169, 216
East Village, gentrification of, 77–78
economic decline, NYC. *See* fiscal crisis (New York City); recessions; stock market
Economic Development Corporation, 170
Economic Development Council, 30, 67
Edsall, Thomas Byrne, 15
education: Bloomberg reform, 185–91; community education councils, 190; neoliberal policy related to, 186–87, 189–90; private-public partnership, 189–90; test score increases, 189; UFT, 22–23, 46
Eichner, Bruce, 123
Eisenberg, Lewis, 220
Eisner, Michael, 124
Ellinghaus, William, 36–38, 45; real estate development, 198

Ellish, Herb, 37
Ellis, Mark, 110
Emergency Financial Control Board (EFCB), 38–41, 46–49; business elite favored by, 40, 49; goals, 38; members, 38–40; powers of, 38–39; watchdog role, 79
eminent domain and Atlantic Yards, 235
Empire State Development Corporation, 118, 212, 214, 219; subsidiaries, 216–17
employment: Dinkins-era layoffs, 121–22; Giuliani-era income, 153; Giuliani-era layoffs, 132–33; immigrants, jobs of, 110–12, 251–52; Koch-era income, 73–74, 82; Koch-era layoffs, 72–73, 88; manufacturing decline/job loss, 3, 12–14; new media jobs, 100; post-9/11 job loss, 246–54; post-9/11 wage loss, 255; trends (1995–2001), 153–54; wage decline (1990s), 149; wage decline (2000–2005), 282; wage-freezes, 38, 45, 47, 144; wage/job freeze proposal (1975), 30–31. *See also* industries of New York City; municipal unions
Ensley, Charles, 24, 257–58
Enterprise Foundation, 180
Esposito, Meade, 87, 89
executive compensation, 200–204; financial sector, 200–201; and Giuliani, 154; stock/stock options, 202–4
exports of services by NYC, 12–14

Fainstein, Susan, 223
Farrakhan, Louis, 135
Farrell, Herman, 118
federal government: airline industry bailout, 249; bailout loans, 40–41, 48; drop in funds, Dinkins-era, 121–22; drop in funds, Koch-era, 69; drop in funds, Lindsay/Beam-era, 57
Feinstein, Barry, 43, 44, 82, 115
Feldman, Sandra, 83, 115, 131
Ferrell, Herman, 207
Ferrer, Fernando, 157, 192–94
Fields, C. Virginia, 192
Fife, Barbara, 120

financial center (New York City), 11–15, 24–27; building/construction (*see* office building construction); central business district (CBD), 24, 28–30; corporate headquarters complex model, 26–30; global city concept, 11, 24; globalization effects (*see* globalization and New York City)

Financial Community Liaison Group (FCLG), 33

Financial Emergency Act (1975), 31, 38

financial sector: downsizing, 121; economic crisis (*see* fiscal crisis [New York City]); executive compensation, 200–204; firms, types of, 24–25, 198–99; job loss (1975–96), 103; mergers and acquisitions fees to, 199–200; post-9/11 job loss, 246–48, 253–54; recession 1990s, effects of, 100, 122; sector growth, 97–99

Fine, Janice, 275

firefighters, Koch-era losses, 73

fire, insurance, and real estate (FIRE): rise/decline (1990s), 97, 102–3; size of, 199

First National City, global investment approach, 35

fiscal crisis (New York City): bond underwriting crisis, 32–35; budget items during, 68–69; and crisis regime, 18, 30–42, 42–49; default (1975), 16, 37, 43–44; economic decline (1974–75), 9, 12–14, 30–35; federal assistance, 40–41; neoliberal reorganization, 18. *See also* bailout

Fishman, Michael, 257

fish market plans, Bronx, 216

Flom, Joseph, 119

Flynn, Thomas, 36, 37

food stamps, 73, 140

Ford, Gerald, 41, 46

foreign direct investment (FDI): increase in, 94–95; services investment, 95–96

Forest City Ratner, 206, 223. *See also* Ratner, Bruce

42nd Street Development Corporation, 124

42nd Street Redevelopment Corporation, 134, 217

Freedom Tower, 215

Freeman, Joshua, 3, 16, 262, 280

Friedman, Stanley, 86–87, 89

Fulani, Lenora, 164

Fuld, Richard, 201

garment industry: post-9/11 losses, 250–51; worker centers, 274

Garth, David, 156

Gehry, Frank, mega-projects, 217, 235

gentrification: Brooklyn areas, 77, 233–34; engineered by business elite, 78; gentrified neighborhoods, 77, 140; Giuliani era, 140; Harlem, 231–32; and income inequality, 106; Lower East Side, 77–78; and racial discrimination, 77–78, 126; real estate values, rise in, 76–77; whites, increase in residents, 77–78, 231–34

Gerard, Karen, 32

Giardino, Alfred, 39

Gibbs, Linda, 183, 195

Giuliani, Rudolph, 131–54; affairs, 142, 145–46; appointments of, 135, 210; Brooklyn Museum incident, 146; budget deficit, 151; and business elite, 144–45, 150–52, 220; campaign contributions to, 144–45, 211; crime control/law enforcement, 134–38, 146; defeat by Dinkins, 91–92, 115, 119; election of 1993, 128–32; election of 1997, 142–45; and homeless, 138–39, 144; job cuts, 132–33; and municipal unions, 131, 144; NYC economy, post-Giuliani, 149–54; poor, status of, 138–40, 144, 149–50, 152–53; popularity, decline in, 146–47; privatization schemes, 141; race relations, 135, 137, 142, 146–47; real estate development under, 133–34, 140; supporters of, 128–32, 143–45; tax exemptions/breaks, 132–33, 150–51; Times Square renewal, 133–34; votes by race/party, 129–30, 143; World Trade Center attacks, 147–48; World Trade Center cleanup, 218–19

global city, NYC as, 5–6, 9–10, 24, 27

globalization: acceleration of (1980s–present), 94–98; economic measures of, 94–95; foreign direct investment (FDI), increase in, 94–96; foreign-

owned U.S. assets, 96; and multilateral organizations, 95
globalization and New York City, 97–113; airline industry decline, 101–2; competitive aspects, 100–101; export of services, 12–14; financial sector, growth of, 97–98; immigration/immigrants, 108–13; NYC economic vulnerability, 13–16, 98; and stock market boom (1990s), 98–100; and telecommunications industry decline, 102
Golden Triangle (politics/real estate/banking), 206–7
Goldin, Harrison, 46
Goldman Sachs: executive compensation, 199–201
Ground Zero area tower, 225
Gompers, Samuel, 262
Gonzalez, Juan, 114, 116, 120
Goodale, Toni, 164
Good Old Lower East Side, 278
Gotbaum, Victor, 23, 32, 42–45, 48, 82–83
Gould, George, 36
government. *See* New York City government
Governor's Island, commercial development, 216, 218
Governor's Island Preservation & Education Corporation, 217
Gowanus, development dispute, 234–35
Grasso, Richard, 211, 220, 221
Great Society programs, 17, 19, 21. *See also* welfare state
Green, Mark, 156–58
Green, Roger, 236
Greenspan, Alan, 98–99
Greenwich Village, Hudson River Park opposition, 227
Gregorian, Vartan, 163
Griffen, Gilroye, 40
Ground Zero, rebuilding, 218–27; Bloomberg criticism, 226; developers involved, 223; incentives/tax breaks, 223–25; LMDC board members, 219–21; Port Authority opposition, 222; residential use, 223–24; size of project, 222; transportation plans, 225
Guzman, Carlos, 257

Hamilton, Charles V., 21
Hammett, Bill, 127
Handlin, Oscar, 108
Hanover, Donna, 145–46
Harding, Ray, 128, 142, 210, 220
Harding, Robert, 210, 219, 226
Harlem: East River Plaza plans, 216; gentrification, 231–32
Harlem Community Development Corporation, 217, 231
Harnett, Joel, 30, 63
Harris, Patricia, 160, 164, 195
Hart-Cellar Act (1965), 108–9
Harvey, David, 18, 202–3
Hasidic Jews, racial violence, 126
Health and Hospitals Corporation: Bloomberg spending increase, 169; Giuliani privatization attempt, 141; strike (1976), 47
Hell on Wheels, 258, 266
Hell's Kitchen/Clinton development, 198, 231
Heritage Foundation, 16
Hernandez-Piñero, Sally, 120, 123, 220, 221, 228
Hevesi, Alan, 157
High Line, transformation plans, 228
Hill, Stanley, 24, 83, 115, 118, 144, 257
Hindery, Leo J., 211–12
homeless: Bloomberg era, 179, 182–83; Giuliani era, 138–39, 144, 150; housing development for, 78–79; Koch era, 73; race-ethnicity of, 150; worker center activities, 274
Home Relief, 1, 16, 139
Horowitz, Dale, 32, 33, 48
Horton, Raymond, 30
hospitals (city): Giuliani privatization attempt, 141; HHC strike, 47; income-producing services, 67; Koch-era closing, 72
Hotel Employees and Restaurant Employees Local 100, 85
housing: Bloomberg era, 171, 177–82; community coalitions for, 277–78; Dinkins era, 123, 126; Giuliani era, 150, 177; Ground Zero project, 223–24; housing projects, first, 16; Koch era, 73; rents, increase over time, 77, 178; rent-stabilized apartments, 178–79; Section 8 vouchers, 177, 181,

housing: Bloomberg era (*cont.*)
183; underground housing conversion,
184. *See also* low-income
neighborhoods; mega-projects
Housing Development Corporation
(HDC), 179–80, 223
Housing Preservation and Development
(HPD), 179–80
Howard Beach, 87
Howard, Philip, 231
Hudson River Park, 215; features of,
227
Hudson Yards: features of, 230–31;
transportation plans, 230
Hudson Yards Infrastructure
Corporation, 230
Hughs, Charles, 24, 144
Human Resources Administration
(HRA), cuts to (1994–95), 138–39
Hunt Commission (1971), 33
Hunters Point, development plans,
216

Icahn, Carl, 79
Immigrant Workers Freedom Ride,
279
immigration/immigrants, 108–13:
borough enclaves, 109; Brooklyn
population, 233; diversity of, 109; first
waves, 108; income of, 110–11; jobs of,
110–12, 251–52; NYC demographics
(1970, 1990), 115; statistics
(1991–2000), 109; suburban residents,
109–10; and underground economy,
111–13, 140; union organizing,
270–72, 278–79; worker centers,
273–75
Impact Schools, 188
income: of immigrants, 110–11; income
decline (1980s–1990s), 107; Koch era,
72–74, 82; low-income employment,
rise in, 107; and shifts in industries
(1989–2000), 105–6; wage freezes, 38,
45, 47
income inequality: and executive
compensation, 200–201; and
gentrification, 106; Giuliani era,
153–54; Koch era, 72; and NYC
industries, 105–7, 254
Industrial and Commercial Incentive
Board (ICIB), 71, 122–23

Industrial and Commercial Incentive
Program (ICIP), 122–23, 171
industrial area development: and
rezoning, 215. *See also* mega-projects
Industrial Development Agency (IDA),
54, 71, 123, 170
industries of New York City: airline
industry decline, 101–2; building/
construction (*see* real estate
development); business services, 103;
competitive aspects, 100–101; decline
(1990s), 101–3; export of services,
12–14; financial sector (*see* financial
center [New York City]); fire,
insurance, and real estate (FIRE), 97,
102–3; and income inequality, 105–7,
254; manufacturing decline and job
loss, 3, 12–14; media/
communications, 102; new media
firms, 100; post-9/11 losses, 246–54;
shifts in (1989–2000), 105–6;
telecommunications services, 27, 102;
tourism, 105
interest groups, 20–23; capitalist class
(*see* business elite)
intermediaries, political influence,
211–12
International Association of Machinists
(IAM), 249
International Brotherhood of Electrical
Workers (IBEW), 83
International Monetary Fund, 95
Internet-related firms. *See* new media

Jack, Hulan, 89, 90, 118
Jackson, Jesse, 85, 88, 91, 114–15; and
African American voter registration,
91, 114; Dinkins support of, 119; strike
supporter, 116
James, Letitia, 235, 270
James, Willie, 267
Javits Convention Center, 105; expansion
plans, 216, 228–29
Jenkins, Steve, 275
Jensen, Michael, 202
jobs. *See* employment
Johnson, Suzanne Nora, 201
Johnson, Thomas, 220
Jones, J. Raymond, 90, 118
Jones, Theodore, 244
Justice for Janitors, 278

Kaplan, Robert, 201
Kelling, George, 134
Kelly, Ray, 161
Keynesian economics, 15
Klein, Joel, 187–88
Koch, Ed, 62–92; budgetary shift under, 68–69; campaign contributions to, 64; campaign costs, 26, 65; city worker layoffs, 72; coalition of, 64–65; crisis regime favoritism, 63–64, 67–70; defeat by Dinkins, 65, 91–92; deputy mayor to Dinkins, 120; developmentalism under, 66, 69; elections, 62–65; income inequality, rise in, 72; and municipal unions, 72–74, 80–86, 92; and no-bid basis contracts, 65; NYC government reorganization, 63–64, 79–80; poor, status of, 65, 73, 75–76, 78–79; popularity decline, 87–88; property class creation, 71; racial violence, 87; real estate development under, 70–72, 76–79, 133; real estate values, rise in, 70, 72; scandals under, 86–87; stock market crash (1987), 87–88; tax exemptions/breaks, 70–72, 123; working-class status, 72–74
Koeppel, William, 145
Kovner, Bruce, 201, 205
Krugman, Paul, 204

Labor Notes, 267–68
labor unions: and Chinatown garment industry, 251; and the crisis, 22–24, 42–51; corruption, 256–58; and Dinkins, 131–32; falling income, 255–56; under Koch, 80–86; union reform, 258–69. *See also* municipal unions
La Guardia, Fiorello: charter revisions by, 19; and welfare state, 3, 16
Lambert, Edward, 201
Landmarks and Preservation Commission, and lobbyists, 209
Langone, Kenneth, 211
Lategano, Cristyn, 142, 145
Latinos: borough presidents, 89; coalitions (1960s–70s), 21–22; decrease and gentrification, 77–78; first union leaders, 85; immigration to U.S., 108–9; under representation and

Democratic Party, 88–91; work stoppage (2006), 279
Lawe, John, 81–82
Lazard Frères, 120
Leadership Academy, 188, 189, 190
Learning to Work, 188
Lefkowitz, Louis, 39
Leroy, Greg, 169
Leventhal, Nathan, 120
Levy, Jill, 189
Lewis, Edward, 220
Liberty Bonds, Ground Zero project financing, 223–25
Libeskind, Daniel, 222
Lifflander, Clay, 133
Lindsay, John, 17, 19, 57; campaign financing, 26; and contract award system, 53
Listening to the City, 223
lobbyists, 208–11; major firms, 209–10; political influence, 209–11
Long Island City, office development, 216
Lopez, Vito, 208, 237
Lorenzo, Frank, 85, 248
Lorquet, Patrick, 259
Louima, Abner, 142, 146
Lower Manhattan Development Corporation (LMDC), 160, 206, 212, 217; members (2001–5), 219–20, 226
low-income neighborhoods: development, historical view, 74–75; housing, abandonment/torching (1970s), 75–76; Koch-era development, 78–79; planned shrinkage approach to, 76, 140
Luchese crime family, 84
Lynch, Bill, 116, 120
Lynn, Frank, 115

machine politics, emergence of, 2–3
Machinists Lodge 340, 271
McKissack & McKissack, 236
McMillian, Josie, 258
Majority Coalition, 116–17, 131
Make the Road by Walking, 274–75
Malloy, Ed, 220
management/ownership fusion, 201–4
Manes, Donald, 86, 89

Manhattan: building boom, 13; building boom collapse (1974), 13–14; central business district, 28–30; CMSA, job status, 103–4; down-zoned area, 215; East River Plaza, 211, 216; East River Science Park, 169, 216; financial activities (*see* financial center [New York City]; financial sector); gentrified areas, 140; Governor's Island development, 216, 218; grid layout (1811), 75; Ground Zero, rebuilding (1811), 75; Ground Zero, rebuilding, 215, 218–27; Harlem gentrification, 231–32; Hell's Kitchen/Clinton development, 231; High Line/Chelsea transformation, 228; Hudson River Park, 215, 227; Hudson Yards, 230–31; Javits Convention Center expansion, 228–29; Randall's Island water park, 216; real estate value, reasons for, 27–28; South Street Seaport upscale housing, 216; Trump Place, 231
Manhattan Institute, 127
mansions, 74, 205
Manton, Thomas, 207
manufacturing: decline in New York, 3, 12–14; garment industry, Chinatown, 250–51
Margolis, David, 38, 64, 86
Markey, Ray, 258
Markowitz, Marty, 237
Master, Bob, 269
Mathew, Biju, 251, 275
Mayer, Martin, 10
mayoral elections: campaign contributions (*see* specific mayors); campaign finance reform law, 65; coalition building, 62; cost/amount spent, 26, 91, 144, 156; union endorsements, split, 63, 79, 81
mayor of New York City: budget, residual power over, 79–80; elections/election financing (*see* mayoral elections; *specific mayors*); La Guardia, strengthening position of, 19. *See also specific mayors*
Mayor's Management Advisory Board (Shinn Commission), 81
Mayor's Management Advisory Committee (MMAC), 37, 45

media industry: NYC position, 102. *See also* new media
mega-projects, 214–42; Atlantic Yards, 235–37; Brooklyn Academy of Music (BAM) area, 238; Brooklyn Bridge Park, 238; Chelsea transformation, 228; Coney Island makeover, 240; DUMBO waterfront development, 238; Ground Zero, rebuilding, 218–27; Harlem gentrification, 231–32; Hell's Kitchen/Clinton development, 231; Hudson River Park, 227; Hudson Yards, 230–31; Javits Convention Center expansion, 228–29; Red Hook development, 239; and rezoning, 215; scope/locations of, 215–16; Trump Place, 231; Williamsburg/Greenpoint high-rises, 237
mergers and acquisitions: and business elite, 199; fees, 199–200
Messinger, Ruth, 142–45
Met Council, 278
Metropolitan Council on Housing, 277–78
Metro Tech, 124
Meyerson, Bess, 87
middle class, income decline (1980s–90s), 106–7
Midtown West, 230
migrations, internal, 108
Miller, Gifford, 164, 192, 208
Miners for Democracy, 262
Minnite, Lorraine, 277
Mitchell-Lama housing, 67
Molinaro, Guy, 210
Molinaro, James, 164, 210
Mollenkopf, John, 192
Montgomery, Velmanette, 235
Morris, Charles, 51
Moses, Robert, and New Deal funds, 3, 16
multilateral organizations, and globalization, 95
Municipal Assistance Corporation (MAC) Act (1975), 33; development/implementation, 35–38; goal of, 36; problems of, 37; recommendations (1978), 67; union pension fund bond purchase, 46–47
municipal bonds: bond underwriting crisis, 32–35; Ground Zero project financing, 223–25; MAC goals, 36

Municipal Labor Committee, 23, 43, 48, 261

Municipal Union-Financial Leadership (MUFL) group, 48–49

municipal unions: agency shop, 47; black leaders, first, 24, 83–84; Bloomberg era, 193, 255–62; coalition bargaining, growth of, 48; collective bargaining, decline of, 81–82, 263; corruption, 84–85; crisis regime, union support of, 31, 42–49; cuts, crisis-era proposals, 37, 43; demonstrations (1975), 42–43; Dinkins era, 115–16; election of leaders, 264–66, 269; Fifth Avenue march (1981), 80; fiscal crisis concessions, 42, 45–46; Giuliani era, 131, 144; growth of, 22–23; immigrant worker organizing, 270–72, 278–279; innovative approaches (1998–2000s), 269–72; Koch era, 72–74, 80–86, 92; Latino leaders, first, 85; leadership transitions, 83–84; membership growth (1980s), 80; pension fund money and bailout, 38, 43, 46–47; political endorsements, split in, 63, 79, 81; post-9/11 status, 255–72; power groups, 22; power shifts and neoliberalism, 263–64; reform failure (2000s), 262–69; reform/insurgencies (2000s), 257–62; women leaders, 83, 84. *See also* strikes

Murphy, Kevin, 202

Nathan, Judi, 145–46

National Action Committee on Labor Law Reform, 16

National Association of Broadcasting Employees and Technicians (NABET), 256

National Urban Summit, 121

Nation of Islam, Giuliani arrests, 135

neoliberal policy: basic structures of, 18; and Business Roundtable, 15–16; crisis regime, 30–42; development of, 15–18; education policy, 186–87, 189–90; and municipal union power shifts, 263–64; NYC economic reorganization, 18; plus social liberalism, 205–6; policy agenda, 25; reforms, types of, 16

Nespoli, Harry, 261

Ness, Immanuel, 282

New Caucus, 259

New Deal, NYC benefits from, 3, 16

New Directions, 258, 264, 266–67

Newfield, Jack, 31, 146, 148, 206, 290

New Housing Marketplace, 179–81, 185

Newman, Dr. Fred, 164

new media: decline of, 100, 166; growth of, 100

New York Building Congress, 214

New York City: capitalist class power (*see* business elite); economic decline (*see* fiscal crisis [New York City]); as financial center (*see* financial center [New York City]); as global city, 5–6, 9–10, 24, 27; globalization effects (*see* globalization and New York City); government (*see* New York City government); historical view, 1–3, 74; immigration/immigrants, 108–13; industries (*see* industries of New York City); interest groups/coalitions, 20–23; and social programs (*see* welfare state); unions (*see* labor unions; municipal unions); uniqueness of, 5–8

New York City government: business elite advisory groups, 67; charter commission reforms, 79–80; Koch-era reorganization, 63–64, 79–80; structure of, 18–19

New York City Investment Fund, 169

New York City Partnership, 67, 122, 123, 132, 180, 198

New York Metro Area Postal Workers Union, 258

New York New Media Association, 100

New York New Visions, 223

New York Taxi Drivers Alliance, 253, 271, 275

New York Telephone (Verizon), 28–29

Nicholas, Henry, 84

Nixon, Richard, New Federalism, 15

Norman, Clarence, 207, 270

Northwest Bronx Community and Clergy Coalition, 274

NYNEX (Verizon), strike (1989), 85–86

O'Connor, John, Cardinal, 85
office building construction:
corporations, common interests of,
28–29; Dinkins era, 123–24; growth of
(1967–73), 13, 28; Koch era, 71–72;
Lindsay era, 58–59
Office of Collective Bargaining (OCB),
81
Office of the Special Comptroller, 63
Offitt, Morris, 159
Ofili, Chris, 146
oil industry, petrodollars, investment of,
10
O'Neal, Stanley, 201, 205
open admissions, CUNY, 21
Operation Condor, 146
Operation Safe Housing, 183
Owens, Major, 119, 235

Painters District 9, 84–85
parent coordinators, 190–91
Park Slope, 126, 233, 234
Parrot, James, 225, 229, 247, 255
Parsons, Richard, 189
Partnership for New York, 132, 169, 191,
198, 210, 212, 218, 225
Pataki, George, and Ground Zero
rebuilding, 219–22, 225
Paterson, Pat, 35
patronage. *See* contract award system
Patterson, Ellmore, 33
Paulson, Henry, 201
payment in lieu of taxes (PILOT), 172
Penn Station, Hudson Yards
development, 230
Pennsylvania Station Redevelopment
Corporation, 217
Peter Cooper Village, sale of, 232
Pierce, Jan, 86
planned shrinkage, 76, 140
Plaza Hotel, condo conversion, 205
police: Dinkins era, 121; Koch-era gains,
73–74; shootings by, 137, 146–47;
wage increases (2000s), 256, 260. *See
also* crime control
Police Benevolent Association, 22
political influence (1970s–2000): county
leaders/clubhouses, 207; Golden
Triangle (politics/real estate/
banking), 206–7. *See also* business
elite; crisis regime

political influence (2000–present),
207–13; county organizations,
207–8; elite organizations, 210,
212–13; intermediaries/bundlers,
211–12; lobbyists, 208–11; of politics/
lobbying/real estate/banking/
corporate power, 212–13
poor/poverty: anti-poverty programs
abolished (*see* welfare state); crisis
regime impact on, 73; planned
shrinkage approach to, 76, 140; rates,
6, 73, 107, 149; working poor, 153. *See
also* homelessness; low-income
neighborhoods
Pope, Sandy, 239, 259
Port Authority: financing of, 221–22;
Ground Zero plans, opposition to, 222;
political influence, 212; World Trade
Center, ownership, 13, 59, 197, 222
postal workers: rebellion (1999), 258;
wage increase (1999), 256
Powell, Adam Clayton, 90
private-public partnership, education,
189–90
privatization: Bloomberg, 162; Giuliani
proposals, 141
Professional Staff Congress, 261
property tax: Bloomberg era, 167,
171–75; drop in revenues (1966–75),
58; exemptions (*see* tax
exemptions/breaks); Giuliani era,
150–51; impact on rent, 30; Koch era,
69–71, 123; property classifications,
71, 150, 174; rate increase (1970s),
29–30
proportional representation, 90
Prudential, tax breaks, 124
public assistance. *See* welfare state
public benefit corporations, 118–19
Public Development Corporation, 54,
123
Public Employee Conference (PEC), 23,
48
Puerto Ricans: migration to U.S., 108.
See also Latinos

Queens: down-zoned areas, 215; Hunters
Point development, 216; Long Island
City development, 216; Queens West,
216, 230; Shea Stadium revitalization,
216, 218

Queens West, 216, 230
Queens West Development Corporation, 217
Quill, Mike, 82, 280
Quinn, Christine, 207–8

race relations: Dinkins era, 125–27; discrimination and gentrification, 77–78, 126; Giuliani era, 135, 137, 142, 146–47; Koch era, 87; police shootings, 146–47. *See also* African Americans; Latinos
Rainbow Coalition, 119, 131
Randall's Island, water park plans, 216
Randel, John, 75
Ratner, Bruce, 134, 206, 213; Atlantic Yards, 235–37; campaign contributions of, 145, 211; developments of, 211; as intermediary, 211
Rattner, Steven, 159
Ravitch, Richard, 81–82, 88
Reagan, Ronald, supply-side economics, 15, 18
real estate (New York City): law of urban rent, 27–28; and social class divisions, 74–75; taxes (*see* property tax). *See also* real estate development; real estate values
Real Estate Board of New York, 25, 30, 122, 132, 218–19
real estate development: Bloomberg era, 169; Dinkins era, 123–24; Giuliani era, 133–34, 140; Golden Triangle (politics/real estate/banking), 206–7; Koch era, 70–72, 76–79; Lindsay era, 58–59; major developers (2000–present), 206, 213, 223, 228; outer boroughs (*see* boroughs; mega-projects); tax expenditures (*see* tax exemptions/breaks); 2005 agenda, 213. *See also* gentrification; housing; mega-projects; office building development
real estate investment trust (REIT), losses (1970s), 10
real estate tax. *See* property tax
real estate values: Bloomberg era, 173; and gentrification, 76–77; Giuliani era, 150–51; high, reasons for, 27–28; Koch era, 70, 72; rise in values, 70, 72,

150–51; superrich privatized spaces, 205
recession: of 1974–75, 9–15; of 1990, 87–88, 100, 121–22; post-9/11, 245–54
Red Hook, development/cruise ship plans, 216, 239
Regional Plan Association, 25, 30, 36, 285
Related Companies, 223, 228, 230
rent control, 66
rent-stabilized apartments, 178–79
Republican Party, Dinkins defeats Koch, 91–92
residential building, tax breaks, 70, 78
Restaurant Opportunities Center, 274–75
Ridgeway, Jim, 284
Rifkind, Simon, 36, 44
Rivera, Dennis, 84–85, 115, 118, 131
Riverdale, down-zoning, 215
Riverside Park, 231
Roberts, Lillian, 24, 258, 265
Roberts, Sam, 119, 120, 163
Robles-Roman, Carol, 161
Rockefeller Brothers Fund, 124, 133, 198
Rockefeller, David, 17, 35, 44–45, 67, 122; real estate projects of, 197–98
Rockefeller, Nelson, 33, 41, 118, 197
Rockrose, 223
Rohatyn, Felix: and crisis regime, 35–36, 37–39, 44–45, 45, 48, 67; Dinkins appointment, 120
Rosenthal, Mark, 257
Ross, Steven, 228
Rudin, Jack, 119, 134
Rudin, Lew, 206
Rudin, William, 206, 226
Rutenberg, Jim, 163

Safir, Howard, 137
sales tax, rise (1970s), 59–60
sanitation: Dinkins-era cuts, 122; Koch-era decline, 72; strike, 42–43; USA, 22, 43; wage increase (2000s), 260
Sassen, Saskia, 11, 27–28, 101, 112
Saunders, Lee, 257–58
Sawhill, John, 40
school vouchers, 187
Schwartz, Frederick A.O., 80
Scott Commission, 32

Section 8 vouchers, 177, 181, 183
securities firms. *See* financial sector
Senior Citizens Rent Increase
    Exemption Program (SCRIE), 181
September 11 attacks: cleanup, 218–19;
    economic impact, 166, 245–54; and
    Giuliani, 147–48. *See also* Ground
    Zero
Service Employees International Union
    (SEIU): Bevona ousted, 257; wage
    increase (1997), 256
services: export by NYC, 12–14; foreign
    direct investment in, 95–96; and U.S.
    economy, 96–97
7 World Trade Center, 222, 225
Seymour, Joseph, 222
Shalala, Donna, 36, 66
Shanker, Albert, 23, 44–45, 48, 82–83
Sharpton, Al, 142, 157
Shaw, Mark, 161, 226
Shea Stadium, revitalization plans, 216,
    218
Sheekey, Kevin, 161, 195
Shelp, Ronald, 123, 132
Shinn, Richard, 35, 37, 66, 81; real estate
    development, 198
Shonfeld, Frank, 84
Shuman, Stanley, 40, 220
Silicon Alley: location of, 100; office
    space rents, 100
Silver, Sheldon, 210, 219
Silverstein, Larry, 213, 221, 222, 225,
    226
Simons, James, 201
Simon, Walter, 15, 34
Simon, William, 41, 46, 47
Sites, William, 278
Skyler, Ed, 161, 195
skyscrapers, development of, 75
Sleeper, Jim, 119
Smeal, Frank, 35
Smiley, Donald, 35
Smith, William, 258
social class: NYC divisions, beginning of,
    74–75. *See also* business elite; middle
    class; poor/poverty; working class
social democratic polity: business elite
    view of, 17–18; elements of, 16–17;
    and La Guardia, 3
social liberalism, within economic
    neoliberalism, 205–6

social services: nonprofit organizations,
    65. *See also* welfare state
Solomon Equities building, 123
Sorkin, Michael, 147
South Street Seaport, 105, 216
Spitzer, Eliot, 137, 211
Stark, Martha, 226
Starr, Roger, 76, 140
Staten Island, down-zoning, 215
Steisal, Norman, 120, 123
Stern, Andy, 257
Stern, Robert, 134
stock market: boom (1990s), 98–100;
    crash (1987), 87–88, 97, 121; slump
    (1974), 11; slump (2000), 96, 100;
    stock options, management/
    ownership fusion, 201–4
strikes: airline industry, 85, 248;
    American Federation of State, 42, 47;
    communication workers, 255–56;
    Daily News strike, 116; DC 37, 22–23;
    Health and Hospitals Corporation, 47;
    NYNEX, 85–86; sanitation workers,
    42–43; teachers, 46; transport workers,
    81–82, 243–44
Stuyvesant Town, sale of, 232
suburbs, immigrant residents,
    109–10
Sullivan, Barry, 123, 124
Sulzberger, Arthur, 133
Sunset Park, 240
Suozzi, Thomas, 211
supply-side economics, 15
Sutton, Percy, 62, 90, 118

Tabajadores en Acción, 274, 277
Tammany, decline of, 19
taxation: *The City in Transition*
    proposals, 66–67; sales tax increase,
    59–60. *See also* property tax; tax
    exemptions/breaks
tax exemptions/breaks: assessment
    reductions, 58, 172–76; Bloomberg
    era, 170–76; Dinkins era, 123–24; and
    fiscal crisis, 58–60; 421a's, 70, 78, 123,
    171; and gentrification, 78; Giuliani
    era, 132–33, 150–51; Ground Zero
    project, 223–25; and income
    inequality, 204; J-51s, 70, 78, 123, 171;
    Koch era, 70–72; Lindsay era, 58–59;
    office building construction, 58–59,

71–72; payment in lieu of taxes (PILOT), 172; for residential building, 70, 78; state authority projects, 13, 59, 72; West Side development projects, 229–30

tax expenditures. *See* tax exemptions/breaks

taxi industry: New York Taxi Workers Alliance, 253, 271; post-9/11 losses, 252–53; restructuring, 251–52

Taylor Law (1968), 51, 82

Taylor, Mark, 237

teachers: Koch-era gains, 73–74, 82. *See also* United Federation of Teachers (UFT)

Teamsters for a Democratic Union (TDU), 267

telecommunications: industry decline, 102; NYC importance in, 27

Temporary Commission on City Finances: formation of, 13–14; Koch-era policy proposals, 66–67

Terry frisk, 137

Thabit, Walter, 126

Thatcher, Margaret, 18

Third World: debt crisis (1980s), 10; as investment opportunity, 10–11

Times Square Business Improvement District (BID), 133–34

Times Square Development Project: and Dinkins, 119, 123, 133; and Giuliani, 124, 133–34; and Koch, 72, 124, 133; state involvement, 134; tax-exempt status, 59, 72; as tourism project, 105, 133–34

Times Square Hudson River Park Trust, 217

Tishman, Robert, 66, 134, 214

Tish, Merryl, 190

Tobias, Robert, 189

Tomson, Louis, 222

tourism: projects of 1990s, 105; Times Square Development, 105, 133–34

Toussaint, Roger, 244, 258, 267

Trade Union Education League, 262

transit fare, increase, 72

Transitional Finance Authority (TFA) bonds, 166, 167

Transnational corporations (TNCs), growth of, 94–95

Transport Workers Union (TWU) Local 100, 22; New Directions, 258–59; strikes, 81–82, 243–44, 280

Trump, Donald, 79, 213

Trump Place, features of, 231

Turner, Doris, 84

Tyler, Gus, 112

underground economy: as crime control mechanism, 138; and immigrants, 111–13, 140; relationship to formal economy, 111; size of, 112

underground housing conversion, 184

Uniformed Firemen's Association, 22

Uniformed Forces Coalition, 256

Uniformed Sanitationmen, 22, 260–61; strike, 42–43

unions. *See* labor unions; municipal unions

UNITE, 251, 272

United Federation of Teachers (UFT), 22–23; contract (2005), 260; insurgency (2005), 259; strike (1975), 46

United Food and Commercial Workers (UFCW), 272

United Public Workers, 43

UNITE-HERE, 270

Uniting for Solutions Beyond Shelters, 180

Urban Development Corporation, 33, 59, 118, 124

Utility Workers, insurgency (2005), 259

Vallone, Peter, 116, 143–44, 157, 210

Van Arsdale, Harry, 23, 44–46, 66, 83

Van Arsdale, Thomas, 83

Vann, Al, 91, 118

Verizon, strike, 255–56

Village Voice, 284

Viniar, David, 201

Vornado Realty, 230

voter registration, African Americans, 91, 114

wages. *See* employment

Wagner, Robert, Jr., 55, 128

Walcott, Dennis, 161

Walker, James, 19

Wallace, Mike, 290

Wall Street. *See* financial sector; stock market
War on Poverty, 17, 21
Washington Consensus, 95
Washington Square, 74
waterfront development: character of projects, 217; and rezoning, 215. *See also* mega-projects
Weaver, Robert, 36
Weil, François, 12
Weingarten, Randi, 189, 261
Weisbrod, Carl, 210, 220, 221, 226
Welch, Jack, 189, 191
welfare state: Bloomberg era, 166; crisis regime cuts, 37–38; Giuliani-era cuts, 138–40, 144, 149–50, 152–53; Great Society-era, 17, 19, 21; Koch-era cuts, 65, 73; La Guardia-era, 3, 16; welfare rights movement, 21
West Side Stadium, 208, 214; MSG protest, 210, 229; rejection of, 228–29
Westway, 198
white backlash codes, 64–65
Whitehead, John, 220
whites: gentrification and increase in, 77–78, 231–34; white flight, 3, 126
Williamsburg/Greenpoint, high-rise projects, 237
Wils, Madelyn, 220, 221
Wilson, Howard, 220, 221
Wilson, James Q., 134
women: CEOs, financial sector, 205; Dinkins appointments, 120; union leaders, first, 83, 84
worker centers, 273–78
Work Experience Program, 139, 144, 152, 272, 285

working class: boroughs population, 7; conditions, Koch-era, 72–74; crisis regime, impact on, 72–74; displacement of, 241–42; and labor unions (*see* labor unions; municipal unions); post-9/11 job loss, 247–48, 255; September 11 volunteers, 148; weakened position of, 281–83; worker centers, 273–78
Working Families Party (WFP), 269–70
World Bank, 95
World Trade Center: city revenue loss estimate, 59; cleanup, 218; planning, 197; profitability to corporations, 28–29; redevelopment (*see* Ground Zero, rebuilding); rental tax incentives, 59; September 11 attacks, 147–48, 166; tax-exempt status, 13, 59
World Trade Organization, 95
Worldwide Plaza, 123
Wright, Deborah, 205
Wright, Richard, 110
Wriston, Walter, 32, 35, 41, 44; real estate development, 198
Wylde, Kathryn, 169

Yankee Stadium project, 216, 218
Yassky, David, 234, 238

Zarb, Frank, 220
Zeckendorf, William, 123
zero tolerance, Giuliani law enforcement, 135–38, 146
zoning: down-zonings, 215; rezoning and mega-projects, 215
Zuckerman, Morton, 134
Zucotti, John, 46
Zukin, Sharon, 147